Drug Policy and the
Criminal Justice System

Drug Policy and the Criminal Justice System

Nancy E. Marion
UNIVERSITY OF AKRON

CAROLINA ACADEMIC PRESS
Durham, North Carolina

ISBN 978-1-61163-778-6
e-ISBN 978-1-53100-007-3

Library of Congress Cataloging-in-Publication Data

Names: Marion, Nancy E., author.
Title: Drug policy and the criminal justice system / Nancy E. Marion.
Description: Durham, North Carolina : Carolina Academic Press, [2018] |
  Includes bibliographical references and index.
Identifiers: LCCN 2018005760 | ISBN 9781611637786 (alk. paper)
Subjects: LCSH: Drug abuse--United States. | Drug traffic--United States. |
  Drug control--United States. | Criminal justice, Administration of--United
  States.
Classification: LCC HV5825 .M2536 2018 | DDC 362.290973--dc23
LC record available at https://lccn.loc.gov/2018005760

Carolina Academic Press, LLC
700 Kent Street
Durham, North Carolina 27701
Telephone (919) 489-7486
Fax (919) 493-5668
www.cap-press.com

Printed in the United States of America

Contents

About the Author

Dr. Nancy E. Marion is a professor of political science and criminal justice at the University of Akron. Her research areas largely revolve around the intersection of politics and criminal justice. She is the author of numerous articles and books that examine how politics affects criminal justice policy.

Drug Policy and the
Criminal Justice System

Chapter 1

Illicit Drug Use and Abuse: An Introduction

Chapter Objective: To provide the reader with an introduction to the problem of illicit drug use and help readers understand why people choose to use drugs. Important terms are introduced to provide a general knowledge of significant ideas related to drug use and abuse.

Introduction

On December 30, 2015, comedian Bill Cosby was arraigned for aggravated indecent assault after being accused of giving a woman drugs and alcohol that rendered her unconscious. He then allegedly sexually abused her without her consent. This was not the only woman who made such allegations against the comedian. In fact, similar charges have been made against Cosby by more than 50 women, all of whom accuse him of using drugs to sexually assault them.[1] Drug abuse has also been behind the downfall of many other popular actors. Charlie Sheen had a very public "meltdown" and was fired from a highly rated comedy show after being accused of using drugs and alcohol to excess. Lindsay Lohan was arrested twice in 2007 for driving under the influence, causing her to lose movie deals. Robert Downey, Jr. battled addictions to heroin, cocaine, and marijuana, spending time in jail and in rehab facilities. Numerous other actors have died because of their drug use (Margaux Hemingway, John Belushi, River Phoenix, Philip Seymour Hoffman, and Heath Ledger), as have musicians (Amy Winehouse, Kurt Cobain, and Whitney Houston). Politicians have even seen their careers affected by drug use (Rob Ford, Joseph McCarthy, Marion Barry, and Ted Kennedy).

It is not only today's celebrities that use drugs and whose lives have been affected by them. Drugs have been used for thousands of years by people in many cultures as a way to alter their consciousness or for medical purposes. Substances such as coca leaves, marijuana, or mushrooms were used to relieve pain or other medical conditions without medical prescriptions or government regulation. Over time this shifted, and now many laws exist to control the manufacture, sale, and use of many drugs. While many argue the drug laws are discriminatory and at times illogical, the intent is to protect users from the harms that could result from excessive use.

This book examines drug use in the US and around the globe and the policies designed to deter, punish, and treat those who use drugs. It also examines the different types of drugs that are used to achieve an altered mental state and political responses to the problems associated with drug use. To start, this chapter provides an introduction into the study of illicit drugs and their impact on users and society as a whole.

Drug Use: The Basics

Today, drug use is often an accepted part of many cultures and a common part of everyday life. Drugs are used as a stimulant to help people stay awake, a depressant to help sleep or to relieve pain, or as a way to relax the body. In many countries, it is common to see people smoking cigarettes or drinking alcohol to make socializing easier or to unwind after a tough day at work. Other people drink endless cups of coffee, colas, or energy drinks throughout their day to maintain mental sharpness or to stay awake. Many others use drugs as part of religious services. Some drugs that were once illegal are becoming more widely accepted, including marijuana, as the public perceives it to be less dangerous than they did in the past.

Some drugs are legal and can be purchased easily. Caffeine in colas, coffees, and other drinks may be purchased by anyone of any age and in any amount. Some drugs, such as nicotine and alcohol, can only be purchased by adults. Other drugs, called **over-the-counter drugs**, can also be sold legally to adults, possessed, and used by them as medicine. In some cases, there are limits on who can purchase them and in what quantities. Millions of people spend money to obtain over-the-counter drugs each day and there are no legal punishments for their use. More information on these drugs is presented in Table 1.1.

Table 1.1 Over-the-Counter Drugs

Over-the-counter drugs (OTCs) are those drugs that are available to adults without a doctor's prescription. Some OTCs are used to relieve general aches and pains, such as headaches, while others help cure simple ailments such as colds, the flu, or constipation. People usually purchase an OTC drug without consulting a physician. Instead, they "self-diagnose" their condition and choose a drug that promises to attack the symptoms. The recommended dosage for these drugs is printed on the package, along with possible side effects.

These drugs have been approved and determined to be safe by the US Food and Drug Administration (FDA). Before being put on the market, a new drug must be thoroughly tested to determine if it is safe enough to sell as an OTC drug. Even once a drug is approved as a safe drug, there are still some possible risks to taking it. Sometimes, the FDA will decide to change a drug from an OTC drug to a prescription drug, or vice-versa. For example, the FDA changed some allergy drugs from being prescription drugs to OTC drugs, including Actifed, Aleve, Benadryl, Claritin, Prilosec, and Zantac.

OTC drugs can be abused. A commonly abused OTC medicine is Dextromethorphan, the active ingredient in many cough and cold medicines, including NyQuil and Robitussin. People can drink cough medicine to get high, which is called "robo-tripping" or "skittling." Those who drink a large amount of cough medicine may feel euphoric, experience color distortions, hallucinations, vomiting, loss of muscle movement, seizures, and drowsiness. If alcohol is also used, the user may overdose. Another drug used to treat the common cold, pseudoephedrine, is often mixed with other substances to make methamphetamine. For many years this drug was available as an OTC drug but it is now highly regulated.

Source: National Library of Medicine. "Over-the-Counter-Medicines." http://www.nlm.nih.gov/medlineplus/overthecountermedicines.html; Etingoff, Kim. 2013. *Abusing Over-the-Counter Drugs*. Broomall, PA: Mason Crest.

Certain drugs are legal only if a user has a prescription from a physician. These prescription drugs are recommended by a doctor to treat a verified medical condition and are used to maintain a person's health or treat an ailment or disease. Prescription drugs are often advertised in popular media outlets. In 2015, there

also illegal to sell drugs to another person. If drugs are sold in a "drug-free zone," such as near a school, the criminal penalties are higher. These crimes are clearly directly caused by drug use.

Other crimes also occur because people use drugs. An illegal substance can affect a user's mood, perception, and behavior, causing a person to lose their inhibitions and act in bizarre ways, or in ways that are not natural for them. They can become aggressive and violent, and do things that put them or others in danger. When a person combines multiple drugs, it can result in unpredictable and dangerous consequences. A user may go so far as to unknowingly attack another person while under the influence of drugs. A person addicted to a drug and feeling symptoms of withdrawal may steal items from stores or homes in order to sell them and make money to buy more drugs. There are often turf wars and gang violence associated with drugs that have led to innumerable injuries and deaths.

Other people use drugs to carry out crimes. They can be used by offenders to sexually abuse another person. When a victim is drugged unknowingly, they may be sexually or physically abused and not even know it. A victim may also be drugged and have their possessions stolen. People can be drugged and used for human trafficking.

How Drugs Are Ingested

There are many ways to ingest or "take" drugs. The mode of ingestion will partly determine the effect that drug will have on the user. The same drug may have different effects on different people in part because of how it was put into the body.

There are five general methods for ingesting a drug. The first is by smoking. When a drug is burned and the smoke inhaled, a user will feel the effect within 7–10 seconds.[12] In some cases, burning a drug in order to smoke it can ruin its psychoactive properties (e.g., powder cocaine). These drugs must be taken in a different manner, such as through in intravenous (IV) injection. This method puts the drug directly into a user's bloodstream. However, the effect is not felt as quickly because the blood containing the drug is diluted with blood that does not contain the drug. If a drug is ingested this way, the user may feel the effects within 15–30 seconds.[13] Drugs can also be injected under the skin (referred to as subcutaneous injection) or into a user's muscle (referred to as intramuscular injection). Not all drugs can be injected. A drug must be water soluble in order to be injected so a drug such as marijuana could not be injected.

Close up of addict smoking marijuana joint © Syda Productions via fotolia.com.

Snorting a drug is another method of ingestion. When a drug is snorted, the substance is absorbed through the nasal passages and then carried through the blood to the heart and the brain. The user will feel the effects within three to five minutes.[14] A drug can also be ingested through contact with a person's skin, eyes, mouth, vagina, or anus (e.g., suppositories). An example of this is a nicotine replacement patch. The time it takes for a user to feel the effects of a drug ingested in this manner will depend on the area of the body where the drug is located, but it generally takes from 3 to 30 minutes.[15]

The final mode of ingestion is to take a drug orally, such as by eating, drinking or swallowing a pill. In this case, the drug is digested in the stomach and then taken into the bloodstream. The effect will depend on the amount of food in the user's system and the dosage consumed. It can take up to 20 to 30 minutes for a user to feel the effects.[16]

Why Do People Use Drugs?

Many people take drugs for medical reasons to cure or treat a medical ailment or condition. Of course, this is necessary and legal. When prescribed correctly, drugs can ease problems that exist in a person's life and make them able to live longer, more productive lives.

However, drugs are also used by people who are not sick. The use of drugs for recreation became a popular trend in the US in the years after World War II. Smoking cigarettes became sexy and it became acceptable to have a drink at lunch.[17] But recreational drug use became more prevalent and more accepted during the 1960s. Young people at the time experimented with a wider variety of drugs and used them publicly. They did so to get high but also as a way to rebel against "the establishment." The use of drugs such as marijuana, LSD, and heroin became widely accepted by younger people.

Even with all the dangers of illicit drugs, people continue to use them. They do so for many reasons. Most young people use drugs and alcohol because of peer pressure. If a person's friends use drugs, that person may be more likely to use drugs.[18] Many times, teen friends will urge other youth to "just try it." This positive reinforcement often encourages a young person to continue to use the drug. In addition, they learn how to purchase illegal drugs and then how to use them. Thus, an individual's association with others who abuse substances tends to be a strong predictor of future drug use.[19]

In general, adults use drugs for recreational purposes because they make the user feel good. They feel happy, relaxed, and blissful after consuming a substance. In some cases, drugs are used by people who are trying to escape from reality or avoid their problems. If people struggle with self-esteem issues or have a difficult time socializing, they turn to drugs to help alleviate the pain they may feel. Others take drugs to alleviate physical pain, either due to an injury or after surgery. Steroids are sometimes used by athletes to improve their athletic performance.

Some individuals are prescribed drugs to relieve mental or physical disorders. These drugs, called psychotherapeutic drugs, are those that are used to alter a person's mood or state of mind. They can be drugs such as pain relievers, stimulants, or antidepressants. When used correctly, psychotherapeutic drugs can help make a person's problems less troublesome and help them to cope with the problems in a more effective manner. For this reason, they are often prescribed to treat people who have been diagnosed with disorders such as depression, schizophrenia, and manic-depression.

Some college students say the drugs help them to focus on their coursework. Examples of these drugs are OxyContin, Vicodin, and certain benzodiazepines.[20] Some of these medications may be addictive for some patients.[21]

A person's family situation may also influence patterns of drug use. Events such as a parental divorce or arrest; a lack of a strong relationship between parents and children; use of drugs by parents and siblings; family disorganization; a lack of parental involvement in the child's activities; a lack of parental discipline; death or absence of a parent; and emotional, physical, and/or sexual abuse are factors that have been found to be linked to drug use. A young person's experience in school plays a role in their drug use choices. Studies have found that if a young person has a negative school experience, they are likely to use drugs. That means that if they have low academic achievement and disciplinary problems, along with frequent absences, they may be more likely to use drugs.[22]

Some have argued that those young people who listen to music or watch television and movies that include drug references or themes will be more likely to use drugs. The effects of the media on behavior of youth have been subject of much concern. Drug use is portrayed in movies, on TV, and in music. Research has found that youths who spend more time watching television and listening to music with drug references are more likely to use drugs.[23]

Those who support the recreational use of drugs argue it is possible for the majority of adults to use drugs responsibly to relax and it will not negatively affect their jobs or other aspects of their lives. They point out that many people legally use alcohol for recreation or relaxation and are able to maintain a job and social relationships. Some point out that recreational drug use is no more of a health risk than other legal activities such as sports (particularly boxing, football, or car racing), or even the legal use of cigarettes.

Theories of Drug Use

There is no single reason why people use drugs. Drug addiction is caused by many factors, which include natural, biological, psychological, and possibly genetic factors.[24] Some theories of drug use and addiction are described below. These theories help us understand why people take drugs, which may help us to make effective policies to reduce drug use and related harms.

Natural Theories

The **natural theories** of drug use and addiction revolve around the idea that drug addictions are a consequence of an innate need in human nature to alter one's consciousness. Dr. Andrew Weil, a well-known physician and supporter of alternative medicines, has for many years presented the argument that a person's desire to get high or alter their state of mind is natural. Dr. Weil points out that children will often spin around in circles until they are dizzy—an early form of altered consciousness.[25] Some people choose to alter their mental state by using drugs, whereas others use other methods, including eating to excess or exercising to achieve a feeling of being high.[26]

Biological Theories

Biological theories for drug addiction are based on the concept that drug addiction is genetic. For many years, some experts have argued that some people have a predisposition to substance abuse caused by a defect in their genetic makeup. A person's genes may affect the level of intoxication they feel after taking drugs, how much a person can tolerate, and how well the user's body metabolizes the drug.[27]

Another biological theory has to do with the role of dopamine on the brain. Dopamine causes a person to feel euphoric. Drugs can cause the body to release two to ten times more dopamine than natural rewards.[28] This means that drug use is perceived as more pleasurable than natural rewards. As a user continues to use drugs, the brain responds by lowering the levels of dopamine in the brain for the same dose. Consequently, the user must use higher doses of drugs in order to achieve the same level of pleasure.

Sociological Theories

Sociological theories for drug use are based on the concept that all behaviors are learned, which affects how people interact with others. One sociological explanation for drug use is the **Anomie Theory**. This theory explains that society defines goals in our culture (particularly monetary success) and the legitimate means to achieve the goals. Most people cannot achieve the goals, thus producing feelings of stress and strain. Those who are unable to attain that societal ideal that is, in fact, achievable only by a few, use drugs as a way to cope with the inability to reach those goals.[29]

Another social learning theory is called **Differential Reinforcement**. This suggests that drug use behavior is reinforced socially through reinforcement and punishment. If people associate with other drug users, the other users will reinforce drug use behaviors. Users will get positive feedback from their friends, reinforcing that behavior, urging continued drug use.[30]

The **Labeling Theory**, attributed to Howard Becker, suggests that individuals can be labeled as drug addicts based on not only their drug use patterns but also based on their race, socioeconomic status, or other characteristics. Once a person is labeled in this way, they take on that identity. By labeling a person as a drug user, it will trigger a person to begin, or to continue, drug use.[31] Many times, those who are labeled as a drug user or addict are members of racial or ethnic minority groups, or of lower economic status. In other words, they are labeled a drug addict based more on their racial or ethnic or economic characteristics rather than their acts.

A related theory, described by Edwin Sutherland, is called **Differential Association**. Sutherland explains that people who associate with others who place a value on deviant behavior will be more likely to exhibit those behaviors. In other words, if a person spends time with drug users, they are likely to also become a drug user.[32]

Under a theory called **Conflict Theory**, drug use is explained by societal divisions and divisions of power that exist in many cultures. Higher rates of crack and heroin use exist in urban areas, according to this theory, because meaningful economic opportunities do not exist for the people who live there. Residents then feel powerless and alienated. Thus, in order to reduce drug use, society must concentrate on making changes to economic and political conditions.[33]

While these theories all provide some understanding about drug abuse, it is still not clear why some people abuse illicit drugs. These theories are only a beginning to fully understanding this behavior.

Drugs in Popular Culture and Sports

Drug use has been depicted in popular culture and the media for many years. While this may mirror trends in society it can also, in turn, influence people's general attitudes toward drugs, as well as their drug use and behavior. From a young age, children see drug use references in cartoons and movies. Although they may not fully understand it, they may be getting messages through the media about drugs from a young age. Some of the messages hint that drug use can be dangerous, but just as many messages imply that drug use is okay—that drugs and alcohol use can help to relieve stress or make social situations easier. Drug use in pop culture may be portrayed as "cool" and give kids an image that they will be cool if they use drugs.[34]

Television shows like *Jersey Shore* and *That 70's Show* depict young adults drinking excessively and smoking marijuana while having fun. The lyrics of popular music often describe drug use. In 1967 the Beatles sang about "Lucy in the Sky with Diamonds," a reference to LSD, and in 1980 Eric Clapton sang about "Cocaine." Amy Winehouse sang that she refused to go to drug rehab in her hit "Rehab" in 2006. Drug use in movies is common as well (e.g., *Up in Smoke, Wolf of Wall Street, Blow*). This sends the message that drugs are needed to have a good time or to "fit in." These shows make drug use seem glamorous, and rarely portray the negative repercussions of drug use.

Many professional athletes have been caught using prescription, recreational, or performance-enhancing substances, sending a message to youth that it is necessary to use drugs to excel at sports. Athletes will sometimes use stimulants, anabolic-androgenic steroids, erythropoietin, and other performance-enhancing (ergogenic) substances as a way to increase their performance. The World Anti-Doping Agency (WADA) and the United States Anti-Doping Agency (USADA), work to halt the use of these drugs by athletes. Other organizations, including the International Olympic Committee, the International Sports Federation, and the National Olympic Committee, have also implemented programs to address this problem.

Many successful athletes have been accused of using performance-enhancing drugs during their careers. Some are outlined in Table 1.2.

Table 1.2 Athletes and Drug Use

Lance Armstrong: After years of denying his drug use, Armstrong admitted in 2013 to using performance-enhancing drugs. He was stripped of his seven Tour de France titles and his Olympic bronze medal from the 2000 Olympics.[35]

Barry Bonds: Bonds was the all-time leader in Major League Baseball for home runs in a single season and in his career, but was accused of using performance-enhancing drugs. He was found guilty of lying to a federal grand jury about his drug use, a conviction that was later overturned.[36]

Marion Jones: Jones excelled in track, winning 5 medals at the 2000 Olympics. After Jones admitted to using steroids, she was sentenced to jail and was forced to give up her medals.[37]

Alex Rodriguez: In 2009, Rodriguez admitted to using performance-enhancing drugs. He was suspended by the Major League Baseball Commission for the entire 2014 season.[38]

Jose Canseco: Canseco admitted to using steroids throughout his baseball career, even writing a book about the extensive use of steroids by other baseball professionals.[39]

Bo Bowling: Bowling, a college football player, was arrested after police found over 100 grams of marijuana, Xanax, steroids, and over $1,000 in his apartment. He was charged with felony and misdemeanor crimes.[40]

Andre Agassi: In 1997, tennis star Agassi admitted that he used crystal methamphetamine after failing a drug test. After claiming that he took the drug unknowingly in a drink, he was given a warning. In his autobiography released years later, he admitted that the excuse was not true.

Floyd Landis: In 2006, Landis tested positive for performance-enhancing drugs after the Tour de France. He was suspended from professional competition through January 30, 2009.[41]

Michael Phelps: The Olympic medal winner in swimming was arrested in 2004 for drunk driving and sentenced to probation. He was also fined and required to speak to high school students about the dangers of drinking and driving. In 2009, a photograph emerged that showed Phelps smoking marijuana. For this, he was suspended from swimming for three months. Phelps was then arrested in 2014, again for drunk driving. This time he was banned from competitions for six months, and lost the opportunity to participate in the World Aquatics Championship in 2015.[42]

Important Terms

There are many terms that will be used in the remainder of the book that are common when studying drugs and drug use. For this reason, it is important to define these terms.

To begin with, it is important to understand what a **drug** is. According to the 1973 National Commission on Marijuana and Drug Abuse, a drug is "any chemical substance which has an action on living tissues."[43] Another definition of a drug is "a chemical that influences biological function (other than by providing nutrition or hydration)."[44] A more detailed definition of a drug is provided by the US Food and Drug Administration, which defines as drug as:

- A substance recognized by an official pharmacopoeia or formulary.
- A substance intended for use in the diagnosis, cure, mitigation, treatment, or prevention of disease.
- A substance (other than food) intended to affect the structure or any function of the body.
- A substance intended for use as a component of a medicine but not a device or a component, part or accessory of a device.
- Biological products are included within this definition and are generally covered by the same laws and regulations, but differences exist regarding their manufacturing processes (chemical process versus biological process.)[45]

In order to ingest these drugs, a person may use an item or items that are collectively called **drug paraphernalia**. The term "drug paraphernalia" refers to any equipment, product, or material that is used to make, use, or hide illicit drugs. Examples include bongs, grow kits, miniature spoons, roach clips, hookahs or syringes.[46] There are two categories of drug paraphernalia. The first is those products that are used by drug users to either ingest drugs or conceal them, such as pipes or containers for hiding drugs. The second type of drug paraphernalia refers to those items that are used by drug traffickers as they prepare illegal drugs for distribution, such as a scale or bags to package the drug.

Under federal law (Title 21 of the Controlled Substances Act), it is illegal for a person to possess, sell, transport, import, or export drug paraphernalia. Under that law, a person who carries out those activities may be punished by time in a facility. In addition, many states have also made these behaviors illegal. Some stores get around the law by selling the products for "tobacco use." A marijuana or hash pipe will be packaged with a disclaimer that the product is intended for use only with tobacco products. This is of particular concern because many of these products are sold to young people. These products are often marketed to them by use of colorful logos, tie-die designs, smiley faces, or even skulls, dragons, and wizards.

Drugs can be categorized as being either a "**hard drug**" or a "**soft drug.**" These terms are used to distinguish a drug based on its addictive potential, potency, and severity of effects on a user, but they are ambiguous terms that have little, if any, scientific basis. Nonetheless, the terms are used by many people to categorize drugs based on their impact. "Soft" drugs are those drugs that are considered to be either non-addictive or only mildly addictive. These are typically the drugs that are more socially acceptable and have lower penalties associated with possession and use. Some examples of drugs considered to be soft drugs are caffeine, alcohol, nicotine, and marijuana.

"Hard" drugs, on the other hand, are those that are considered to be highly addictive and potentially harmful to the user, to the extent of possibly causing the user's death. Examples of hard drugs include opiates such as heroin and morphine, cocaine, crack, and amphetamines (including methamphetamine and crystal meth).[47]

The argument has been made that the use of "soft" drugs such as marijuana, alcohol, and tobacco make a user more likely to use "harder" or more harmful drugs such as cocaine and heroin. This is called the **Gateway Hypothesis**, and the "soft" drugs called **Gateway Drugs**.

The effect that a drug has on a user depends partly on the **purity** of the drug, which refers to the concentration of the active ingredient in an illegal drug, as opposed to impurities or adulterants. Illicit drugs are often "cut" by sellers so they can have more product to sell and can make more money. For instance, starch may be added to heroin to increase the amount of the drug a dealer has for sale. The purity of a drug may affect the price of the drug. Usually those drugs that have higher purity cost more. The purity will also influence the effect of the drug on the user. A drug with less adulterants will have a stronger effect, but may also lead to an overdose. Additives can make the drug toxic, or it may make it more difficult to counteract a possible overdose as the doctors do not know what the person ingested.

If a person owns, controls, or uses an illicit drug, they are considered to be in **possession** of a drug. If a person is convicted of drug possession, they could be fined or incarcerated, depending on the state, the law in that state, the drug involved, and the amount of the drug. The criminal background of the person may also play a role.[48]

The use of a drug, either licit or illicit, in a way that is not prescribed by a physician is considered to be **drug abuse**. This can include using a drug when there is no medical condition, or in a way that is not following the appropriate dosage. It also refers to using a substance to achieve an altered state of mind, or to "get high," as opposed to using it to treat a medical condition. When a drug is abused, it can result in significant psychological and physical changes in a user's personality and physical body.

A person who becomes dependent on a drug in such a way that they are unable to stop using it is considered to have an **addiction**. An addicted person will use a drug repeatedly, often for reasons other than to maintain their health. According to the National Institute on Drug Abuse (NIDA), part of the National Institutes of Health, addiction is "chronic, relapsing brain disease that is characterized by compulsive drug seeking and use, despite harmful consequences. It is considered a brain disease because drugs change the brain; they change its structure and how it works. These brain changes can be long lasting and can lead to many harmful, often self-destructive, behaviors."[49] In other words, it is a disease of the brain that makes a person unable to control their consumption of a substance. An addiction can range from mild to severe. Those with only a mild addiction often respond more quickly to treatment and are more successful after treatment. On the other hand, those with a severe addiction face a more difficult time with recovery and treatment.

Sometimes, addicts may begin to use a second drug to either replace the original drug to which they have formed an addiction, or they may use two drugs at the same time. This is called a **cross-addiction** or **cross-tolerance**. For example, a marijuana user who cannot purchase marijuana may instead use alcohol. Or that addict may use both drugs at the same time. An addict may use two drugs to boost the effects on the body or to cancel the effect of one drug by using another. These addicts are considered to be cross-addicted.

Cross-tolerance may then occur when that abuser becomes tolerant to one drug but then becomes addicted to a new drug. For example, a person may develop a tolerance to alcohol but then may also create a tolerance to a tranquilizer drug. This can happen even if the person never used the tranquilizer. Or a person who uses heroin may become tolerant to other narcotics.

Cross-addictions can be extremely dangerous. The use of two or more drugs at the same time may have an even more powerful effect than one might expect. There is an increased possibility of an unintended overdose, even though the quantity of each substance, when used alone, may have been safe.[50]

While most people who use a drug do not become addicted or dependent on it, others become addicted quickly. Some people can drink a glass of wine with dinner but do not become addicted to alcohol, whereas others become addicted very quickly. Some people would label these individuals as having an "**addictive personality**." It is not possible to predict if a person who uses a drug will become addicted or dependent on it, and it is unknown why some become addicted and others do not. But scientists have shown that there are some characteristics that may be related to the likelihood that a person will become addicted to drugs. The more risk factors a user has, the higher the probability that they will become addicted to using a drug.

Many experts do not rely on the term "addictive personality" to describe addicts, claiming that it is too vague and nonscientific. Instead, they would rather describe these individuals as "vulnerable to addiction" or "at higher risk for addiction." Other health professionals use the term "dependence."

Dependence occurs when a person is unable to control his or her drug use. When a person is dependent on a drug, they will crave that drug; if they do not use it, they may experience withdrawal symptoms. There are two forms of dependence. The first is physical dependence, which occurs when a user's body, after an extended use of a drug, will begin to rely on that drug's presence. When the drug is no longer ingested, a person's body will react with withdrawal symptoms. These symptoms vary, but can include sweating, chills, fever, nausea, or headaches. If a user does not experience withdrawal symptoms after long-term or heavy use of a drug, it is not considered to be a physically addicting drug.[51]

The second type of dependence is psychological (or behavioral) dependence. This effects how a person feels from halting the use of a drug that is not physically addicting. This can be more of a "habit" than an addiction,

If a person is dependent on a drug, they are not necessarily addicted to it. A person who is dependent on a drug will still be in control of their drug use. After a period of non-use, their desire for the drug will disappear. If a person is addicted, they are unable to stop their drug use. They are often unable to keep a job or maintain relationships. The terms are often used to mean the same thing, but they are quite different.[52]

An addiction or dependence on a drug can affect the user's relationship with friends and family members. The term "codependency" refers to the behaviors that people develop if they are living with a person who is abusing drugs that allow the abuser to continue his or her behavior. In these situations, the non-drug abuser is often forced to ignore their own needs and put the needs of the abuser at the forefront. Co-dependents help an abuser maintain their addiction. They will often even make excuses to others for missed events, or act to maintain peace in the home, regardless of how it affects others.[53]

Sometimes an addiction can be linked to a particular drug. Some substances are more addictive than others and the likelihood that a drug will cause a chemical dependence in the user is called **addiction liability**. Those drugs with a higher addiction liability score have been identified as have a higher likelihood of addiction than those drugs with a lower score. For example, heroin has a higher addiction liability score than marijuana.

Heroin is more addictive than alcohol. This could be because those drugs that enter the bloodstream more quickly have a greater initial effect. Drugs can be categorized based on their potential for addiction.

There is no scientific evidence that proves that a certain characteristic or trait on the part of the user will lead to addiction, nor will the use of a particular drug. Even though experts have identified many characteristics that may predispose an individual to becoming addicted, none have been proven. More research needs to be done to fully understand the connection between personality and drug abuse.

The concept that an addict has a medical illness or condition that is the cause of the addiction (as opposed to a choice the user is making to use the drug) is referred to as the **Disease Model of Addiction**. According to this theory, addicts are unable to control their drug use and therefore should receive medical treatment as opposed to being punished. In other words, there are biological reasons underlying the addiction, similar to any other kind of medical condition. This also means that an addict needs to be treated in order to overcome the addiction. The disease model of addiction seeks to remove any stigma associated with addiction.

Not everyone agrees with this model. Critics argue that this theory gives addicts a way to escape responsibility for their behavior. These critics argue that addicts choose to use drugs and that changes that occur in the brains of addicts are the result of sustained drug use rather than the brain causing the drug use.[54] They argue that drug use is evidence of a weak moral character, and those who use drugs should be punished for their actions.

A person's withdrawal symptoms may be related to their **tolerance** to a drug. Over time, a drug user may not experience the same feeling of being "high" if they ingest the same amount of a drug. They may become desensitized to the effects of the drug. A person's body will adapt to a particular dosage so the individual will need to use more of the drug to experience the desired effect. This is referred to as tolerance.[55]

Over time and continued use, a person's body will become used to a drug and will develop a tolerance. In many situations, a drug tolerance can be reversed. If a person does not use the drug for a period of time, the drug's effect may be felt if the user begins to use again. When a small quantity of a drug produces the same effects as did a larger dose in the past, it is called **reverse tolerance**. This could happen, for example, if an incarcerated drug user leaves prison and returns to using the same dosage as they did prior to entering the facility. Their tolerance for the drug has "reversed," so that a smaller amount of the drug has a big impact. Reverse tolerance has commonly been blamed for drug overdoses of former inmates.[56]

All of these topics related to drug use have been studied for many years, and continue to be studied even today. Our knowledge about drug use and the effect of drugs is continually growing as new drugs are created and existing drugs are used in new ways. The study of how drugs affect a user's biological systems is called **pharmacology**. A pharmacologist will study the chemical properties of drugs, the effects of drugs on a user, and any potential medical uses of drugs.[57]

Many of these drug activities take place in what has been termed **High-Intensity Drug-Trafficking Areas (HIDTAs)**. Certain places within the US have been identified as high-intensity drug-trafficking areas. If given this designation, the area will be given more federal assistance to fund programs to alleviate drug-related problems. The program also supports more cooperation between the federal, state, and local law enforcement agencies in an effort to fight the drug trade.

The government has identified 28 communities as HIDTAs, which includes 60 percent of the nation's population. This includes places such as New York City, Newark, Miami, Houston, Los Angeles, and the southwest border region with Mexico. Two new HIDTA areas are Puerto Rico and the Washington, DC/Baltimore area.

The communities that receive funding will spend money on programs that deter drug use or treatment programs such as drug courts or education. Other funded programs include the Domestic Marijuana Investigation Project, the

National Methamphetamine and Pharmaceuticals Initiative, and the Domestic Highway Enforcement Program.

Conclusion: This Book

Although much is known about illicit drugs and their use, many questions remain. Who uses illegal drugs and why? What is the link between crime and drugs? What laws or policies have been passed to ban drugs, or to permit them? What can be done to reduce the harms caused by illicit drugs? This book examines illicit drug use and abuse in the US. It begins by detailing patterns of drug use in the US to determine the exact nature of the problem. It then provides a short history of drug use in the US and abroad. In chapters 4 and 5, the types of drugs that are commonly used are detailed, with summaries given of their production and effects on the users. The focus of chapter 6 is marijuana. Extra attention is given to this drug because of the publicity it is currently receiving as states opt to legalize its use for either recreation or medical purposes. Chapter 7 examines the laws that have been passed by the government that attempt to reduce the availability and use of illicit drugs (and in the long run, the social and economic harms related to drug use). In some cases, the laws passed by Congress were political reactions to the problems rather than fact-based reactions.

The links between drugs and crime are provided in chapter 8. Drugs are the basis of many types of crimes, and these links are defined more fully here. The international components of drugs and drug trafficking are given attention in chapter 9. Since many users and addicts are in need of treatment, these options are described in chapter 10. The final chapter provides a conclusion to the ideas presented throughout the book and makes some recommendations for the future.

Important Terms

Addiction
Addictive Liability
Addictive Personality
Anomie Theory
Biological Theories
Conflict Theory

Cross-Addiction
Cross-Tolerance
Dependence
Differential Association
Differential Reinforcement
Disease Model of Addiction

Drug

Drug Abuse

Drug Paraphernalia

Gateway Drug

Gateway Hypothesis

Hard Drug

High-Intensity Drug-Trafficking Areas

Labelling Theory

Natural Theories

Over-the-Counter Drug

Pharmacology

Possession

Purity

Quasi-legal Drug

Reverse Tolerance

Sociological Theories

Soft Drug

Tolerance

Withdrawal

Review Questions

1. Outline some of the harms that come from using illicit drugs. What other harms can you think of?

2. How do people "take" or ingest drugs?

3. What are some reasons why people use illegal drugs?

4. There are many theories as to why people choose to use illegal drugs. What are some of those theories?

5. How are drugs portrayed in sports and in popular culture?

6. What is the disease model of addiction? Do you agree with this approach?

Endnotes

1. Stern, Marlow. November 24, 2014. "Bill Cosby's Long List of Accusers (So Far): 18 Alleged Sexual Assault Victims between 1965–2004." *The Daily Beast*, http://www.thedaily beast.com/articles/2014/11/24/bill-cosby-s-long-list-of-accusers-so-far-17-alleged-sexual-assault-victims-between-1965-2004.html; Michael McLaughlin. May 17, 2016. "Model Drags Hugh Hefner into Sexual Assault Lawsuit against Bill Cosby." *The Huffington Post*. http://www.huffingtonpost.com/entry/chloe-goins-bill-cosby-hugh-hefner-lawsuit_us_573 b773de4b0646cbeeb360d.

2. Kaiser Family Foundation. "Total Number of Retail Prescription Drugs Filled at Pharmacies" http://kff.org/other/state-indicator; "Retail Prescription Drugs Filled at Pharmacies (annual Per Capita)." http://kff.org/other/state-indicator/retail-rx-drugs-per-capita.

3. Colvin, Rod. 2008. *Overcoming Prescription Drug Addiction: A Guide to Coping and Understanding*. Omaha, NE: Addicus Books.

4. Substance Abuse and Mental Health Services Administration. 2012. National Survey on Drug Abuse and Health; Justice Policy Institute. 2008. "Substance Abuse Treatment and Public Safety." Washington, D.C. http://www.justicepolicy.org.

5. Federal Bureau of Prisons. "Offenses." https://www.bop.gov/about/statistics; Carson, E. Ann and Sabol, William J. 2012. "Prisoners in 2011." U.S. Department of Justice, Office of Justice Programs, Bureau of Justice Statistics. http://bjs.gov/content/pub/pdf/.

6. Sentencing Project. "Incarceration." http://www.sentencingproject.org/issues/incarceration.

7. Drug Policy Alliance. "Wasted Tax Dollars." http://www.drugpolicyalliance.org.

8. Gholipour, Bahar. 2013. "Illegal Drugs are Cheaper, Stronger than Ever." *Livescience* http://www.livescience.com; Office of National Drug Control Policy. 2015. National Drug Control Strategy, Data Supplement. www.whitehouse.gov/sites/default/files.

9. National Institute of Health, National Institute on Drug Abuse. "Drugs of Abuse." https://www.drugabuse.gov/drugs-abuse.

10. Barth, Kelly. 2007. *Drug Abuse.* Detroit: Greenhaven Press; Coalition on Drug Abuse. *Symptoms and Signs of Drug Abuse.* http://drugabuse.com/library/symptoms-and-signs-of-drug-abuse/.

11. DrugAbuse.org. 2013. "The Link between Drug Abuse and STDs." http://www.drugs abuse.org/the-link-between-drug-abuse-and-stds/; Mayo Clinic. "Sexually Transmitted Diseases." http://www.mayoclinic.com/health/sexually-transmitted-diseasees-stds/DS01123; Substance Abuse and Mental Health Services Administration. 2007. "Heavy Drinking and Drug Use Linked to Higher Rates of Sexually Transmitted Diseases among Young Adults." https://nsduhweb.rti.org/respweb/homepage.cfm http://www.samhsa.gov/newsroom/advisories/0703281912.aspx.

12. "Heroin." Center for Substance Abuse Research. http://www.cesar.umd.edu/cesar/drugs/heroin; "Ways of Taking Drugs." Alcoholrehab.org. http://alcoholrehab.com/drug-addiction/.

13. "Cocaine: Ingestion Methods." 2008. http://ecstasy.com.ua/cocaine/cocaine-ingestion-methods. "Ingesting Meth." https://www.crystalmethaddiction.org/ingesting-meth.

14. "About Heroin." http://www.aboutheroin.com/snorting.heroin.

15. "Ways of Taking Drugs." Alcoholrehab.org. http://alcoholrehab.com/drug-addiction/.

16. "Ways of Taking Drugs." Alcoholrehab.org. http://alcoholrehab.com/drug-addiction/.

17. Jonnes, Jill. 1999. *Hep-cats, Narcs, and Pipe Dreams: A History with Illegal Drugs.* Baltimore, MD; Johns Hopkins University Press.

18. Partnership for Drug Free Kids, "Top 8 Reasons Why Teens Try Alcohol and Drugs." http://www.drugfree.org/resources/top8; Akers, Ronald L. 1969. *Deviant Behavior: A Social-Learning Approach.* Belmont, CA: Wadsworth.

19. Faupel, Charles E., Gret S. Weaver, and Jay Corzine. 2014. *The Sociology of American Drug Use.* New York: Oxford University Press; Crowley, Thomas J. 1981. "The Reinforcers for Drug Abuse: Why People Take Drugs." In *Classic Contributions in the Addictions,* ed. Howard Shaffer and Milton Earl Burglass, 367–381. New York: Brunner/Mazel.

20. Cooper, Aaron. 2011. "College Students Take ADHD Drugs For Better Grades." CNN. http://www.cnn.com/2011/09/01/health/drugs.

21. Drugs.com. "Psychotherapeutic Agents." http://www.drugs.com/drug-class/psychotherapeutic-agents.html; Strauss, Abbey. "An Introduction to Medications and Side Effects." *Bipolarbearexpress.* http://web.archive.org/web/20121210063908/http://fastlaunch.tripod.com/bipolarbearexpress/id10.html.

22. Isralowitz, Richard E., and Peter L. Myers. 2011. *Illicit Drugs*. Santa Barbara, CA: Greenwood.

23. Mayo Clinic. "Drug Addiction: Risk Factors." http://www.mayoclinic.org/diseases-conditions/drug-addiction/basics/risk-factors/con-20020970; National Institute on Drug Abuse. "Preventing Drug Use among Children and Adolescents (In Brief): What Are Risk Factors and Protective Factors?" http://www.drugabuse.gov/publications/preventing-drug-abuse-among-children-adolescents/chapter-1-risk-factors-protective-factors/what-are-risk-factors; Time to Act: The Partnership at Drugfree.org. "Is Your Teen at Risk for Drug Use: Risk Factors." http://timetoact.drugfree.org/think-learn-risk-factors.html; Wright, Douglas A., and Michael Pemberton. 2004. "Risk and Protective Factors for Adolescent Drug Use: Findings from the 1999 National Household Survey on Drug Abuse." Rockville, MD: Department of Health and Human Services, Substance Abuse and Mental Health Services Administration, Office of Applied Studies.

24. Morrison, Wayne. 1995. *Theoretical Criminology: From Modernity to Post-Modernism*. London: Cavendish.

25. Weil, Andrew. 1983. *The Natural Mind*. Boston: Houghton Mifflin.

26. Weil, Andrew. 1983. *The Natural Mind*. Boston: Houghton Mifflin; Weil, Andrew. 1986. *The Natural Mind: A New Way of Looking at Drugs and the Higher Consciousness*. Boston: Houghton-Mifflin.

27. National Institute of Health, National Institute on Drug Abuse. "Drug Facts: What is Marijuana." https://www.drugabuse.gov/publications/drugfacts.

28. Marion, Nancy E. 2015. "Theories of Drug Addiction" in Nancy E. Marion and Willard M. Oliver, eds. *Drugs in American Society*. Santa Barbara: ABC-CLIO, pp. 891–894.

29. Marion, Nancy E. 2015. "Theories of Drug Addiction" in Nancy E. Marion and Willard M. Oliver, eds. *Drugs in American Society*. Santa Barbara: ABC-CLIO, pp. 891–894; Merton, Robert. 1938. "Social Structure and Anomie." *American Sociological Review*, 3:672–682.

30. Marion, Nancy E. 2015. "Theories of Drug Addiction" in Nancy E. Marion and Willard M. Oliver, eds. *Drugs in American Society*. Santa Barbara: ABC-CLIO, pp. 891–894.

31. Becker, Howard S. 1953. *Becoming a Marihuana User*. Indianapolis: Bobbs-Merrill.

32. Marion, Nancy E. 2015. "Theories of Drug Addiction" in Nancy E. Marion and Willard M. Oliver, eds. *Drugs in American Society*. Santa Barbara: ABC-CLIO, pp. 891–894.

33. Akers, Ronald L. 1969. *Deviant Behavior: A Social-Learning Approach*. Belmont, CA: Wadsworth; Bandura, Albert. 1969. *Principles of Behavior Modification*. New York: Holt, Rinehart and Winston; Crowley, Thomas J. 1981. "The Reinforcers for Drug Abuse: Why People Take Drugs." In *Classic Contributions in the Addictions*, ed. Howard Shaffer and Milton Earl Burglass, 367–81. New York: Brunner/Mazel; Currie, Elliott. 1985. *Confronting Crime: An American Challenge*. New York: Pantheon Books; Currie, Elliott. 1993. *Reckoning: Drugs, the Cities, and the American Future*. New York: Farrar, Straus and Giroux; De Fiebre, Christopher M., and Allan C. Collins. June 2002. "Exploring the Genetic Commonality of Alcohol and Tobacco Abuse." *Science Blog*. http://www.sciencebog.com/community/older/2002/G/2002156.html; Faupel, Charles E., Greg S. Weaver, and Jay Corzine. 2014. *The Sociology of American Drug Use*. New York: Oxford University Press; Tierney, John J. 2006. *Criminology: Theory and Context*. Harlow, UK: Longman; Tierney, John J. 2009. *Key Perspectives in Criminology*. Maidenhead, UK: Open University Press; Wilson, William. 2002. *Central Issues in Criminal Theory*. Oxford: Hart.

34. Manning, Paul. 2007. *Drugs and Popular Culture: Drugs, Media and Identity in Contemporary Society*. Portland, OR: Willan Publishing.

35. Macur, Juliet. January 17, 2013. "For Armstrong, a Confession Without Explanation." New York Times. http://www.nytimes.com/2013/01/18/sports/cycling/lance-armstrong-confesses-to-using-drugs-but-without-details.html.

36. ESPN, 2007. Barry Bonds Steroids Timeline. http://www.nytimes.com/2013/01/18/sports/cycling/lance-armstrong-confesses-to-using-drugs-but-without-details.html.

37. Shipley, Amy. October 5, 2007. Marion Jones Admits to Steroid Use. *Washington Post.* http://www.washingtonpost.com/wp-dyn/content/article/2007/10/04/AR2007100401666.html.

38. Weaver, Jay. November 5, 2014. "Alex Rodriguez's DEA Confession: Yes, I used steroids from fake Miami doctor." *Miami Herald.* http://www.miamiherald.com/sports/mlb/article3578762.html.

39. Jose Conseco: Biography. http://www.biography.com/people/jose-canseco-17180940#steroid-scandal.

40. Wright, Scott. February 11, 2009. OSU's Bo Bowling Charged with Drug Possession. *NewsOK.* http://newsok.com/article/3345039.

41. Associated Press, October 28, 2009. "Agassi says he used Crystal Meth in '97." ESPN. http://www.espn.com/sports/tennis/news/story?id=4600027.

42. Sparks, Griffen. October 8, 2014. "Michael Phelps Seeks Treatment for Substance Abuse Following DUI Arrest." Brookhaven Hospital. http://www.brookhavenhospital.com/michael-phelps-seeks-treatment-for-substance-abuse-following-dui-arrest/.

43. National Commission on Marijuana and Drug Abuse. 1973. The Report of the National Commission on Marihuana and Drug Abuse.http://www.druglibrary.org/schaffer/library/studies/nc/ncmenu.htm.

44. Kleiman, Mark A. R., Jonathan P. Caulkins, and Angela Hawken, 2011. *Drugs and Drug Policy* (New York: Oxford University Press).

45. US Food and Drug Administration, Feb. 2, 2012. "Drugs@FDA Glossary of Terms." http://www.fda.gov/Drugs/InformationOnDrugs/ucm079436.htm.

46. Hollen, Kathryn H. 2008. "Paraphernalia." *Encyclopedia of Addictions.* Santa Barbara, CA: Greenwood.

47. Drug and Alcohol Rehab Solutions for Addiction. "Hard and Soft Drugs: How Are They Different?" http://www.drug-and-alcohol-rehab-info.com/addiction/index.php/hard-and-soft-drugs/; Levinthal, Charles E. 2012. *Drugs, Behavior, and Modern Society.* Boston: Allyn and Bacon.

48. Cornell University Law School. "Penalties for Simple Possession." http://www.law.cornell.edu/uscode/text/21/844; Laws.com. "Drug Possession Explained in Depth." http://criminal.laws.com/drug-possession.

49. National Institutes of Health, National Institute on Drug Abuse. September 2014. "The Science of Drug Abuse and Addiction: The Basics." https://www.drugabuse.gov/publications/media-guide/science-drug-abuse-addiction-basics.

50. Johnson, Marilys C. 1999. *Cross-addiction: The Hidden Risks of Multiple Addictions.* New York: Rosen Pub. Group; West, James W. 2010. "What Is Cross Addiction?" Betty Ford Center. http://www.bettyfordcenter.org/treatment/doctors-office/what-is-cross-addiction.php.

51. Karr, Justin. 2007. Drug Abuse. Detroit: Greenhaven Press; Friedman, Lauri S. 2012. *Drug Abuse.* Detroit: Gale. "Alcohol or Drug Withdrawal." WebMD. http://www.webmd.com/mental-health/addiction.

52. Colligan, L. H. 2011. *Drug Dependence.* New York: Marshall Cavendish Benchmark; Klosterman, Lorrie. 2008. *Drug Dependence.* New York: Marshall Cavendish Benchmark; National Institute on Drug Abuse. US Department of Health and Human Services. "Is There

a Difference between Physical Dependence and Addiction?" *Principles of Drug Addiction Treatment: A Research-Based Guide*. http://www.drugabuse.gov/publications/principles-drug-addiction-treatment-research-based-guide-third-edition/frequently-asked-questions/there-difference-between-physical-dependence.

53. AllAboutCounseling.com. "Codependency." http://www.allaboutcounseling.com/codependency.htm; Beattie, Melody. 1986. *Codependent No More: How to Stop Controlling Others and Start Caring for Yourself*. Center City, MN: Hazelden Foundation; Becker, Robert A. 1989. *Addicted to Misery: The Other Side of Co-dependency*. Deerfield Beach, FL: Health Communications; Lancer, Darlene. 2012. *Codependency for Dummies*. Hoboken, NJ: John Wiley and Sons.

54. Halpern, John H. 2002. "Addiction Is a Disease." *Psychiatric Times* 19(10): 54–55; Schaler, Jeffrey A. 2002. "Addiction Is a Choice." *Psychiatric Times* 19(10): 54, 62; White, William. 2000a. "Addiction as a Disease: Birth of a Concept." *Counselor Magazine* 1(1): 46–51, 73; William White, 2000b. "The Rebirth of the Disease Concept of Alcoholism in the 20th Century." *Counselor Magazine* 1(2): 62–66; William White. 2001. "Addiction Disease Concept: Advocates and Critics." *Counselor Magazine* 2(1): 42–46; William White. 2007. "A Disease Concept for the 21st Century." AddictionInfo: Alternatives to 12-Step Treatment. http://www.addictioninfo.org/articles/1051/1/A-Disease-Concept-for-the-21st-Century/Page1.html; Ketcham, Katherine, and William Asbury. 2000. *Beyond the Influence: Understanding and Defeating Alcoholism*. New York: Bantam Books.

55. National Institute on Drug Abuse. 2007. "The Neurobiology of Drug Addiction, 6: Definition of Tolerance." http://www.drugabuse.gov/publications/teaching-packets/neurobiology-drug-addiction/section-iii-action-heroin-morphine/6-definition-tolerance.

56. Gurman, Sadie. 2016. "Heroin Overdose Antidote Offers Hope for Vulnerable Inmates." *Daily Herald*. http://www.dailyherald.com/article/10260322/news/; Binswanger, I.A., Nowels, C.O., Corsi, K.F., Long, J., Booth, R.E. & Steiner, J.F. 2012. "Return to Drug Use and Overdose After Release from Prison: A Qualitative Study of Risk and Protective Factors." *Addiction Science and Clinical Practice*. 7:3.

57. Hitner, Henry, 2012. *Pharmacology: An Introduction*. New York: McGraw-Hill; Rosenfeld, Gary C. 2014. *Pharmacology*. Baltimore: Lippincott Williams and Wilkins.

Chapter 2

Patterns of Drug Use

Chapter Objective: This chapter provides information on who uses illicit drugs and what types of drugs. There are different sources that provide an estimate as to the amount and patterns of drug use, the results of which are each discussed. Drug use among various populations is described.

Introduction

It is estimated that 1 in 20 adults, which is a quarter of a billion people from ages 15–64 years old, admitted to using at least one illicit drug in 2014.[1] Who uses drugs, and what types of drugs they use, changes over time as some drugs become more popular amongst users and others lose their popularity. It is important to know who is using these substances and to what extent so that new policies can be implemented to address the problems associated with their use. We will then be able to target prevention programs to focus on the drugs being used and direct them to the right audience. This chapter will provide a description of drug use patterns. This will show not only who is using illicit drugs, but also what drugs are being used and how drug use changes over time. It will show if more people are using drugs now than in the past and if so, which ones. Demographic differences in use and abuse will become clear.

Sources for Drug Use Information

Information on illicit drug use is often difficult to collect and track simply because the use of these drugs is illegal and therefore kept secret. Most drug users could face criminal penalties for using the drug so they tend to hide it, making the true nature of its availability and use unknown. It is not possible to trace production or sales of illegal drugs as is done with a legal product. Drugs are bought and sold surreptitiously and not assembled in any official manner. Users do not disclose what they purchase and use and sellers do not report their income from drug sales. Clearly, it can be difficult to know who is using what type of drug and how often.

Instead, we must rely on anecdotal or indirect evidence to estimate drug use. Officials attempt to estimate statistics on drug use using self-report surveys in which respondents are asked about their drug use. The surveys can also focus on a particular population (e.g. youth, or residents in a certain part of the country, or a certain ethnic background). While this can provide valuable information, survey data like this can be of limited value because people may not tell the truth. They may tell untruths about how often they use drugs, or underestimate how often or the amount that is used. At the same time, some respondents may also over-report their drug use.

There are five main sources that collect information on drug use and patterns that will be included here. The information in this chapter will be based on results from the Monitoring the Future Program (National Institute on Drug Abuse/National Institutes of Health), Drug Use Forecasting (ADAM I and ADAM II, by the National Institute of Justice), Youth Risk Behavior Survey (Centers for Disease Control and Prevention), the National Survey on Drug Use and Health (Substance Abuse and Mental Health Services Administration), and the Drug Abuse Warning Network (SAMHSA). Each of these sources and their findings are described below.

One agency that collects information on drug use patterns and makes it available to researchers and the public is the **National Clearinghouse for Alcohol and Drug Information (NCADI)**, overseen by the Center for Substance Abuse Prevention, which is part of the Substance Abuse and Mental Health Services Administration of the US Department of Health and Human Services. The Clearinghouse, which is based in Rockville, Maryland, houses the world's largest collection of current information on drugs and substance abuse. The Clearinghouse disseminates information through publications (brochures, fact sheets, monographs, pamphlets, and posters) and a computerized information service that can be used by parents, teachers, youth, communities, and prevention/treatment professionals, usually at no charge. The materials kept in the Clearinghouse originate from many other federal agencies including the Center for Substance Abuse Prevention, the Center for Substance Abuse Treatment, the National Institute on Alcohol Abuse and Alcoholism, and the US Departments of Education and Labor.[2]

Monitoring the Future Study

Monitoring the Future is a survey that is conducted by the National Institute on Drug Abuse, which is part of the National Institutes of Health. Originally the survey reported behaviors only for twelfth graders but in 1991 students in eighth and tenth grade were added to the survey group. The survey asks about 50,000 students in about 400 public and private schools to complete a questionnaire about their drug use. Follow-up surveys are sent to respondents through the age of 55 to provide information about their continued drug use patterns. Because the study began in 1975, it provides a longitudinal analysis of drug use patterns.

The survey is conducted each year by the Institute for Social Research at the University of Michigan. The questions ask for information on the respondent's use of illegal drugs, alcohol, tobacco, psychoactives, pharmaceuticals, and inhalants during the last 30 days, the last year, and in their lifetime. They ask questions pertaining to the age when the person first used a drug, the frequency with which they use, quantity of use, beliefs about risks, and expected future use. They link drug use with other outcomes such as college enrollment and completion, employment, marriage, parenthood, and future drug use.

The 2015 survey shows that overall drug use (for both illicit and licit drugs) declined from 2014. There was a significant decline in the number of youth consuming cigarettes and alcohol, hitting the lowest level since the survey has been taken. The use of synthetic marijuana, heroin, ecstasy, sedatives, and prescription drugs (for non-medical uses) all declined.[3]

People continue to become more tolerant toward the use of marijuana, according to the report. The perceived risk of smoking the drug among eighth, tenth, and twelfth graders is the lowest level ever recorded in the survey. Respondents in tenth and twelfth grades showed less disapproval of others who smoked marijuana. In addition to this, there were low levels of perceived risk among twelfth graders for the use of sedatives and amphetamines, even though the reported use of these drugs is declining.[4]

The 2015 findings show that about half of the students who reported using an electronic vaporizer are using them to experiment with tobacco, and one-third reported that they enjoy the taste of vaporizers. There was a far lower number of students reporting a perceived risk in using e-cigarettes as compared to traditional cigarettes. The use of cigarillos (small cigars) is down, as is the use of hookahs to smoke tobacco. Another form of tobacco, smokeless tobacco, is also declining.[5]

The substance that is most widely used by youth, according to the 2015 survey, is alcohol. Even though alcohol use has been in decline since the 1980s, it is still used frequently by middle and high school students. Two out of three students, or 64%, reported that they consumed alcohol by the end of their high school careers. One quarter (25%) indicated that they consumed alcohol by eighth grade. About half (47%) of twelfth graders and 11% of eighth graders indicated that they have been drunk at least once in their life. There was also a decline in the number of youth reporting binge drinking from previous years.[6]

The 2016 survey results shows that drug use (alcohol, cigarettes, illicit drugs, synthetic drugs, and prescription drugs) continues to decline among eighth, tenth, and twelfth graders. However, there is a high rate of e-cigarette use. Table 2.1 shows the percent of youth who have used drugs over the previous year.

The results of the survey provide great insight into drug use by the youth population. But the data are somewhat limited. Those students who drop out of high school are not included in the sample used. Unfortunately, this is a population that typically has a high rate of drug use. Moreover, because the survey is self-administered, there can be issues with reporting distortions (i.e., students report more or less drug use than is accurate). This is of particular concern because the respondent's name and address are listed on the cover sheet to enable the researchers to follow up with that respondent at a later time.

Drug Use Forecasting (DUF/ADAM)

In 1987, the **Drug Use Forecasting** (DUF) Program, supported by the National Institute of Justice, began to collect information on drug use by using self-reported surveys alongside urine specimens from juvenile and adult arrestees. This was done in 23 different sites at four times a year. The data collected was not based on a statistically representative sample and no information was gathered concerning alcohol use, drug access, or drug markets.

This program was successful for many years. In 1997, the DUF Program was redesigned and became the **Arrestee Drug Abuse Monitoring** (ADAM) Program. ADAM incorporated a more advanced sampling design and improved the method for collecting more accurate data. ADAM conducted face-to-face interviews along with urine samples in 35 booking facilities across the nation. Interviewers collected basic arrest data from booking information to provide sufficient identifying information that the arrestee could be matched to census data representing all bookings into the jail. The program was terminated in 2003, but reinstated in 2006, this time as **ADAM II**. This time, only ten sites were used. In recent years, the number of sites was reduced to five. The sites included were Atlanta, Georgia (Fulton County); Chicago, Illinois (Cook County); Denver, Colorado (Denver County); New York, New York (Borough of Manhattan); and Sacramento, California (Sacramento County).

Table 2.1 Percent of Youth Reporting Use over Past Year

Drug	Percent of Youth Reporting Use
Alcohol	58.2
Marijuana/Hashish	34.9
Small Cigars	15.9
Amphetamines	7.7
Adderall	7.5
Heroin	5.4
Synthetic cannabinoids	5.2
Tranquilizers	4.7
Cough Medicine	4.6
Vicodin	4.4
Hallucinogens	4.2
OxyContin	3.7
Sedatives	3.6
Ecstasy	3.6
LSD	2.9
Hallucinogens Other than LSD	2.9
Cocaine	2.5
Ritalin	2.0
Inhalants	1.9

Source: National Institute on Drug Abuse, June 2016. "Drug Facts: High School and Youth Trends." Available at https://www.drugabuse.gov/publications/drugfacts/high-school-youth-trends.

This analysis was expanded in the **International Arrestee Drug Abuse Monitoring (I-ADAM) program**. Here, officials use same surveys in other countries such as Australia, Chile, England, Scotland, South Africa, the Netherlands, Malaysia, and Taiwan to learn more about drug use worldwide.

The researchers ask arrestees about the events surrounding their arrest, as well as questions about how often they used alcohol, marijuana, crack cocaine, powder cocaine, heroin, and methamphetamine (as primary drugs) and when. Information is collected for the time period before the arrest and the arrestee's lifetime use. For each of the primary drugs, information is then collected on the drug market (where the drug was purchased). Other information concerning the transaction (cash versus noncash) is gathered, as are details about the amount of drug purchased, the location of the purchase (e.g., public or private setting), and whether the drug dealer was a new one or regular contact.

At the end of the interview, a urinalysis is performed as a way to estimate the amount of drug used and to verify the information provided by the arrestee. The urinalysis tests for 10 different illegal drugs. Data is collected from adult male arrestees at all sites; information from female and juvenile arrestees is collected from fewer sites.[7]

The 2013 ADAM II report showed that the percentage of arrestees who tested positive for drug use ranged from a low of 63% in Atlanta to a high of 83% in Chicago and Sacramento. Twelve percent of arrestees had multiple drugs in their system in Atlanta, whereas that figure was 50% in Sacramento. The most commonly used drug was marijuana. Those testing positive for marijuana use reported that they had little trouble purchasing the drug.[8]

The arrestees testing positive for cocaine declined in 2013, a trend that began in 2000. In all cities except New York, there was a decline in the self-reported use of crack cocaine. However, the proportion of arrestees who tested positive for opiates was significant in all of the testing sites. This was a particular problem in the Denver and Sacramento sites. These two sites also saw significant increases in the use of methamphetamines.[9]

When it came to the costs of drugs and the market for drugs, ADAM discovered that users spend about $100 billion a year on cocaine, heroin, marijuana, and meth, a figure that has remained stable over the past ten years. In 2010, users spend more money on marijuana than cocaine, which was opposite of the trend just ten years earlier. Table 2.2 gives more detailed information on drug costs.

Youth Risk Behavior Survey

The Youth Risk Behavior Surveillance System was developed in 1990 as a way to track high-risk behavior and illegal substance abuse of students in grades 9–12. It monitors behaviors that could lead to death, disability, and social problems, such violent acts, sexual behavior, tobacco and alcohol use, unhealthy dietary patterns, and inadequate physical activity. The survey is carried out every other year by the Centers for Disease Control and Prevention. The survey has collected information on over 3.8 million students since it began.

Table 2.2 Average Cost of Illicit Drugs (in billions of 2010 Dollars)

	2000	2005	2010
Cocaine	55	44	28
Heroin	23	22	27
Marijuana	22	30	41
Meth	8	23	13
Total (All 4 Drugs)	108	119	109

Source: Office of National Drug Control Policy, Office of Research and Data Analysis, Prepared by Rand Corporation. February 2014. *What America's Users Spend on Illegal Drugs: 2000–2010*. Available at https://www.whitehouse.gov/sites/default/files/page/files/wausid_report_final_1.pdf.

The 2015 results indicate that 30.7 percent of females and 33.8 percent of males have tried smoking cigarettes; 5.0 percent of females of 8.0 percent of males reported that they smoked an entire cigarette before the age of 13; 9.7 percent of females and 11.8 percent of males report that they currently smoked cigarettes, with 2.2 percent of females and 2.4 percent of males reporting they smoke cigarettes daily. Moreover, 43.6 percent of females and 46.1 percent of males tried vapor products.[10]

When it comes to alcohol use, 65.3 percent of females and 59.1 percent of males have had at least one drink of alcohol. 33.5 percent of females and 32.2 percent of males reported that they currently used alcohol.[11]

More males (39.8 percent) than females (37.5 percent) reported that they have ever used marijuana. Similarly, more males (23.2 percent) than females (20.1 percent) currently use marijuana. The same pattern is true of synthetic marijuana (10.3 percent of males and 7.9 percent of females). In fact, males reported using all types of drugs more than females. This is shown in Table 2.3.[12]

National Survey on Drug Use and Health

Each year, the US Department of Health and Human Services, specifically the Substance Abuse and Mental Health Services Administration, conducts a survey of 70,000 young people between the ages of 12 and 17 as a way to track their behaviors regarding substance use. The survey is an attempt to collect information on patterns of alcohol, tobacco, and illegal substance use and abuse. Households across the US are chosen randomly and a professional interviewer visits the home. Participation is voluntary.

Table 2.3 Percent of Youth Reporting Use of Drugs

Drug	Male	Female
Cocaine	6.3	3.8
Ecstasy	6.0	3.9
Heroin	2.7	1.2
Methamphetamine	3.6	2.3
Steroids without a Prescription	4.0	2.7
Prescription Drugs without a Prescription	17.8	15.6
Inhalants	7.2	6.6
Hallucinogenic Drug	8.0	4.6

Source: Centers for Disease Control and Prevention, High School Youth Risk Behavior Survey, 2015. Available at http://www.cdc.gov/healthyyouth/data/yrbs/pdf/2015/ss6506_updated.pdf.

The 2014 survey shows that 27 million people (aged 12 and older) in the US used an illicit drug within the month prior to the survey. This is about 1 in 10 Americans and reflects an increase when compared to previous years. The increase seems to be largely the result of an increase in the number of people using marijuana and nonmedical use of prescription pain relievers. The results show that 8.4 percent of people aged 12 or older were current marijuana users; 1.6 percent of people aged 12 or older were nonmedical users of pain medication. Other results show that:

- 66.9 million people used a tobacco product
- 139.7 million people drank alcohol
- 22.8 percent of underage people used alcohol; 13.8 percent were binge drinkers
- 21.5 million people had a substance abuse disorder (17 million with an alcohol use disorder; 7.1 million with an illicit drug use disorder, and 2.6 million with both an alcohol use and illicit drug use disorder.[13]

Drug Abuse Warning Network (DAWN)

The **Drug Abuse Warning Network (DAWN)** gathers information on drug-related emergency department visits to hospitals and medical facilities and deaths related to drugs (from coroners and medical examiners) nationally and for specific cities. This includes any deaths that are either directly or indirectly

Girl overdosed surrounded with drugs and alcohol © phoenix021 via fotolia.com.

related to substance use, and any visit to an emergency department if the event was directly caused by drug use. It also includes those in which drugs were a contributing factor but not the primary cause of the event, like accidental consumption of drugs, adverse reactions, overdoses, suicides, or accidents resulting from drug use. The original DAWN program was discontinued in 2011, but SAMHSA is currently developing other sources of data on drug-related emergency room visits.

The DAWN reports show trends in drug use, the emergence of any new drugs, or new drug combinations. The report also has information regarding the use of illegal substances such as club drugs, cocaine, heroin, marijuana, stimulants, and alcohol when used by a minor. The study includes information on use of prescription drugs, over-the-counter medications, dietary supplements, and inhalants, but does not collect information on drugs that are used in the treatment of medical conditions (e.g., respiratory therapy, chemotherapy, radiation therapy), vaccines, dietary supplements, vitamins, and other over-the-counter pharmaceutical products. For every visit, information on the patient's sex, age, and race/ethnicity are collected. Information is also provided for the disposition of each case (if the patient was treated and released, admitted to the hospital intensive or critical care unit, or died).[14]

In 2011, there were over 125 million emergency room visits, and about 5 million of those were related to drugs. This was an increase of 100 percent since 2004. The age group with the highest number of visits was those aged 18–20. Specifically, about 1.25 million of those visits (51%) involved illicit drugs; about 1.24 million (51%) involved nonmedical use of pharmaceuticals, and .61 million (25%) involved drugs combined with alcohol.[15] About 20 percent of the visits involved in a serious medical condition that resulted in admission to the hospital, transfer to another facility, or even death.[16]

The number of methamphetamine-related visits to emergency rooms in 2011 was 102,961. The majority of those visits also included another drug, such as marijuana or alcohol. In 6 of 10 of the visits because of meth use, patients were treated and released.[17] The number of emergency department visits that involved the consumption of energy drinks doubled between 2007 and 2011 from 10,068 to 20,783. About 1 in 10 visits resulted in hospitalization.[18]

Patterns of Illegal Drug Use

The results of these surveys show some general patterns or trends about drug use. First, it is clear that drug use tends to begin during a person's adolescent years, then peak in early adulthood and decline in middle to late adulthood. Youth and those in early adulthood are more likely to use illegal drugs than those in other populations. The use of alcohol tends to be highest around age 21, whereas the use of illicit drugs and marijuana tends to crest earlier (between the ages of 18 and 20). Legal drug use and abuse rises again in the elderly populations, particularly with prescription drugs. This could be because of the chronic ailments that tend to occur as a body ages, and the pain associated with those medical conditions. However, there is also a rise in drug abuse by older people as they become addicted to legal, prescription drugs or turn to illicit drugs to help with pain maintenance.

It is also the case that, on the whole, males are more likely to use drugs than females. This was made very clear in the results of the Youth Risk Behavior Survey. Males were more likely to use every category of drug than females, and males are more likely to end up in an emergency room or overdose. Fewer females than males use marijuana, but females are quicker to start taking cocaine and use higher amounts than men. Females use methamphetamine at an earlier age than men. When they use heroin, women tend to use smaller quantities and are less likely to inject it than men.[19]

Close up of addicts using drug pills © Syda Productions via fotolia.com.

When it comes to racial differences, Caucasians reportedly use all types of drugs more often than any other racial/ethnic group. Conversely, African Americans report comparatively low patterns of illegal drug use.

Differences in drug use patterns are also evident by region of the country in which people live. Those living in the West and in urban areas are more likely to use illegal drugs than those living in other parts of the country.

Drug Use Patterns by Group

Drug use patterns vary by ethnic background, gender, and age. This is described below.

African Americans and Drug Use

America's War on Drugs had led to increases in the number of peopled arrested and imprisoned for street-level drug offenses and longer penalties for drug users and sellers. Many anti-drug policies passed by Congress in the past 30 years have disproportionately affected minority groups. Although statistics show that the rates of drug use are comparable across all races, and that African

Americans are no more likely to use or sell drugs than whites,[20] they also show that minorities are far more likely to be stopped by police, searched, arrested, prosecuted, convicted, and incarcerated for drug law violations than are white Americans. African Americans and Latinos also have higher arrest and incarceration rates than whites for drug offenses. Some experts argue that the higher arrest rates can be explained by discretionary practices by law enforcement officials who tend to focus their activities on urban areas, lower-income communities, and communities of color. They also cite unfair treatment by the criminal justice system.

The 2015 Youth Risk Behavior Survey shows that the percent of African American youth who ever drank alcohol was lower than for whites or Hispanics. When it came to the percent of youth who reported that they ever used marijuana, 45% blacks and Hispanics reported this behavior whereas only 35% of whites did. Only 4.7% of black youth reported using hallucinogenic drugs, whereas 6.4% of whites and 6.8% of Hispanics did. Hispanic youth were more likely to use cocaine and ecstasy (8.0% and 6.1%), which were higher than whites' (4.1% and 4.3%) and Blacks (3.8% and 6.1%).[21]

The 2014 National Survey on Drug Use and Health, the number of African Americans (ages 12 and older) who reported that they used illegal drugs within the previous month was 20.4%. That number for the national average was 10.2%. This means that more African Americans reportedly used illegal drugs than other ethnic groups. The rate of binge drinking (defined as consuming five or more drinks at one time) among African Americans was 21.6%, as compared to the national average of 23%. This can be interpreted to mean that African American men are less likely to binge during than other groups. Finally, African Americans from ages 12 to 20 who reported using alcohol within the past month was 17.3%, compared to the national average of 22.8%. This means that African Americans tend to drink less than other groups.[22]

Statistics also show that African Americans are more likely to be arrested and sent to prison for drug-related offenses when compared to other ethnic groups.[23] The higher imprisonment rates are thought to be a result of increasingly harsh sentencing structures that have resulted from the War on Drugs.[24] The disparity in arrest rates for African Americans may also be the result of police departments that face pressure to increase the number of people arrested for drug offenses. It has been argued that some police departments are more likely to arrest residents from low income or minority communities because they provide easy arrests and convictions.[25]

One of the most obvious examples of disparity in sentencing for laws was the federal laws for sentencing those convicted of crack cocaine versus those convicted of powder cocaine. Under the law, the penalties for possession of crack were 100 times harsher when compared to the punishments for powder cocaine. African Americans were typically more likely to use crack cocaine and were often sentenced to much longer penalties than whites, who were more likely to use powder cocaine. This discrepancy was eventually changed in the Fair Sentencing Act, passed by Congress and supported by President Obama.

It has been argued that socioeconomic factors have crucial influence on drug use by African Americans. The crux of this argument is that factors such as poverty, high unemployment, and lack of opportunities for education increase the likelihood that someone will use drugs. Other factors presumed to impact drug use include access to drugs or an "urban lifestyle." Other research shows that blacks are more likely to abuse alcohol and illegal drugs if they feel they have been treated unfairly, discriminated against, or both.[26]

African Americans are less likely than other groups to need treatment for alcohol use, but are more likely to need treatment for illicit drug use.[27] However, treatment options are not as readily available as they are for whites who use drugs. There is a larger "treatment gap" for African Americans, which is the discrepancy between the number of individuals who are seeking treatment and those who actually receive it. This means that fewer African Americans are able to participate in treatment they need to overcome their drug use patterns. To compound matters, there is some evidence to indicate that the drug treatment programs that are available to minority groups may not be specifically geared toward their needs and are not effective. Many researchers agree that a successful treatment program for African Americans should include culturally sensitive treatment targeted for this population, including a spiritual component.[28]

One organization that works to make drug laws more equitable is the **National African American Drug Policy Coalition** (**NAADPC**). This group is comprised of leaders from nine African American professional organizations. The organization has chapters in major cities across the country who each attempts to address the issue of drug abuse in the African American community. The group monitors both state and federal laws and makes recommendations for more effective laws that are fair to all groups and that focus on education, prevention, treatment, and research. They also work to educate policymakers, judges, and other community leaders about effective anti-drug programs.

Latinos/Hispanics and Drug Use

Across the US, Latinos represent the largest and fastest growing minority group. According to SAMHSA, in 2014 among persons aged 12 or older, the rate of current illicit drug use among Hispanics was 8.9%. This rate was lower than the rate for the nation, (10.2%). Additionally, the rate of binge alcohol use among Hispanics was 24.7%. This rate was higher than the national average, which was 23%.

Findings from the 2005 Monitoring the Future Study show that twelfth grade Hispanic students had the highest rate of use for crack, heroin, ice, and Rohypnol.[29] Other research shows that overall drug use among Hispanic youth has increased dramatically, and Latino teens abuse alcohol and drugs more than any other ethnic group. Since 2008, the use of drugs by Hispanic teens has increased 20%, use of marijuana increased by 25%, and use of ecstasy is up 36%. These results show that Hispanic teens are 40% more likely to use illicit drugs than whites and 30% more than blacks.[30]

Research shows that treatment for Hispanics and Latinos should include intrapersonal factors such as drug resistance skills, personal self-management skills, and general social skills. Another important factor in successful treatment is the family context and other family factors such as family support and communication (better relationships) between the parent and child. The school environment is also an area of concern for Hispanic youth in treatment because of the high drop-out rate found in this population.[31]

Native Americans and Substance Abuse

The American Indian/Alaska Native (AI/AN) populations in the US face particular problems. They are more likely to have higher rates of smoking tobacco than other groups. Statistics show that 29.2% of the AI/AN population smoke tobacco, compared to 16.8% of the general population. AI/AN women have the highest rates of smoking when compared to other groups, with 26% reporting that they smoked during pregnancy.[32] They also have higher rates of illegal drug use, with methamphetamine use a particular concern. Native American youth are particularly susceptible to these behaviors.

According to the 2014 National Survey on Drug Use and Health, the rate of illegal drug use among AI/AN groups was 14.9%, whereas the national average was 10.2%. Almost 22% of AI/AN between the ages of 12 and 20 reported they used alcohol in the previous month, compared to 22.8% of other groups. The rate of past-month underage binge drinking was 14.3% for AI/AN, compared to the national average of 13.8%. This means that AI/AN groups use more illegal drugs and see more underage binge drinking, but have about the same rate of alcohol use. It is also interesting to note that in 2010, Native Americans experienced the highest rate of drug-induced death (17.1%).[33]

A study by experts at Colorado State University found that in the years between 2009 and 2012, 56.2% of AI eighth graders and 61.4% of tenth graders had used marijuana. The numbers for the nation as a whole were 16.4% and 33.4%. The survey also showed that AI students had rates of heroin and Oxy-Contin use that were about 2–3 times higher than the national averages. AI youth are also using alcohol and drugs earlier than other youth.[34]

AI/AN populations are seeking treatment for their drug abuse. In 2010, 2.5% of admissions to treatment facilities were AI/AN adults, although they make up only 0.9% of the population. However, most AI/AN adults are referred to treatment programs by the criminal justice system. They are less likely to be referred to treatment programs by other adults.[35]

Female Drug Use

Women face different issues with regard to drug use and abuse then males. There are both biological differences as well as cultural differences that may influence a female's drug use patterns. It is not surprising, then, that many studies have found that females use drugs differently than men. They tend to use smaller amounts of drugs and for a shorter time before becoming addicted. Women may also be more sensitive to the effects of drugs, and may be more likely to need emergency care than men.[36] Females often use drugs because of low self-esteem, peer pressure, or depression.

Female Alcohol Use

According to the National Institute on Alcohol Abuse and Alcoholism, women tend to drink less alcohol and have fewer alcohol-related problems and symptoms of dependency than do men. However, when it comes to heavy users, females are the same or even surpass males when it comes to the number of problems that can result from excessive drinking.[37]

To increase the chance of being effective, treatment for female alcoholics should include different incentives than treatment used for males. Most female alcoholics seek treatment for their alcohol use after they experience family problems caused by their drinking. They are often encouraged by other family members to seek that treatment. Fewer women participate in treatment programs because of contact with the criminal justice system than men. Those women who do not seek treatment programs for their alcohol problems are likely to claim that they do not have childcare as the reason why they cannot participate.

Alcohol use by women is particularly dangerous if the woman is pregnant. If a pregnant woman uses alcohol, it passes to the unborn baby, causing miscarriage, stillbirth, or serious disorders for the child. This condition is termed **fetal alcohol spectrum disorders** (FASDs). Children with FASDs will often have abnormal facial features, a small head, shorter-than-average height, low body weight, poor coordination, hyperactive behavior, difficulty paying attention, and poor memory. Because of these issues, they often have learning disabilities and difficulty in school. Some children have speech and language delays, low IQs, and problems with vision and hearing. Other children have problems with their heart, kidney, or bones.[38]

When a pregnant woman uses drugs, it can be risky to both the woman and the child. The use of any drug during pregnancy may result in serious consequences to the child. The exact effects will depend on the drug used, and the amount ingested. An unborn baby could become addicted to a drug the mother uses while pregnant, and may also suffer from withdrawal symptoms after birth. This is called **neonatal abstinence syndrome** (**NAS**). A child may also suffer from **fetal alcohol syndrome**, a spectrum of disorders that may result if a pregnant woman drinks alcohol. The symptoms vary, but can include a small head size, low body weight, low IQs, slowed growth, low intelligence, and problems with sight or hearing. Some infants may have missing fingers or toes, facial deformities, or small brains.[39] They may also have developmental delays and have problems learning in school and have difficulties controlling their emotions.

A pregnant woman who uses IV drugs risks transmitting diseases such as HIV to the baby. Pregnant women who use drugs risk miscarriage, premature delivery, small birth weight, and other health concerns.

Women who smoke cigarettes may also affect the health of the child. The chemicals the woman ingests when she smokes tobacco (including nicotine) may deprive the baby of oxygen and cause it to abort. A child born to a mother who smoked may have a low birth weight, slower development, and learning difficulties. A 2013 study by the Women's Health Initiative showed that smoking while pregnant led to an increased risk of spontaneous abortion, premature birth, stillbirth, and tubal ectopic pregnancy. Smoking while pregnant can also cause asthma among infants and young children or Sudden Infant Death Syndrome (SIDS).[40]

Many sources have found, however, that fewer women than men smoke cigarettes. In 2008, about 21.1 million (18.3 percent) females chose to smoke, compared to 24.8 million (23.1 percent) males. Although fewer women smoke than men, the percentage difference between them has decreased. More women are choosing to smoke, and, along with that, they have more smoking-related diseases. Females who smoke tobacco may experience multiple health problems, including lung cancer, chronic obstructive pulmonary disease (COPD), emphysema, or chronic bronchitis. Women who smoke also double their risk for developing coronary heart disease. Cigarette smoking also causes a person's skin to wrinkle earlier and deeper, making smokers appear older than they are.[41]

Like males, many females begin smoking as teenagers to look "cool" or to fit in with peers. Some begin to smoke as a way to rebel against their parents or society as a whole. Some females smoke as a way to maintain a low weight because cigarettes dull a person's sense of taste. In recent years, there has been a decline in young women who are smoking cigarettes.[42]

It is more difficult for women to quit smoking than men. Females tend to metabolize nicotine faster than males. This also means that treatment options like patches and gum tend to be more effective for females.[43]

Seniors and Drug Use

Elderly men and women abuse prescription drugs more than any other age group. This is because they often take more than one prescription medicine each day and take them for long periods of time. This is made worse when seniors see more than one doctor, each of whom may prescribe a different medication. The elderly become dependent on drugs that are prescribed to them by a physician for ailments related to aging (joint pains or sleeping problems). They may also have prescription drugs for depression or loneliness.[44]

Older Americans are also using nonprescription drugs more frequently. A recent study by the Substance Abuse and Mental Health Services Administration reported an increase in illicit drug use by adults 50 years of age and older, particularly by women between the ages of 60–64.

Researchers have found that about 4.7 percent of older adults admit to using an illegal drug in the previous year. Overall, older men had a higher rate of drug use for all types of drugs when compared to women, but women were more likely to use non-medical drugs than men. Women admitted to using drugs for self-medication to cope with loneliness and stress. The prescription drugs most commonly abused by older people are benzodiazepines (diazepam, alprazolam, clonazepam, and lorazepam) and opiates (oxycodone, hydrocodone, morphine, and methadone).[45]

Alcohol can have significant interactions with some prescribed medications. When seniors mix alcohol with their prescribed medications, either intentionally or inadvertently, or overuse their prescribed medications, there can be serious consequences including a possible overdose or death.

Conclusion

It is difficult to know the exact numbers of people who are using illicit drugs. Those who use these substances try to maintain secrecy about their behaviors and may not want to admit to using illegal drugs. Many organizations try to estimate drug use through surveys or emergency room visits. These studies provide information on drug use in general, but also patterns of drug use over time. This information can help experts create more effective treatment programs for drug abusers that help them to become drug-free and productive citizens.

Important Terms

Arrestee Drug Abuse Monitoring (ADAM)

Drug Abuse Warning Network (DAWN)

Drug Use Forecasting (DUF/ADAM)

Fetal Alcohol Syndrome

International Arrestee Drug Abuse Monitoring (I-ADAM)

Monitoring the Future Study

African American Drug Policy Coalition (NAADPC)

National Clearinghouse for Alcohol and Drug Information (NCADI)

National Survey on Drug Use and Health

Neonatal Abstinence Syndrome (NAS)

Youth Risk Behavior Survey

Discussion Questions

1. What are the different sources of information on drug use? What information is found in each one?

2. What source on drug use patterns is most reliable and why? How could you design a better way to collect information on drug use?

3. What are patterns of drug use among seniors?

4. What are some characteristics of drug use among African Americans?

5. What are some dangers if females use alcohol while pregnant?

6. Describe the trends in drug use by Native Americans.

Endnotes

1. United Nations Office on Drugs and Crime, 2016. World Drug Report. https://www.unodc.org/wdr2016/en/drug-use.html.

2. "National Clearinghouse for Alcohol and Drug Abuse Information." Substance Abuse and Mental Health Services Administration. http://www.cocommunity.net/agency/national-clearinghouse-alcohol-and-drug-information.html. NCADI. http://ncadi.samhsa.gov/; "SAMSHA: National Clearinghouse for Alcohol and Drug Information." US Department of Health and Human Services. http://www.dhs.state.il.us/page.aspx?item=4843.

3. Johnston, L.D., O'Malley, P.M., Miech, R.A., Bachman, J.G., & Schulenberg, J.E. 2016. *Monitoring the Future National Survey Results on Drug Use, 1975–2015: Overview, Key Findings on Adolescent Drug Use.* Ann Arbor: Institute for Social Research, The University of Michigan. http://monitoringthefuture.org/pubs/monographs/mtf-overview2015.pdf.

4. Johnston, L.D., O'Malley, P.M., Miech, R.A., Bachman, J.G., & Schulenberg, J.E. 2016. *Monitoring the Future National Survey Results on Drug Use, 1975–2015: Overview, Key Findings on Adolescent Drug Use.* Ann Arbor: Institute for Social Research, The University of Michigan. http://monitoringthefuture.org/pubs/monographs/mtf-overview2015.pdf.

5. Johnston, L.D., O'Malley, P.M., Miech, R.A., Bachman, J.G., & Schulenberg, J.E. 2016. *Monitoring the Future National Survey Results on Drug Use, 1975–2015: Overview, Key Findings on Adolescent Drug Use.* Ann Arbor: Institute for Social Research, The University of Michigan. http://monitoringthefuture.org/pubs/monographs/mtf-overview2015.pdf.

6. Johnston, L.D., O'Malley, P.M., Miech, R.A., Bachman, J.G., & Schulenberg, J.E. 2016. *Monitoring the Future National Survey Results on Drug Use, 1975–2015: Overview, Key Findings on Adolescent Drug Use.* Ann Arbor: Institute for Social Research, The University of Michigan. http://monitoringthefuture.org/pubs/monographs/mtf-overview2015.pdf.

7. Office of National Drug Control Policy, Executive Office of the President. 2013. "Adam II: 2012 Annual Report." http://www.whitehouse.gov/sites/default/files/ondcp/policy-and-research/adam_ii_2012_annual_rpt_web.pdf; Office of National Drug Control Policy, Executive Office of the President. 2013. "NIJ's Drugs and Crime Research: Arrestee Drug Abuse Monitoring Programs." http://www.nij.gov/topics/drugs/markets/adam/Pages/welcome.aspx.

8. Office of National Drug Control Policy. January 2014. *Adam II: 2013 Annual Report: Arrestee Drug Abuse Monitoring Program II.* https://www.whitehouse.gov/sites/default/files/ondcp/policy-and-research/adam_ii_2013_annual_report.pdf.

9. Office of National Drug Control Policy. January 2014. *Adam II: 2013 Annual Report: Arrestee Drug Abuse Monitoring Program II.* https://www.whitehouse.gov/sites/default/files/ondcp/policy-and-research/adam_ii_2013_annual_report.pdf.

10. Centers for Disease Control and Prevention, High School Youth Risk Behavior Survey, 2015. http://www.cdc.gov/healthyyouth/data/yrbs/pdf/2015/ss6506_updated.pdf.

11. Centers for Disease Control and Prevention, High School Youth Risk Behavior Survey, 2015. http://www.cdc.gov/healthyyouth/data/yrbs/pdf/2015/ss6506_updated.pdf.

12. Centers for Disease Control and Prevention, High School Youth Risk Behavior Survey, 2015. http://www.cdc.gov/healthyyouth/data/yrbs/pdf/2015/ss6506_updated.pdf.

13. Center for Behavioral Health Statistics and Quality. 2015. *Behavioral Health Trends in the United States: Results from the 2014 National Survey on Drug Use and Health.* (HHS Publication No. SMA 15-4927, NSDUH Series H-50). http://www.samhsa.gov/data/.

14. US Department of Health and Human Services, Substance Abuse and Mental Health Services Administration. Substance Abuse and Mental Health Data Archive. http://www.icpsr.umich.edu/icpsrweb/SAMHDA/series/97; US Department of Health and Human Services, Substance Abuse and Mental Health Services Administration, Center for Behavioral Health Statistics and Quality. 2011. *Drug Abuse Warning Network Methodology Report, 2011 Update.* http://www.samhsa.gov/data/2k13/DAWN2k11ED/rpts/DAWN2k11-Methods-Report.htm#methods-2.1.

15. Substance Abuse and Mental Health Services Administration, *Drug Abuse Warning Network, 2011: National Estimates of Drug-Related Emergency Department Visits.* HHS Publication No. (SMA) 13-4760. DAWN Series D-39. Rockville, MD: Substance Abuse and Mental Health Services Administration, 2013. http://store.samhsa.gov.

16. Substance Abuse and Mental Health Services Administration. July 3, 2014. "The Dawn Report: Alcohol and Drug Combinations Are More Likely to Have a Serious Outcome Than Alcohol Alone in Emergency Department Visits Involving Underage Drinking." http://www.samhsa.gov/data/.

17. Substance Abuse and Mental Health Services Administration. June 19, 2014. "The Dawn Report: Emergency Department Visits Involving Methamphetamine: 2007–2011." http://www.samhsa.gov/data/.

18. Substance Abuse and Mental Health Services Administration. March 13, 2014. "The Dawn Report: 1 in 10 Energy Drink-Related Emergency Department Visits Results in Hospitalization." http://www.samhsa.gov/data/.

19. National Institute on Drug Abuse. July 2015. "Sex and Gender Differences in Substance Abuse." https://www.drugabuse.gov/publications/research-reports/substance-use-in-women/sex-gender-diffrences-in-substance-use.

20. DrugPolicy.org. "Race and the Drug War." http://www.drugpolicy.org/race-and-drug-war; Mitchell, Ojmarrh. 2009. "Is the War on Drugs Racially Biased?" *Journal of Crime and Justice* 32(2): 49–75.

21. Centers for Disease Control and Prevention, High School Youth Risk Behavior Survey, 2015. http://www.cdc.gov/healthyyouth/data/yrbs/pdf/2015/ss6506_updated.pdf.

22. Substance Abuse and Mental Health Services Administration. February 18, 2016. Racial and Ethnic Minority Populations. http://www.samhsa.gov/specific-populations/racial-ethnic-minority.

23. Urbina, Ian. June 3, 2013. "Blacks Are Singled Out for Marijuana Arrests, Federal Data Suggests." *New York Times.* http://nytimes.com/2013/06/04/us/marijuana-arretst-four-times-as-likely.

24. McWhorter, John. 2011. "How the War on Drugs Is Destroying Black America." *Cato's Letter* 9(1): 2–6; Venugopal, Arun. August 16, 2013. "The Shift in Black Views of the War on Drugs." *National Public Radio.* http://www.npr.org/blogs/codeswitch/2013/08/16/212620886/the-shift-in-black-views.

25. Knafosaki, Saki. September 17, 2013. "When It Comes to Illegal Drug Use, White America Does the Crime, Black America Gets the Time." *Huffington Post.* http://www.huffingtonpost.com/2013/09/17/racial-disparity-drug-use_n_3941346.html.

26. Hunt, Haslyn E. R. November 14, 2012. "Study: Unkindness Linked to Alcohol, Drug Abuse in Black Populations." *Purdue University News.*http://www.purdue.edu/newsroom/releases/2012/Q4/study-unkindness-linked-to-alcohol,-drug-abuse-in-black-populations.html.

27. Substance Abuse and Mental Health Services Administration. February 21, 2013. Need for and Receipt of Substance Use Treatment among Blacks. http://www.samhsa.gov/data/sites/default/files/NSDUH124/sr124-african-american-treatment.htm.

28. Britt, Alice B. 2004. "African Americans, Substance Abuse and Spirituality." MinorityNurse.com. http://www.minoritynurse.com/article/african-americans-substance-abuse-and-spirituality.

29. US Department of Health and Human Services, SAMHSA. "Drug Abuse among Hispanics." http://store.samhsa.gov/product/Drug-Abuse-Among-Hispanics/SMA07-4288.

30. MetLife Foundation. 2012. The Partnership Attitude Tracking Study: Hispanic Teens and Parents. www.drugfree.org.

31. US Department of Health and Human Services, SAMHSA. "Drug Abuse among Hispanics." http://store.samhsa.gov/product/Drug-Abuse-Among-Hispanics/SMA07-4288.

32. Campaign for Tobacco-Free Kids. November 13, 2015. "American Indian/Alaska Natives & Tobacco Use." https://www.tobaccofreekids.org/research/factsheets/pdf/0251.pdf.

33. Substance Abuse and Mental Health Services Administration. February 18, 2016. "Racial and Ethnic Minority Populations." http://www.samhsa.gov/specific-populations/racial-ethnic-minority.

34. National Institute on Drug Abuse. September 11, 2014. "Substance Use in American Indian Youth Is Worse Than We Thought." https://www.drugabuse.gov/about-nida/noras-blog/2014/09/substance-use-in-american-indian-youth-worse-than-we-thought.

35. Center for Behavioral Health Statistics and Quality. November 7, 2012. "Almost Half of American Indian and Alaska Native Adult Substance Abuse Treatment Admissions Are Referred Through the Criminal Justice System." http://www.samhsa.gov/data/sites/default/files/Spot107AIANAdultCJAdmissions/Spot107AIANAdultCJAdmissions.pdf.

36. National Institute on Drug Abuse. September 2015. "Drug Facts: Substance Use in Women." https://www.drugabuse.gov/publications/drugfacts/substance-use-in-women.

37. US National Institute on Alcohol Abuse and Alcoholism, US Department of Health, US Department of Health and Human Services. 2011. "Women and Alcohol." Washington, DC.

38. Center for Disease Control and Prevention. 2010. "Fetal Alcohol Spectrum Disorders." http://www.cdc.gov/ncbddd/fasd/alcohol-use.html.

39. US Department of Health and Human Services, Centers for Disease Control and Prevention. "Smoking and Tobacco Use." http://apps.nccd.cdc.gov/osh_faq/topic.aspx?TopicID=8.

40. American Lung Association. 2013. "Women and Tabaco Use." http://www.lung.org/stop-smoking/about-smoking/facts-figures/women-and-tobacco-use.html.

41. American Congress of Obstetricians and Gynecologists. 2011. "Tobacco Use and Women's Health," Number 503. http://www.acog.org/~/media/Committee%20Opinions/Committee%20on%20Health%20Care%20for%20Underserved%20Women/co503.pdf?dmc=1&ts=20131114T1456437926; National Institutes of Health, National Cancer Institute. 2006. "Women, Tobacco and Cancer: An Agenda for the 21st Century." Washington, DC: US Department of Health and Human Services.

42. Samet, Jonathan M., and Soon-Young Yoon. 2010. Gender, Women and the Tobacco Epidemic. Geneva: World Health Organization.

43. National Institute on Drug Abuse. July 2015. "Substance Use in Women." https://www.drugabuse.gov/publications/research-reports/substance-use-in-women/summary.

44. Aging Care. 2012. "Seniors and Prescription Drug Addiction." http://www.aging care.com/Articles/seniors-and-Prescription-Drug-Addiction-133459.htm; May, Luella. 2010. "Statistics Show Drug Abuse in Seniors is Rising." *NaturalNews.com*. http://www.naturalnews.com/028858_seniors_drug_abuse.html##ixzz2oAKRGTrL; Partnership for Drug-Free Kids. 2011. "Elderly at Risk for Prescription Drug Abuse." http://www.drugfree.org/jointogetherddiction/elderly-at-risk-for-prescription-drug-abuse.

45. Johns Hopkins Medicine Alerts. 2012. "Drug Abuse and the Elderly." http:///www. johnhopkinshealthalerts.com/reports/prescription_drugs/3363–1.html.

Chapter 3

History and Laws

Chapter Objective: After reading this chapter, the student should have a better understanding of the laws pertaining to illicit drugs in the US and how the past laws have helped to define current laws.

Introduction

For many years, the federal government has passed legislation to regulate the manufacture, transportation, sale, possession, and use of drugs in the US. These laws have evolved over time, often becoming more harsh for users. It has been argued that many of the laws banning the recreational use of drugs are examples of morality policies, as they attempt to regulate an individual's personal morals or behaviors.[1] They are statements based on what the majority of individuals in a society agree to be fundamentally right and wrong[2] and become an expression of societal norms of conduct.[3] The laws prohibiting drug use are also statements about the dangers of these substances and in essence are limiting an individual's ability to make choices about their own lives.[4] Whether this is true or not, we have many laws regarding the use of drugs. This chapter provides an analysis of those laws. This is important not only to understand current laws about drugs, but also to understand the background of our laws today.

Early History

From the Civil War era (about the mid-1800s) until the early 1900s, the use of drugs such as morphine, cocaine, and opium was legal and they were commonly used. These drugs were regularly prescribed by doctors to patients who suffered from a myriad of ailments ranging from heartburn to depression to headaches. Cocaine was used as a customary stimulant and as a cure for many illnesses. It was, for many years, an ingredient in the popular drink Coca-Cola (see Table 3.1). Heroin, first discovered in 1898, was used to relieve pain, to help people sleep, and to cure coughing. Opium was often referred to as "God's own medicine"[5] and its use was common, as shown in Table 3.2.

Table 3.1 Coca-Cola

During the 1880s, it was thought that coca could be used as an alternative to alcohol and could cure many ailments. Many products began to include small amounts of cocaine as an ingredient, including drinks. One drink at the time contained not only cocaine but also extracts of the African kola nut (caffeine), thus giving it the name "Coca-Cola." The new drink was marketed as a "temperance drink" because it contained no alcohol.

The original formula for the drink was developed in 1887 by John Styth Pemberton, a manufacturer of patent medicine from Georgia. Pemberton based his new drink on the successful Vin Mariani, a drink that contained wine and coca. Pemberton's new drink was sold for a nickel for an 8-ounce bottle. He marketed it with the pitch:

> This 'Intellectual Beverage' and Temperance Drink ... makes not only a delicious, exhilarating, refreshing and invigorating Beverage ... but a valuable Brain Tonic, and a cure for all nervous affections—Sick Head-ache, Neuralgia, hysteria, Melancholy, &c. The peculiar flavor of COCA-COLA delights every palate; it is dispensed from the soda fountain in same manner as any of the fruit syrups.

Asa Griggs, an American manufacturer and philanthropist, bought the formula for the new drink from Pemberton and changed the ingredients slightly to improve its quality. Eventually, cocaine was removed from the drink in 1906. In 1909, the US Bureau of Food and Drugs brought a suit against the Coca-Cola company because they claimed the drink contained no coca and very little cola. In 1919, officials from the Coca-Cola Company assured the US government that they changed the recipe to remove coca, thereby settling the disagreement.

Source: Hoy, Anne H. 1986. *Coca-Cola: The First Hundred Years*. Atlanta: Coca Cola Company; Martin, Jeff. 2001. *Coca-Cola: The History of an American Icon*. Orland Park, IL: MPI Media Group.

Table 3.2 Opium in the US

Large numbers of Chinese immigrants first came to the US in hopes of striking gold in the California gold rush in 1848, alongside many other Chinese immigrants who came to the US to work as laborers as the transcontinental railroad was constructed. Many of the Chinese immigrants began to smoke opium during their free time to escape the drudgery of their jobs, even though many did not use drugs before coming to the US. The drug was available at local Chinese stores or from small shopkeepers in San Francisco's Chinatown. Many of the immigrants became addicted to the opium. It is estimated that about 15 percent of the Chinese immigrants in the US at that time smoked opium on a daily basis.

An Opium Den, Chinatown, San Francisco, California. The New York Public Library's Robert N. Dennis collection of stereoscopic views via wikimedia commons.

In the 1870s, the practice of smoking opium began to spread beyond the immigrant Chinese community. Public smoking shops and opium dens opened in Nevada and California, and in many cities, including Chicago, St. Louis, New York, and New Orleans. These stores allowed non-Chinese individuals to smoke the drug. In the beginning, most of the non-Chinese patrons who frequented the smoke shops were lower class, young people. It was not long before people from the middle and upper classes began frequenting the opium dens. This was frightening to many, who argued that opium use could lead to the physical and moral decline of young people.

Opium users went to these dens because raw or poorly refined opium is difficult to keep lit while being smoked. In an opium den, there would be someone there to help keep the drug lit and tend to the users. Smokers would usually lie on the floor in a circle, with their heads resting on another's hip, or on a pillow. The smoker would inhale the drug through a special pipe, with their head elevated and tilted on its side. This was necessary because the opium would cause the user to fall asleep.

In the 1870s, when the economy fell into a depression, many people felt threatened by the immigrants because they saw the immigrants as taking jobs from the more-deserving native-born workers. It was thought that the Chinese immigrants were using opium as a way to harm the US. Those living in the US alleged that the Chinese smoked the drug with white women in exchange for sexual favors; others linked opium use with prostitution and gambling. Some went so far as to accuse the Chinese of poisoning whites with the drug, even mixing it with candy that they gave to young children as a way to get them hooked.

In 1875, some local governments passed new laws to crack down on opium use and opium dens. One of those new laws was the Smoking Opium Exclusion Act of 1909. This law was the first federal law to limit the importation of narcotics into the US, and it was also the first time the federal government legislated recreational drug use.

Source: Booth, M. 1996. *Opium: A History*. New York: St. Martin's Press; Courtwright, David T. 2001. *Dark Paradise: A History of Opiate Addiction in America*. Cambridge, MA: Harvard University Press; Dikotter, Frank, Lars Laamann, and Zhou Xun. 2004. *Narcotics Culture: A History of Drugs in China*. Chicago: University of Chicago Press.

Drug use was often popular among musicians in the early 1900s. Jazz music was popular in the US at this time, and those in the jazz music scene claimed that drugs helped to spur their creative thought. It was thought that the use of marijuana would allow musicians to reach a certain level of musical ability that they would not attain when sober. In the words of some, they became "hot" after using drugs. Many said that marijuana helped them to produce higher quality jazz, by loosening their inhibitions, and to generate more creative music.[6]

Many dangerous drugs were routinely found in patent medicines that were common at this time. Patent medicines were tonics, syrups, and other concoctions that were sold throughout the US until the early twentieth century as medicine and cure-alls for various ailments. They became widely used because, at that time, most Americans did not have easy access to medical care so they relied on traditional healing methods and patent medicine to feel better. The patent medicines were frequently sold by traveling salesmen and through mail-order companies that promised the formula would cure common diseases and illnesses such as arthritis, or even make babies stop crying. These mixtures often included opium or cocaine so the users would frequently become addicted. Many consumers quickly realized that the claims being made about the products were false and misleading. They discovered that they were ingesting dangerous drugs after people died from using the products. To prevent this, Congress passed the Pure Food and Drug Act in 1906 that required the seller to inform the user of the medicine's ingredients.[7]

Pure Food and Drug Act (1906)

The **Pure Food and Drug Act** of 1906 required that vendors place labels on any food, medicine, or other products that were sold to, and consumed by, the general public. Moreover, the law also made it illegal for a person to transport mislabeled foods or drugs across state lines. If a person was caught doing so, the products could be seized and the owner punished through fines and imprisonment. Officials from the Public Health Service (the precursor to the Food and Drug Administration) were responsible for ensuring that all medicines were labeled before being sold to the public.[8] Clearly this law was intended to ensure that consumers were aware of the ingredients in medicines.

Smoking Opium Exclusion Act (1909)

The first federal law that restricted the flow of drugs into the US was the **Smoking Opium Exclusion Act** of 1909. Prior to this, similar laws to ban opium smoking had been passed by local governments but these laws were largely in-effective. Many people turned to the federal government for help. This was not a popular suggestion since at the time, the government did not regulate social problems like drugs.

Despite these concerns, Congress passed the new law that banned the im-portation of opium that was used for smoking. The punishment for violating the law was a fine of up to $5,000 or a sentence of two years in prison. But this did not stop the use of opium in the US. Just a few months after the law was passed, smugglers on the West Coast were able to hide the drug in shipments of ordinary goods. Nonetheless, the ban on opium made the drug less available for users, thus increasing the prices. Selling opium became a profitable business, giving more incentive for traffickers to import the drug. Other users simply switched to using other, more potent forms of opium, like morphine and heroin, which were not included in this legislation.[9]

Webb-Kenyon Act (1913)

Around this time, many states had passed laws or were considering laws to ban alcohol. Anti-liquor advocates such as the Anti-Saloon League of America (ASL) and the Woman's Christian Temperance Union fought for the passage of local laws to ban the use of alcohol in some fashion. When a state passed a prohibition law, bootleggers from "wet" states would smuggle alcohol into the "dry" state at a hefty profit. The **Webb-Kenyon Act** made it a federal crime to transport alcohol from a wet state into a dry state, with harsh penalties for those found to be doing so. The law was vetoed by President Taft, an opponent of prohibition. However, there was enough support in Congress for the bill. They overrode his veto and it became law.[10]

New York State Legislature: Boylan Act (1914)

An example of a state-level law to regulate drug use was the **Boylan Act** that was passed in 1914 by the New York State Legislature. This was passed in re-sponse to an increased use of cocaine and opiates by residents in that state and was intended to reduce the availability and use of opiates for recreation. Under the law, addicts could be placed in state institutions to receive treatment and ultimately "cure" them. Since most of the opiates at the time were prescribed by physicians, this law only increased the availability of the drugs on the black market. Thus, the law was eventually overturned.[11]

Harrison Narcotics Act (1914)

The first major anti-drug law passed by the federal government was the **Harrison Narcotics Act**, passed in 1914. This law placed restrictions on opiates and cocaine in the US. According to the new law, every person who purchased narcotics would have to keep records for up to two years tracking their drug purchases. Local revenue offices were also required to keep copies of all orders placed for narcotics, and pharmacists could only sell medications that contained opium, cocaine, or their derivatives to individuals who had a doctor's prescription for them. Any patent medicine that contained more than very small amounts of morphine, cocaine, opium, and heroin could no longer be sold through the mail or in stores. Any retail dealer or physician who dispensed the drugs were required to have a tax stamp in order to sell the drugs. Additionally, every person that sold narcotics had to register with the federal government. The stamps were issued by the Treasury Department, which also had the task of administering the law. Any person who violated the law could be punished by a fine of up to $2,000 or a sentence of up to five years in prison.[12]

Upon passage of this law, many physicians became leery of prescribing narcotic drugs at all. Instead, both patients and addicts were forced to turn to the black market for their drugs and supplies. At the same time, many addicts sought out treatment, a positive unintended consequence of the law.

Whitney Act (1917)

Despite federal action to limit the availability of drugs, states continued to pass their own laws in this area. The New York Legislature passed the **Whitney Act** in 1917 that permitted doctors to treat addicts as they saw fit. This meant that doctors could provide maintenance prescriptions to addicts if it was intended to wean that person off of the drugs. Moreover, any addicts who were found to be breaking the drug laws could be paroled to the care of a physician for outpatient treatment instead of being sent to a correctional facility.

However, it became clear that some doctors were prescribing excessive amounts of drugs as a way to make a large profit. Because of this law, narcotics remained widely available in New York.

1917, 1919: Prohibition

One of the major federal actions to regulate drug use in the US was the Eighteenth Amendment to the US Constitution, which created **Prohibition**. The law was passed by Congress on December 18, 1917, then ratified by the required 36 states by January 16, 1919, becoming effective one year later, on January 16, 1920. The amendment made the sale, manufacture, and distribution of alcohol illegal.

The amendment itself was rather short and consisted of only three short sections. In Section 1, the manufacture, sale, or transportation of intoxicating liquor was made illegal, as was the importation and exportation of alcohol into and out of the United States and all of its territories. Section 2 mandated that Congress and the states both had the power (concurrent power) to enforce the law. The final section informed people that the amendment would become effective upon ratification by enough states within seven years.[13]

On October 28, 1919, members of Congress passed the Volstead Act, over President Woodrow Wilson's veto. The act provided details about the implementation of the Eighteenth Amendment (how the prohibition would be carried out). The Volstead Act provided for criminal penalties for violating Prohibition and put the IRS in charge of investigating and charging anyone who violated the law.

During the years of Prohibition, it was clear that people wanted to continue to use alcohol. There was a proliferation of secret drinking establishments called speakeasies and alcohol was made in stills hidden in basements or outdoors. There was no oversight of these hidden stills, and many people were poisoned and seriously injured from additives in the alcohol. Bootleggers were arrested for illegal trafficking. Violence erupted over turf wars for the black market. Organized crime developed and thrived as they provided a prohibited product to the public.[14]

Franklin D. Roosevelt, as a candidate for a second term as governor of New York before becoming president, called for a repeal of the Eighteenth Amendment and Prohibition. He thought it was best to allow states to choose if they would allow consumption of alcohol. Prohibition was repealed by the Twenty-First Amendment, passed in 1933.[15]

Narcotic Drugs Import and Export Act (1922)

The **Narcotic Drugs Import and Export Act**, also known as the Jones-Miller Act, was a law that governed international commerce in controlled substances. It was originally passed to address concerns related to drug smuggling into China, but it also was directed at narcotics control in the US. At this time, some business owners were concerned that morphine from foreign countries was being trafficked to China through the US and Japan. American business owners were afraid that the trafficking could harm American economic interests in China.

The new law created tougher restrictions on the importation of narcotics. These drugs could not be imported into the US unless they were intended to be used as medicine. The act also created the Federal Narcotics Control Board that would determine if drug exports were legal and if drug imports were necessary under the provisions of the law. The implementation of the law was given to the Treasury Department's Narcotic Division. Violators of the act faced fines of up to $5,000 and up to ten years in prison (double what was established in the Harrison Act). If the violators were foreigners, they could be deported.

Porter Narcotic Farm Act (1929)

The **Porter Narcotic Farm Act** was passed because federal prisons were becoming filled with drug addicts who were being incarcerated for violations of the Harrison Act. The Porter Narcotic Farm Act created two prison-based hospitals called "narcotic farms" that were used to treat those who were addicted to drugs as well as carry out research into drug addictions. The first farm was located in Lexington, Kentucky, and opened in 1935. The second was located in Fort Worth, Texas, and opened in 1938. The US Public Health Service and the Federal Bureau of Prisons oversaw the operations of the prison-based hospitals.

The farm in Kentucky was referred to as "Narco" and housed about 1,500 inmates. They had a working farm that included cows and other animals as well as food crops. Inmates worked on the farm and had other work responsibilities within the institution. The farms attracted celebrites battling addictions. Peter Lorre and Sammy Davis Jr. spent time there, as did William S. Burroughs.

Inmates addicted to drugs who were sentenced to federal prisons could be transferred to the farm or they could be sentenced to it directly. Addicts could also volunteer to be admitted to the farm as a way to receive treatment. Unfortunately, the success rates were not high. It was estimated that somewhere between 70 and 90 percent of the inmates returned. In addition, there were many ethical questions about the research being conducted and the farms reverted back to prisons in 1975.[16]

Marihuana Tax Act (1937)

The 1937 **Marihuana Tax Act** effectively prohibited the recreational use of marijuana in the US. Under this law, marijuana was treated the same as other controlled substances such as opiates and cocaine. While the act did not outwardly ban the use of the drug, it regulated it to the extent that it in essence made it illegal.[17]

The Marihuana Tax Act required that anyone who sold the drug had to purchase a stamp from the Treasury Department. The cost of the stamps varied. Those who produced the drug and medical professionals had to pay $1 per year, but those who sold the drug but were not medical professionals had to pay $5 for the stamp. Those who imported the drug had to pay $24. Moreover, every sale or transfer of marijuana was taxed $1 per ounce. Interestingly, the federal government would not issue any stamps necessary to sell the drug legally, making commerce in the drug impossible.[18]

In addition to the taxes, there was a registration requirement. Under the law, anyone who grew, transported, prescribed, or sold marijuana had to register with the federal government. This ensured that they paid the tax. However, because the drug was illegal in most states, those people who registered were then subject to prosecution.

Although the law allowed for marijuana to be used as a medicine, this was rarely done. This meant that medical treatments that included marijuana were pulled from the market by 1939.

Anyone who violated the provisions of the law could be fined up to $2,000 and faced a possible sentence of five years in prison. About 1,000 individuals were arrested each year for violating the law in the five years after the law was passed and federal officials reportedly destroyed about 60,000 tons of marijuana.[19]

Food, Drug, and Cosmetic Act (1938)

The 1938 **Food, Drug, and Cosmetic Act** was a law passed by Congress to protect the food supply and the quality of legal drugs in the US. The law required that consumable products be labeled to accurately reflect their contents. The law also set standards to ensure the safety of medicines. It also prohibited false or exaggerated claims about the effects a product would have. All drugs labels had to have directions for safe use. It also required that all drugs receive premarket approval by the FDA before being sold to the public.[20]

Opium Poppy Control Act (1942)

At the beginning of WWII, it was still legal to grow opium poppies in the US. This became an issue because the traditional opium trafficking routes were disrupted during the war, leading to a shortage of imported heroin. Concerns were raised that domestic opium production would increase to make up for the gap. In response, Congress passed the **Opium Poppy Control Act** that placed strict controls on the production of domestic opium. The new the law required that opium poppy growers in the US register with the government and obtain a license to do so. The law also placed limits on the amount of opium the growers could produce.[21]

Boggs Act (1951)

After World War II, many more people were addicted to narcotics. The trafficking routes had opened up again so illegal drugs were readily available on the black market. This meant that there were more drugs available and there was consequently more drug use by young people. Congress responded with a tough new anti-drug law called the **Boggs Act**. Passed in 1951, this was the first drug-related federal legislation passed by Congress since the 1937 Marihuana Tax Act.

The law was first introduced by Louisiana Representative Hale Boggs. The new law set mandatory minimum sentences for drug offenses. It stipulated that any person who knowingly imported or brought any opiates, cocaine, or marijuana into the US could be fined up to $2,000 and be given a possible term of imprisonment between two and five years. This potential punishment also applied to anyone who knowingly received, concealed, bought, sold, transported, or conspired to traffic in these drugs. Any person who committed these offenses more than once (i.e., a repeat offender) could face harsher penalties. Specifically, those convicted of a second offense faced 5 to 10 years in prison, and those convicted of subsequent violations could face 10 to 20 years in prison. Moreover, the new law provided that anyone convicted more than once would not be eligible for suspended sentences or granted probation. The strict provisions of this law took sentencing discretion away from judges, ensuring that guilty offenders could not get away with a slap on the wrist.

Because the law criminalized the purchase and transportation of illegal drugs, it allowed for the prosecution of users, as opposed to those who were trafficking or smuggling the drugs. Thus, even though the law was intended to attack smugglers, addicts and users also were subject to the mandatory sentences.

President Truman backed the bill, calling it a useful anti-drug measure. To determine the effectiveness of the new bill, Truman appointed an interdepartmental committee on narcotics to advise him on the implementation and effectiveness of the law. The committee was comprised of representatives from multiple federal agencies, including the departments of Treasury, State, Defense, Justice, and Agriculture, and from the Federal Security Agency. The head of the committee was Harry Anslinger, the commissioner of the Bureau of Narcotics. In the end, the committee made no recommendations nor took any actions.[22]

After only a few years, it became clear to experts that the tougher enforcement outlined in the Boggs Act did not reduce addiction rates across the country. The enhanced punishments did not seem to halt traffickers from importing heroin into the US or stop people from using drugs.[23]

Durham-Humphrey Amendment

When this law was passed, the Food and Drug Administration (FDA) was given the task of categorizing drugs as prescription or over-the-counter drugs. This amendment also limited the sale of prescription drugs to circumstances where the drug was medically necessary and prescribed by a physician.

An important provision of the **Durham-Humphrey Amendment** provided a definition of "prescription drug." According to the Amendment, if a drug had the potential of being habit-forming or was a new drug that required labelling under the Food, Drug, and Cosmetic Act of 1938, it was a prescription drug. Such drugs had to include the warning "Caution: Federal law prohibits dispensing without prescription."

Narcotic Control Act (1956)

In 1956, the Senate Judiciary Subcommittee carried out a study on narcotics addiction and illicit drug traffic in the US. They heard testimony from hundreds of witnesses and discovered that there were more drug addicts than ever before in the nation, as well as more drug trafficking than ever before. It was reported in the media that the rates of drug addiction had tripled in the years after World War II ended.[24] In response, the Congress passed the **Narcotic**

Control Act of 1956. This new law increased penalties for offenders convicted of drug trafficking and dealing that were set in the Boggs Act.

Both the minimum and maximum sentences for offenders who were trafficking and possessing drugs such as opiates, cocaine, and cannabis were increased. For a first offense, an offender could face between five and ten years in prison and a second-time offender could be sent to prison for a period of between 10 and 20 years. If an adult was caught selling heroin to minors, they could be sentenced to death.

The new minimum sentence for importing illicit narcotics was increased to five years in prison, with a maximum of 20 years. The possible punishments for repeat offenders were also raised to a minimum of 10 years and a maximum of 40 behind bars. The maximum fines for these offenses were raised from $2,000 to $20,000. The act allowed narcotic agents to carry weapons and arrest offenders without a warrant.

In addition to this, the act included provisions to increase the ability of law enforcement to use surveillance against suspects and apprehend them. As a way to increase the surveillance of possible drug traffickers, the law mandated that anyone identified as an addict, users, or anyone with a drug-related offense had to register with the Treasury Department before leaving the country.

The Counterculture and Drugs

To some extent, the Narcotic Control Act was the government's reaction to the more open use of drugs by those in the counterculture that was occurring about this time. Starting in the late 1950s, a **counterculture** emerged among youth that opposed the values of mainstream society. They opposed materialism, protested against the Vietnam War, lived in communes, and practiced free love. A key part of the counterculture was the use of psychoactive drugs like LSD.

One of the leaders of the movement was Timothy Leary, a former Harvard professor who said that individuals should take LSD as a way to "tune in, turn on, and drop out." Leary began a church called the League of Spiritual Discovery whose members used LSD as a sacrament. In 1964, Ken Kesey organized a group of people he called the Merry Pranksters to travel across the country in a psychedelically painted school bus. On the way they took LSD. Leary and Kesey became legends in the drug counterculture and later inspired many young people to experiment with psychoactive drugs.

More support for drug use came from authors. Jack Kerouac used amphetamines while writing *The Subterraneans* and *On the Road*. Kerouac believed that amphetamines were helpful in maintaining the creative process because they helped him to write smoothly and naturally. Another author, Allen Gins-berg, did not use drugs himself, but wrote about drug use and culture in 1957 *Howl*, in which he glorified the rebellious character of those who used illicit drugs. Another author, William S. Burroughs, wrote a book called *Junkie*, in which he described his life as an opiate addict during the 1940s and 1950s. In it, he described traveling freely and living a lifestyle of a beatnik, or someone who rejected traditional societal roles of the times. He also wrote *Naked Lunch* in which he describes his drug use experiences.[25]

The government responded to the counterculture's use of drugs by passing new laws to tighten their control over these substances. One of those was the Drug Abuse Control Amendments.

Drug Abuse Control Amendments (1965)

During the early to mid-1960s, the number of Americans using ampheta-mines, barbiturates, and hallucinogens continued to grow. The public's concern with this trend only expanded after actress Marilyn Monroe died from a bar-biturate overdose. The **Drug Abuse Control Amendments** of 1965 amended the 1938 Food, Drug, and Cosmetic Act to expand the number of substances that were regulated by the federal government. Instead of just limiting am-phetamines and barbiturates, the new legislation targeted all drugs that were depressants (containing barbiturates), stimulants (containing amphetamines), or hallucinogens. The amendments required that any person who was involved in the transfer of these drugs needed to register with the government. They would then be subject to regular inspections. The law also included a provision to crack down on the production of counterfeit drugs.

As the law was written, if a person possessed these drugs without the required license or a prescription from a physician, they could be sentenced for a federal crime. Medical practitioners were exempt from prosecution if they could show that they were using the drugs as part of their medical practice. The penalty for a person convicted of possessing the drugs was a maximum of two years' imprisonment along with a $5,000 fine. Any repeat offenders could face up to six years in prison and a fine of up to $15,000.

The amendments also gave FDA officials the power to carry firearms, serve warrants, seize drugs, and make arrests without warrants through a new agency called the Bureau of Drug Abuse Control. The bureau's enforcement respon-sibilities were limited to depressants and stimulants. The enforcement of laws regarding narcotics and marijuana remained under the Bureau of Narcotics in the Treasury Department.

Narcotic Addict Rehabilitation Act (1966)

A presidential commission that was established in 1962 recommended a civil commitment system for federal drug offenders. This recommendation was turned into policy in the 1966 **Narcotic Addict Rehabilitation Act** (NARA) that was signed into law by President Johnson (Public Law 89-793). The act allowed for rehabilitation and treatment for drug addicts as opposed to punishment, which was a different approach to dealing with addicts than in the past. The law allowed for those addicted to drugs to be committed civilly (instead of being sent to prison) before a trial or before sentencing. This was the first law to provide for alternative methods of punishments and treatment programs for drug offenders.

Under NARA, addicted offenders could be civilly committed to treatment programs if it was deemed that they were likely to succeed. If an offender could prove that they were addicted to a substance, they would be provided with treatment for up to three years in lieu of prison. Even addicts who did not commit a crime could volunteer to be committed and treated if they sought to be cured. In order to carry this out, federal funds would be allocated to local government to establish treatment centers.

The program had mixed results. Many addicts were found to be unsuitable for treatment and sent to jail or prison. Other offenders who had been sent to programs did not comply with the programs and were returned to prison. However, in the end, the law was significant because it provided judges with a choice to put addicts into a treatment program instead of sending them to jail.[26]

Comprehensive Drug Abuse Prevention and Control Act (1970) (Controlled Substances Act)

During the Nixon administration, drugs continued to be used openly by middle-class youth and many Vietnam War veterans were returning home who were using drugs or addicted to drugs. To some, these trends signaled the need for additional federal laws against drugs. Congress responded and passed the **Comprehensive Drug Abuse Prevention and Control Act**, also known as the Controlled Substances Act (CSA), which was signed by President Nixon in 1970. The new law consolidated previous federal anti-drug laws into one comprehensive law, making it one of the most significant pieces of federal legislation on psychoactive drugs. The law cracked down on drug law violators but also required additional education programs designed to prevent youth from trying drugs, more research into drug addiction, and rehabilitation programs with medical treatment for those who were addicted to drugs.

Title I of the act focused on rehabilitation programs relating to drug abuse, placing an emphasis on treatment and education on the dangers and harms related to drug use. Part of this title authorized the federal government to provide monetary grants to state and local governments, and for contracting with private organizations, to create educational materials about drug abuse. There were also funds available for evaluating the effectiveness of the materials. Other sections helped pay for research into the best treatment alternatives for those addicted to narcotics.

Title II of the act, which was also known as the Controlled Substances Act (CSA), allowed the government to control the manufacture and distribution of controlled substances. This section of the law grouped all drugs into five classes, or schedules, based on their potential for abuse, their medical potential, and the potential of the drug to generate psychological and physical dependence. Other considerations were the chemical composition and safety of the drug. Table 3.3 outlines the drug categories.

Schedule I drugs are substances identified as having a high potential for abuse but with no medical value. Examples of these drugs were heroin, marijuana, and LSD. Other examples are peyote, methaqualone, and 3.4-methylene-dioxymethamphetamine, otherwise known as ecstasy. Schedule II drugs are drugs that still had a high potential for abuse, and can lead to severe psychological or physical dependence on the part of the user. These drugs were noted to have some limited medical use. Examples of these drugs include opiates such as hydromorphone, methadone (Dolophine), meperidine (Demerol), oxycodone (OxyContin, Percocet), fentanyl (Sublimaze, Duragesic), morphine, opium, and codeine. Schedule II stimulants include amphetamine (Adderall), methamphetamine (Desoxyn), and methylphenidate (Ritalin). Amobarbital, glutethimide, and pentobarbital are examples of Schedule II depressants.

Schedule III drugs are thought to have less potential for abuse than those in Schedules I and II, and were considered to have acceptable use in medical treatment. Use of these drugs can lead to moderate or low physical dependence or high psychological dependence. Examples of Schedule III narcotics include combination products containing less than 15 milligrams of hydrocodone per dosage unit (Vicodin), products containing not more than 90 milligrams of codeine per dosage unit (Tylenol with Codeine), and buprenorphine (Suboxone). Examples of Schedule III nonnarcotics include benzphetamine (Didrex), phendimetrazine, ketamine, and anabolic steroids such as Depo-Testosterone.

Drugs on Schedule IV and V were considered to have even lower potential for abuse and more medical functions. Drugs placed in Schedule IV of the CSA are those substances that have a low potential for abuse relative to the drugs found in Schedule III, Schedule II, or Schedule I. Examples of the drugs placed in this category include alprazolam (Xanax), carisoprodol (Soma), clonazepam (Klonopin), clorazepate (Tranxene), diazepam (Valium), lorazepam (Ativan), midazolam (Versed), temazepam (Restoril), and triazolam (Halcion).

The last schedule of drugs, Schedule V substances, are those that have a low potential for abuse relative to substances listed in the above categories. They consist primarily of preparations containing limited quantities of certain narcotics such as cough syrups that contain no more than 200 milligrams of codeine per 100 milliliters or per 100 grams. These are products such as Robitussin AC, Phenergan with Codeine, and ezogabine.

Those drugs categorized as either Schedules I or II became tightly regulated, and it became illegal to distribute them without permission from the attorney general. Potential penalties for violating these laws were also strongest for Schedule I and II drugs, with penalties ranging up to 15 years in prison and a fine of up to $25,000. If it involved a repeat offender, the possible sentences could be doubled. The penalty for violating the law involving Schedule III drug was up to five years in prison and a $15,000 fine, while for a Schedule IV drug the punishments could be up to three years in prison and a $10,000 fine, and for Schedule V drugs the maximum potential sentence was one year in prison and a fine of up to $5,000. The act also allowed punishments of up to a year in prison and a fine of up to $5,000 for the possession of controlled substances and the penalties for repeat possession offenses were doubled.

The Controlled Substances Act also set punishments for those who trafficked in drugs. The law set a 10-year minimum sentence, with a maximum sentence of life, for offenders convicted of large-scale trafficking. There was also a maximum fine of $100,000 for this offense. For repeat offenders, these sentences could be doubled. Any individuals convicted of importing Schedule I and II drugs faced prison sentences of up to five years in prison and fines of up to $15,000.

To enforce the new laws, law enforcement officials were given the authority to carry weapons, search property, arrest offenders without warrants, confiscate property, and enter a premises to investigate an offense upon a warrant issued by a judge.

Table 3.3 Controlled Substances Act (CSA) (1970)

Schedule I: High potential for abuse; no medical use in the US, and a lack of accepted safety for use under medical supervision: heroin, LSD, marijuana, Methaqualone, mescaline, psilocybin, peyote, rohypnol, Bufotenine, Hashish and oil, PCP, MDMA (ecstasy), Methadone, Gamma-Hydroxybutyrate (GHB)

Schedule II: Substance has a high potential for abuse, has a currently accepted medical use in the US with severe restrictions, and abuse may lead to severe psychological or physical dependence: Cocaine, Codeine, Hydrocodone, Morphine, Methamphetamine, Phencyclidine (PCP), Amobarbital, Secobarbital, Pentobarbital, Percocet, Ritalin, Percodan, Demerol, Opium, Oxycodone, THC, Dexedrine

Schedule III: Substance has a potential for abuse (less than Schedule I or II), has currently accepted medical use in the US, and may lead to moderate or low physical dependence or high psychological dependence: codeine with aspirin; Hydrocodone with aspirin; Vicodin, Anabolic steroids, Nandrolone, Testosterone, Marinol

Schedule IV: Substance has a low potential for abuse as compared to Schedule III, has currently accepted medical use in the US, and abuse may lead to limited physical and psychological dependence: Valium/Diazepam, Phenobarbital, Diazepam, Xanax/Alprazolam, Darvon/Propoxyphene, Triazolam/Halcion, Fenfluramine, Phentermine, Chloral Hydrate, Restoril/Temazepam, Chlordiazepoxide/Librium

Schedule V: Substance has a low potential for abuse as compared to Schedule IV, has currently accepted medical use in the US, and abuse has a narrow scope for physical and psychological dependence: cough medicines with codeine

Source: Controlled Substances Act, PL 91-513.

Rockefeller Drug Laws (Early 1970s)

The **Rockefeller Drug Laws** were a series of laws that were passed during the 1970s by the New York State Legislature during Governor Nelson Rockefeller's administration. The laws were passed after it was thought that the existing anti-drug treatment policies had failed, and many people believed that drug use was becoming uncontrollable. These new laws were very harsh and set high punishments for anyone convicted of using illicit drugs in New York state. The laws created mandatory minimum sentences for drug users of 15 years to life in prison with no probation/parole, and no plea bargaining. Governor Rockefeller's supporters backed the new laws, but many others did not. Many of the original laws were repealed or changed over time.[27]

Drug Abuse and Treatment Act (1972)

President Nixon signed the **Drug Abuse and Treatment Act** of 1972 as a way to reorganize federal drug agencies and make the federal government's response to drug abuse more effective. He established a new office, the Special Action Office of Drug Abuse Prevention, that would be found within the Executive Office of the President. This agency was given the responsibility to oversee all major federal drug-abuse prevention programs, education, treatment, rehabilitation, training, and research.

In addition, a second new agency created in the law was the National Drug Abuse Training Center. This agency was tasked with developing, conducting, and supporting training programs related to drug abuse prevention. A third agency created in the bill was the National Institute on Drug Abuse (NIDA). This new agency would be housed within the National Institute of Mental Health and was given the responsibility to administer drug abuse programs assigned to the Secretary of Health, Education, and Welfare.

Nixon also created four new advisory bodies when he signed the new law. The president's goal was to have experts who would provide him with counsel and recommendations about the nation's drug policies. These four new agencies were the Drug Abuse Strategy Council, the National Advisory Council on Drug Abuse, a Federal Drug Council, and the National Advisory Council on Drug Abuse Prevention.[28]

National Minimum Drinking Age Act (1984)

In 1984, Congress passed the **National Minimum Drinking Age Act** that mandated states set their legal drinking age for alcohol at 21 years. According to the law, if a state did not set the drinking age at 21, they would not receive federal funds for highway construction. The goal of the law was to decrease fatalities caused by drunken driving, a goal that was met by the law.[29]

Aviation Drug-Trafficking Control Act (1984)

The **Aviation Drug-Trafficking Control Act**, signed by President Reagan, was intended to increase the penalties for, and thus deter, smuggling of illicit drugs. This bill, officially known as "An Act to Amend the Federal Aviation Act of 1958 to Provide for the Revocation of the Airman Certificates and for Additional Penalties for the Transportation by Aircraft of Controlled Substances, and for Other Purposes," established increased penalties for any pilot whose aircraft contains, transports, or attempts to transport illegal substances. A pilot found guilty of these offenses would possibly lose their license for five years, as opposed to the one-year penalty that existed previously. Moreover, the law gave officials in the Federal Aviation Administration (FAA) the power to strip an aircraft of its registration if it was found to be used for transporting illegal substances.[30]

In 1988, this law was amended to provide $2.7 billion for anti-drug activities, part of which went to fund the aircraft registration system so that an aircraft could not be registered to a fictitious person, or a name that was not identifiable. Moreover, a person could not use a false or nonexistent address nor a post office box to register an aircraft. A person could not change the registration markings assigned to a plane. The FAA was required to create a method to track any time a plane was sold to another person. The new bill also required the FAA to establish a method for timely and adequate notice of any transfer of ownership of aircraft.[31]

Anti-Drug Abuse Act (1986)

The Anti-Drug Abuse Act of 1986 (P.L. 99-570), also known as the Drug-Free America Act, was an attempt to attack and eliminate drug use across the US. To do this, the law gave the president new powers to increase taxes on any goods that were imported from countries that were not cooperating in efforts to curb drug production and trafficking. The law also permitted law enforcement to seize assets of drug dealers, and new anti-money laundering provisions were established. Probably some of the most controversial parts of the new law reestablished federal mandatory minimum guidelines for both drug possession and trafficking.

The law was signed by President Reagan in October 1986. As he signed the law he said,

> Well, today it gives me great pleasure to sign legislation that reflects the total commitment of the American people and their government

to fight the evil of drugs. Drug use extracts a high cost on America: the cost of suffering and unhappiness, particularly among the young; the cost of lost productivity at the workplace; and the cost of drug-related crime. Drug use is too costly for us not to do everything in our power, not just to fight it but to subdue it and conquer it.[32]

The new law was comprised of 6 titles (chapters) and numerous subtitles, as shown in Table 3.4.

Table 3.4 Provisions of the Anti-Drug Abuse Act

Title I: Drug-Free Federal Workplace Act of 1986: amended the act that originally established the concept of a drug-free workplace. This time, some terms were defined more clearly. It also mandated that an employer is not legally obligated to hire an applicant or keep an employee who uses a controlled substance.

Sign in Des Moines, Iowa by Tony Webster via wikimedia commons.

Title II: Drug-Free Schools Act of 1986 (the Zero-Tolerance Act): established national programs designed to maintain drug-free school environments that are conducive to learning. Under the law, schools could require students to refrain from using illegal drugs as a condition of admission or continued enrollment. It was also legal for schools to require and conduct drug testing of its students or applicants.

Title III: Substance Abuse Services Amendments: amended the Public Health Service Act to extend block grant programs.

Title IV: Drug Interdiction and International Cooperation Act of 1986

Subtitle A: International Forfeiture Enabling Act: allows for seizure of any property by law enforcement that was related to an unlawful drug activity and was derived from the proceeds of the illegal activity or was used in the commission of the activity.

Subtitle B: Mansfield Amendment Repeal Act: repealed the law that required certain reports to Congress regarding international narcotics control activities.

Subtitle C: Narcotics Traffickers Deportation Act: Revised the federal law regarding the deportation of people who were convicted of violating controlled substances laws.

Subtitle D: Customs Enforcement Act of 1986: Revised the Tariff Act of 1930 regarding, among other things, the reporting of vessel arrivals, aviation smuggling, the seizure of conveyances, the exchange of information with foreign customs and law enforcement officers, and information regarding inspections and preclearance in foreign countries. The act increased the possible criminal and civil penalties for violations. The possible fine was set at up to $5,000, or a prison sentence of up to two years, or both. Moreover, the act amended the Controlled Substances Import and Export Act to make it unlawful for any US citizen on board any aircraft to manufacture, distribute, or possess with intent to manufacture or distribute a controlled substance. Criminal penalties were established for someone who operated an aircraft without lights and for illegal fuel installations aboard aircraft.

Subtitle E: Maritime Drug Law Enforcement Prosecution Improvements Act of 1986: makes it illegal for a person on board a US vessel to knowingly manufacture, distribute, or possess a controlled substance with the intent to manufacture or distribute.

Title V: Anti-Drug Enforcement Act

Subtitle A: Drug Penalties Enhancement Act of 1986: Amended the Controlled Substances Act to increase the criminal penalties for violating drug laws.

Subtitle B: Drug Possession Penalty Act of 1986: Amended the Controlled Substances Act to establish minimum penalties for possession offenses.

Subtitle C: Continuing Drug Enterprise Penalty Act of 1986: Amended the Controlled Substances Act to establish a minimum life sentence and multimillion-dollar fines for those individuals or organizations that engage in continuing criminal drug enterprises. If a killing results from a violation of the act, a procedure was described for the imposition of the death penalty.

Subtitle D: United States Marshals Service Act of 1986: Revised some provisions of federal law relating to the US Marshals Service.

Subtitle E: Controlled Substances Import and Export Penalties Enhancement Act of 1986: amended the Controlled Substances Import and Export Act to increase the penalty for violations from a maximum of 15 years in prison to a minimum of five years and a maximum of 40 years in prison. In cases where a death results from substance use, the penalty would be set at 20 years to life in prison. The act also increases the fines for violators from $125,000 to $2,000,000 for an individual, and $5,000,000 for an organization. There were also enhanced penalties for subsequent offenses.

Subtitle F: Juvenile Drug Trafficking Act of 1986: Amends the Controlled Substances Act to establish punishments for any person who was at least 21 years of age and employs a person who is under the age of 21 in the trafficking of a controlled substance.

Subtitle G: Chemical Diversion and Trafficking Act of 1986: amends the Comprehensive Drug Abuse Prevention and Control Act to require manufacturers, distributors, importers, and exporters of certain substances to maintain complete records of their transactions. The law also prohibits the distribution or export of such substances unless the recipient or purchaser presents the distributor with a certification of lawful use. The law also directs the attorney general to maintain an active system to curtail the diversion of precursor chemicals that are used to manufacture controlled substances, both domestically and internationally.

Subtitle H: Money Laundering Crimes Act of 1986: Establishes criminal penalties for financial transactions involving the proceeds of some form of unlawful activity for the purpose of either facilitating such activity or concealing its nature. The act also sets forth procedures for the civil and criminal forfeiture of any property involved in such unlawful financial transactions.

Subtitle I: Controlled Substances Technical Amendments of 1986: Makes technical amendments to the Controlled Substances Act.

Subtitle J: Controlled Substances Analogs Enforcement Act of 1986: Amends the Controlled Substances Act to establish penalties for the manufacture or possession of a designer drug with the intent to distribute. The law also makes it illegal to knowingly or intentionally possess a designer drug.

Subtitle K: Asset Forfeiture Amendments Act of 1986: Amends federal law concerning the forfeiture of assets involved in unlawful controlled substance activities.

Subtitle L: Exclusionary Rule Limitation Act of 1986: Amends the federal criminal code so that any evidence that was obtained as a result of a search or seizure shall not be excluded in a US district court on the ground that it violated the Fourth Amendment to the Constitution, if the search or seizure was undertaken in with a reasonable belief that it was legal.

Title VI: Public Awareness and Private Sector Initiatives Act of 1986: declares that an agency may contract for property or services that are designed to warn of the dangers of illegal drug use without complying with any requirement for competition in federal procurement, so long as at least 50 percent of actual, reasonable costs of providing the property or service is being donated to the federal government.

Source: "Congress Clears Massive Anti-Drug Measure." 1987. In *CQ Almanac 1986*, 42nd ed., 92–106. Washington, DC: Congressional Quarterly. http://library.cqpress.com/ cqalmanac/cqal86–1149752; Reagan, Ronald. September 15, 1986. "Message to Congress Transmitting Proposed Legislation to Combat Drug Abuse and Trafficking." http://www. reagan.utexas.edu/archives/speeches/1986/091586b.htm; Library of Congress. S2849 Drug-Free America Act (1986). Available at https://www.govtrack.us/congress/bills/99/ s2849#summary.

Anti-Drug Abuse Act Amendments (1988)

Amendments to the Anti-Drug Abuse Act of 1986 were passed by Congress in 1988 as drug use continued to rise across the nation. This new law again increased many penalties for drug use, even providing for the death penalty in murder cases that involved drug-trafficking organizations. Those who possessed a small amount of crack cocaine faced a sentence of five to 20 years. In addition to increasing punishments, the law also had provisions providing for treatment. Specifically, it provided that about half of the $2.8 billion allocated for the program be spent on program geared toward decreasing demand, including educational and treatment programs.

In addition, the amendment created the Office of National Drug Control Policy (ONDCP) that would be responsible for creating and implementing the nation's anti-drug use policies. The head of the ONDCP would be known as the nation's drug czar and would be a cabinet-level position. This person would serve as an advisor to the president on any matters related to illicit drugs, and would coordinate all federal drug-control programs across the nation. The ONDCP has the duty to publish the National Drug Control Policy each year. This report outlines the administration's efforts and success at reducing illicit drug use, manufacturing and trafficking, drug-related crime and violence, and drug-related health consequences. It provides an outline for the nation's goals and strategies to control and reduce illicit drug use.[33]

Drug Kingpin Death Penalty Act (1987, 1994)

The **Drug Kingpin Death Penalty Act** was passed by Congress to address violence associated with the drug trade. Under the law, the death penalty could be imposed against a person when an individual other than a participant in a criminal act dies. The government must show that the act was intentional and caused the individual's death. It also applies if the person killed was a judge, law enforcement officer, or an employee of a correctional institution.

In 1994, the law was amended to allow for the death penalty against an individual who was considered to be a "drug kingpin," and who either played a significant role in the drug trade or who had control of the drug network. It was not necessary for that person to have actually carried out the crime that resulted in death. The death penalty was also authorized for those defendants who were convicted in federal court of murder that was committed while the offender was engaged in a "continuing criminal enterprise" that involved either large quantities of a controlled substance or $20 million in receipts over a one-year period. In short, the defendant in this situation did not have to commit the murder him/herself but either ordered it, know about it, or was part of the organization whose members carried out the murder.[34]

Chemical Diversion and Trafficking Act (1988)

This new law restricted access to precursor chemicals and tableting machines that are used to make other drugs. It required that companies keep detailed records about imports and exports on any transactions that include these materials. Before this, many of the primary chemicals used in the manufacture of cocaine in South America were purchased in the US.

Drug-Free Workplace Act (1988)

The **Drug-Free Workplace Act** of 1988 requires that federal contractors and the grantees both provide drug-free workplaces as a condition of receiving the contract or grant from the federal government. The regulations do not apply to people or organizations that do not have, nor intend to apply for contracts/grants from the federal government. The act also does not apply to subcontractors. If a federal contractor fails to maintain a drug-free workplace, the payment for that contract may be halted and the contract terminated.

According to the law, a "drug-free workplace" is a federal site where employees are prohibited from manufacturing, distributing, dispensing, possessing, or using a controlled (illegal) substance. As part of the law, all employees must be made aware that the site is a drug-free site, and the punishments for violating the policy must be provided. There must also be drug-free awareness programs available to employees that can educate them about the dangers of drug use in the workplace, as well as drug counseling that is available for anyone who might need it.[35]

International Narcotics Control Act (1989)

The **International Narcotics Control Act** of 1989 (PL 101-213) was signed into law by President George H. W. Bush on December 13, 1989. The intent of the new law was to reduce the trafficking of illicit drugs into the US by providing financial support to governments that were actively fighting against both the production and trafficking of cocaine. The bill provided federal funds to combat the international drug trade, with particular attention given to preventing the production of cocaine in South America (but some funds were also available for Mexico). Under the bill, Congress authorized $115 million in 1990 for international narcotics control assistance with an additional $125 million to be used for military and law enforcement assistance to the South American countries of Colombia, Peru, and Bolivia because of their role in producing the majority of the world's cocaine. The money was meant to provide those countries with more support in their anti-drug efforts, but it was also hoped that it would strengthen relationships between their governments and the US.

The bill also focused on crop substitution programs that would provide alternate employment for those people who grow coca crops. Some policies supported the eradication of coca crops, increased enforcement of narcotics laws, and rehabilitation, treatment, and education programs for users.

This bill was reauthorized in 1992 as the International Narcotics Control Act of 1992, and signed into law (Public Law 102-583).[36]

Crime Control Act (1990)

The **Crime Control Act** of 1990 is an anti-crime bill that was signed by President George H. W. Bush. The bill included provisions in multiple areas, including crime prevention, money laundering, child abuse, prisons, child pornography, and anti-drug measures. One of the anti-drug measures included in the bill was Title VIII, which covered rural drug enforcement. This section allocated money for assistance for drug enforcement in rural areas. Additional funds were made available to local police departments so they could fight drug use.

Another section of the bill was Title XV, the Drug-Free School Zones Act. This provision required the US attorney general to develop policies for establishing and maintaining drug-free school zones. These policies could then be used by local school districts to develop their own drug-free school zones. To support the Drug-Free School Zones, Congress authorized $15 million in federal funds. The money could be spent on a variety of things, such as setting geographic boundaries for drug-free schools and posting signs that identify these areas as drug-free school zones. Other examples include drug-abuse education and prevention programs for children and youth and enforcement policies meant to end the use of alcohol and drugs in the drug-free zones.

Another key provision was Title XIX, or the Anabolic Steroids Control Act of 1990. This provision added anabolic steroids to Schedule III of the CSA. This categorization made it illegal for a person other than a doctor to prescribe, dispense, or distribute anabolic steroids and that the use of the drug would be for a recognized therapeutic purpose. It also increased the potential fines and prison terms for knowingly distributing or possessing steroids if there was an intent to distribute those drugs for a reason other than medical treatment.

The Chemical Diversion and Trafficking Act was another critical provision of the law. This was Title XXIII, and it added specified substances to the list of precursor chemicals subject to controls imposed by that act. A similar provision was the Drug Paraphernalia Act, found in Title XXIV. This amended the CSA to make it illegal to sell, offer for sale, or to use the mail to transport, or import or export, drug paraphernalia.

Title XXVI, the Licit Opium Imports Act, required that the president review the US narcotics raw material policy to determine if it would be advisable to continue the reliance on the rule by which at least 80 percent of US imports of narcotics raw material must come from India and Turkey; and to report the results of such review to Congress by April 1, 1991.

Title XXVII, Sentencing for Methamphetamine Offenses, required that the US Sentencing Commission amend the sentencing guidelines pertaining to offenses revolving around smoking crystal methamphetamine.

Finally, Title XXVIII, Drug Enforcement Grants, authorized appropriations for fiscal years 1991 and 1992 for grants under the drug control and system improvement grant program (Edward Byrne Memorial Programs).[37]

Andean Trade Preference Act (1991)

Many people became concerned with the massive influx of illicit drugs into the US from countries such as Bolivia, Colombia, and Peru. To address this concern, President Ford reached out to leaders of these countries in the hopes of increasing cooperation with them and to limit both the production and shipment of drugs. The subsequent president, Jimmy Carter, did the same. He announced that the president of Colombia had promised to give the drug problem high priority. Carter also promised to establish a commission comprised of government officials from both countries that would work to coordinate their efforts regarding international cocaine trafficking. President Reagan allocated $10 million to purchase aircraft that would be used for efforts regarding the interdiction and eradication of drugs.[38]

President George H. W. Bush signed the **Andean Trade Preference Act** (ATPA) in December 1991. The new law provided financial assistance for four Andean countries (Bolivia, Colombia, Ecuador, and Peru) to assist them in their fight against drug production and trafficking. The intent of the law was to help these countries develop alternative means of production so that they would rely less on drug production and trafficking. The law also designated certain export products to come into the United States duty-free. Congress agreed to increase the number of Andean-produced items exempted from tariffs from about 5,600 to about 6,300.

The original act has been amended since first being passed. The law was amended in 2001 when Congress passed the Andean Counterdrug Initiative, which was an attempt at preventing narcotics shipments from entering the US. The ATPA was again amended in 2002 by the Andean Trade Promotion and Drug Eradication Act (ATPDEA), passed during the George W. Bush administration. This new law reauthorized the original act, but also designated additional products as duty-free.

The permitted exemptions were set to expire on December 31, 2006, but Congress passed a bill to reauthorize the act for an additional six months, extending the expiration to June 30, 2007. At that point, Congress passed a bill allowing for an additional eight-month extension on duty-free goods, then passed a third extension for ten months. Some analysis shows that Bolivian officials did not appear to be cooperating, so in November of 2008, President Bush asked Congress to remove Bolivia from the agreement. A new plan that covered only products from Ecuador was eventually passed.[39]

Alcohol, Drug Abuse, and Mental Health Reorganization Act (ADAMHA) (1992)

The **Alcohol, Drug Abuse, and Mental Health Reorganization Act** (ADAMHA) (PL 102-321) was signed into law by President George H. W. Bush on July 10, 1992. When he did this, the existing federal alcohol, drug abuse, and mental health research and services programs were restructured in order to support research into substance abuse and mental health, as well as increase social services to those impacted by drug use.[40]

One thing that was done under the law was the rearrangement of the Alcohol, Drug Abuse, and Mental Health Administration (ADAMHA). This agency was originally established by President Nixon in 1974 and incorporated the Department of Health and Human Services. The ADAMHA Act integrated three research institutes into the National Institutes of Health: the National Institute on Alcohol Abuse and Alcoholism; the National Institute on Drug Abuse; and the National Institute of Mental Health. President Bush explained that when these three research agencies were brought into the NIH, there would be a more efficient exchange of information and sharing of expertise and knowledge within the drug research community.[41] In the long run, these increased communications would improve the quality of research being carried out to address the needs of those addicted to drugs.

Another goal of the reorganization was to provide more effective and comprehensive services to any defendant who was identified as having mental illness and addictive disorders. Bush believed the reorganization would allow the federal government to provide assistance to state and local organizations as they provide services to addicts. Bush wanted to increase the quality of mental health and substance abuse services for those who suffer from mental illness and addictive disorders.

There were two other notable provisions of this Act pertaining to funds. The first provision created a federal grant program to provide substance abuse treatment for addicts. To qualify for money, states would have to assess their current programs and develop ways to improve them.

The second provision banned the use of federal funds for needle sxchange programs. President Bush believed that such programs only encouraged more drug use rather than reducing the transmission of disease.[42]

The new law passed by Congress required states to enforce laws that would bar the sale of tobacco products to minors. Although most states had laws to prohibit such sales, many were not enforcing them.

Domestic Chemical Diversion Control Act (1993)

This bill eliminated the loophole for purchasing the drugs required to make methamphetamines through over-the-counter sales. However, the law applied to products that contained ephedrine but not pseudoephedrine. As a result, those who wanted to produce meth simply switched to using pseudoephedrine.

Violent Crime Control and Law Enforcement Act (1994)

The **Violent Crime Control and Law Enforcement Act** of 1994 was comprehensive law that made numerous changes in the criminal justice system. Signed by President Clinton, the bill had many provisions related to drugs. One of those was related to drug courts. Title V of the act created a grant program to states to created drug courts. These courts provide special services to offenders who are suffering from drug addictions and who have been identified as having strong potential for rehabilitation.

Drug treatment for inmates was also part of the bill. The law made $383 million available to prison officials to fund drug treatment programs within the facility. The bill required the director of the Administrative Office of the US Courts (Administrative Office) to establish a program of drug testing for federal offenders who were placed on post-conviction release.

Title XVII of the 1994 law allocated federal money to be used for drug enforcement in rural areas. To keep with that effort, the Attorney General was mandated to establish a Rural Drug Enforcement Task Force. Training for the officers serving on the Task Force was to be provided by the Federal Law Enforcement Training Center (FLETC).

In other provisions of the bill:

- Provided grants to local governments for education and prevention programs related to the use and sale of illegal drugs by juveniles.
- Defined that the death penalty could be imposed for specified drug-related offenses, particularly related to drug trafficking.
- Defined penalties for inmates who trafficked drugs within a federal prison and for drug dealing in "drug-free" zones.
- Established penalties for using children to distribute drugs near school and playgrounds.[43]

Comprehensive Methamphetamine Control Act (1996)

The use of methamphetamine increased throughout the early 1990s, leading to an increase in violent crime and deaths. Because of this, Congress passed the **Comprehensive Methamphetamine Control Act** of 1996. The law focused on limiting the availability of the precursor chemicals needed to manufacture meth. It also focused on limiting the trafficking of meth and importation of it from other countries.

The law made it illegal to possess the chemicals needed for making methamphetamine. It also increased the penalties for possessing these chemicals. If a person was found to be in violation of the law, they could be sentenced to a term in prison of up to ten years and face a possible fine of up to $30,000, or both. In addition, law enforcement could now confiscate any over-the-counter products (such as medications to treat cold and allergy symptoms) if it was thought that they were being used to manufacture methamphetamines. The new law also increased the penalties associated with possession, manufacture, trafficking, or sale of methamphetamine itself. These were to be set by the US Sentencing Commission.

The law permitted some over-the-counter sale of medications that contained pseudoephedrine as long as they were sold in blister packs. The thought was that this form of packaging would make processing the pills more difficult, thereby discouraging meth producers from making the meth. Instead, major producers simply got their drugs from sources in Mexico or Canada, where bulk purchases of ephedrine and pseudoephedrine were legal.[44]

Another part of this law established a Methamphetamine Interagency Task Force. This new agency, which would be headed by the US attorney general, would design, implement, and evaluate any education, prevention, and treatment practices regarding methamphetamines and other synthetic stimulants.[45]

Hillory J. Farias and Samantha Reid Date-Rape Drug Prohibition Act (2000)

In 2000, GHB (or gamma-hydroxybutyric acid) became an illegal Schedule I drug when President Clinton signed the **Hillory J. Farias and Samantha Reid Date-Rape Drug Prohibition Act** of 2000. Samantha Reid was a 15-year-old Michigan girl who unknowingly consumed the drug after it was slipped into her Mountain Dew. She later died because she stopped breathing. Hillory Farias was a 17-year-old high school senior in Texas who also died as a result of GHB being slipped into her soft drink. The drug can still be used for legitimate medical purposes.

Making GHB a Schedule I drug makes it a crime to possess, manufacture, or sell the drug or any of the precursor chemicals that are used to make the drug. It also increased the penalties for any unauthorized manufacturing or distribution of the drugs.

A person convicted of these offenses could face up to 20 years in prison.

Combat Methamphetamine Epidemic Act (2005)

The popularity of methamphetamine rose and fell over many years. It was a popular drug in the late 1960s as part of the counterculture's acceptance of drug use, but then waned after the Controlled Substances Act of 1970 was passed. It became popular again in the 1990s after Mexican drug cartels manufactured mass quantities of the drug and began to distribute it in California and Southwestern states. It was also made easily in small, home-based labs that relied on readily available over-the-counter cold medications. The drug's use once again fell after provisions in the PATRIOT Act limited the availability of over-the-counter medications.

The **Combat Methamphetamine Epidemic Act** of 2005 was another attempt by Congress to restrict access to the precursor drugs used to manufacture the drug. The law mandates that a pharmacy must ensure that the drugs are sold only by the pharmacist, and that any person purchasing it provide a photo identification. Records must be kept of who purchases the drug and when. No person is permitted to purchase more than 7.5 grams of the drug within a 30-day period.

After the law was passed, forty states then passed laws that limited sales of medications containing pseudoephedrine. Two states, Oregon and Mississippi, passed laws to make these products only available with a doctor's prescription. The new law has not stopped the production of meth. Instead, producers simply use a smaller amount of the drug in a "one pot" method.[46]

Fair Sentencing Act (2010)

When Congress passed the Anti-Drug Abuse Act of 1986, they made the sentences for offenders convicted of possessing crack cocaine more harsh than the sentences for those convicted of possessing powder cocaine. This meant that offenders arrested for possession of crack cocaine could be sentenced to much longer penalties than those who were arrested for possessing powder cocaine. Many opponents to this scheme argued this discrepancy was racist because crack cocaine offenses were more often committed by black offenders whereas powder-cocaine offenses were most often committed by white offenders. Congress reduced the disparity in 2010 in the **Fair Sentencing Act**, which was signed by President Obama.

The goal of the new law was to improve the fairness and equity of the sentencing process with regards to cocaine and reduce the sentencing disparity between the punishments required for conviction of crack offenses and powder cocaine offenses. The law eliminated the five-year mandatory minimum prison sentence that had been the requirement for federal offenders convicted of possessing five grams or more of crack cocaine. It also reduced the mandatory sentences for conviction of possessing crack cocaine. This would bring them more in line with the punishments for conviction of powder cocaine.[47]

Synthetic Drug Abuse Prevention Act (2012)

Drug manufacturers began to producing synthetic marijuana and giving it names like K2 or Spice. The drugs were extremely dangerous with tremendous health risks. Nonetheless, the drugs were popular among high school youth.[48] The law passed in 2012 increased regulations of these drugs (Subtitle D of Title XI of the Food and Drug Administration Safety and Innovation Act (P.L. 112-144)). When this was signed into law, 26 types of synthetic cannabinoids were placed into Schedule I of the Controlled Substances Act.[49] In addition, many states also passed laws to place limits on synthetic marijuana products.

Conclusion

Over the past 100 years, there have been many bills passed to stop drug importation, use, possession, and manufacture. Each of the new laws focuses on different drugs or drug-related problems. Nonetheless, even with increased regulation and increased penalties, people continue to use illegal drugs. There is no doubt that Congress will continue to pass new laws to regulate drug use, but they will probably not be effective in stopping illegal drug use.

Important Terms

Alcohol, Drug Abuse, and Mental Health Reorganization Act
Andean Trade Preference Act
Anti-Drug Abuse Act
Anti-Drug Abuse Act Amendments
Aviation Drug-Trafficking Control Act
Boggs Act
Boylan Act
Chemical Diversion and Trafficking Act
Combat Methamphetamine Epidemic Act
Comprehensive Drug Abuse Prevention and Control Act
Comprehensive Methamphetamine Control Act
Counterculture
Crime Control Act
Domestic Chemical Diversion Control Act
Drug Abuse and Treatment Act
Drug Abuse Control Amendments
Drug Kingpin Death Penalty Act
Drug-Free Workplace Act
Durham-Humphrey Amendment
Fair Sentencing Act
Food, Drug, and Cosmetic Act
Harrison Narcotics Act

Hillory J. Farias and Samantha Reid Date-Rape Drug Prohibition Act
International Narcotics Control Act
Marihuana Tax Act
Narcotic Addict Rehabilitation Act
Narcotic Control Act
Narcotic Drugs Import and Export Act
National Minimum Drinking Age Act
Opium Poppy Control Act
Porter Narcotic Farm Act
Prohibition
Pure Food and Drug Act
Rockefeller Drug Laws
Smoking Opium Exclusion Act
Synthetic Drug Abuse Prevention Act
Violent Crime Control and Law Enforcement Act
Webb-Kenyon Act
Whitney Act

Discussion Questions

1. One of the most important pieces of legislation passed by Congress to control illicit drugs was the Comprehensive Drug Abuse Prevention and Control Act, passed in 1970. What were the elements of this law?

2. Why was the Harrison Narcotics Act important to limiting drug use in the US?

3. If you were in Congress and wanted to pass a bill related to drug use, what would it include?

4. Congress has passed many laws over time to regulate illicit drugs. What laws do you think are most or least effective?

5. What laws are supported by Republican or Democratic presidents? How do they differ, if at all?

6. Are laws regulating drug use a type of morality policy?

Endnotes

1. Bowen, Elizabeth A. 2012. "Clean Needles and Bad Blood: Needle Exchange as Morality Policy." *Journal of Sociology and Social Welfare* 39(2): 121–141; Mooney, Christopher Z. 2000. "The Decline of Federalism and the Rise of Morality-Policy Conflict in the United States." *Publius* 30: 171–188; Knill, Christoph. 2013. "The Study of Morality Policy: Analytical Implications from a Public Policy Perspective." *Journal of European Public Policy* 20(3): 309–317.

2. Omori, Marisa K. 2013. "Moral Panics and Morality Policy: The Impact of Media, Political Ideology, Drug Use, and Manufacturing on Methamphetamine Legislation in the United States." *Journal of Drug Issues* 43(4): 517–34.

3. Tatalovich, R., and B. W. Daynes. 1998. *Moral Controversies in American Politics: Cases in Social Regulatory Policy.* Armonk, NY: M.E. Sharpe.

4. Bowen, Elizabeth A. 2012. "Clean Needles and Bad Blood: Needle Exchange as Morality Policy." *Journal of Sociology and Social Welfare* 39(2): 121–141; Hawdon, J. E. 2001. "The Role of Presidential Rhetoric in the Creation of Moral Panic: Reagan, Bush, and the War on Drugs." *Deviant Behavior* 22: 419–445.

5. Terry, Charles E., and Midred Pellens. 1928. "San Francisco Law Against Opium Smoking, 1857." In Steven R. Belenko, ed. *Drugs and Drug Policy in America.* Westport, CT: Greenwood Press, p. 14–15.

6. Fachner, J. 2003. "Jazz, Improvisation and a Social Pharmacology of Music." *Music Therapy Today* 4(3): 1–26. http://musictherapyworld.net; Wills, G. I. 2003. "Forty Lives in the Bebop Business: Mental Health in a Group of Eminent Jazz Musicians." *British Journal of Psychiatry* 183: 255–59; Winnick, C. 1960. "The Use of Drugs by Jazz Musicians." *Social Problems* 7(3): 240–53.

7. Courtwright, David T. 2001. *Dark Paradise: A History of Opiate Addiction in America.* Cambridge, MA: Harvard University Press; Morgan, H. Wayne. 1974. *Yesterday's Addicts: American Society and Drug Abuse, 1865–1920.* Norman: University of Oklahoma Press.

8. Courtwright, David T. 2001. *Dark Paradise: A History of Opiate Addiction in America.* Cambridge, MA: Harvard University Press; Hilts, Philip J. 2003. *Protecting America's Health: The FDA, Business, and One Hundred Years of Regulation.* New York: Alfred A. Knopf; Morgan, H. Wayne. 1974. *Yesterday's Addicts: American Society and Drug Abuse, 1865–1920.* Norman, OK: University of Oklahoma Press; Musto, David F. 1987. *The American Disease: Origins of Narcotics Control.* Expanded Edition. New York: Oxford University Press; Swann, John P. "History of the FDA." http://www.fda.gov/oc/history/historyoffda/default.htm.

9. Courtwright, David T. 2001. *Dark Paradise: A History of Opiate Addiction in America.* Cambridge, MA: Harvard University Press; Musto, David F. 1987. *The American Disease: Origins of Narcotics Control.* Expanded Edition. New York: Oxford University Press.

10. Murdock, Catherine Gilbert. 1998. *Domesticating Drink: Women, Men, and Alcohol in America, 1870–1940.* Baltimore: Johns Hopkins University Press; Pegram, Thomas P. 1998. *Battling Demon Rum: The Struggle for a Dry America, 1800–1933.* Chicago: Ivan R. Dee.

11. Belenko, Steven R., ed. 2000. *Drugs and Drug Policy in America: A Documentary History.* Westport, CT: Greenwood Press; King, Rufus. 1972. *The Drug Hang-Up: America's Fifty-Year Folly.* Springfield, IL: Bannerstone House; Musto, David F. 1987. *The American Disease: Origins of Narcotics Control.* Expanded Edition. New York: Oxford University Press.

12. Courtwright, David T. 2001. *Dark Paradise: A History of Opiate Addiction in America.* Cambridge, MA: Harvard University Press; "Harrison Narcotics Tax Act." http://www.princeton.edu/~achaney/tmve/wiki100k/docs/Harrison_Narcotics_Tax_Act.html; Musto, David F. 1987. *The American Disease: Origins of Narcotics Control.* Expanded Edition. New York: Oxford University Press.

13. Engdahl, Sylvia. 2012. *Prohibition.* Detroit: Greenhaven Press; Gordon, Ernest B. 1943. *The Wrecking of the Eighteenth Amendment.* Francestown, NH: Alcohol Information Press; Peck, Garrett. 2009. *The Prohibition Hangover: Alcohol in America from Demon Rum to Cult Cabernet.* New Brunswick, NJ: Rutgers University Press.

14. Mappen, Marc. 2013. *Prohibition Gangsters: The Rise and Fall of a Bad Generation.* New Brunswick, NJ: Rutgers University Press;

15. Andersen, Lisa M. F. 2013. *Politics of Prohibition: American Governance and the Prohibition Party, 1869–1933.* New York: Cambridge University Press; Engdahl, Sylvia. 2012.

Prohibition. Detroit: Greenhaven Press; Nishi, Dennis. 2004. *Prohibition*. San Diego, CA: Greenhaven Press; Peck, Garrett. 2009. *The Prohibition Hangover: Alcohol in America from Demon Rum to Cult Cabernet*. New Brunswick, NJ: Rutgers University Press.

16. Acker, C. J. 1997. "The Early Years of the PHS Narcotic Hospital at Lexington, Kentucky." *Public Health Reports* 112: 245–47; Ball, J. C., W. O. Thompson, and D. M. Allen. 1970. "Readmission Rates at Lexington Hospital for 43,215 Narcotic Drug Addicts." *Public Health Reports* 85: 610–16; Burroughs, W. S. 2003. *Junky: The Definitive Text of "Junk" (50th Anniversary Edition)*. New York: Penguin Books; Campbell, N. D. 2006. "A 'New Deal' for the Drug Addict: The Addiction Research Center, Lexington, Kentucky." *Journal of the History of Behavioral Sciences* 42: 135–157; Campbell, N. D., J. P. Olsen, and L. Walden. 2008. *The Narcotic Farm: The Rise and Fall of America's First Prison for Drug Addicts*. New York: Abrams; Edwards, G. 2010. "Seeing America—Diary of a Drug-Focused Study Tour Made in 1967." *Addiction* 105: 984–90; Kolb, L., and W. F. Ossenfort. 1938. "The Treatment of Addicts at the Lexington Hospital." *Southern Medical Journal*. 31: 914–20.

17. Schaffer Library of Drug Policy, The Marijuana Tax Act of 1937. http://www.drug library.org/SCHAFFER/hemp/taxact.

18. Newton, David. 2017. *Marijuana: A Reference Handbook*. Santa Barbara: ABC-CLIO.

19. U.S. Customs and Border Protection, (2016, October 6) "Did you know … Marijuana was once a legal cross-border import?" https://www.cbp.gov/about/history; Marion, Nancy E. (2014). *The Medical Marijuana Maze* (Durham, North Carolina: Carolina Academic Press).

20. "The 1930 Food, Drug, and Cosmetic Act." US Food and Drug Administration. http://www.fda.gov/AboutFDA/WhatWeDo/History/ProductRegulation/ucm132818.htm; Hillstrom, Kevin. 2012. *US Health Policy and Politics: A Documentary History*. Washington, DC: CQ Press; Kleinfeld, Vincent A. 1949. "Federal Food, Drug, and Cosmetic Act: Judicial and Administrative Record, 1938–1949." Chicago: Commerce Clearing House; US Food and Drug Administration. "FDA History—Part II: The 1938 Food, Drug, and Cosmetic Act." http://www.fda.gov/aboutFDA/WhatWeDo/History/origin/ucm054826.htm.

21. Chouvy, Pierre-Arnaud. 2010. *Opium: Uncovering the Politics of the Poppy*. Cambridge, MA: Harvard University Press; United Nations Office on Drugs and Crime. "The Suppression of Poppy Cultivation in the United States." http://www.unodc.org/unodc/en/data-and-analysis/bulletin/bulletin_1950–01–01_3_page003.html.

22. Truman, Harry S. November 2, 1951. "Executive Order 10302—Interdepartmental Committee on Narcotics." Online by Gerhard Peters and John T. Woolley. *The American Presidency Project*. http://www.presidency.ucsb.edu/ws/?pid=78436; Truman, Harry. 1951. "Statement by the President Upon Signing Bill Relating to Narcotics Laws Violations." Online by Gerhard Peters and John T. Woolley, *The American Presidency Project*. http://www.presidency.ucsb.edu/ws/?pid=13984.

23. Belenko, Steven R., ed. 2000. *Drugs and Drug Policy in America: A Documentary History*. Westport, CT: Greenwood Press; Musto, David F. 1987. *The American Disease: Origins of Narcotic Control*. Expanded Edition. New York: Oxford University Press; Rowe, Thomas C. 2006. *Federal Narcotics Laws and the War on Drugs: Money Down a Rat Hole*. Binghamton, NY: Hawthorn Press.

24. Musto, David. 1987. *The American Disease: Origins of Narcotic Control*. New York: Oxford University Press; Davenport-Hines, Richard. 2001. *The Pursuit of Oblivion: A Global History of Narcotics 1500–2000*. London: Weidenfeld and Nicholson.

25. Boon, Marcus. 2002. *The Road of Excess: A History of Writers on Drugs*. Cambridge, MA: Harvard University Press.

26. Martin, William R., and Harris Isbell, eds. 1978. *Drug Addiction and the US Public Health Service*. Rockville, MD: National Institute on Drug Abuse; Musto, David F. 1987. *The American Disease: Origins of Narcotic Control*. Expanded Edition. New York: Oxford University Press; White, William L. 1998. *Slaying the Dragon: The History of Addiction Treatment and Recovery in America*. Bloomington, IL: Chestnut Health Systems.

27. Gray, M. 2009. "A Brief History of New York's Rockefeller Drug Laws." *Time*. http://content.time.com/time/nation/article/0,8599,1888864,00.html; Kohler-Hausmann, J. 2010. "'The Attila the Hun Law': New York's Rockefeller Drug Laws and the Making of a Punitive State." *Journal of Social History* 44: 71–95; Mann, B. 2013. "The Drug Laws That Changed How We Punish." *Morning Edition*. http://www.npr.org/2013/02/14/171822608/the-drug-laws-that-changed-how-we-punish; New York Civil Liberties Union. 2009. *The Rockefeller Drug Laws: Unjust, Irrational, Ineffective*. New York, NY: NYCLU Press.

28. "Drug Abuse Prevention: New Programs Approved." 1973. In *CQ Almanac 1972*, 28th ed., 03-162-03-166. Washington, DC: Congressional Quarterly. http://library.cqpress.com/cqalmanac/cqal72-1250269; Nixon, Richard. March 21, 1972. "Statement About the Drug Abuse Office and Treatment Act of 1972." Online by Gerhard Peters and John T. Woolley. *American Presidency Project*. http://www.presidency.ucsb.edu/ws/?pid=3782; "Presidential Statement to Congress: Nixon on Drug Control Programs." 1972. In *CQ Almanac 1971*, 27th ed., 11-94-A-11-98-A. Washington, DC: Congressional Quarterly. http://library.cqpress.com/cqalmanac/cqal71-869-26707-1255187; Research Foundation for the State of New York University. "Drug Abuse Office and Treatment Act of 1972." https://portal.rfsuny.org/portal/page/portal/The%20Research%20Foundation%20of%20SUNY/home/What_we_do/Federal_Laws_and_Regulations/Antidiscrimination/Drug_Abuse_Office_and_Treatment_Act_of_1972.

29. Hanson, David J. "The National Minimum Drinking Age Act of 1984." http://www2.potsdam.edu/hansondj/youthissues/1092767630.html; Liebschutz, Sarah F. 1985. "The National Minimum Drinking Age Law." *Publius* 15(3): 39–51; Palicz, K. "Legislative Analysis of the National Minimum Drinking Age Act." National Youth Rights Association. http://www.youthrights.org/research/library/legislative-analysis-of-the-national-minimum-drinking-age-act/?sid=; Reagan, Ronald. July 17, 1984. "Remarks on Signing a National Minimum Drinking Age Bill." Online by Gerhard Peters and John T. Woolley. *American Presidency Project*. http://www.presidency.ucsb.edu/ws/?pid=40164.

30. Aviation Drug-Trafficking Control Act of 1984. Public Law 98–499. http://www.gpo.gov/fdsys/pkg/STATUTE-98/pdf/STATUTE-98-Pg2312.pdf; Reagan, Ronald. October 19, 1984. "Statement on Signing the Aviation Drug-Trafficking Control Act." Online by Gerhard Peters and John T. Woolley. *The American Presidency Project*. http://www.presidency.ucsb.edu/ws/?pid=39283.

31. "Congress Clears Massive Anti-Drug Measure." 1987. In *CQ Almanac 1986*, 42nd ed., 92–106. Washington, DC: Congressional Quarterly. http://library.cqpress.com/cqalmanac/cqal86-1149752; "Election-Year Anti-Drug Bill Enacted." 1989. In *CQ Almanac 1988*, 44th ed., 85–111. Washington, DC: Congressional Quarterly. http://library.cqpress.com/cqalmanac/cqal88-1141196; US Department of the Treasury. 2013. "Treasury Designates Head of Aviation Drug Smuggling Operation." http://www.treasury.gov/press-center/press-releases/Pages/tg1857.aspx.

32. Reagan, Ronald. October 27, 1986. "Remarks on Signing the Anti-Drug Abuse Act of 1986." Online by Gerhard Peters and John T. Woolley. *American Presidency Project*. http://www.presidency.ucsb.edu/ws/?pid=36654.

33. White House, Office of National Drug Control Policy. http://www.whitehouse.gov/ondcp/about; Huggins, Laura E., ed. 2005. *Drug War Deadlock: The Policy Battle Continues.* Stanford, CA: Hoover Institution Press; Padwa, Howard, and Jacob A. Cunningham. 2010. "Anti-Drug Abuse Acts." In *Addiction: A Reference Encyclopedia.* Santa Barbara, CA: ABC-CLIO. http://ebooks.abc-clio.com/reader.aspx?isbn=9781598842302&id=A1857C-734.

34. "Bush Signs Stripped-Down Crime Bill." 1991. In *CQ Almanac 1990*, 46th ed., 486–99. Washington, DC: Congressional Quarterly. http://library.cqpress.com/cqalmanac/cqal90-1113148; "Election-Year Anti-Drug Bill Enacted." 1989. In *CQ Almanac 1988*, 44th ed., 85–111. Washington, DC: Congressional Quarterly. http://library.cqpress.com/cqalmanac/cqal88-1141196; "Expansion of the Federal Death Penalty." *Capital Punishment in Context.* http://www.capitalpunishmentincontext.org/issues/expansion; "H.R. 696–103rd Congress: Drug Kingpin Death Penalty Act." 1993. http://www.govtrack.us/congress/bills/103/hr696.

35. Cornell University Law School. 41 USC Chapter 81, Drug-Free Workplace. http://www.law.cornell.edu/uscode/text/41/subtitle-IV/chapter-81; US Department of Labor, Office of the Assistant Secretary for Policy. "Drug-Free Workplace Act of 1988." http://www.dol.gov/elaws/asp/drugfree/screen4.htm.

36. Bush, George. 1989. "Statement on Signing the International Narcotics Control Act of 1989." Online by Gerhard Peters and John T. Woolley. The American Presidency Project. http://www.presidency.uscb.edu/ws/?pid=17942; United Nations Office on Drugs and Crime. 2010. "The Global Cocaine Market." World Drug Report 2010. http://www.unodc.org/documents/wdr/WDR_2010/1.3_The_globa_cocaine_market.pdf.; International Narcotics Control Act of 1989. Pub. L. 101-231; International Narcotics Control Act of 1989. Pub. L. 101-231.

37. Bill Summary and Status: S. 3266, Library of Congress, Thomas. http://thomasl.loc.gov/cgi-bin/bdquery/z?d101:SN03266:@@@L&summ2=m&; Biskupic, Joan. May 19, 1990. "Election-Year Crime Measure Starts Moving Right on Cue." *CQ Weekly* 1555–58. http://library.cqpress.com/cqweekly/WR101409301; "Bush Signs Stripped-Down Crime Bill." 1991. In *CQ Almanac 1990*, 46th ed., 486–99. Washington, DC: Congressional Quarterly. http://library.cqpress.com/cqalmanac/cqal90-1113148; Seghetti, Lisa M., 2007. "Federal Crime Control: Background, Legislation, and Issues." Washington, DC: Congressional Research Service.

38. "Congress Clears Foreign Aid Authorization Bill." 1986. In *CQ Almanac 1985*, 41st ed., 41–61. Washington, DC: Congressional Quarterly. http://library.cqpress.com/cqalmanac/cqal85–1147153; "Presidential Address: Bush Anti-Drug Proposal Slated to Add $2.2 Billion." 1990. In *CQ Almanac 1989*, 45th ed., 33-C-36-C. Washington, DC: Congressional Quarterly. http://library.cqpress.com/cqalmanac/cqal89–851–25637–1136979; "Presidential Address: Bush Anti-Drug Proposal Slated to Add $2.2 Billion." 1990. In *CQ Almanac 1989*, 45th ed., 33-C-36-C. Washington, DC: Congressional Quarterly. http://library.cqpress.com/cqalmanac/cqal89–851–25637–1136979; "Presidential Statement: Carter Proposes Drug Law Revision." 1978. In *CQ Almanac 1977*, 33rd ed., 41-E-43-E. Washington, DC: Congressional Quarterly. http://library.cqpress.com/cqalmanac/cqal77–863–26256–1200540; "Congress Clears Massive Anti-Drug Measure." 1987. In *CQ Almanac 1986*, 42nd ed., 92–106. Washington, DC: Congressional Quarterly. http://library.cqpress.com/cqalmanac/cqal86–1149752; "Presidential Address: Bush Anti-Drug Proposal Slated to Add $2.2 Billion." 1990. In *CQ Almanac 1989*, 45th ed., 33-C-36-C. Washington, DC: Congressional Quarterly. http://library.cqpress.com/cqalmanac/cqal89–851–25637–1136979; "Presidential Statement: Carter Proposes Drug Law Revision." 1978. In *CQ Almanac 1977*, 33rd ed., 41-E-43-E. Washington, DC: Congressional Quarterly. http://library.cqpress.com/cqalmanac/cqal77–863–26256–1200540.

39. "Andean Trade Program." http://export.gov/peru/u.s.perutradepromotionagreement/andeantradepreferenceact/index.asp; Office of the US Trade Representative, Executive Office of the President. "Andean Trade Preference Act." http://www.ustr.gov/trade-topics/trade-development/preference-programs/andean-trade-preference-act-atpa; US Customs and Border Protection. 2013. "Andean Trade Preference Act (ATPA)—Expiration of Duty-Free Treatment." https://help.cbp.gov/app/answers/detail/a_id/325/~/andean-trade-preference-act-%28atpa%29-expiration-of-duty-free-treatment; US International Trade Commission. 2011. *Andean Trade Preference Act: Impact on U.S. Industries and Consumers and on Drug Crop Eradication and Crop Substitution, 2011.* http://www.usitc.gov/publications/332/pub4352.pdf.

40. Bush, George. July 10, 1992. "Statement on Signing the ADAMHA Reorganization Act." Gerhard Peters and John T. Woolley. *The American Presidency Project.* http://www.presidency.ucsb.edu/ws/?pid=21218; Bush, George. October 1,1992b. "Proclamation 6482—Mental Illness Awareness Week, 1992," Gerhard Peters and John T. Woolley. *The American Presidency Project.* http://www.presidency.ucsb.edu/ws/?pid=47409.

41. Bush, George. 1992a. "Statement on Signing the ADAMHA Reorganization Act." July 10. Gerhard Peters and John T. Wooley, *The American Presidency Project.* http://www.presidency.ucsb.edu/ws/?pid=21218; Bush, George. 1992b. "Proclamation 6482—Mental Illness Awareness Week, 1992." October 1. Gerhard Peters and John T. Wooley, *The American Presidency Project.* http://www.presidency. Uscb.edu/ws/?pid=47409.

42. Bush, George. 1992a. "Statement on Signing the ADAMHA Reorganization Act." July 10. Gerhard Peters and John T. Wooley, *The American Presidency Project.* http://www.presidency.ucsb.edu/ws/?pid=21218; Bush, George. 1992b. "Proclamation 6482—Mental Illness Awareness Week, 1992." October 1. Gerhard Peters and John T. Wooley, *The American Presidency Project.* http://www.presidency. Uscb.edu/ws/?pid=47409.

43. H.R. 3355 (103rd), Violent Crime Control and Law Enforcement Act of 1994. http://www.govtrack.us/congress/bills/103/hr3355; McCollum, Bill. 1995. "The Struggle for Effective Anti-Crime Legislation—An Analysis of the Violent Crime Control and Law Enforcement Act of 1994." *University of Dayton Law Review* 20 (Winter).

44. Cunningham, J. K., I. Borjoquez, O. Campollo, L. M. Liu, and J.C. Maxwell. 2010. "Mexico's Methamphetamine Precursor Chemical Interventions: Impacts on Drug Treatment Admissions." *Addiction* 105: 1973–83; Cunningham, J. K., and L. Lon-Miu. 2009. "Impact of US and Canadian Precursor Regulation on Methamphetamine Purity in the United States." *Addiction* 104: 441–53.

45. "Crime Prevention Legislation Takes Aim at Multiple Targets, Including Drugs, Fraud, and Crimes Against Children and the Elderly." 1997. In *CQ Almanac 1996*, 52nd ed., 5-38-5-42. Washington, DC: Congressional Quarterly. http://library.cqpress.com/cqalmanac/cqal96-1092382; Federal Register. "Comprehensive Methamphetamine Control Act of 1996; Possession of List I Chemicals, Definitions, Record Retention, and Temporary Exemption from Chemical Registration for Distributors of Combination Ephedrine Products." http://www.gpo.gov/fdsys/pkg/FR-1997-02-10/pdf/97-3086.pdf.; Library of Congress. "Bill Text Versions 104th Congress (1995–1996) S. 1965." http://www.gpo.gov/fdsys/pkg/BILLS-104s1965es/pdf/BILLS-104s1965es.pdf.

46. Congressional Subcommittee on Criminal Justice, Drug Policy, and Human Resources. 2005. *Fighting Meth in America's Heartland: Assessing Federal, State, and Local Efforts.* Washington, DC: US Government Printing Office.

47. Federal Crack Cocaine Sentencing. *The Sentencing Project: Research and Advocacy for Reform.* http://sentencingproject.org/doc/publications/dp_CrackBriefingSheet.pdf;

Gotsch, K. 2011. "Breakthrough in U.S. Drug Sentencing Reform: The Fair Sentencing Act and the Unfinished Reform Agenda." http://sentencingproject.org/doc/dp_WOLA_Article. pdf; Lesniewski, Niels, and Keith Perine. March 22, 2010. "Senate Votes to Narrow Disparity in Cocaine Sentences, but Some Black Caucus Members Aren't Satisfied." *CQ Weekly* 700. http://library.cqpress.com/cqweekly/weeklyreport111-000003618148; Mauer, M. December 27, 2010. "Beyond the Fair Sentencing Act." *The Nation* 1–2. http://mfile.narotama.ac.id/ files/Jurnal/Jurnal%20Berkeley%20University%202010-2011%20(pdf)/Beyond%20the%20 Fair%20Sentencing.pdf; Perine, Keith. October 19, 2009. "Sentencing Disparity Proves Hard to Crack." *CQ Weekly* 2348. http://library.cqpress.com/cqweekly/weeklyreport111-000 003225314; "S 1410: Smarter Sentencing Act of 2013." https://www.govtrack.us/congress/ bills/113/s1410/text; "Sentencing Reform Starts to Pay Off." August 1, 2013. *New York Times.* http://www.nytimes.com/2013/08/02/opinion/sentencing-reform-starts-to-pay-off.html? adxnnl=1&adxnnlx=1385743247-NgP56G7AsqeEpceb4mE7gA; Stern, Seth. June 5, 2006. "Meth vs. Crack: Different Legislative Approaches." *CQ Weekly* 1548–54. http://library.cqp-ress.com/cqweekly/weeklyreport109-000002240935; Stern, Seth. November 19, 2007. "Lighter Crack Penalties: Much Support, No Action." *CQ Weekly* 3464–65. http://library.cqp-ress.com/cqweekly/weeklyreport110-000002630674; Stern, Seth. August 3, 2009. "Bill to Equalize Sentencing for Crack Cocaine Approved." *CQ Weekly* 1856. http://library.cqpress. com/cqweekly/weeklyreport111-000003184530; Stern, Seth. August 2, 2010. "Cleared Bill Would Reduce Disparity in Crack, Powder Cocaine Sentences." *CQ Weekly* 1877. http:// library.cqpress.com/cqweekly/weeklyreport111-000003716172.

48. Monitoring the Future Study: High School and Youth Trends. National Institute of Health, National Institute of Drug Abuse. https://www.drugabuse.gov/publications/ drugfacts/; "What are Synthetic Cannabinoids?" November 2015. National Institute of Health, National Institute of Drug Abuse; https:www.drugabuse.gov/publications/drugfacts.

49. Sacco, L. N., and K. Finklea. September 16, 2013. "Synthetic Drugs: Overview and Issues for Congress." *Congressional Research Service.* http://www.fas.org/sgp/crs/misc/R42066. pdf.

Chapter 4

The Types of Drugs: Stimulants and Depressants

Chapter Objective: This chapter introduces two primary categories of illicit drugs: stimulants and depressants. The effects of these drugs, types of drugs, and use patterns are described.

Introduction

Illicit drugs are psychoactive substances, which means that they can change the brain's function and have an effect upon a person's mood, perception, and consciousness. Many of these drugs are used for medical reasons but they are often used recreationally as well. Generally speaking, illicit drugs can be categorized based on their physiological, psychological, and behavioral effects on users. The drugs can be grouped into stimulants, depressants, opiates, hallucinogens, antidepressants, and steroids. This chapter describes two categories of drugs, stimulants and depressants, including their effects on the user, possible withdrawal symptoms, and treatment options.

Stimulants

Stimulants, also known as speed or uppers, are drugs that speed up the body's central nervous system and elevate a person's mood so they feel euphoric, more alert, and energetic. When a person uses these drugs, they are able to fight off fatigue and stay awake for longer periods of time than normal. Stimulants are also known to suppress a user's appetite. Other effects of stimulant use include an increase in blood pressure, heart rate, and respiration. If taken in high doses, stimulants may cause heart arrhythmias (irregular heart-beats) and seizures.

Some stimulants can be highly addictive, depending on the drug and how it is ingested. When a stimulant is smoked, snorted, or injected into the body, it can produce an immediate and intense high known as a "rush" or a "flash." These extreme feelings are what makes a user want to use the drug again. Often, tolerance to these drugs builds quickly so that a user must ingest more of the drug to experience the rush associated with the drug. Many users will often binge on these drugs, even for days at a time, until delirium, psychotic behavior, or a lack of a drug will prevent a user from continuing. The user typically crashes, which is characterized by a withdrawal period that includes a deep depression, feelings of anxiety, craving the drug, and extreme exhaustion. There may also be other symptoms including tremors, dizziness, chest pains, vomiting, paranoia, agitation, panic, and aggression. These symptoms are made worse if the user combines a stimulant drug with another drug such as alcohol.

Some stimulant drugs are used for legitimate medical reasons and are often prescribed and used under medical supervision. For example, they can be used to treat obesity because they suppress appetites and increase a person's metabolism. Stimulants are also used to treat those who suffer from attention-deficit hyperactivity disorder. These individuals are often prescribed Ritalin as a treatment.

There is no specific medication to treat an addiction to stimulants. It is thought that reducing the stimulant gradually along with therapy is effective to help users avoid relapse.

Many stimulants, such as caffeine and nicotine, are not prohibited and are legally available. Others are illegal but are available on the street through the black market. These include cocaine, crack, and methamphetamine. Some stimulants are natural and others are made in laboratories. Examples of stimulants include caffeine, nicotine, cocaine (and crack), amphetamines, and methamphetamines.

Caffeine

Caffeine is one of the oldest stimulants known and the most widely used drug in the world. It is a mild drug that is used to increase energy levels, reduce fatigue, and increase alertness. Caffeine is a naturally occurring drug that is found in over 60 plants, such as coffee beans and kola nuts. It is commonly found in coffees, teas, and sodas. The exact effects on a user will vary according to the individual and the amount of caffeine consumed. It is also available in over-the-counter products such as No-Doz. It is thought that caffeine consumption by children and teens should be limited.

Even though it is a naturally occurring drug, caffeine can still be dangerous. If a person ingests too much caffeine, they could suffer from a caffeine overdose (sometimes called **caffeinism**). If a person ingests excessive amounts of caffeine, defined as 250 to 750 milligrams (found in 2 to 7 cups of coffee) or more, they may experience restlessness, dizziness, nausea, headaches, tense muscles, sleep disturbances and insomnia, stomach irritation, irregular or rapid heartbeats, anxiety attacks, drowsiness, ringing ears, diarrhea, vomiting, light flashes, and difficulty breathing. Extreme use can cause convulsions, respiratory failure, and even death.[1]

Most people consume caffeine in coffee and other common beverages. It is difficult to know the exact amount of caffeine in a cup of coffee as there are many types and blends. However, an eight-ounce cup of coffee, on average, contains about 100 to 200 milligrams of caffeine. Most tea contains about half of the amount of caffeine that is found in coffee. Sodas have less caffeine than coffee and tea, and cocoa contains very little caffeine at all.

Many people believe that caffeine is addicting, but it does not meet the criteria for an addictive substance as outlined in the American Psychiatric Association's *Diagnostic and Statistical Manual of Mental Disorders*. Many users report feeling physical discomfort (e.g., headaches and a lack of energy) if they do not use caffeine regularly but for the most part the symptoms are mild and do not have the negative consequences in a user's life that characterize an addiction.

Energy Drinks

Energy drinks are a relatively new product on the market that purport to help the user experience hours of energy, improved concentration, and even weight loss. They have a high amount of caffeine along with sugar and in some cases some vitamins or herbal supplements. The drinks generally contain between 80 and 300 mg of caffeine per 8-ounce serving, with some brands marketing their products in 16- to 24-ounce containers, making their products much more intense. Typically, these beverages contain three to five times the caffeine found in a can of soda of an equivalent size.

The first energy drink on the market was Red Bull, which came out in 1997. Now there are many different varieties of energy drinks, some of which are carbonated like a soda. For more information about caffeine amounts in these drinks see Table 4.1. Because many energy drinks are sold as dietary supplements as opposed to beverages, they are not regulated by the Food and Drug Admin-

Table 4.1 Caffeine Levels in Popular Energy Drinks

Red Bull	80 milligrams per 8.3-ounce serving
Tab Energy	95 mg per 10.5-oz. serving
Monster and Rockstar	160 mg per 16-oz. serving
No Fear	174 mg per 16-oz. serving
Fixx	500 per 20-oz. serving
Wired X505	505 mg per 24-oz. serving
In comparison:	
Brewed coffee	200 milligrams per 12-oz. serving
Instant coffee	140 mg per 12-oz. serving
Brewed tea	80 mg per 12-oz. serving
Mountain Dew	54 mg per 12 oz. serving
Dr. Pepper	41 mg per 12-oz. serving
Pepsi Cola	38 mg per 12-oz. serving
Coca-Cola Classic	34.5 mg per 12-oz. serving
Canned or bottled tea	20 mg per 12-oz. serving

istration (FDA). This means that the manufacturers are not legally required to provide information about the total amount of caffeine in the drink. Energy drinks are often served cold or with ice so they are easy to consume.

Energy drinks are becoming very popular but they can be dangerous. Some users have had adverse reactions to the high doses of caffeine, and some have even died after using these products. The high doses of caffeine in these products have been associated with headaches, heart attacks, miscarriages, irregular heartbeats, diarrhea, vomiting, and even psychotic disorders. The FDA has released adverse-event reports for both Monster Energy and Rockstar Energy, two popular brands of energy drinks. Users of 5-Hour Energy Shots, another energy drink brand, have also reported adverse reactions. The reports serve as a warning to users that these products may cause harm to others, even though there is no proof that the product caused the harm.[2]

In recent years, some users have started to combine energy drinks and alcohol. The caffeine found in the energy drinks counteracts the depressant nature of the alcohol. These drinks are called an "energy cocktail." Examples include a Vodka Bull (Red Bull and vodka), Chambull (Red Bull and Champagne), and Bullgarita (Red Bull and tequila). A typical alcoholic energy drink contains the equivalent of six beers and five cups of coffee in a 23.5-ounce can. These drinks, as described in Table 4.2, can have devastating effects on users. Research shows that those who consume these drinks are three times more likely to binge drink than those who do not mix the two substances. In addition, people who drink energy drinks with alcohol are more likely to be sexually victimized or drive with a drunk driver.[3]

Table 4.2 Four Loko

In 2005, after watching other students at Ohio State University mix alcohol and caffeine, Chris Hunter, Jason Freeman, and Jeff Wright created Four Loko. The "four" in the name refers to its four primary ingredients: alcohol, caffeine, taurine, and guarana. The three students created a company they called Phusion LLC, and began selling 23-ounce cans of Four Loko at locations around the college. Four Loko was a malt liquor-based concoction that contained up to 12 percent alcohol and came in eight fruit flavors.

As the drink became popular around colleges in the Midwest, there were many concerns about the product's health risks. There were multiple reports that the drink was adversely affecting the health of students, resulting in hospital visits or even death. Doctors reported that Four Loko's caffeine masked its alcoholic effects, leading drinkers to consume more than they normally would. By November 2009, the Food and Drug Administration (FDA) notified Phusion and other small makers of alcoholic caffeinated drinks that it would begin investigating the safety of their products. Despite the FDA investigation, Four Loko's popularity grew. In the summer of 2010, rap artists such as Killah Kid Kriz ("Loko Is My Liquor") and Ricosuave glorified the drink in their lyrics. Ricosuave's "So Loko (4 Loko Anthem)" included the line: "I know Jesus turned water into wine/But he woulda turned it into Four Loko at a party of mine."

Use of the drink began to decline in September 2010 after a party at a New Jersey College where 17 students and six visitors became sick after ingesting Four Loco. The following month, nine students at Central Washington State University were hospitalized after mixing Four Loko with other alcoholic drinks. Soon other institutions banned the drink, including Ramapo College, Boston University, and the University of Maryland. Despite these actions, reports of deaths after consumption of Four Loko began to increase. The parents of a Florida man who killed himself blamed their son's death on Four Loko and filed suit against Phusion. Four Loko was also blamed for a fatal auto accident in Maryland.

In an effort to protect their product, Phusion contacted presidents and deans of student life at colleges and universities around the country and offered to fund on-campus alcohol education programs that would include instruction on how to use Four Loko responsibly. This plan had little effect as universities continued to ban the drink. On November 17, 2010, Phusion announced it would remove caffeine from Four Loko. Then in March 2014, the company agreed to stop production, after it had been sued by the attorneys general of 20 states.

Source: The Week Staff. November 24, 2010. "The Rise and Fall of Four Loko." http://theweek.com/article/index/209434/the-rise-and-fall-of-four-loko.

For young people, these drinks can be dangerous. There is some evidence of a link between the use of stimulants and sudden unexplained deaths among young people.[4] One 19-year-old teen, Alex Morris, who typically drank two cans of *Monster* every day for three years, went into cardiac arrest and died one day in 2012. His mother claimed that the high levels of caffeine in the drink caused her son's heart failure. Another teenager, 14-year-old Anais Fournier, drank two 24-oz. cans of *Monster* and went into cardiac arrest and died. Officials at *Monster* claimed that there were no lab tests to determine what may have caused Fournier's death. Other lawsuits against *Monster* clam that the company targets its drinks to children, who may be more susceptible to its effects.[5]

A report released by the Substance Abuse and Mental Health Services Administration (SAMHSA) in 2013 indicated that the number of emergency room visits involving energy drinks had doubled between 2007 (when there were approximately 10,000 visits) and 2011 (more than 20,000 visits). The symptoms reported by patients included arrhythmia, increases in blood pressure and, in rare cases, cardiac arrest. These hospital visits were each brought on by either the use of energy drinks alone or from a combination of energy drinks and another drug or alcohol.[6]

Nicotine

Another stimulant drug is **nicotine**, which is a naturally occurring drug found in the tobacco plant and its products such as cigarettes (shredded tobacco leaves), cigars (whole tobacco leaves), pipe tobacco, smokeless tobacco products (snuff and chewing tobacco), and gums. Nicotine is a stimulant that is colorless, poisonous, and highly addictive. When a user smokes a cigarette or other tobacco product, dopamine is released into the brain. Users feel an immediate rush but it quickly subsides within a few minutes.

Nicotine is one of the most addictive drugs known and is one of the most heavily abused drugs. According to SAMHSA, about 72.9 million Americans age 12 or older used tobacco products in 2006.[7] Approximately 22 percent of Americans were cigarette smokers in 2011, a decrease since 2002.[8] It seems that adolescents and young adults are not smoking cigarettes as much now as in the past. This makes tobacco second only to alcohol as the most widely abused addictive drug. A new trend in consuming nicotine is an electronic cigarette, or an e-cigarette. These are described in Table 4.3.

There are many risks associated with the use of tobacco and nicotine. Tobacco use will increase the heart rate, respiration, and blood pressure of the user upon use. Long-term effects of tobacco use include a decreased sense of smell and taste, frequent colds, bleeding gums and frequent mouth sores, wheezing, coughing, bad breath, yellow-stained teeth and fingers, gastric ulcers, chronic bronchitis, emphysema, heart disease, chronic obstructive pulmonary disease (COPD), stroke, and cancer. Women who smoke while pregnant can cause long-term health problems for their babies.

If used in excess, nicotine can be fatal. A person would only need to ingest only a drop or two of pure nicotine (about 50 mg) to cause death. One cigarette contains anywhere from .5 to 15 mg of nicotine.[9]

A person who stops smoking may experience symptoms of nicotine withdrawal. The exact symptoms will vary from one person to the next, but common symptoms include impatience, irritability, and aggressive behavior. Most people will crave the drug for weeks after quitting.[10]

Table 4.3 E-Cigarettes

E-cigarettes, or "electronic cigarettes," are battery-powered cigarettes that often look like traditional cigarettes, but the user inhales a vapor instead of smoke. The device has a heating element in one end that heats a liquid solution that is vaporized and then inhaled. The liquid solution, and thus the vapor, often contains nicotine along with other flavorings. When a person uses an e-cigarette in this fashion, it is referred to as "vaping."[11]

Not all liquids contain nicotine and thus can be used to replace cigarettes or help a user to quit using cigarettes. They provide a smoker with the feeling that they are smoking a cigarette but they are not. In addition, even though e-cigarettes may contain nicotine, it may be less that what is in a traditional cigarette. E-cigarettes do not contain other chemicals found in cigarettes such as tar and carbon monoxide. For this reason, groups such as The American Association of Public Health Physicians have recommended that e-cigarettes be used as a safe alternative for those who are not able to quit using tobacco. On the other hand, the World Health Organization issued a statement in July 2013 in which they pointed out that the effectiveness of e-cigarettes to assist with smoking cessation has not yet been proven. They recommended that consumers do not rely on e-cigarettes until more research has been done.

Even though e-cigarettes have been on the market since the early 2000s, the safety of the product has been questioned. Critics argue that the liquid solution used in an e-cigarette contains the same chemicals that are in cigarettes. In some cases, they could be worse because different ingredients can be added to the liquid. It has been pointed out that use of an e-cigarette may make a user, particularly a younger person, more comfortable with cigarettes, so they will be more comfortable using tobacco cigarettes. Moreover, since many e-cigarettes contain nicotine, the addictive chemical in tobacco, users may become addicted to the drug even without smoking tobacco products. Many states have passed laws to regulate the use and sale of e-cigarettes, especially to minors. Other laws limit the places where e-cigarettes can be used.

Source: Holmes, Rick. December 15, 2013. "E-cigarettes: Savior or Menace?" *MetroWest Daily News*. http://www.metrowestdailynews.com/editorspick_mobile/x915453088/Holmes-E-cigarettes-Savior-or-menace; Sohn, Emily. January 30, 2011. "How Safe Are E-Cigarettes?" *ABC News*. http://abcnews.go.com/Technology/safe-cigarettes/story?id=12789204; Eyb, Lynette. December 26, 2013. "The Global Battle over E-Cigarettes." *Global Post*. http://www.salon.com/2013/12/26/the_global_battle_over_e_cigarettes_partner/.

Shisha

Another way tobacco is ingested is a product called **shisha**, a tobacco mixture that is flavored and smoked in a hookah or water pipe. Shisha is often sweetened with honey, molasses, fruit, and other ingredients. The tobacco mixture is heated in the pipe and the smoke passes through water to cool it before it is inhaled by the user. The use of shisha is relatively new in the US but it has been used in other parts of the world for many years. In recent years, the use of shisha was introduced by Arab Americans, and its use is spreading across the US, particularly among young people.

It is thought that smoking shisha through a hookah pipe removes the toxic compounds typically found in tobacco. The perception is that when the tobacco smoke passes through the water it is filtered so that the dangerous chemicals are removed. This is not the case. A hookah allows many of the harmful ingredients in tobacco to remain in the smoke, including toxins and nicotine. The smoke from shisha has the equivalent amount of tar and nicotine as is found in 20 cigarettes. Shisha smoke may also contain high levels of carbon monoxide. Those who use shisha face the same risks as they do by smoking tobacco. According to the American Cancer Society, the same types of cancer, such as of the lung, mouth, and gums, have been linked to smoking a hookah pipe.

Not surprisingly, a person who uses shisha will experience the same effects as those who use nicotine. This includes increases in blood pressure and heart rate. However, because of the high level of carbon monoxide, a user may lose consciousness. This can become worse, though, because the shisha compound may be mixed with other drugs such as narcotics. Smoking shisha through a hookah may also result in other health problems for a user. When many people use a hookah, they may pass a hose from one person to the next to inhale the smoke. Using an unclean hose in this manner can spread infections from one person to the next, including anything from a simple cold to more serious ailments such as herpes or tuberculosis.

Gutka

Another way to ingest tobacco is **gutka** (ghutka or betel quid). This is a sweet, chewable, smokeless tobacco product that is often mixed with spicy and fruity ingredients. Gutka may also contain parts of the areca nut and have other flavors mixed in such as cardamom, turmeric, cloves, saffron, and mustard seed. Gutka is typically packaged in small tins and a small quantity of the product is placed between the user's teeth and gums or lip. The user is able to then suck or chew on the drug, spitting out small pieces of tobacco or other ingredients. Gutka is popular and used commonly in Asia and in India, but has not been widely used in the US. In recent years, the popularity of the drug is rising, particularly among immigrants from India.[12] Gutka is currently not regulated as a tobacco product in the US, but it is recognized that, as a tobacco product, use of gutka could cause cancer and have other long-term effects.

Cocaine

Cocaine is a naturally occurring stimulant that can be extracted and refined from the coca plant that is grown primarily in the Andean region of South America. There, coca leaves have been chewed for many years as a mild stimulant and a medicine. Millions of people there still chew leaves every day. The coca plant is processed in secret labs and turned into cocaine, a white powder that has a bitter taste (See Table 4.4). The powder is then smuggled into the US and around the world for distribution. The powder is often diluted or "cut" with other ingredients by dealers as a way to stretch the supply.

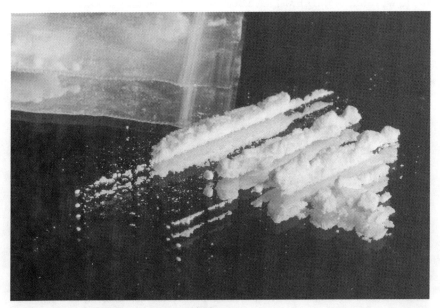

Cocaine on mirror © Pavel Chernobrivets via fotolia.com

Table 4.4 Coca Plant

The coca plant is a flowering bush with oval-shaped leaves that grows in the Andes region of South America. The plant has been used in traditional medicine and religious ceremonies in that region for thousands of years. Bags of coca leaves are commonly sold in the markets. People regularly chew the coca leaves to achieve a very mild euphoric feeling that includes numbness in the mouth, an increased heart rate, and faster breathing. It is also common to drinking coca tea. Coca is used in food products such as granola bars, cookies, and candy. Users in that country claim that the coca leaf has a positive benefit for physical, mental, and social health. It has been used to alleviate fatigue, hunger, and thirst, and to relieve the pain of headache, rheumatism, and wounds. It has become a cash crop for Argentina, Bolivia, and Peru, and there has been a movement in these countries to expand the legal markets of the crop, recommending its use in salads and other foods.

The coca leaf is not cocaine, but it contains the raw material to manufacture cocaine. Outside of South America, most countries do not make a distinction between the coca leaf and any other form of cocaine. Thus, the possession of coca leaves is illegal in most places.

Source: Cortes, Ricardo. 2012. *A Secret History of Coffee, Coca & Cola.* New York: Akashia Books; Cortes, Ricardo. January 13, 2013. "The Condemned Coca Leaf." *New York Daily News.* http://www.nydailynews.com/opinion/condemned-coca-leaf-article-1.1238569?.

Cocaine became popular in the 1980s because it was thought to be a "safe" drug that was not addictive. Further, since the drug was ingested by snorting or inhaling as opposed to injecting, there was no need to share needles, thereby lessening the chance that diseases would be transmitted between users. In the 1990s, the dangers of the drug became more apparent and the drug became less popular.

There are many ways to ingest cocaine. As a powder, it can be snorted or inhaled by users. When cocaine is snorted, it reaches the brain quickly—in about 1–3 minutes. The high that results lasts about a half hour. When cocaine in the powder is burned, it does not vaporize or turn into a smoke. This means that powder cocaine cannot be smoked because the heat destroys the drug. In order to smoke cocaine, it must be turned into freebase cocaine. When powder cocaine is formed into freebase cocaine it is known as **crack**, which then can be vaporized into a smoke and ingested that way.

Freebase cocaine is extremely dangerous to manufacture. The process requires the use of ether, which is extremely flammable. The drug vaporizes at a very low temperature so that the user can inhale the heated vapor and get an immediate feeling of being high. The "rush" is intense, lasting about five minutes. In this form, the drug provides a user with a more intense effect with a smaller amount of the drug needed.

Crack cocaine is made when cocaine hydrochloride is dissolved in water and mixed with baking soda. The resulting solution is then boiled or heated in a microwave. It is then cooled, often in ice or in a freezer, resulting in a yellowish-white product. Small chunks of the hardened drug, called rocks, are broken off and heated in a small pipe or on a piece of foil. When the "rocks" are heated, vapors are released that the user inhales. The rocks make a "cracking" sound when they are burned, giving the drug the name "crack." Some users mix crack with other drugs such as tobacco or marijuana. When crack is used, the drug hits the brain in seconds, flooding the brain with dopamine. The high feeling peaks in 3–5 minutes after use and lasts about 15 minutes. A user may experience feelings of depression when the drug wears off.

Cocaine can also be converted into a liquid form which is then injected into a user's body with a needle or syringe. If the cocaine is injected, the effect is almost immediate. The user will feel the effects within 15 to 30 seconds, with a high peaking in 3 to 5 minutes. When ingested this way, the effects of the drug last for about 15 to 20 minutes.

Crack cocaine is extremely addicting. People who use cocaine feel a sense of euphoria, excitement, alertness, well-being, and increased confidence. They often have a heightened sense of energy and do not feel the need to eat or sleep regularly. This means that users will not eat or sleep for days at a time. Other symptoms a user may experience after using cocaine are increased heart rate and blood pressure, muscle spasms, and convulsions. In high doses, cocaine will cause hallucinations and convulsions. Seizures, cardiac arrest, and respiratory failure have also been reported, along with depression, paranoia, and psychosis. If the cocaine was snorted, users may suffer from damage to the nasal membranes sometimes referred to as "cocaine nose." These users may lose their sense of smell, suffer from nosebleeds, or have difficulty swallowing. It is common for users to develop a tolerance to cocaine, meaning that they must ingest more of the drug to achieve the desired effect.[13]

Cocaine is categorized as a Schedule II drug under the federal Controlled Substances Act. This means it has some recognized medical use alongside a high potential for abuse. Medically, the drug used to be used as an anesthetic medication. Common street names for cocaine include blanca, coca, coke, flake, nieve, perico, and snow.

During the 1970s and 1980s, cocaine in a powder form was used primarily by whites and the upper classes. On the other hand, crack, because it is typically much cheaper than powder cocaine, was more likely to be used by those living in poorer neighborhoods and more by black Americans. In 1986, when Congress passed new laws to establish mandatory sentences for possession of cocaine, an offender who possessed 500 grams of powder cocaine would receive a five-year sentence, but an offender that had only 5 grams of crack would receive that same sentence. Some critics quickly pointed out that the punishments set by Congress in the new law were racially biased. In 2009, Congress addressed those concerns and passed the Fair Sentencing Act. Under the new law, the ratio is 18 to1 between the amounts of cocaine and crack that are punishable by mandatory sentences. Congress explained the difference in sentences by the higher dangerousness that crack has when compared to powdered cocaine.

Most of the cocaine available on the street today originates from South American countries, particularly Colombia, Peru, Bolivia, and Ecuador. Here, drug cartels produce and distribute cocaine for the US. The cartels also traffic cocaine into Europe, Australia, and Canada. This has not only devastated natural resources in Colombia, but is also the source of much violence.

Amphetamines

Another category of stimulant drugs is the **amphetamines**. These drugs are synthesized from adrenaline and ephedrine and are more toxic and more difficult for a user's body to metabolize. This means that a user will feel the effects for a longer time than cocaine. Some of the effects of this drug are an increased energy level and alertness, increased attention, a greater sense of confidence, well-being, and euphoria. The drug acts as an appetite suppressor for some people. After using amphetamines, users may appear to be hyperactive, agitated, anxious, or exhausted. Users may also experience high blood pressure, irregular heartbeat, nausea, and vomiting. If amphetamines are used over prolonged periods of time, users may exhibit irrational and paranoid behavior, psychotic episodes, or aggressiveness.[14] Amphetamines have recognized medical purposes and are often used to treat depression, obesity, attention disorders, and narcolepsy. They can also be used to improve the concentration of people with attention-deficit hyperactivity disorder (ADHD).

Withdrawal symptoms from amphetamines include headaches, muscle cramps, fatigue, sleep disturbances and nightmares, and depression. Users will

Illegal drug lab © wellphoto via fotolia.com.

often continue to use amphetamines not only to avoid the withdrawal symptoms but also to feel the rush experienced when they use the drug.

Methamphetamine

One type of amphetamine is **methamphetamine**, or "meth." Meth is a powerfully addicting drug that is not naturally occurring but instead a synthetic drug made in laboratories. It was originally created in the 1960s and 1970s as a medicine but made its way onto the black market, where it was used by college students who claimed it allowed them to concentrate for longer periods of time. It then became popular as a recreational drug because it made users more outgoing and able to socialize more comfortably.

Meth is an odorless, tasteless drug that comes in many forms. It can be a powder, which can be smoked, snorted, or injected. It can also be dissolved in water or alcohol and injected, which intensifies its effects. "Crystal meth" or "ice" is a smokeable form of methamphetamine that is popular because it is not injected into the body. It is a concentrated form of methamphetamine that resembles small pieces of translucent glass. The "rocks" can be smoked and produce a more intense high. A newer form of meth originates from Thailand and is called "ya ba" (or "yaba"). This is a pill that can either be taken orally or crushed and then snorted. If the drug is taken orally, the effects are not as intense but last longer.

When used, the drug typically has a rapid onset and lasts about six to eight hours.[15] Meth can cause feelings of alertness, heightened energy levels, and an overall sense of well-being. However, after about eight hours, the "high" that users feel begins to disappear and users will start to "crash." This is when many users will often re-use the drug to avoid withdrawal. This cycle of binge and crash is called a "run" and may go on for many days, during which time a user may not eat or sleep. Some users during this time may experience hallucinations, anxiety, and paranoia, or continually repeat behaviors. This is sometimes referred to as "**tweaking**." This may also involve a capacity to carry out violent acts.[16]

If meth is used for an extended time, a user may experience hallucinations, paranoia, or obsessive picking of the skin. Acute users may also experience irregular heart rhythm, heart attacks, or stroke. They may experience irreversible damage to their brain. People addicted to meth find it difficult to maintain employment or care for their children. A common symptom in meth addicts is "meth mouth," a condition caused by drying up of a user's gums and salivary glands, causing enamel on the teeth to rot and the teeth to decay.[17]

Meth is easily manufactured in a home, apartment, garage, car, or any other place. These manufacturing sites are called **meth labs**. The drug is made by combining ephedrine (a natural form of the drug) or pseudoephedrine with common household products such as drain cleaner and table salt. These precursor drugs that are used to make meth, pseudoephedrine and ephedrine, are found in decongestants that are sold as over-the-counter drugs. The chemicals used are toxic and highly flammable.

During the 1980s, it was very easy to purchase the ingredients needed to make meth and labs were common. Because of this, the drug was readily available on the street at a very low cost. As a way to reduce the manufacturing of meth, many states and the federal government passed laws regulating the sale of pseudoephedrine. The Combat Methamphetamine Epidemic Act of 2005 placed limits on the availability and sale of products containing the drug.

A newer method for making meth in a home lab is called "shake and bake." This requires that pseudoephedrine be ground into a powder, which is combined with other ingredients that are readily available in stores such as camping fuel, lithium, and/or lye (crystal drain opener). These ingredients are mixed together and then poured into an empty soda bottle. The bottle is shaken for between an hour and up to five hours. The liquid is separated from solid material, which is meth. This process is extremely dangerous as the chemicals used are highly explosive. One of those chemicals, lithium, explodes if it comes into contact with water. Once the chemicals are placed inside the bottle, deadly ammonia gas builds up and must be released. If not, the bottle will explode. Now, massive quantities of meth are produced in Mexico, where drug traffickers have industrial-sized manufacturing sites (called "super-labs") and organized smuggling operations.

Meth is a Schedule II drug under the Controlled Substances Act. It has recognized medical purposes and is prescribed for conditions such as narcolepsy, a sleep disorder. But it also has a high potential for abuse.

Statistics show that almost 5 percent of the population over the age of 12 have tried meth at least once. Most users are Caucasians in their 20s and 30s with a high school education or better. Users are equally divided between males and females and have a wide variety of occupations.[18]

Meth addiction imposes intense costs to the social structure of society, but there are also environmental costs. For every pound of meth that is produced, there are about 6 pounds of toxic waste that is dumped into fields and streams and finds its way into the food and water supply.[19]

Bath Salts and Synthetic Cannabis

Bath salts are synthetic stimulants that are often sold at convenience stores, head shops, or online. They are referred to as "bath salts" because some of the compounds are white crystals that resemble Epsom salts. These products contain one or more of three chemicals that have stimulant and hallucinogenic properties: mephedrone, methylone, or MDPV, or derivatives of these chemicals. Some bath salts are synthetic substances that mimic the mild stimulant found in khat,[20] a Schedule I drug in the US. The problem with these products is that street chemists are continually making new forms of these drugs to keep them "legal." As quickly as legislatures ban the product, chemists will make a slight change to the chemical compounds so it can be considered legal.

Synthetic cannabis is also very popular. This is comprised of dried plant leaves or herbal mixtures that have been sprayed with synthetic designer cannabinoids. It was created to mimic marijuana and is marketed as fake (and therefore legal) weed. The synthetic spray that is used is made up of many different compounds, but is chemically different enough from marijuana that the laws regulating marijuana (and cannabinoids) do not apply. The sprayed plant leaf material is sold in small bags or packets under names like K2, Spice, vanilla sky, black mambo, cloud 9, ivory wave, or purple wave. These drugs are not regulated by the DEA and can be sold to anyone of any age.

Synthetic cannabis packs are often labeled as potpourri or herbal incense and carry the warning "Not for Human Consumption."[21] Despite the warning, people continue to use the drugs. They are snorted, smoked, or injected into the body and can affect a person in many ways. Users may hallucinate, experience cardiovascular problems, heart palpitations, seizures, tremors, kidney failure, nausea, and headaches. Some effects are unpredictable and can include hyper-aggressive behavior including paranoia, panic attacks, and violent acts.[22] Some users have committed suicide after using the drug. Users typically have no memory of their reactions once the drug wears off. The high from the drug can last up to nine hours.[23]

Spice has been categorized as a Schedule I drug by the federal government. It is also illegal under most state laws. It is difficult to argue that these new drugs are safe. One 2013 crime spree carried out by a man in Tampa, Florida, after using bath salts, clearly demonstrates the harmful effects that these drugs can have. This is described in Table 4.5.

Table 4.5 Effects of Using Bath Salts

Charlie "Chris" Bates, after ingesting bath salts, entered an apartment complex around 11:00 and found some students watching football on television. He tied up four men and raped four women. After leaving the apartment, Bates then approached a female who was sitting on the front porch of her house. He forced her to go inside with him and forced her to undress and kiss him. When the female began to pray and recite Bible verses, Bates apologized and left. He stumbled to another apartment complex where there was a party with about 25 people in attendance. At gunpoint, Bates forced the partiers to go into a bedroom. He fired his weapon once into the floor, then left. On his way out, Bates encountered another man, fired several shots at him, but ran on.

Police heard the gunshots and saw Bates running away but were unable to find him. By the next morning, there was a full manhunt in progress, with 100 officers looking for him, including some by helicopter. Eventually, two police officers found him and exchanged gunfire. Bates was killed. An autopsy of Bates' body showed that he had heavy amounts of illegal "bath salts" in his body when he died.

In 2012, a man was shot and killed by police officers after he refused to stop eating the face of another homeless man. The man had removed his clothing and was eating the other man's face, a behavior that officials said was consistent with ingesting bath salts.

In another incident in 2011, a 48-year-old woman in Panama Beach, Florida, tried to kill her 71-year-old mother with a machete after taking bath salts. She ran away after police were called, leaving her mother uninjured.

Source: Sullivan, Dan. December 6, 2013. "Test Finds Bath Salts Chemical in Tampa Rampage Suspect's System." *Tampa Bay Times*. http://www.tampabay.com/news/ publicsafety/crime/medical-examiner-suspect-in-september-rampage-had-bath-salts-in-his-system/2155836; "Face Eating Cannibal Attack May be Latest in String of 'Bath Salts' Incidents." June 1, 2012. ABC News. http://abcnews.go.com/Blotter/face-eating-cannibal-attack-latest-bath-salts-incident/story?id=16470389.

Ecstasy

Ecstasy is another type of methamphetamine that is also categorized as a synthetic hallucinogen. Ecstasy was first synthesized in Germany in 1912 and was used in the US in the 1970s as a way to treat psychiatric patients. The drug is now commonly used by young people at raves or nightclubs because of the perception that it is a safe drug. Ecstasy causes the brain to flood with serotonin, the body's "happy chemical." Those who use the drug report feeling a sense of euphoria and sensual arousal. The drug also produces an energizing effect. Some users will experience blurred vision, a fast heart rate, distorted perception and memory, and high blood pressure. Some users feel anxious and depressed long after using the drug. The effects typically last from three to four hours.

Ecstasy can make it difficult for a user's body to regulate its internal temperature. Many users are susceptible to overheating, dehydration, and organ damage. Users must continue to drink water to prevent this from happening. Ecstasy can build up in a person over time, leading to a toxic amount of drug in the body. This is complicated when users mix ecstasy with other drugs such as caffeine, cocaine, or alcohol.

Ecstasy is a Schedule I drug according to the CSA. It is listed as having no recognized medical use, however some physicians are using it to treat patients with posttraumatic stress disorder.

Users who have been using the drug for a long time may have withdrawal symptoms upon quitting the drug. They often feel fatigued, have no appetite, feel depressed, and have a difficult time concentrating.

The drug is called many names such as adam, beans, hug, love drug, MBDB, MDEA, molly, X, and XTC.[24] According to the Drug Enforcement Administration, most ecstasy available in the US is manufactured in Mexico.

Khat

Khat (pronounced "cot") is a stimulant drug found in the East African shrub *Catha edulis.* It has been used by indigenous people for many centuries who chew the leaves or dry them to make a tea, paste, or flaky substance that is smoked. The drug has been known to increase a user's energy and suppress their appetite. It can also produce a sense of euphoria and elation. In larger doses, the user may experience manic behavior, hallucinations, delusions, increased heart rate, exhaustion, hyperactivity, insomnia, and gastric disorders. If used over a long term, the drug may cause tooth decay and gum disease, constipation, ulcers, and inflammation of the stomach. Users may also experience an increase in blood pressure, irregular heartbeat, heart attacks, and strokes. Once ingested, the effects peak after about three hours, but can last up to 24 hours.[25] Khat users sometimes experience withdrawal symptoms after ceasing to use the drug. The symptoms include a depressed mood, irritability, trembling, loss of appetite, nightmares, and difficulty sleeping.

Khat is not used for medical reasons in the US, but in parts of Europe and East Africa it is legal. It is sometimes grown there and smuggled to the West.[26] Because of this, khat has been widely available in the US since 1995, but there is no reliable estimate of how prevalent it is in this country.

The street names for khat include Abyssinian tea, African salad, catha, chat, kat, and oat.[27]

Depressants

Depressants, also called sedatives or downers, are drugs that slow down the normal functions of a person's central nervous system. They can make a user less aware of what is going on around them. They can also reduce a person's energy level and lower a person's pulse, blood pressure, and breathing to produce a sense of calm and help to alleviate anxiety, induce sleep, and reduce stress. They can also cause a user to experience slurred speech. When overused,

depressants can cause death. Examples of depressants include alcohol, barbiturates, opiates (opium, morphine, heroin, codeine, methadone, Demerol,
Percodan), sedatives, and tranquilizers (benzodiazepines). One depressant,
methaqualone, was often used by college students in the 1960s and 1970s who
referred the pills as "ludes." Pharmaceutical companies stopped marketing the
drug in 1984. Two commonly used date rape drugs, gamma hydroxybutyric
acid (GHB) and flunitrazepam (Rohypnol), are depressants.

Depressants may be swallowed, injected, smoked, inhaled, or snorted. If
prescribed by a physician for medical reasons, these drugs are usually very safe.
However, if used for a long time or with a higher dosage than needed, depressants may be very addictive. Those who have used the drugs for a long time
will experience withdrawal symptoms as severe as seizures or even death. For
this reason, a person attempted to withdraw from abuse of depressants should
consult with a medical professional.

Depressant drugs go by many different names on the streets. They include
Flunitrazepam, which has been called forget-me-pill, Mexican valium, R2,
roche, roofies, roofinol, rope, rophies, and GHB, which has been called G,
Georgia home boy, grievous bodily harm, or liquid ecstasy.

Alcohol

Alcohol is the most widely or commonly used depressant drug. It is easily
available and legal in some circumstances. Drinkable alcohol is ethanol alcohol.
Alcohol affects brain functioning, lowers inhibitions, and impairs a person's
judgment, coordination, reflexes, vision, and memory. Some users become
violent, causing assaults and homicides. If used to excess, alcohol may also
cause periods of memory loss referred to as blackouts. Vomiting may occur,
which may cause a user to choke or suffocate if they aspirate on their own
vomit. Alcohol poisoning results in respiratory depression, coma, and possibly
death. The long-term effects of alcohol use can be serious. It can cause cirrhosis
of the liver, heart disease, cancer, and brain damage.

Alcohol is produced by fermenting or distilling fruits, vegetables, or grains.
Major types of alcoholic beverages include distilled spirits (e.g., whiskey, vodka,
and gin) or fermented beverages (e.g., beer and wine).

For most adults, moderate (social) drinking (1 to 2 drinks a day for men,
1 for women) is not considered harmful, and may even be a health benefit to
a person's cardiovascular system. Drinks are defined as 5 ounces of wine, 12
ounces of beer, or 1 to 3 ounces of distilled spirits. Many people binge drink,
which means they drink five or more drinks at a time. This behavior is
described in Table 4.6.

Table 4.6 Binge Drinking

Binge drinking refers to a consuming five or more drinks at one time, generally with the intent of getting drunk. A binge drinker can then go weeks or even months before having another alcoholic drink. Binge drinking is the most common form of excessive alcohol use in the US. It is estimated that one in six adults in the US binge drinks about four times a month, drinking about eight drinks per sitting.

According to the Centers for Disease Control, binge drinkers tend to be young adults between the ages of 18 and 29. In addition, almost 90 percent of the alcohol consumed by under-aged youth is through binge drinking. More men than women tend to binge drink. Many people binge drink because it allows them to feel more comfortable in a social setting, or because of peer pressure. Some people binge drink to relax after a hard day at work or to forget their problems.

There are some serious short-term and long-term effects for those who binge drink. It can result in accidents and injuries, alcohol poisoning, unsafe sexual activity, and criminal behavior. It can also result in missed work or school. Long-term, serious results include pancreatitis, alcoholic liver disease, hepatitis, and possibly stomach ulcers and cancer. Suggestions to prevent binge drinking include increased education about the dangers of the behavior.

Source: Centers for Disease Control and Prevention. "Fact Sheets: Binge Drinking." http://www.cdc.gov/alcohol/fact-sheets/binge-drinking.htm; Centers for Disease Control and Prevention. 2012. "Binge Drinking: Nationwide Problems, Local Solutions." http://www.cdc.gov/vitalsigns/BingeDrinking/; Centers for Disease Control and Prevention. 2012. "Vital Signs: Binge Drinking Prevalence, Frequency and Intensity among Adults." *Morbidity and Mortality Weekly Report* 61(1):14–19.

When a user is unable to stop using alcohol, they are considered to be an alcoholic, or to suffer from alcoholism. It is estimated that about 10 to 15 percent of people who drink alcohol become addicted. There are two types of alcoholism: acute and chronic. A person with acute alcoholism will experience occasional episodes of intoxication. A chronic alcoholic will experience a pattern of long-term abuse of the drug. If not treated, alcoholism can lead to the death of the abuser.

There are generally three recognized stages of alcoholism: early, middle, and late. In early alcoholism, the abuse is often not recognized because the user appears to be drinking socially. Alcoholics in this stage seem to have increased pleasure from drinking and will then develop a greater tolerance for alcohol than others. They may continue to drink after everyone else has stopped, or may hide how much alcohol they drink. An alcoholic in this stage is not easily identified.

The middle stage of alcoholism is indicated by a higher number and more severe hangovers that are caused by drinking to excess. A person may exhibit shakiness, agitation, sweating, an upset stomach, headaches, thirst, and feelings of guilt or shame. They may also have memory lapses.

In late stages of alcoholism, the user's behavior deteriorates and health issues become apparent. The addict may experience withdrawal symptoms if they stop drinking and may even crave alcohol. They may experience nausea and diarrhea, mental confusion, hallucinations, and seizures along with increased heart rate, rapid breathing, disorientation, and blackouts. In serious cases, delirium tremens may develop. Long-term use of alcohol may result in dementia, heart failure, or cirrhosis of the liver, leading to the user's death.[28]

The amount of alcohol that is in a person's body is measured by their **blood-alcohol content**, or BAC. This is a measure of the percentage of alcohol that is present in a person's blood as measured in grams per 100 milliliters. If a person has a BAC of .08 or more, it means that they have .08 grams of alcohol in their blood (or 8/100 of 1 percent alcohol). At this stage, they are considered to be legally drunk. In all states in the US, a person with a BAC over .08 is not permitted to drive cars, aircrafts, or boats. They are also not permitted to operate heavy machinery.[29]

In most cases, if a person's BAC is between .01 and .05, they will appear to others that they have not had any alcohol to drink. However, there is alcohol in their blood, and this would be detected through a blood test. If a person's BAC is between .03 and .12, they will show some mild effects of alcohol consumption, such as being more talkative and have lower inhibitions. They may be more relaxed and have difficulty concentrating on a complex task. Along with these symptoms, a person at this level of intoxication will have impaired judgment and an increased reaction time. A person with a BAC in this range is considered to be legally drunk.

When a person's BAC increases to .09–.25, they will exhibit a lack of coordination, an impaired judgment, and a higher reaction time. A person with a BAC of .18 to .30 will experience confusion, dizziness, and vision problems. A person at this level may also have difficulty walking and have slurred speech. They may experience memory loss or "blackout." When the BAC is between

.27 and .40, the user may not be able to stand or walk. They may vomit or experience incontinence. If a person has a BAC of .35 and .50, they may lose consciousness, fall into a coma, or even die from respiratory paralysis.[30]

A BAC is measured through a breathalyzer test. A drinker blows into a device that measures the amount of alcohol in their breath. The results of this test are considered to be accurate and are often used as evidence in a courtroom. A BAC can also be determined through a blood test or through a urinalysis. A person's BAC is affected by the amount of alcohol they drink but also by other factors such as their gender (women are usually affected more by alcohol), the amount of food in the stomach, the size of the individual, and any medications they may be taking.

A relatively mild withdrawal symptom of alcohol is a hangover. The symptoms include a dry mouth, sleep disturbances, body aches, diarrhea, dizziness, fatigue, nausea, and mild headaches, trembling, anxiety, depression, and sensitivity to light and sound. These symptoms can occur within a few hours after a person stops using the drug. The intensity of the symptoms depends on the amount of alcohol consumed, but also on the characteristics of the user. Users who are older are more likely to experience hangover symptoms for longer times than do younger users. Females also have worse hangovers than males, and those who smoke cigarettes or other tobacco products tend to have more serious hangover symptoms.

There are no cures for hangovers, despite myths that black coffee, raw eggs, chili peppers, steak sauce, vitamins, or fatty foods will help. The only real cure is bed rest and liquids. A person suffering from a hangover may be absent from work or school, or may have lowered work performance and productivity.[31]

Many celebrities have died because of addictions to or abuse of alcohol. Errol Flynn (actor) died of acute alcoholism; Jeff Hanneman (musician) died of cirrhosis of the liver; Jimi Hendrix (musician) passed away due to respiratory arrest caused by an overdose of alcohol and barbiturates; Jack Kerouac (author) died of cirrhosis of the liver after a lifetime of drinking.

Barbiturates, Sedatives, and Tranquilizers

Barbiturates are depressants. Because they slow down a person's central nervous system and brain activity, they are used to treat anxiety, agitation, insomnia, muscle tension, and to aid in alcohol or drug withdrawal. They can also be used to help a person who suffers from epilepsy. Not surprisingly, the possible side effects of barbiturates include drowsiness, impaired judgment, diminished motor skills, amnesia, slurred speech, slowed reactions, and decreased reflex reactions. In higher doses, side effects may include vertigo, nightmares, aggression, coma, cardiorespiratory arrest, and an altered perception of time and space. Serious side effects include anemia, impaired liver function, headaches, blurred vision, and depression.

The first barbiturate was invented in 1832. The formal name was chloral hydrate, but most knew it as a "mickey." It was put into a person's drink and caused them to pass out. In 1864, a German scientist, Johann Freidrich Wilhelm Adolf von Baeyer, discovered barbituric acid, leading to barbiturates. These turned out to be highly addictive. The need to have a safer drug led to the creation of benzodiazepines, and drugs like Valium. Doctors thought these drugs were safer for patients than earlier drugs.

Barbiturates are a Schedule II drug under the CSA. Medically, they are often used for mild sedation, but can also be used as an anesthetic or an anticonvulsant. Some barbiturates have a high potential for abuse, both physical and psychological. Some barbiturates are less addictive, and have thus been identified as a Schedule III or IV drug in the CSA. Barbiturates can be injected into a vein or muscle, or can be taken orally through a pill form.

When used recreationally, barbiturates make the user feel relaxed and euphoric. Some users report feeling less anxiety and have a loss of inhibitions. Over time, a user can become physically and psychologically addicted to barbiturates and build up a tolerance to the drug so more is needed for the same effect. Someone addicted to barbiturates may experience withdrawal symptoms and must go through detox treatment in order to cleanse the body of the drug.[32] Symptoms of withdrawal include insomnia, tremors, convulsions, dizziness, irrational fears, and rapid mood changes. Over-use of barbiturates can lead to an overdose. This becomes even more serious if barbiturates are used with drugs such as alcohol or opiates. Many celebrities who have passed away as a result of a barbiturate overdose include Marilyn Monroe, Judy Garland, and Jimi Hendrix.

Barbiturates are called many names, including barbs, reds, re birds, phennies, tooies, yellows, and yellow jackets. Some examples of barbiturates include phenobarbital, amobarbital, and secobarbital.

Tranquilizers

The term "**tranquilizers**" also refers to antianxiety medication. "Tranquilizers" is a term introduced in 1953 to describe drugs that have a calming effect.

Tranquilizers come in two varieties. Minor tranquilizers (anxiolytics) are used for sedation and to treat anxiety. Today, these drugs are called antianxiety medications. Major tranquilizers (neuroleptics) were developed to treat psychiatric disorders including schizophrenia. These drugs combat hallucinations and other delusions, and make a user feel less stress and fear. They make users feel peaceful.

The first antianxiety drug that was developed was meprobamate, called Miltown, named after the location of the company that introduced it. It became popular because the toxic dose was high (the amount needed before death occurred), and it seemed to work well for patients. However, the drug made some people very drowsy and affected their motor reflexes so they were unable to drive or carry out other tasks. It also was quickly addictive. In response, this drug was replaced by a class of antianxiety drugs called benzodiazepines (described below).

According to the National Survey on Drug Use and Health conducted by SAMHSA, about 2.1 million people aged 12 and older used tranquilizers for nonmedical reasons in 2012. About 4 percent of people in 2012 who used an illicit drug for the first time used a tranquilizer. Over half of the users obtained their drug from a friend or relative. Of the people seeking treatment for drug use in 2012, about 458,000 sought treatment for tranquilizer use.[33]

Benzodiazepines

Like barbiturates, **benzodiazepines** are a type of sedative or tranquilizer. They help people sleep. A widely used tranquilizer is Xanax, but other examples are Valium, Ativan, and Librium. On the street, these drugs are called candy, tranks, and benzos.

Benzodiazepines are the most prominent of the minor tranquilizers and one of the most frequently prescribed drugs. They were introduced in the early 1960s and used to reduce anxiety. Side effects include drowsiness and reduced alertness, with physical dependency possible if the drugs are used for an extended period.

Benzodiazepines have been used successfully as medications and have been shown to be a relatively safe drug and less likely to cause a fatal overdose. But they can also be misused. Medications used to treat anxiety or depression are typically in the top five most frequently reported drugs in cases of drug-related deaths. Often, these victims have ingested far more than the suggested dosage or have been used in combination with other drugs such as alcohol.

GHB and Flunitrazepam (Rohypnol)

Two types of benzodiazepine are gamma-hydroxybutyrate (also called GHB, liquid X, and easy lay) and Flunitrazepam (also called, Rohypnol or roofies). These drugs are largely tasteless, colorless, and odorless, so they can easily be slipped into a victim's drink and ingested unknowingly. The victim will quickly

feel the effects of the drug, becoming weak, confused, dizzy, or even unconscious. This allows the offender to sexually abuse the victim without their
knowledge or consent. Because of this, these drugs are commonly referred to
as date rape drugs. The effects last for hours, depending on the amount
ingested, the size of the victim, if there is food in their stomach, their tolerance,
and if there are other drugs present. Alcohol may often make the effects of the
drug stronger. Since the drugs are rapidly eliminated from the body it is difficult
to prove that the victim was drugged. For these reasons, the victim may not
report the offense to officials.

Although these drugs have been made illegal, they can still be purchased
easily on the black market.[34] They are fairly common and reportedly are being
used more frequently. They can be found at parties, on college campuses, and
in nightclubs. A person who ingests a predatory drug may feel extremely relaxed,
sleepy, dizzy, nauseous, have burry vision, experience seizures, sleepiness, trou-
bled breathing, tremors, sweating, vomiting, and a slow heart rate. Other symptoms include feeling drunk, problems with speech, difficulty with motor
movements, confusion, stomach problems, hallucinations, lost sense of time
and identity, distorted perceptions of sight and sound, feeling out of control,
and impaired motor function. Finally, convulsions, out-of-body experiences,
memory problems, numbness, loss of coordination, and aggressive or violent
behavior are symptoms as well.

As a way to reduce the victimization associated with these drugs, manufacturers are now coloring the pills with a dye that can alert drinkers that the drug
has been added to their drink. However, offenders have responded to this by
ordering blue-colored tropical drinks.[35] More information on these drugs is
presented in Table 4.7.

Table 4.7 Date Rape Drugs

Flunitrazepam, or Rohypnol, is illegal in the US but smuggled in from
other countries where it is used as a sleep aid. This drug also goes by
many names, such as lunch money, Mexican valium, mind erasers, R-
2, rib, roach, roopies, roofies, rope, riffies, or whitey. Rohypnol is typically sold in a pill form that can be crushed and dissolved in a drink very
quickly. When a victim ingests the drug, it normally takes about 30 min-

utes for them to feel the effects, which can last for many hours. A person who has ingested Rohypnol may exhibit slurred speech, loss of muscle control, difficulty with motor skills, nausea, confusion, dizziness, sleepiness, and low blood pressure. They may also feel a loss of inhibitions and impaired judgment.

The second commonly used date rape drug is GHB. This drug is often sold in a liquid form so it is easy to pour quickly into a victim's drink, but it also can be found as a pill or white powder. The drug can make drinks taste salty. Once ingested, a user may feel symptoms in as quickly as 15 minutes, and can exhibit them for up to four hours. The symptoms of GHB include drowsiness, dizziness, nausea, and loss of consciousness, seizures, difficulty breathing, tremors, sweating, vomiting, and a slow heart rate. An overdose of the drug can result in a coma or death. GHB is legal in the United States to treat a disorder called narcolepsy, but only when prescribed by a physician. GHB can be easily manufactured and found in the US.

The third date rape drug is ketamine, also known as black hole, bump, green, jet, K, k-hole, Kit Kat, purple, special K, or super acid. This drug is usually in the form of a liquid or a white powder. The effects of ketamine include a loss of memory, distorted perception of sight and sound, a confused sense of time, feelings of being out of control, problems breathing, convulsions, vomiting, loss of coordination, and slurred speech. Ketamine is used in the United States medically as an anesthetic for animals. It is stolen from veterinary clinics and then sold on the streets.

Source: "Rohypnol: Physiological Effects." June 20, 2009. *Controlled Substances*. http://ecstasy.com.ua/rohypnol/rohypnol-physiological-effects; Crawford, Emily. 2004. *Risk Perception and Drug-Facilitated Sexual Assault*. Oxford, OH: Miami University.

Inhalants

Inhalants are products that are intentionally inhaled by the user that produce a feeling of being high. Over 1,000 substances can be categorized as inhalants, many of which are products found in most homes and are cheap to buy. Since they are household products, the products are not regulated under the Controlled Substances Act. Many states have passed laws that discourage minors from buying the products but they are often legal to purchase.

Inhalants have many of the same characteristics as the drugs described above. They are similar to depressants because they suppress the central nervous system and decrease a user's respiration rate and blood pressure. At the same time, they are similar to hallucinogens because they lead to a distorted perception of time and space.[36]

Inhalants can be ingested in many ways. One popular way is to soak a cloth with the substance which is then held close to the nose so it can be inhaled. This is called "**huffing**." Another method is to place the cloth soaked with the product in a container which is then held close to the face so the fumes can be inhaled. Users may also simply paint or rub the chemicals onto their skin or clothing so the fumes can be inhaled. In a method called "**bagging**," users place a soaked cloth into a paper or plastic bag, allow the fumes to concentrate, then inhale them. This method has been blamed on suffocation deaths because of displacement of oxygen in the lungs.

Poppers are one type of nitrite-based inhalants that are popular. These are more likely to be used by older adolescents or even adults. Poppers were first developed as a heart medication and were available in small glass vials. These vials were easily broken, or popped, to allow the person to inhale the drug.[37] Because poppers are readily available and easy to find, adolescents often believe they are safe drugs.

Poppers are inhaled, so these drugs will reach a user's brain more quickly when compared to other drugs. The duration of the high from inhaling a popper is short, so users will often repeat the process multiple times to extend the effect. A user will experience an immediate or sudden feeling of being high, but then may experience feelings of drowsiness, lightheadedness, and agitation as the drug wears off. A user may experience slurred speech, nausea, and headaches, or they may experience impaired motor coordination. Some may lose consciousness. Users may also have watery eyes or a rash around the mouth. Chronic inhalant users may exhibit signs such as anxiety, excitability, irritability, or restlessness. Some users will suffer irreversible physical and mental damage from using poppers.

When used over a long term, a user may experience more serious effects. Because of the chemicals in the inhalants, users may suffer from bone marrow, kidney, or liver damage. They may also experience memory and intellectual impairment. The potential psychological and neurological damage resulting from using inhalants can be extreme and tragic, causing long-term health ailments or even death. In some cases, a first-time user may experience asphyxiation or heart failure, also known as the sudden sniffing death syndrome.

Because there are so many different kinds of inhalants with so many types of chemicals, it is hard to categorize them. However, there are four general types of inhalants:

- Volatile solvents: liquids that vaporize at room temperature and include paint thinners and removers, dry-cleaning fluids, gasoline, glues, and felt-tip markers;
- Aerosols: sprays that contain propellants and solvents. This includes spray paints, deodorant and hair sprays, vegetable sprays used for cooking, and fabric-protector sprays. Before these substances can be ingested, the gas must be separated from the other material. This can be done by spraying into a balloon. Aerosols are prevalent in most household products;
- Gasses: found in many household products including butane lighters, propane tanks, whipped cream dispensers, and refrigerants. Gasses can also be found in aerosols and dispensers (whippets), lighters, and nitrous oxide or chloroform that are used in medical settings;
- Nitrates: have effects somewhat similar to anesthetics and are primarily used as sexual enhancers. Common nitrates are poppers.

Long-term use of inhalants may lead to mild withdrawal symptoms, although there are typically no significant withdrawal symptoms.[38]

There are many street names for inhalants, including: air blast, ames, amys, bang, bolt, boppers, bullet, bullet bolt, buzz bomb, discorama, highball, hippie crack, huff, kick, laughing gas, locker room, medusa, moon gas, Oz, pearls, poor man's pot, poppers, quicksilver, rush, Satan's secret, shoot the breeze, snappers, snotballs, spray, Texas shoe shine, thrust, toilet water, and whippets.

Methaqualone (Quaalude)

"Quaalude" is a brand name for the synthetic depressant **methaqualone**. At one time, Quaaludes were thought to be non-addictive and were thought to be safer to use than other drugs. Because of this, they were often used as an alternative to barbiturates and were prescribed by physicians for sedation and to help people sleep better. Quaaludes made users have a pleasant feeling, as if they were drunk. Quaaludes were in great demand, especially on college campuses. Students would mix Quaaludes with wine in a trend called "luding out." The drug was sometimes referred to as the "love drug" because it lowered a user's inhibitions for sexual behavior.

In 1977, 23 year-old Freddie Prinze, from the TV series *Chico and the Man*, was addicted to Quaaludes. He took a dozen pills and then shot himself. Later that year, 42-year-old Elvis Presley died from taking too many drugs, including Quaalude and Valium. Five years later, comedian John Belushi, of *Blues Brothers* fame, died of an overdose of Quaalude he took to relieve anxiety from his cocaine habit.

In 1973, the drug was placed in Schedule II of the CSA because it was thought to have some medical value. This changed in early 1980s, when Quaaludes were removed from the market after many people died after using the drug. It was then rescheduled as a Schedule I drug, primarily because the medical use was no longer recognized and it still had a high potential for abuse. In 1984, Congress passed a law that made possession of Quaalude illegal. After that, it became harder to find on the street. Today, methaqualone is not manufactured by any pharmaceutical company but it is still available through the black market. That means that the drug is either manufactured in secret labs or smuggled into the US from other countries.

Other formal names of Quaalude include Cateudil, Dormutil, Hyminal, Isonox, Melsed, Melsedin, Mequelone, Mequin, Methadorm, Mozambin, Optimil, Parest, Renoval, Somnafac, Toquilone Compositum, Triador, and Tuazole. Quaalude also has informal names that include: bandits, Beiruts, blou bulle, disco biscuits, ewings, flamingos, flowers, genuines, lemmon 714, lemons, lennons, lovers, ludes, mandies, qua, Quaaludes, quack, quad, randy mandies, soaper, sopes, sporos, vitamin Q, and wagon wheels.[39]

Conclusion

There are many kinds of illicit drugs that have a variety of effects on users. It is important to know the effects of each drug so that a user in distress can be treated correctly, and so that long-term treatment can be provided to them. This chapter provided a review of the types of drugs that are currently being used for non-medical purposes so that we have a better understanding of the impacts illegal drugs are having on those who use them.

Important Terms

Alcohol

Amphetamine

Bagging

Barbiturates

Bath Salts

Benzodiazepines

Blood-Alcohol Content

Caffeinism

Cocaine

Crack

Date Rape Drugs

Depressants

E-cigarettes

Ecstasy

Energy Drinks

GHB

Gutka

Huffing

Inhalants

Khat

Meth Labs

Methamphetamine

Methaqualone

Nicotine

Poppers

Shisha

Stimulants

Synthetic Cannabis

Tranquilizers

Tweaking

Review Questions

1. What is the difference between a stimulant drug and a depressant? What are the general effects of these drugs?

2. Give some examples of stimulant drugs. What are the effects of these drugs?

3. Provide some examples of depressant drugs. What might happen to you if you ingested one of these drugs?

4. What are some of the dangers of taking stimulant and depressant drugs?

Endnotes

1. National Institutes of Health. "Caffeine." MedLine Plus. http://www.nlm.nih.gov/medlineplus/caffeine.html; "Caffeine." WebMD. http://www.webmd.com/vitamins-supplements/ingredientmono-979CAFFEINE.aspx?activeIngredientId=979&activeIngredientName=CAFFEINE; Chambers, Kenneth P. 2009. *Caffeine and Health Research*. New York: Nova Biomedical Books.

2. DeNoon, Daniel J. November 16, 2012. "More Deaths, Illnesses Linked to Energy Drinks." *WebMD News Archives*. http://www.webmd.com/diet/news/20121116/more-deaths-illness-energy-drinks.

3. Doheny, Kathleen. 2008. "Energy Drinks: Hazardous to Your Health?" WebMD. http://www.webmd.com/food-recipes/news/20080924/energy-drinks-hazardous-to-your-health; Rath, Mandy. 2012. "Energy Drinks: What Is All the Hype? The Dangers of Energy Drink Consumption." *Journal of the American Academy of Nurse Practitioners*. 24(2); Williams, Brian, and Tom Costello. October 25, 2012. "Caffeine Drinks Pose Hidden Danger, Report Says." Video News Report. New York: NBCUniversal Media, LLC.

4. Gould, Madelyn S., Timothy Walsh, Jimmie Lou Munfakh, Marjorie Kleinman, Nai-hua Duan, Mark Olfson, Laurence Greenhill, and Thomas Cooper. 2009. "Sudden Death and Use of Stimulant Medications in Youths." *American Journal of Psychiatry* 166: 992–1001.

5. "Lawsuit Blames Monster Energy Drinks for California Teen's Death." June 26, 2013. Fox News. http://www.foxnews.com/health/2013/06/26/lawsuit-blames-monster-energy-drinks-for-california-teen-death/; American Academy of Pediatrics. 2011. "Sports Drinks and Energy Drinks for Children and Adolescents: Are They Appropriate?" *Pediatrics* 127(6): 1182–89. http://pediatrics.aappublications.org/content/127/6/1182.full?sid=1af2837a-6401-426a-a9fa-cc73b9321c39.

6. Society for Cardiovascular Angiography and Interventions. "Energy Drinks and the Heart: Know the Risks." http://www.scai.org/SecondsCount/Disease/detail.aspx?cid=135 410fb-a293-43e0-82c6-ec0bcc47125f; Heneman, K., and S. Zidenberg-Cherr. "Nutrition and Health Info-Sheet for Health Professionals: Some Facts about Energy Drinks." http://cns.ucdavis.edu/ content/FactSheets/EnergyDrinks.pdf; Malinauskas B. M., V. G. Aeby, R. F. Overton, *et al.* 2007. "A Survey of Energy Drink Consumption Patterns among College Students." *Nutr J* 6: 35–42; Seifert, S. M., J. L. Schaechter, E. R. Hershorin, *et al.* 2011. "Health Effects of Energy Drinks on Children, Adolescents, and Young Adults." *Pediatrics* 127(3): 511–28; Substance Abuse and Mental Health Services Administration. 2013. "Update on Emergency Department Visits Involving Energy Drinks: A Continuing Public Health Concern." *The DAWN Report.* http://www.samhsa.gov/data/ 2k13/DAWN126/sr126-energy-drinks-use.htm; US Food and Drug Administration. 2012. "Dietary Supplements." http://www.fda.gov/Food/DietarySupplements/default.htm; Wolk, B. J., M. Ganetsky, and K. M. Babu. 2012. "Toxicity of Energy Drinks." *Current Opinion in Pediatrics* 24: 243–51; Health Day News. February 1, 2013. "Energy Drinks Pose Risks to Teens, Study Finds." http://www.healthfinder.gov/News/Article.aspx?id =673034.

7. Centers for Disease Control. 2011. "Targeting the Nation's Leading Killer: At a Glance." http://www.cdc.gov/chronicdisease/resources/publications/aag/osh.htm; US Department of Health and Human Services. 1986. *The Health Consequences of Involuntary Smoking: A Report of the Surgeon General.* http://profiles.nlm.nih.gov/ps/access/NNBCPM.pdf; US Department of Health and Human Services, Substance Abuse and Mental Health Services Administration, Center for Behavioral Health Statistics and Quality. 2012. "Results from the 2012 National Survey on Drug Use and Health: Summary of National Findings." http://www.samhsa.gov/data/NSDUH/2012SummNatFindDetTables/NationalFindings/NSDUHresults2012.htm#ch4.

8. Substance Abuse and Mental Health Services Administration (SAMHSA), Office of Applied Studies. 2007. *Results from the 2006 National Survey on Drug Use and Health: National Findings.* DHHS Publication No. SMA 07-4293.

9. American Lung Association. "General Smoking Facts." http://www.lung.org/stop-smoking/about-smoking/facts-figures/general-smoking-facts.html.

10. US Department of Health and Human Services, Centers for Disease Control and Prevention. http://apps.nccd.cdc.gov/osh_faq; US Department of Health and Human Services, National Institute on Drug Abuse. 2006. *Research Report Series: Tobacco Addiction.* NIH Publication No. 06-4342.

11. Dale, Lowell. 2011. "What Are Electronic Cigarettes?" Mayo Clinic. http://www.mayoclinic.com/health/electronic-cigarettes/AN02025.

12. Centers for Disease Control and Prevention. "Betel Quid with Tobacco (Gutka)." *Smoking and Tobacco Use.* http://www.cdc.gov/tobacco/data_statistics/fact_sheets/smokeless/betel_quid/; Gupta P. C., and C. S. Ray. 2003. "Smokeless Tobacco and Health in India and

South Asia." *Respirology* 8(4): 419–31; National Cancer Institute, National Institutes of Health. "Smokeless Tobacco." http://www.cancer.gov/cancertopics/tobacco/smokeless-tobacco; Varughese, A. 2003. "Gutka—A Silent Killer." *The Nicotine Challenger*. http://www.tobaccoprogram.org/pdf/tnc/spring03/page7.pdf.

13. US Department of Health and Human Services, National Institute on Drug Abuse. 2004. *Research Report Series: Cocaine Abuse and Addiction*. NIH Publication No. 99-4342. http://www.nida.gov.

14. Drugs.com. "Amphetamine." http://www.drugs.com/amphetamine.html; Menhard, Francha Roffe. 2006. *The Facts about Amphetamine*. New York: Marshall Cavendish Benchmark.

15. National Institutes of Health. "Methamphetamine." MedlinePlus. http://www.nlm.nih.gov/medlineplus/methamphetamine.html.

16. Sheff, David. 2008. *Beautiful Boy: A Father's Journey through His Son's Addiction*. Boston: Houghton Mifflin; Sheff, Nicholas. 2007. *Tweak: Growing Up on Amphetamines*. New York: Atheneum Books.

17. US Department of Health and Human Services, National Institute on Drug Abuse. 2006. *Research Report Series: Methamphetamine Abuse and Addiction*. NIH Publication No. 06-4210.

18. Substance Abuse and Mental Health Services Administration. 2013 National Survey on Drug Use and Health. http://www.samhsa.gov.

19. Methamphetamine Laboratory Identification Hazards: Fast Facts. National Drug Intelligence Center, December 2003. US Department of Justice. http://www.justicee.gov/archive/ndic/pubs7.

20. Anderson, David, Susan Beckerleg, Degol Hailu, and Axel Klein. 2007. *The Khat Controversy*. New York: Berg.

21. Goodnough, Abby. July 16, 2011. "An Alarming New Stimulant, Legal in Many States." *New York Times*. http://www.nytimes.com/2011/07/17/us/17salts.html?pagewanted=all; McMillen, Matt. 2011. "'Bath Salts' Drug Trend: Expert Q & A." WebMD. http://www.webmd.com/mental-health/features/bath-salts-drug-dangers; Snyderman, Nancy. October 19, 2011. "Bath Salts Drugs Causing Alarm." *Nightly News*. New York: NBCUniversal Media LLC.

22. "America's New Drug Problem: Snorting 'Bath Salts.'" January 24, 2011. FoxNews.com. http://www.foxnews.com/health/2011/01/24/americas-new-drug-problem-snorting-bath-salts/.

23. US Department of Health and Human Services, National Institute on Drug Abuse. 2010. "Club Drugs (GHB, Ketamine, and Rohypnol)." http://www.drugabuse.gov/publications/drugfacts/club-drugs-ghb-ketamine-rohypnol; Yuodelis-Flores, C. 2014. "The New Club Drugs: Designer Drugs & Legal Highs. Synthetic Cannabinoids and Cathinones." Northwest AIDS Education and Training Center; http://depts.washington.edu/nwaetc/presentations/uploads/84/club_drugs_and_hiv.pdf; Olive, M. Foster. 2004. *Designer Drugs*. Philadelphia: Chelsea House Publishers.

24. Schroeder, Brock E. 2004. *Ecstasy*. Philadelphia: Chelsea House Publishers.

25. Anderson, David, Susan Beckerleg, Degol Hailu, and Axel Klein. 2007. *The Khat Controversy: Stimulating the Debate on Drugs*. New York: Berg.

26. World Health Organization. 2006. "Assessment of Khat." http://www.who.int/medicines/areas/quality_safety/4.4KhatCritReview.pdf.

27. US Department of Justice, Drug Enforcement Administration. 2008. http://www.usdoj.gov/deahttp://www.drugabuse.gov/publications/drugfacts/khat; US Department of

Justice, Drug Enforcement Administration. 2013. http://www.deadiversion.usdoj.gov/drug_chem_info/khat.pdf.

28. Fingarette, Herbert. 1988. *Heavy Drinking: The Myth of Alcoholism as a Disease*. London: University of California Press; Gifford, Maria. 2011. *Alcoholism*. Santa Barbara, CA: Greenwood Press; Jellinek, E. M. 1960. *The Disease Concept of Alcoholism*. New Haven, CT: Hillhouse Press.

29. "Alcohol Impaired Driving: Overview of the Law and Police Practices." 2013. *Supreme Court Debates* 16(2): 7–11.

30. "Blood Alcohol." WebMd. http://www.webmd.com/mental-health/alcohol-abuse/blood-alcohol?page=2; Centers for Disease Control and Prevention. "Effects of Blood Alcohol Concentration." http://www.cdc.gov/Motorvehiclesafety/Impaired_Driving/bac.htmlp; Kiesbye, Stefan. 2011. *Drunk Driving*. Detroit: Greenhaven Press; Parks, Peggy J. 2010. *Drunk Driving*. San Diego, CA: Reference Point Press; Wilson, Mike. 2007. *Drunk Driving*. MI: Greenhaven Press.

31. "Hangovers." Mayo Clinic. http://www.mayoclinic.com/health/hangovers/DS00649; Sutton, Amy L. 2007. *Alcoholism Sourcebook*. Detroit: Omnigraphics; US Department of Health and Human Services, National Institutes of Health, National Institute on Alcohol Abuse and Alcoholism. 2011. "Beyond Hangovers: Understanding Alcohol's Impact on Your Health." Washington, DC; Vander Ven, Thomas. 2011. *Getting Wasted: Why College Students Drink Too Much and Party So Hard*. New York: New York University Press.

32. Henn, Debra, Deborah de Eugenio, and David J. Triggle. 2007. *Barbiturates*. New York: Chelsea House.

33. US Department Health and Human Services, US Public Health Service, Substance Abuse and Mental Health Services Administration. 2013. "Results from the 2012 National Survey on Drug Use and Health." http://www.samhsa.gov/data/NSDUH/2012SummNatFind DetTables/Index.aspx.

34. "Sedative, Hypnotic or Anxiolytic Dependence." *MD Guidelines*. http://www.md guidelines.com/sedative-hypnotic-or-anxiolytic-dependence.

35. iCAN Foundation Crime Victims Assistance Network. "Predatory Drugs." http://www.ican-foundation.org/resources/predatory-drugs/; US Department of Health and Human Resources, Office on Women's Health. 2008. "Date Rape Drugs Fact Sheet." http://www.womenshealth.gov/publications/our-publications/fact-sheet/date-rape-drugs.html.

36. National Institute on Drug Abuse. July 2012. *Inhalant Abuse*. http://www.drugabuse.gov/publications/research-reports/inhalants; US Department of Health and Human Services, National Institute on Drug Abuse. March 2005. *Research Report Series: Inhalant Abuse*. NIH Publication No. 05-3818.

37. Hartney, Elizabeth. May 16, 2014. "What Are Poppers?" http://addictions.about.com/od/designerdrugs/g/What-Is-Poppers.htm.

38. Duncan, Jhodie Rubina, and Andrew John Lawrence. 2013. "Conventional Concepts and New Perspectives for Understanding the Addictive Properties of Inhalants." *Journal of Pharmacological Sciences*. 122.

39. Carroll, Marilyn. 1985. *Quaaludes: The Quest for Oblivion*. New York: Chelsea House Publishers; Gass, Justin T. 2008. *Quaaludes*. New York: Chelsea House Publishers; "The Quaalude Lesson." *Frontline*. http://www.pbs.org/wgbh/pages/frontline/meth/faqs/quaaludes.html; Ziemer, Maryann. 1997. *Quaaludes*. Springfield, NJ: Enslow Publishers.

Chapter 5

The Types of Drugs: Opiates, Hallucinogens, and Others

Chapter Objective: This chapter introduces other categories of illicit drugs, including opiates, hallucinogens, antidepressants, and steroids. Like the stimulant and depressant drugs introduced in chapter 4, these drugs have serious short- and long-term effects on users.

Introduction

Opiates and hallucinogens are commonly used drugs that have quite different effects on a user's body than the drugs discussed in chapter 4. The use of both opiates and hallucinogens has been rising in recent years, raising concerns among experts. Antidepressant and steroid abuse has also been on the rise.[1] The reasons why people use these drugs, the health risks posed by these drugs, and treatment options for addicts are discussed in this chapter.

Opiates

The term "**opiates**" refers to all products and derivatives of the opium poppy. This includes morphine and codeine, the natural opiates. Heroin, another drug from the poppy plant, is a semisynthetic drug that is the most commonly abused illegal substance. Other substances that are derived from the poppy plant include oxycodone (painkillers OxyContin and Percocet), each of which is used medically and legally for pain relief and other medical purposes. Thebaine is another opiate, but it acts more like a stimulant than a depressant so it is not a drug that is frequently abused. However, it is a highly addictive substance that is used to make other drugs. Other drugs that are made from the opium plant are widely abused, including hydromorphone (used to treat pain but highly addictive), ketobemidone (a drug similar to morphine), tildine (used to treat pain but has been linked to coma, convulsions, and respiratory distress in large doses), and hydrocodone (a Schedule II drug used to treat coughs and pains). Drugs that mimic the activity of opium and are chemically similar to opiates, but are lab-created (synthetic) are called opioids. These include anileridine (similar to Demorol), Meperidine (sometimes used for pain relief following surgery), Dextropropoxyphene, Pentazocine, Butorphanol, LAAM (used as a maintenance drug for those addicted to narcotics), and Methadone (used to treat narcotics addicts). Scientists attempting to create a new drug that would mimic the effects of opium produced fentanyl, an entirely synthetic but extremely powerful drug. Fentanyl can be hundreds of times more potent than heroin.

Opium comes from the seedpods of the *Papaver somniferum* poppy. When the plant is grown in the West, it is a low-morphine-producing variety; when it is grown in the Mediterranean regions of the world, primarily in Afghanistan, it produces a much stronger drug. Most opium comes from poppies grown in Afghanistan and in South America, in areas considered to be the Golden Triangle or the Golden Crescent. Poppies are also cultivated in Mexico (the leading supplier of heroin to the US)[2] and Colombia. Poppies from Colombia are grown mostly in the Andes Mountains.[3]

The poppy plant grows to about four feet tall with a long stem and a brightly colored flower that is usually purple, red, pink, or white, as portrayed in the movie *The Wizard of Oz*. The plant matures in about three months. A flower blooms at the top of the plant, the petals of which eventually fall off, revealing a one- to three-inch green seedpod about the size as a walnut that is full of poppy seeds. The pod, or bulb, is slashed or punctured. Inside the pod is a milky-white fluid or sap that is collected and dried. Sometimes it is boiled until it becomes a dark brown waxy or gummy resin. The dried substance is raw opium, sometimes called "blac." In this form, the opium can be can be dried and rolled into a ball, or crushed into a powder. The opium can also be processed to create solidified morphine. If morphine is heated at 185 degrees for six hours, it becomes an impure heroin product. This product can then be treated to remove any impurities and then further refined to form a product that looks like small white flakes. The flakes are dried under pressure to produce heroin.

Opiates release tension and anxiety in a user and create a sense of euphoria along with physical and mental relaxation. At the same time, the use of opiates

A poppy field in Afghanistan by davric via wikimedia commons.

causes constructed pupils in the eyes, slurred speech, drowsiness, and a release of histamine in the body. They may also cause a user to have difficulty concentrating, confusion, nausea, vomiting, constipation, and slowed breathing. Those who are addicted to narcotic drugs may suffer withdrawal symptoms such as fever, increased blood pressure, diarrhea, involuntary twitching, runny nose, insomnia, and depression upon ceasing to use the drug. The exact effect of the opiate depends on the person, the mode of administration, and the dose consumed.

Many opiates have recognized medical uses and are typically used in the medical field for treating patients. Opiates are useful for suppressing coughs so it is commonly prescribed as a cough medicine. Many opiates have analgesic (pain reducing) properties, so they are used in hospitals and by doctors to relieve severe pain. They have a sedating effect on a user so that they are calming and induce sleep. They are also prescribed as anti-diarrheals. Each year, about 600 tons of opium is imported into the US for legal, medical uses.[4]

Opiates may be ingested orally but they are generally smoked, sniffed, snorted, or injected. Some users inject the drug under the skin in a process called subcutaneous injection, referred to as "skin-popping." When this is done, the drug is absorbed more slowly into the body, producing a lower degree of euphoria. When injected, the effects of the drug last much longer. Some opiates are delivered via lozenges that allows user to dissolve it in their mouth or inserted rectally in suppositories.

Pure opiates cause relatively little damage to a user, but the opiates sold on the streets usually contain contaminants that can cause serious damage or even death to the user. Unlike stimulants, opiates do not produce a psychotic state when used in a pure form and have the ability to reduce or eliminate psychotic symptoms in mental patients.

Since the 1990s, prescription pain relievers such as OxyContin, Vicodin, and Percocet have become popular drugs used for non-medical purposes. Tolerance builds quickly to opiates, so overdoses are common. The initial symptoms of an opiate overdose include pinpoint pupils, confusion, convulsions, and cold, clammy skin. A user could experience respiratory depression and death. Users can experience other health problems like infections from using dirty needles. Some users experience damage to their internal organs resulting from adulterants that have been added to the drug. It is not uncommon for users to contract HIV or hepatitis, or to suffer from inflammation of tissues around their heart or brain.

Opiates cause physical dependence so when a user stops using the drug, they may experience discomfort. Withdrawal from opiates can be difficult. It sometimes takes between a week and 10 days for a user to be free of the drug. Beginning symptoms include yawning, watery eyes, runny nose, sweating, and restlessness. Secondary symptoms can be flu-like symptoms, severe depression, nausea, vomiting, insomnia, cramps, restlessness, diarrhea and vomiting, chills, and goose bumps. The withdrawal is uncomfortable but not life threatening. Street names for opium include ah-pen-yen, Buddha, chillum, Chinese molasses, Chinese tobacco, Gee, pen yan, when-sehh, and ze.

Morphine

A derivative of opium, **morphine** is one of the most powerful natural pain relievers that exists. The drug was first extracted from opium in 1803 by Friedrich Wilhelm Adam Serturner who called it "morphine" after Morpheus, the Greek god of dreams. The drug quickly became used as a legal analgesic that most patients could use safely. When a user injects morphine, he or she feels the effects almost immediately. This makes it attractive as a recreational drug.

Today, morphine is available in an oral form, as suppositories, or as an injectable drug. It is a Schedule II drug under the Controlled Substances Act. Some of the street the names for morphine include M, sister morphine, vitamin M, and morpho.

Morphine addiction is very serious and the withdrawal process must be gradual or it may result in a stroke, heart attack, or death of the user. Withdrawal symptoms include diarrhea, runny nose, yawning, sweating, headaches, irritability, loss of appetite, body aches, severe abdominal pain, nausea, vomiting, and severe drug cravings. Morphine addiction is often treated with naloxone and naltrexone that block its effect, or methadone.

Codeine

Codeine is the primary psychoactive element in opium and a mild version of morphine. It is widely used as a legal pain reliever because, even though it is less powerful, it also causes less drowsiness. Consequently, codeine is often prescribed for mild to moderate levels of pain. The drug is also effective at treating diarrhea and is an effective cough suppressant. It is the most widely used narcotic in the world. Users often experience constipation, drowsiness, itching, nausea, vomiting, and dry mouth. In small amounts, codeine can produce a sense of well-being and warmth. If larger doses are consumed, the user may feel dizziness, confusion, and cold and clammy skin. Serious reactions may include seizures and unconsciousness.

In tablet form, codeine is a Schedule II drug under the Controlled Substances Act because of its medicinal qualities. At the same time, codeine is highly addictive. If it is compounded with another drug such as acetaminophen or aspirin or other drugs, it is a Schedule III drug. As a cough medicine, it is considered to be a Schedule V drug.

Common street names for codeine include Captain Cody, Cody, schoolboy, doors and fours, pancakes and syrup.

Heroin

A drug that is derived from morphine is **heroin**. Discovered in 1874, heroin has the same general effects as morphine but it is more potent. It is a powerful, fast acting drug that is highly addictive but used as a recreational drug. Because it is so powerful, it has a high potential for an overdose.

Heroin was used in the early twentieth century as a pain medication. It was then used as a treatment for those addicted to morphine. After realizing that it was even more addictive than morphine, heroin was made illegal in 1914. Today, it is considered by the US government to have no medical purpose and is found in Schedule I of the Controlled Substances Act.

When sold on the black market, heroin is often cut by dealers with additives such as starch, flour, lactose, sugar, talcum powder, baking powder, powdered milk, acetaminophen, or a number of other ingredients as a way to stretch the drug. It has even been known to be mixed with other drugs like methamphetamine, PCP, or cocaine. This makes it very dangerous. This becomes even more dangerous since today's illegal heroin is a much higher quality than in the past. Street heroin in the past was about 5 percent pure heroin. Today, the heroin available on the street is up to 90 percent pure. The majority of the heroin produced in Colombia is much more pure than Mexican heroin and is sold primarily in the US.

One type of heroin is **black tar heroin**, which appeared in the 1980s. This is a low grade heroin that has impurities, causing the dark color. It is made with cheaper ingredients in the production stage and is less refined. Since it does not require any complex or expensive lab equipment to make, black tar heroin is relatively easy to make. The drug can be either a dark black, gooey, tar-like substance or a lighter brown, powdery substance, depending on the ingredients used. Since the drug is made in Mexico, black tar heroin is most frequently found in the western and southern areas of the US. The potency of black tar heroin is about the same as regular heroin but because of the impurities, there is a higher risk of side effects. Because black tar heroin is often dissolved in water and injected, and must be heated before injecting, some potential viruses are killed before being injected into the body. Black tar heroin can also be ground into a powder that can be snorted, dissolved into water and used as nose drops (called "water looping"), drunk, heated on foil and the smoke inhaled, or used as a suppository. Because heroin is typically injected, users often share needles. This can cause the spread of HIV and hepatitis. New forms of the drug are being created that can be snorted or smoked. This form of heroin is quick, easy, and cheap to make and requires less equipment and expertise. Much of this product is made with mobile cooking operations which can be packed up to evade law enforcement. Because of the impurities, black tar heroin is typically only about 65–85 percent pure.

The short-term effects of heroin are similar to those of other opiates. A user will experience a sudden rush of euphoria and relaxation. Users will often "nod off" or start to doze. Other effects of the drug include drowsiness, poor motor coordination, fresh needle marks or tracks, slow or slurred speech, facial itching and scratching, dry mouth, deepening of voice, constricted pupils, impairment of night vision, and dizziness. Heroin users may also have mood changes, an inability to concentrate, apathy, mental confusion, giddiness, fearfulness, and anxiety. If a user ingests too much heroin, it can lead to respiratory depression, clammy skin, seizures, and possibly coma and death. If used over a long period, heroin can lead to heart or liver disease and other pulmonary disorders. Those who inject the drug may experience collapsed veins or infections.

Users quickly develop a tolerance to heroin. If the drug is not used regularly (within a few hours), users will experience withdrawal symptoms that include diarrhea, vomiting, muscle and bone pain, agitation, and intense craving. Serious withdrawal from heroin can lead to death.[5]

Heroin addiction in the US continues to rise. In April 2014, the FDA approved the drug Naloxone that can counteract the effects of a heroin overdose. Now, family, caregivers, and emergency workers can have the drug. This will provide time to get the user to a hospital for care. The product provides voice instructions for application.[6]

There have been many celebrities who have been addicted to heroin and died from it. One of those was Sid Vicious (John Ritchie), who played bass guitar for the punk band the Sex Pistols. Kurt Cobain, another rock star, was addicted to heroin before he took his own life. In 1993, actor River Phoenix died from a mixture of cocaine and heroin often called a "speedball." Another actor who died from using speedball was John Belushi. Rock star Jim Morrison of the Doors died in his bathtub of a heart attack brought on by an overdose of heroin. Singer Janis Joplin also died of a heroin overdose, furthered by an addiction to alcohol. More recent deaths related to heroin overdose include the 2014 death of Philip Seymour Hoffman, a celebrated actor and director, and Cory Monteith, an actor from the hit television series *Glee*, who died in 2013.

Street names for heroin include black tar (or negra), boy, brown, dope, H, henry horse, jones, junk, scag, and smack.

Syrup

Syrup is a recreational drug that is often linked to the hip-hop community. The concoction begins with prescription-strength cough syrup that contains codeine and promethazine, although it can be made over-the-counter cough medicine. This is combined with soda (Sprite, 7-Up, or Mountain Dew), a sports drink, or Kool-Aid. Since the cough syrup is purple, the mixture often has a purple hue. For this reason, it is sometimes called purple drank, purple jelly, Texas tea, or purple Sprite.[7]

When consumed, it makes the user feel sedated or have an altered state of consciousness. Other symptoms include constricted pupils, a raspy voice, slurred speech, a slowed heartbeat, loss of balance, and constipation. It can also, in the long term, cause weight gain and tooth decay, largely because of the sugar in the soda. Because of the codeine in the cough syrup, heavy users may experience cardiac arrest and death.[8]

Syrup is linked to Houston in the 1960s when a music producer in the city, DJ Screw, made use of syrup popular. There are many references to syrup in hip-hop lyrics. Two songs, "Sippin' on Some Syrup" and "Rainbow Colors" describe the effects of syrup.

Table 5.1 Use of Syrup

There have been many hip-hop artists and athletes who have had run-ins with syrup. DJ Screw, who made the substance popular, died in 2000 of an overdose of codeine, promethazine, and alcohol. Big Moe, a rapper who released two albums having syrup as the theme (*City of Syrup* and *Purple World*), died in 2007 at the age of 33, after suffering a heart attack that left him in a coma. It was rumored that he used purple drank before his death. Pimp C, a rapper from Texas and a member of the group UGK, died in 2007 in a California hotel. The Los Angeles County Coroner's Office concluded he died from effects of using promethazine and codeine. They noted that while he had the substance in his system but it was not enough to cause his death. However, Pimp C had a history of sleep apnea, which may have been aggravated by the cough medication. Rapper 2 Chainz was arrested in the LA International Airport in 2013 and charged with possession of marijuana, promethazine, and codeine.

In October 2012, rapper Lil Wayne was hospitalized after he suffered seizures while flying in his private jet that were later blamed on a migraine and dehydration. On March 15, 2013, Lil Wayne was again hospitalized, this time after suffering from seizures after an alleged syrup binge. He was admitted to Cedars-Sinai Medical Center after being found unconscious and shaking uncontrollably. Doctors later reported that they had found codeine in Lil Wayne's body and pumped his stomach three times to remove the drugs. Lil Wayne has admitted publicly that he uses syrup. He often describes his experiences with the drug in his music. He has also discussed the difficulties in experiencing withdrawal symptoms upon quitting the drug.

Professional athletes have also been found to have addictions to syrup. One of those, Terrance Kiel, was a football player with the San Diego Chargers in 2006 where he was arrested for attempting to send a case of cough syrup to a friend. He was charged by prosecutors with two felony counts of transporting a controlled substance and three counts of possession of a controlled substance for sale. He pled guilty, ending his football career. Kiel was killed in a car accident two years later. He was 27.

In July 2008, another sports figure, Johnny Jolly, a member of the Green Bay Packers NFL team, was driving and was pulled over by police for excessively loud music. In the drink holder the police found a Dr. Pepper bottle, and beside it were two Styrofoam cups that contained soda and ice. The police officers noted that there was a strong odor of codeine coming from the containers. They also found 200 grams of codeine in the car. The charges against Jolly were initially dismissed but were later refiled in December 2009 after the Houston Police Department received equipment with which the police could retest the cup's contents. Then the contents of the cup tested positive for codeine, the charges against Jolly were reinstated.

In 2005, police in Alabama arrested JaMarcus Russell, a former quarterback with the Oakland Raiders. He was charged with possession of codeine syrup without a prescription.

Source: Reid, Shameem. February 28, 2008. "Lil Wayne on Syrup: 'Everybody Wants Me to Stop ... It Ain't That Easy.' *MTV.com*. http://www.mtv.com/news/articles/1582520/lil-wayne-on-syrup-everybody-wants-me-stop.jhtml; Sullivan, Tim. July 6, 2008. "Kiel Left Little as Memorial to Himself." *Union Tribune*. http://www.uts-andiego.com/sports/sullivan/20080706–9999–1s6sullivan.html; MJD. July 5, 2005. "JaMarcus Russell Arrested; Not Likely to Be Employed Soon." *Yahoo Sports*. http://sports.yahoo.com/nfl/blog/shutdown_corner/post/JaMarcus-Russell-arrested-not-likely-to-be-empl?urn=nfl,253790.

Oxycodone

Oxycodone is a semisynthetic opiate and powerful painkiller often used for cancer patients. It is sometimes mixed with aspirin to make Percodan, or it is mixed with acetaminophen to make Percocet. Another drug, OxyContin, is a sustained-release formula of oxycodone that is used to treat serious and chronic pain. Common street names for oxycodone include hillbilly heroin, kicker, OC, and oxy.[9]

Oxycodone is less potent than morphine, but more potent than codeine. It is made from thebaine, a naturally occurring ingredient in opium. The drug has accepted medical uses but is also highly addictive. Thus, it is classified as a Schedule II drug under the Controlled Substances Act.

Some users crush Oxycodone pills into a powder and snort or inject them. In essence, what is intended to be medicine released over a 12-hour period is ingested all at once. Users will experience a rapid and intense rush after using oxycodone. They typically also experience intense feelings of well-being, relaxation, drowsiness, and sleepiness. Side effects are common and include dizziness, nausea, constipation, and sweating. If a user overdoses, it can lead to coma and death. Tolerance and physical dependence to oxycodone occurs quickly, so users will need more of the drug to achieve the desired effect.

Oxycodone is only available if a patient has a doctor's prescription. While it is heavily regulated, it is also sought after by addicts. Oxycodone is often abused, to the point of reaching epidemic proportions. The number of people addicted to oxycodone continues to increase. Addicts will often commit crimes in order to get the drug. They may commit prescription fraud or break into pharmacies in order to get the drug. Others steal the drug from relatives or friends, or sell their own prescription drugs on the black market. Some addicts will "doctor shop," going from doctor to doctor to find someone who will prescribe the drug to them.

Non-Opiate Analgesics

Non-opiate analgesics have no psychoactive effects. They have a pain-killing effect, but it is much weaker than opiates. Nonetheless, these drugs can still be misused. They are used each day by millions of people for recreation as many believe there are few, if any, risks to using these drugs. However, this is a myth. If abused, a person can experience liver problems, damage to the stomach lining, or even death. Examples of non-opiate analgesics include acetylsalicylic acid (marketed as Aspirin), acetaminophen, and ibuprofen.

These mild analgesics are readily available over the counter (OTC) without a doctor's prescription. An example of this is aspirin, which is generally safe for adults. Some children who use aspirin can develop Reye's Syndrome, a liver disorder. Stronger analgesics require a doctor's prescription. Analgesics may be taken orally (by mouth), through the rectum or nose, or injected, intravenously or topically. They can be taken on a regular schedule or as needed to manage pain.

Another OTC analgesic is acetaminophen, which relieves fever and common pains like headaches, but it does not reduce inflammation. Acetaminophen does not cause stomach problems as found with aspirin, so it is safe for children. But in large doses, like aspirin, it can also cause liver damage.

The third is type of OTC analgesic is nonsteroidal anti-inflammatory drugs (NSAIDs). These drugs are often used for those suffering from arthritis because they reduce pain and swelling. Examples are ibuprofen (Advil or Motrin) and naproxen (Aleve). These drugs have few side effects and are safe for most users but long-term use could lead to kidney and/or liver damage.[10]

Some patients who are unable to ingest drugs orally can use patches that administer analgesics slowly, over a long period of time. Some patience can also use topical analgesics, which can be applied directly to the part of the body where the pain is located. This way, there is less medicine throughout the body and a lower potential for causing side effects. Topical medicine can be applied by a cream, lotion, or spray.[11] Users sometimes combine these drugs with other drugs, such as antihistamines. When combined with other drugs, they are considered to be compound analgesics.

Hallucinogens and Psychedelics

Hallucinogens (psychedelics) are drugs that distort a person's senses and warp their awareness or perception of people and events, or even cause hallucinations (seeing or hearing things that are not real or that do not exist). Hallucinogens produce an unreal perception of sight, smell, taste, touch, or hearing in the user. Examples of these drugs are LSD, Psilocybin, Phencyclidine (PCP), mescaline, peyote, ketamine, and psilocin.[12] Hallucinogens can be either naturally occurring or manufactured in a lab. The naturally occurring ones are derived from plants and fungi.

College students in the 1960s and 1970s made the use of hallucinogenic drugs popular, but the use of these drugs declined for a short time. The results of the National Survey on Drug Use and Health, from the Substance Abuse and Mental Health Services Administration (part of the US Department of Health and Human Services), show that the number of first time users of hallucinogens has remained about the same since 2002. In 2014, the results of the study show that there were 936,000 people aged 12 and over who used a hallucinogenic drug for the first time within the previous 12 month period. Further, 1.2 million people (0.4 percent of the population) reported that they used a hallucinogen in the previous month. This number has also remained about the same since 2002. More males than females reported that they used a hallucinogen within the past month.[13]

Hallucinogens are sometimes used by people in nightclubs as a way to alter their mood or state of mind. For this reason, these drugs are called psychedelics or club drugs. Others use hallucinogens for religious reasons. The American Indian Religious Freedom Act Amendment of 1994 (AIRFA) allowed Native American Church members to ingest a form of the drug peyote as a religious sacrament during all-night prayers.[14]

Legitimate medical uses for hallucinogens exist. Some hallucinogens, such as PCP and ketamine, were developed to serve as general anesthetics. They cause the user to feel detached from his or her surroundings. The drug dextromethorphan is used as a cough suppressant. Some hallucinogens are regarded as stimulants because they elevate heart rate, blood pressure, and body temperature.[15] Some users may experience withdrawal symptoms if they stop using the drug.

LSD

Lysergic acid diethylamide, or **LSD**, is a powerful synthesized psychoactive substance. It was originally created in 1930 by Albert Hoffman as he experimented with a fungus (Ergot). During his experiments, he accidentally spilled some of the drugs on his hands and ingested it. He experienced hallucinations, feelings of dissociation from time and place, and distorted perceptions. This was the first known LSD trip.

The drug was tested by the US military in the 1940s as a possible brainwashing agent. It was then used in the 1950s for psychotherapy and to treat schizophrenia, alcoholism, and other diseases. It was thought that patients would be able to recall repressed memories by using the drug. Medical professionals also learned that LSD could be used to help patients who were terminally ill because it helped to relieve the pain and helped them sleep better. In the 1960s, LSD became popular as a recreational drug even though it was banned. Timothy Leary advocated its use, as described in Table 5.2.

For most people, LSD use is unlikely to cause an addiction and there is no physical addiction or withdrawal. LSD is not an addictive drug and most users can stop using it without any withdrawal symptoms (or very slight symptoms), but it does produce a tolerance in the user. This means that LSD users will need to ingest more of the drug to achieve the same effect. The higher dose may lead to permanent neurological damage or even an accidental overdose. LSD can also be psychologically habit forming.

Table 5.2 Timothy Leary (1920–1996)

Timothy Leary was a major figure in the 1960s counterculture who publicly advocated for the use of psychoactive drugs, and LSD in particular.

Leary was born in Massachusetts in 1920, and attended Holy Cross College, West Point, and the University of Alabama. In each school,

Leary faced disciplinary problems but he was able to earn a PhD in psychology from the University of California, Berkeley. Leary became the director of psychological research at the Kaiser Foundation Hospital, and then became a faculty member at Harvard University. During a trip to Mexico in 1960, Leary took psilocybin and enjoyed the experience. He then introduced his fellow researchers to the drug, which at the time was legally available for psychiatric research. Leary also gave the drug to prison inmates and divinity students.

In 1962, Leary gave the drug to undergraduate students and was fired. He moved to New York and lived on a country estate in Millbrook, New York, a hippie commune. Here he took psychoactive drugs and meditated. His house was raided by police after he was arrested and convicted on marijuana charges in Texas. Throughout, Leary called on others to "tune in, turn on, and drop out," meaning that they should tune in and turn on to the magical world of the psychedelic drug and drop out of mainstream society.

Leary was asked to speak about his drug use to the US Senate in 1966. Leary told the Senators that he took LSD or psilocybin 311 times over a six-year period, and that there was nothing to fear from the drug. He explained that the primary reason why the senators were afraid of the drug was because they were old fogeys who associated the word "drug" with dope fiend, dope addict, or criminal. Leary asked Congress to legalize LSD for responsible adults who would then be able to use the drugs for serious purposes such as spiritual growth, pursuit of knowledge, or personal development.

In 1967, Leary established the League of Spiritual Discovery, a quasi-religious group that used LSD as its sacrament. Leary claimed that the hallucinations caused by the drug expanded his consciousness. Leary also went around the country with a light-and-sound show that he used to expound the virtues of psychedelic drugs. Leary became well-known amongst the counterculture.

In 1970, Leary ran for governor of California. But he was convicted on a marijuana charge and sentenced to 10 years in prison. Leary soon escaped from the prison by climbing up a rooftop and telephone pole and then crossing over barbed wire before dropping onto a highway. He was able to get to Algeria and then to Afghanistan, where he was arrested and deported to the US. He served 42 months in prison. Upon his release

Leary began to teach on college campuses and continued to advocate for experimentation with drugs. Leary also worked in virtual reality, designed computer games, and started a software company. When he was diagnosed with inoperable cancer, he claimed to be thrilled with the prospect of dying. He passed away in 1996 at the age of 75 from prostate cancer.

Source: Lattin, Don. 2010. *The Harvard Psychedelic Club: How Timothy Leary, Ram Dass, Huston Smith and Andrew Weil Killed the Fifties and Ushered in a New Age for America.* New York: HarperOne; Leary, Timothy. 1990. *Flashbacks: A Personal and Cultural History of an Era: An Autobiography.* New York: St. Martin's; Mansnerus, Laura. 1996. "Timothy Leary, Pied Piper of Psychedelic 60's, Dies at 75." *New York Times*, June 1, 1 and 12.

LSD is usually found as crystals which can be crushed into a powder and then formed into tablets or thin squares of gelatin. This is then dissolved, diluted and applied to small squares of paper or pressed into sugar cubes. The term "blotter acid" refers to the small, single-dose squares of paper on which LSD has been applied. When ingested, the user will feel the effects of the drug within 20 to 90 minutes but they peak within one to two hours. The effects usually last for about 12 hours, sometimes longer.

The effects a user will feel after taking LSD vary and can be difficult to predict. The effects will vary depending on the user's mood or frame of mind, their surroundings or setting, or the drug itself. Typically, a user may experience perceptual distortions, elevated body temperature, increased heart rate and blood pressure, and insomnia. Some users report that they can "see" sounds and "hear" colors or lights (called a "**crossover sensation**"). Some patients report that they have a new perception of time, so that a few seconds may feel like an hour. Other users have intense hallucinations, leading to feelings of panic, despair, and fear of insanity. These effects that a user experiences are called a "**trip**."

LSD can be a very dangerous drug and is categorized as a Schedule I drug under the CSA. It is recognized has having no medical value and a high potential for abuse. It causes hallucinations that can lead the user to perform bizarre and dangerous behaviors that can lead to injury to themselves or to others. In some cases, users have jumped off of the roof of a tall building believing they can fly. Or they may think they are being attacked by their friends and "fight off" their attackers. These events are more likely to happen if the user ingests a high dose. A negative experience such as this is referred to as a "bad trip."[16]

Many users have begun to mix LSD with other illicit drugs such as marijuana, or even with legal drugs such as a prescription drug. This practice can make the unpredictable effects of LSD even more dangerous. The combination of the drugs may produce a very different effect.

Some users experience "**flashbacks**" after using LSD. These are brief episodes in which the user experiences effects of the drug even though they have not taken it. When this happens, a user may experience hallucinations many years after using LSD. This may involve not only hallucinations, but also halos of color or sparkling lights. Most people who experience flashbacks were heavy users of the drug but this is not always the case. Table 5.3 gives more information on flashbacks.

Other substances in this category are peyote, a small button-shaped cactus that is dried and eaten, and San Pedro, a cactus that has hallucinogenic effects. The effects of these plants come from their main active alkaloid, mescaline. LSD goes by numerous street names, including acid, blotter, blotter acid, dots, mellow yellow, microdot, pane, paper acid, sugar, sugar cubes, trip, window glass, window pane, and zen.

Table 5.3 Flashbacks

People who use hallucinogenic drugs, particularly LSD, may have flashbacks, which are perceptual and visual distortions, time distortion, or other physical symptoms that appear after the use of the drug has stopped, sometimes months after the drug was last used. Flashbacks usually occur without warning and for unknown reasons. There is some evidence they might be a form of seizure or the result of neuronal destruction caused by drug use.

While flashbacks will usually stop over time, some can be prolonged, recurrent, and unpleasant. When flashbacks happen frequently, they can be considered to be symptoms of a hallucinogen persisting perception disorder (HPPD). These can also be associated with panic, anxiety, and depression. A person experiencing HPPD is aware that the altered perceptions are not real, but this does not mean they are any less distressing. Some anxiolytic drugs have been shown to provide relief to HPPD.

Some medical professionals deny that drug-induced flashbacks are real. Some psychologists argue that a past, vivid drug experience can later give rise to momentary memory flashes of the original experience. Others argue that even though the drug is no longer being ingested by the user, trace amounts of that drug remain in the body. As it is released, it causes a short burst of hallucinations. Critics argue that this possibility is unlikely and that there will be sufficient amounts of drug in the body to cause continuing flashbacks. It is more likely that the initial drug use caused a permanent change in the brain.

Source: *Psychedelics and Hallucinogens.* 2005. New York: Films Media Group.

Psilocybin and Psilocin (Mushrooms)

Psilocybin and psilocin are the hallucinogenic substances found in some mushrooms found in South America and the southwestern US. They were first identified in 1958 by **Albert Hoffman**, although they were used by Native Americans and Mexicans for hundreds of years.

Psilocybe Semilanceata mushrooms, freshly picked in highland Norway and photographed on a piece of rock by Scienceman71 via wikimedia commons.

The effects of psilocybin or psilocin on users depend on the type of mushroom consumed, the processes used to extract the drug, and the dosage. The effects are similar to those experienced by a person who has taken mescaline or LSD. They include nausea and drowsiness, hallucinations, and distorted perceptions. Some users report feeling anxiety and agitation, even panic, and may display psychotic behavior.[17] The effects from mushrooms are not as intense and do not last as long. The effects usually last about 4–6 hours, depending on the dose taken. Adolescents and young adults tend to abuse these drugs as they are popular at raves and nightclubs.

Street names for psilocybin drugs include boomers, God's flesh, hippieflip, hombrecitos, las mujercitas, little smoke, Mexican mushrooms, musk, sacred mushroom, magic mushrooms, silly putty, and simple simon.

Peyote and Mescaline

Mescaline is the agent found in peyote, a small spineless cactus that grows in the southwestern US, specifically in Texas and in the northern part of Mexico. The top of the cactus contains the hallucinogenic substance mescaline in small, disc-shaped "buttons" that are sliced from the cactus and dried. The buttons are chewed or they are soaked in water to produce an intoxicating liquid that can be mixed with other beverages or injected. Most often, users will ingest between 300 and 500 mg, about the amount contained in 6 buttons. The user will feel the effects within an hour or two and last for about 12 hours. Mescaline is usually ingested orally as a powder, tablet, capsule, or liquid. A user can inject the liquid mescaline, but this is not a popular way to use it. Users typically ingest between 300 and 500 mg, approximately the amount contained in 3–6 peyote buttons. The user will feel the effects within an hour or two and then gradually disappear within 10–12 hours.

The effects of peyote differ, depending on the user, the situation, the dose, the potency and the user's experience with the drug. The effects can include an altered visual perception, an increased body temperature, heart rate, and blood pressure. There may also be nausea, loss of appetite, sleeplessness, numbness, weakness, and body tremors. Some users have experienced terrifying thoughts and anxiety, fear of insanity, fear of death, or fear of losing control. Some users have experienced "flashbacks," when they experience hallucinations long after ingesting the drug.

Mescaline was used by the indigenous people of North America for thousands of years. Today, the American Southwest Indians in the Native American Church are permitted to use it as part of their religious and ceremonial rites. For others, it is classified as a Schedule I drug, so its availability is limited to use with a doctor's prescription. Peyote is not as popular amongst drug users as other drugs. This may be because peyote has a bitter taste and can be grown in only a limited area of the country.[18]

Salvia

Salvia, or salvinorin A or divinorin A, is a naturally occurring hallucinogen that is a member of the mint family, so it is sometimes called magic mint (or Sally D). The plant is grown mostly in Mexico and South America. Typically, the leaves are dried and then smoked. The drug is popular among teenagers and young adults because it produces hallucinogens, visions, and visual perception alteration that is similar to those experienced with LSD. The effects are felt by the user within a minute or two after ingestion. The effects are intense and are usually over within an hour.

DMT and Bufotenine

The hallucinogens **DMT** and bufotenine were first synthesized in 1931. The chemicals are naturally present in plants and animals including toads (in the venom), moth larvae, fish, and grubs in the Amazon rain forest. If the drug is injected or smoked, it creates powerful hallucinations. The drug can also be ingested in yage, a drink made from a vine in the Amazon rain forest, and yopo, a snuff used by South American Indian tribes. However, the drug is most often ingested by toad licking or toad smoking as the effective ingredient is found in their venom. Often, licking the toad does not work because the substance breaks down in the stomach acid. Instead, the venom is harvested off the skin of the toads and smoked. DMT is used by indigenous Amazonian Amerindian cultures in religious ceremonies and for healing purposes.

DMT can be inhaled, injected, or swallowed. When it is inhaled, the user can feel the effects quickly, but they are shorter in duration, lasting only about 15 minutes. A user can smoke the drug by adding DMT crystals to marijuana to produce a product called a "green screen." If the drug is smoked, they will feel high in about one minute after use. The initial intense rush, called a "blast off" will occur and then the user will black out. The effects last about 15 minutes.

Those who inject the drug will also have a powerful, yet different, experience. These users may feel as if they have left their bodies, or even enter into a different world or realm. If the drug is taken orally, it must be combined with a monoamine oxidase inhibitor (MAOI), or it has no effect. When it is taken this way, the user will experience visual and auditory hallucinations that will continue for a long time. The drug can also be snorted, resulting in many of the same effects.

The effects of the drug will vary depending on the dose taken. Some users will experience only mild psychedelic effects, whereas others will experience more powerful hallucinations that involve traveling to different realms, encounters with spiritual beings, or different time periods. Physically, users will experience an increased heart rate and blood pressure, dilated pupils, dizziness, amnesia, diarrhea, and possible seizures. It does not appear that users will build a tolerance to the drug.

DMT is not readily available on the black market and because of that it tends to be expensive. It has been classified as a Schedule I drug under the Controlled Substances Act. This indicates that the federal government has defined it as having no legitimate medical uses and a high potential for abuse. Common street names for DMT are God agent, God drug, the businessman's lunch, Dimitri, and special LSD.[19]

Ibogaine

Ibogaine is a hallucinogenic drug that comes from the African shrub *Tabernanthe iboga*, which grows in the Congo Basin. The flower of the plant is yellowish or pinkish white that yields a small, oval, yellow-orange fruit about the size of an olive. The plant is used by indigenous groups as a stimulant, for healing or in initiation ceremonies. In high doses it is a powerful psychedelic.

In the early 1900s, ibogaine was used to treat asthenia, or weakness. In the late 1930s, the drug was more commonly used to treat fatigue, depression, and infectious diseases. In 1955, ibogaine was given to morphine addicts at the US Addiction Research Center as part of their drug treatment program. Other research showed that ibogaine could be effective in treating those addicted to nicotine, alcohol, methamphetamine, and cocaine. Some evidence indicates it can be useful in treating other compulsive behaviors. Despite the possible medical benefits associated with this drug, ibogaine is categorized as a Schedule I substance under the Controlled Substances Act as a drug that is likely to cause dependence or other harm for users.

The drug itself can be found in the bark of the plant's root. The bark is scraped off the root and then eaten. It can also be dried and pounded into a powder. Users of the drug may experience different symptoms. In small doses, ibogaine can cause an increased sense of colors, with some users reporting seeing spectrums or rainbow-like auras to appear around objects. Other users are able to stay awake and alert for days after consuming the drug. With a higher dose, the user will experience slight nausea, dizziness, and a lack of muscular control. If one gram is consumed, the user may experience hallucinations that can last for days.

Even at small amounts, the drug has many serious side effects. It can cause nausea, vomiting, uncoordinated movements, and exhausting psychedelic experiences that last over twenty-four hours. In larger doses, the drug can cause cardiac arrhythmias or death.[20]

PCP

Phencyclidine, known as **PCP**, is a synthetic drug that was originally created in 1926, but was used primarily by doctors in the 1950s as an anesthetic. Physicians discovered that they could perform surgery on a patient while the patient remained conscious. But patients reported visual disturbances, depression, and confusion that lasted for days afterwards. Because of this, these drugs are sometimes grouped with hallucinogens. For many years after this, these drugs were used as a veterinary anesthetic, but this was discontinued in 1978.

PCP is easy and inexpensive to manufacture. On the black market these drugs are called the peace pill, angel dust, hog and trank, wack, wet, and rocket fuel. If a cigarette has been sprayed with PCP (or dipped into PCP), it can be referred to as a leak, amp, lovely, fry stick, toe tag, or happy stick. PCP is sometimes sprayed on marijuana so it can be smoked. When this is done, it is called supergrass or killer joints.[21]

PCP is available as a tablet, powder, and liquid. Some users dissolve the powder in water or alcohol and spray it onto another product such as marijuana or tobacco, which is then smoked. In this form, it is called "embalming fluid." The drug can also be injected. In its pure form, PCP is yellowish oil, but when sold on the street it can be tan or brown because of additives. Most of the time, however, it is found as a white powder. PCP usually has a bitter taste.

PCP is a Schedule II drug in the CSA. It has recognized medical purposes, mainly as a painkiller, but it is highly addictive. Users will often have a psychological dependence on the drug, will crave the drug, and experience compulsive drug-seeking behaviors.

PCP has been called "the world's most dangerous drug" because of the intense side effects it causes. It is much more dangerous than other hallucinogens. Users will often be unable to feel pain, as if their arms and legs are numb, and have poor or impaired muscle coordination, as if they are drunk. A user's speech is often slurred, they may be dizzy, stagger when they walk, and have bloodshot eyes. It is not uncommon to have shallow breathing, sweating, and feeling of being unattached or in a trance. Others who use the drug report nausea, vomiting, blurred vision, and drooling. Many times, users will report periods of blackout and not remember their actions while under the effects of the drug. PCP use is also linked to hostile or violent behavior or even suicidal thoughts. With higher doses, a user may become comatose, have convulsions, or even die.

Ketamine

Ketamine is a drug that was originally developed for use on the battlefields in the Vietnam War as an anesthetic, but today is used as an animal tranquilizer by veterinarians. It is stolen from veterinary clinics and imported from Mexican pharmacies and diverted for illicit recreational use. It is popular by those attending dance clubs and raves.

Ketamine is less potent that PCP and is sometimes used to treat PTSD or depression. It acts quickly on the body and causes the user to have a short burst of energy, but they may also become dizzy and have a sense of euphoria. It also causes feelings of detachment from pain or their environment, but can also cause delirium, high blood pressure, and depression. In high doses, it can cause an experience temporary paralysis, anxiety, hyperventilation, black-outs, and psychosis, or experiences similar to a bad trip on LSD. Long-term, heavy use may cause damage to memory and irreversible damage to the lining of the bladder and urinary tract.[22] Ketamine can cause amnesia that can make users vulnerable to becoming the victim of an unwanted sexual event. Because of this, is it sometimes used as a date rape drug.

The drug is manufactured to be used as an injectable liquid, but it is also evaporated into a white powder so it can be snorted or sprinkled on marijuana and smoked. How the drug is ingested affects how quickly a user feels the effects.

It does not appear that a ketamine user will establish a dependency on the drug, but a user can develop a high tolerance to ketamine quickly. The drug goes by many street names, including cat valium, green, flatliners, jet, K, kaddy, Kate, ket, kéta k, Kit Kat, khole, liquid E, liquid G, mauve, purple, special K, special LA coke, super K, super acid, super C, tac et tic, and vitamin K.

Marijuana

Marijuana is the most widely used illegal drug in the world. The psychoactive agent is found in the leaves of the cannabis plant and is delta 9-

tetrahydrocannabinol (THC). The THC is most concentrated in the flowering tops or buds of the plant. The leaves are commonly smoked but can also be eaten in cookies, brownies, or other food products.

Those who use the drug report having changes in perception, feelings of relaxation, and a distorted sense of time. Some become paranoid and experience impaired memory with difficulty concentrating and slowed reaction time. There will be moderate increase in a user's heart rate, and they may experience red eyes, a dry mouth, and increased appetite. More information on marijuana is provided in chapter 6.

Antidepressant Drugs

Antidepressant drugs are often prescribed to patients who have been diagnosed with having moderate to severe depression. For these patients, it becomes difficult to carry out daily tasks and activities that bring pleasure. They often have abnormal brain functioning that is triggered by stress or significant, traumatic life events. Antidepressants reduce the symptoms associated with depression but do not cure it.[23] For the most part, these drugs do not make users feel high but alter perception and mood. Examples include Prozac, Zoloft, and Paxil.

Antidepressants were popular during the 1950s as a form of treatment, but sales of the drug were limited throughout this time and into the 1960s. It was thought that these drugs caused serious and dangerous interactions with some foods and other drugs, so people did not want to use them. Over time, more types of antidepressant drugs were developed that had fewer side effects and the drugs became more widely used. Today, antidepressants are used for many symptoms and are used by many people of all ages. Many antidepressants relieve pain or act as an anti-inflammatory. Some can be useful to treat patients suffering from social anxiety, anxiety disorders, agitation, obsessive compulsive disorders, and posttraumatic stress disorder.

Nicotine is considered by some to be an antidepressant because it helps the body release dopamine. Low doses of caffeine are also thought to be an antidepressant. It seems that people who use caffeine in small amounts exhibit fewer symptoms of depression.

Some antidepressants cause dizziness, anxiety, nausea, insomnia, restlessness, decreased sex drive, headaches, weight gain, tremors, sweating, sleepiness or fatigue, dry mouth, diarrhea, and constipation. They can also cause suicidal thoughts, especially in young people. For older patients, the drugs cause a greater risk of falling, leading to a higher risk of fractures. For users who are pregnant, the drugs can cause a miscarriage, birth defects, or withdrawal symptoms for their newborns.[24]

Withdrawal symptoms include tremors, restlessness, mild respiratory problems, and crying. They also include anger, anxiety, panic, confusion, memory lapses, nightmares, tinnitus, shaking, balance problems, gastrointestinal problems, headaches, or sweating.[25]

Steroids and Other Performance-Enhancing Drugs

Steroids are synthetic derivatives of testosterone, the naturally occurring male sex hormone present in men and in a smaller extent also in women. Use of these drugs can promote muscle growth, so they can enhance a person's athletic performance and improve a person's body shape. They do not make people feel high, but can make users feel euphoric, friendly, and have more energy. At the same time, they can also make users feel more aggressive and increase sexual desire. They can also cause hair growth and a deepening of the user's voice.

Steroids can be injected into the body or used via a nasal spray, skin patches, or creams. Some are taken orally in a pill form. Low doses of steroids can be effectively used to treat some medical conditions, such as angioedema, a painful skin disease. They have also been used to treat patients suffering from advanced breast cancer, menopause, and the wasting effects of AIDs (nausea and lack of appetite).

Women who use steroids are more likely to experience increased muscle development and a decrease in body fat. They may also see more changes in their voice, more facial hair, irregular or absent menstrual cycles, and shrinking of the breasts. Male users may experience premature balding, impotence, or gynecomastia (an abnormal enlargement of breasts). Common side effects also include high blood pressure, reduced sperm count, and testicular atrophy. In both men and women, steroid use is associated with acne, liver problems, and cardiovascular disease, and a reduced level of good cholesterol.

Steroids are not physically addictive in the same way that other drugs are. However, they may be psychologically addictive as the user may find the results rewarding and may not want to stop using them. This may be especially true for athletes who strive for a more muscular body or who want to excel in their sport. For non-athletes, the effect of a better body may be rewarding to a person with low self-esteem. For these reasons, the abuse of steroids has grown significantly among high school and college students who are seeking to increase their body's muscle mass, allowing them to improve their athletic performance.

Steroids have been categorized as a Schedule III drug under the CSA. Street names include Arnolds, gear, gym candy, juice, pumpers, roids, stackers, and weight trainers.[26]

Conclusion

The drugs described in this chapter may have recognized medical benefits if used with the assistance of a licensed physician. However, it is common for opiates, hallucinogens, antidepressants, and steroids to be abused for their euphoric (and other) effects. The harmful effects of using these drugs can be serious and life-long. Those addicted to these drugs may seek treatment, but many will reuse the drug either to prevent withdrawal symptoms or to seek the euphoric feelings that come along with use. Because of the dangers these substances hold, most of them are categorized as Schedule I drugs, which controls their legal availability and use. Regardless, they are readily available on the black market, where they are cheap and available to those who want them.

Important Terms

Antidepressants

Black Tar Heroin

Codeine

Crossover Sensation

DMT

Flashbacks

Hallucinogens

Heroin

Ibogaine

Ketamine

LSD

Marijuana

Mescaline

Morphine

Non-opiate Analgesics

Opiates

Oxycodone

PCP

Peyote

Psilocybin and Psilocin

Salvia

Steroids

Syrup

Trip

Review Questions

1. What is an opiate and what are the effects on a person who uses an opiate?

2. What are the different types of products that are derived from the poppy plant?

3. Explain what syrup is and why it is a concern to officials.

4. Describe what a hallucinogenic drug might do to a user.

5. List some different types of hallucinogenic drugs.

6. Why would a person choose to use steroids? What are the benefits (and consequences) of using these substances?

Endnotes

1. Perez, Evan. Feb 4, 2014. "Ready Access, Low Cost, Pill-like High: Heroin's Rise and Fatal Draw." CNN. http://www.cnn.com/2014/02/02/US/heroin-use-rising; NPR. November 2, 2013. "With Rise of Painkiller Abuse, a Closer Look at Heroin." http://www.npr.org/2013/11/02/24259489; Volkow, Nora D. May 14, 2014. "America's Addiction to Opiods: Heroin and Prescription Drug Abuse. National Institute of Justice, National Institute of Drug Abuse. https://www.drugabuse.gov/about-nida/legislative; Hendrick, Bill. October 19, 2011. "Use of Antidepressants on the rise in the US." WebMD. http://www.webmd.com/depression/news/20111019/.

2. Office of National Drug Control Policy. "The International Heroin Market." http://www.whitehouse.gov/ondcp/global-heroin-market.

3. Young, R. 2012. "World in Brief: Wiping out Opium." *Crime & Justice International* 18(3): 19.

4. In recent years, the term "narcotic" is has been used to refer to all illegal drugs, or those drugs that are deemed to be harmful. Thus, many drugs, including marijuana, PCP, amphetamines, and others have been included in antinarcotics legislation even though they are not truly narcotics.

5. US Department of Health and Human Services, National Institute on Drug Abuse. 2005. *Research Report Series: Heroin Abuse and Addiction.* NIH Publication No. 05-4165. http://www.nida.gov.

6. Kroll, David. April 3, 2014. "FDA Rapidly Approves Naloxone Auto-Injector for Heroin and Prescription Opioid Overdose." *Forbes.* http://www.forbes.com/sites/davidkroll/2014/04/03/fda-rapidly-approves-naloxone-auto-injector-for-heroin-and-prescription-opioid-overdose/.

7. US Department of Justice, National Drug Intelligence Center. 2011. "Drug Alert Watch." http://www.justice.gov/archive/ndic/pubs43/43924/sw0008p.pdf.

8. "Effects of Purple Drank Abuse." Narconon International. http://www.narconon.org/drug-abuse/purple-drank-effects.html; "Signs and Symptoms of Purple Drank Abuse." Nar-

conon International. http://www.narconon.org/drug-abuse/purple-drank-signs-symptoms.html.

9. Drugs.com. "Oxycodone." http://www.drugs.com/pro/oxycodone.html; Pinsky, Drew. 2004. *When Painkillers Become Dangerous: What Everyone Needs to Know about OxyContin and Other Prescription Drugs*. Center City, MN: Hazelden Foundation.

10. Jasmin, Luc. 2013. "Over-the-Counter Pain Relievers." http://www.nim.nih.gov/medlineplus/ency/article/002123.htm.

11. Knott, Laurence, and Gurvinder Rull. 2013. "Opioid Analgesics." http://www.patient.co.uk/print/513.

12. Bayer, Linda N. 2000. *Strange Visions: Hallucinogen-Related Disorders*. Philadelphia: Chelsea House Publishers.

13. Substance Abuse and Mental Health Services Administration. (2915, October 30). "Hallucinogens" https://www.samhsa.gov.

14. Clark, W. H. 1968. "Religious Aspects of Psychedelic Drugs." *California Law Review* 56(1): 86–99.

15. Bayer, Linda N. 2000. *Strange Visions: Hallucinogen-Related Disorders*. Philadelphia: Chelsea House Publishers; National Institute on Drug Abuse. September 2013. "Hallucinogens and Dissociative Drugs." Research Report Series. http://www.drugabuse.gov/publications/research-reports/hallucinogens-dissociative-drugs/director.

16. US Department of Health and Human Services, National Institute on Drug Abuse. 2001. *Research Report Series: Hallucinogens and Dissociative Drugs*. NIH Publication No. 01-4209.

17. US Department of Health and Human Services, National Institute on Drug Abuse. 2001. *Research Report Series: Hallucinogens and Dissociative Drugs*. NIH Publication No. 01-4209. http://www.nida.gov.

18. Center for Substance Abuse Research, University of Maryland. "Peyote." http://www.cesar.umd.edu/cesar/drugs/peyote.asp; Chouvy, Pierre-Arnaud. 2010. *Opium: Uncovering the Politics of the Poppy*. Cambridge, MA: Harvard University Press; Epps, Garrett. 2009. *Peyote vs. the State: Religious Freedom on Trial*. Norman: University of Oklahoma Press; Olive, M. Foster. 2007. *Peyote and Mescaline*. New York: Chelsea House; Partnership for Drug-Free Kids. "Peyote." http://www.drugfree.org/drug-guide/peyote; "Peyote to LSD: A Psychedelic Odyssey." 2012. A&E Television Networks, LLC. New York: Films Media Group; Ross-Flanigan, Nancy. 1997. *Peyote*. Springfield, NJ: Enslow Publishers; Steinberg, Michael K., Joseph J. Hobbs, and Kent Mathewson. 2004. *Dangerous Harvest: Drug Plants and the Transformation of Indigenous Landscapes*. New York: Oxford University Press.

19. Drug Enforcement Administration, Office of Diversion Control, Drug and Chemical Evaluation Section. 2013. "N,N-Dimethyltruptamine (DMT)." http://www.deadiversion.usdoj.gov/drug_chem_info/dmt.pdf; Shaffer Library of Drug Policy. "Dimethyltryptamine (DMT)." http://www.druglibrary.org/schaffer/dea/pubs/abuse/chap5/dmt.htm; Substance Abuse and Mental Health Services Administration. 2008. "Use of Specific Hallucinogens: 2006." National Survey on Drug Use and Health Report. http://www.samhsa.gov/data/2k8/hallucinogens/hallucinogens.htm.

20. Ali, Syed F. 1998. *The Neurochemistry of Drugs of Abuse: Cocaine, Ibogaine, and Substituted Amphetamines*. New York: New York Academy of Sciences; Alper, Kenneth R., and Stanley Glick, eds. 2001. *Ibogaine: Proceedings from the First International Congress*. San Diego: Academic Press; Alper, K. R. 2001. "Ibogaine: A Review." *The Alkaloids: Chemistry*

and Biology 56: 1–36; Vastag, Brian. 2005. "Ibogaine Therapy: A 'Vast, Uncontrolled Experiment.'" *Science* 308(5720): 345–46.

21. National Institute on Drug Abuse. Research Report Series. *Hallucinogens and Dissociative Drugs* (NIH Publication number 01-4209). Washington, DC: National Institutes of Health; National Institute on Drug Abuse. 2013. "PCP/Phencyclidine." http://www.drug abuse.gov/drugs-abuse/pcpphencyclidine.

22. World Health Organization. 2006. *Critical Review of Ketamine.*

23. "Depression Medications (Antidepressants)." http://webmd.com/depression/ depression-medications-antidepressants; Dudley, William. 2008. *Antidepressants.* San Diego, CA: Daniel A. Leone; Hecht, Alan, and David J. Triggle. 2011. *Antidepressants and Antianxiety Drugs.* New York: Chelsea House; National Institute of Mental Health. 2005. *Medications for Mental Illness* (NIH Publication No. 02-3929). Bethesda, MD: National Institute of Mental Health. http://www.nimh.nih.gov/health/publications/medications/ summary.shtml.

24. "Depression: Dealing with Medicine Side Effects." http://www.webmd.com/ depression/managing-the-side-effects-of-antidepressants.

25. Glenmullen, Joseph. 2005. *The Anti-depressant Solution: A Step-by-Step Guide to Safely Overcoming Antidepressant Withdrawal, Dependence, and "Addiction."* New York: Free Press.

26. National Institute on Drug Abuse. 2012. "Drug Facts: Anabolic Steroids." http:// www.drugabuse.gov/publications/drugfacts/anabolic-steroids; National Institute on Drug Abuse. 2012. "Steroids, Anabolic." http://www.drugabuse.gov/drugs-abuse/steroids-anabolic.

Chapter 6

Medical Marijuana and Recreational Marijuana

Chapter Objective: After reading this chapter, the student will have a better understanding of the drug called marijuana. The public perception of this drug, both as a medical and recreational substance, is rapidly changing as it is legalized in many parts of the country. This controversy is reviewed here in light of an analysis of how legalized marijuana is being implemented in Colorado.

Introduction

Marijuana is the most commonly abused illicit drug in the US. It has been used both for medical reasons and for recreational purposes for hundreds of years around the globe. Recently, marijuana has been at the forefront of the drug legalization debate as many states have passed laws, or are considering new laws, to legalize or decriminalize the drug. This chapter looks at marijuana in more detail, with a focus on the recent trend toward legalizing and decriminalizing medical and recreational marijuana, despite the continued federal policies that prohibit them.

History

Marijuana has been part of the world's cultures for many years. In every part of the world, marijuana has been used for either recreation or as a medicine, or both. It was used in early Chinese and Greek cultures as a medical treatment for various ailments. It was also used by early Egyptians, Romans,

Cannabis sativa by Rotational via wikimedia commons.

and Africans for similar reasons. It was used by ancient Jews, Christians, and Muslims, who may have used it recreationally as alcohol use was banned in the Quran.

In 1492, Christopher Columbus brought cannabis plants to America in his ships. Cannabis became a major commercial crop alongside of tobacco in Jamestown in 1611. The early settlers relied on **hemp** fiber as an important export, so in 1619, officials in the Virginia colony declared that all citizens were required to grow hemp. Those who did not faced criminal penalties.

George Washington grew cannabis for its hemp at his plantation home in Mount Vernon in the 1760s. There is some evidence that Washington also grew cannabis both for medicinal reasons and for recreation. The second and third presidents of the US, John Adams and Thomas Jefferson, also grew cannabis for hemp.[1]

When cannabis plants are grown for hemp, they are grown for the fibrous parts of the plant. These fibers are extremely strong and durable and make excellent cords, ropes, and even clothing. Hemp fibers have been used for centuries. The Chinese used hemp fibers in fabric and in fishing nets in 1000 BCE. The Chinese used paper made from hemp beginning around 200 BCE. In fact, the world's oldest piece of paper dates back to around 500 BCE and was comprised of hemp fibers. More information on hemp is found in Table 6.1.

Table 6.1 Hemp

Hemp is the fibrous product found in the *Cannabis sativa* plant, one of the world's oldest sources of fiber. The strong fibers from the plant were traditionally used for paper and textiles, and it was also used to make rope because of its great strength, as well as its natural resistance to rot and decay. The leaves of this variety of plant have very little THC, and because of that, it cannot be used as a psychoactive drug.

Because *Cannabis sativa* is known as a type of marijuana plant, the government has passed laws prohibiting its cultivation in the US even though it can be used for food or fuel. In addition, the seeds of the plant can be used for oils that are used in paints and other materials. The hemp seed also has high nutritional value with high levels of fatty acids (linoleic acid-omega-6 and alpha-linolenic acid-omega-3), vitamin B, and dietary fiber. Hemp is used as an ingredient in many foods, such as energy bars, salad dressing, milk, and protein shakes. Hemp is also found in cereal, frozen waffles, and ice cream. The oil from the hemp seed contains gamma-linolenic acid (GLA), which is used to treat ailments such as neurodermatitis, arthritis, and premenstrual syndrome.

The hemp plant can also be used in the manufacturing of other essential products such as biodegradable plastics and fuels. The fibers from the hemp plant can be mixed with other materials such as fiberglass to make stronger materials used in building projects, or in composite panels for automobiles that are stronger and more resistant in crashes.

The hemp plant is easy to grow and thrives in all types of soils. It requires little or no pesticides, and is fully biodegradable. Many other products now grown for industrial manufacturing produce a large amounts of waste and have other negative impacts on the environment. In fact, many European countries and Canada continue to issue licenses to farmers so they can grow the hemp plant. They are able to exempt it from international drug laws because it produces such high-quality fiber.

Sources: Arizona Industrial Hemp Council. http://www.azhemp.org/Archive/Package/History/history.html; Bourrie, Mark. 2003. *Hemp: A Short History of the Most Misunderstood Plant and Its Uses and Abuses.* Buffalo, NY: Firefly Books; Conrad, Chris. 1997. *Hemp for Health: The Medicinal and Nutritional Uses of Cannabis Sativa.* Rochester, VT: Healing Arts Press; Hemp Industries Association. http://

www.thehia.org/; Ranalli, Paolo. 1999. *Advances in Hemp Research*. New York: Food Products Press; Rothenberg, Erik. 2001. *A Renewal of Common Sense, The Case of Hemp in the 21st Century*. Available at http://www.azhemp.org/Archive/Package/renewal.pdf.

In the US, marijuana was used in the 1800s as a legal drug for treating the pain of migraine headaches and for insomnia. For many years after that, marijuana was one of the most widely prescribed medicines. The use of marijuana only increased during Prohibition and throughout the 1920s, when the consumption of alcohol was illegal. Around this time, many individual states began to criminalize marijuana use and possession. In 1924, Louisiana passed an anti-marijuana law, triggering the arrest of many people for the sale or possession of marijuana in New Orleans. They faced fines of $50 to $1,000 and possible imprisonment for 30 days to six months. New Mexico passed an anti-marijuana law in 1923 and Colorado in 1927.[2]

The federal government also began to criminalize marijuana during these years. The Congress passed the **Marihuana Tax Act** in 1937 that in essence made recreational use of marijuana illegal in the US. The law required that anyone who imported the drug, produced it, or sold it had to purchase a stamp from the Treasury Department. In addition, anyone who grew, transported, prescribed, or sold marijuana had to register with the federal government. However, since marijuana was illegal in most states, anyone who registered with the federal government may be subject to prosecution by the states.[3]

The federal government reinforced the anti-marijuana message through a campaign to discredit the drug. One way they did this was to produce a movie entitled *Reefer Madness*, produced in collaboration with the Federal Bureau of Narcotics. The movie, released in 1936, supported the idea that marijuana is a "demon weed" that affects the personalities of people who smoke it. It clearly shows that people who smoke marijuana go insane and experience psychotic behavior. More information on the movie is presented in Table 6.2.

The perception of marijuana as a demon drug was not a popular one. In 1937, New York's Mayor Fiorello La Guardia commissioned a report about the effects of using marijuana. The research was completed by the New York Academy of Medicine and concluded that earlier reports describing the negative effects of marijuana were not true. They found that there may be therapeutic effects that can be attributed to the drug, and that marijuana use leads users to be calm and relaxed.

The commission report only angered some in the federal government, most notably Harry Anslinger of the Federal Bureau of Narcotics. For the remainder of his career, he supported anti-marijuana laws and policies.

Table 6.2 *Reefer Madness*

Reefer Madness (originally called *Tell Your Children*) was a movie produced by the US Federal Bureau of Narcotics in 1936 about a couple who sell marijuana, Mae Coleman and Jack Perry. Perry convinces some college students, Bill Harper and Jimmy Lane, to try marijuana. Because Jack has no marijuana, they drive to his dealer to get more. While there, Jimmy asks for a cigarette but is given a joint instead. On the way back to the apartment, Jimmy hits a pedestrian, who is killed.

Bill then begins to have an affair with Blanche. Jimmy's sister, Mary, goes to Mae's apartment to look for Jimmy. Another friend at the apartment, Ralph, offers Mary a cigarette, which turns out to be marijuana. Ralph then makes a pass at Mary. When she refuses, he tries to rape her. Meanwhile, Bill hallucinates that Mary stripped for Ralph and begins a fight with Ralph. As they are fighting, Jack tries to break them up and hits Bill with the butt of his gun, knocking him unconscious. When he does that, the gun accidentally fires, killing Mary. Jack quickly puts the gun in Bill's hand then wakes Bill up. Bill believes he shot Mary. Bill is put on trial for murder, but during this time Ralph goes insane with guilt.

Jack then decides to kill Ralph so he will not tell the police the truth. Jack ends up killing Ralph by punching him to death. The police arrest Ralph, Mae, and Blanche. Mae tells the police what really happened, and they release Bill from prison. Blanche, who was asked to testify against Ralph, commits suicide by jumping out a window. Ralph is then committed to an asylum.

The movie reflected the attitudes about marijuana use that were popular at the time and showed viewers about the dangers associated with using marijuana. In the 1960s, *Reefer Madness* became a favorite cult movie among young drug users.

Sources: Hoerl, Arthur. 1936. *Reefer Madness*. San Diego, CA: Legend Films; Scott Miller. "Inside Reefer Madness: Background and Analysis." http://www.newlinethea-tre.com/reeferchapter.html.

In 1970, the **Comprehensive Drug Abuse Prevention and Control Act** classified marijuana as a Schedule I drug, meaning that it had no recognized medical use and a high potential for abuse. Other drugs in this category include LSD, heroin, hashish, and hallucinogens. The importation, cultivation, possession, use, sale, and distribution of marijuana were made illegal under federal law in the US.

The use of marijuana for recreation decreased through the early and mid-1900s, but increased during and after the Vietnam War. Many returning soldiers had used the drug in Asia and continued to do so upon returning home.

The federal government continued to oppose the legalization of marijuana. As a way to enhance that view, President Nixon formed a committee to study the effects or possible dangers of the drug, called the National Commission on Marijuana and Drug Abuse (also called the Shafer Commission). Nixon fully expected the committee would announce the perils and risks associated with the drug. Instead, the committee's final report indicated that marijuana may not be as dangerous as once thought. Nixon, along with many other officials in the government, largely ignored the committee findings and continued to support harsh punishments for marijuana.

A few years later, in 1975, a man named Robert Randall was arrested for using marijuana, which he claimed to use to treat glaucoma. Randall used the "medical necessity" defense in court to argue that his marijuana use was a justification for breaking the law. A federal court agreed, and the criminal charges against Randall were dropped. In 1976, he became the first American to be granted legal access to marijuana for medical reasons.

In order to supply Randall with the drug he needed, the federal government began to provide him with marijuana. It instituted a new program, the **Compassionate Investigational New Drug Program** (CIND), which could explore the potential benefits of medical marijuana. Under the program, certain physicians identified by the government were given the ability to prescribe medical marijuana to some of their patients only on a trial basis. In the beginning, there was an extensive process for patients to enroll in the program so there were only a dozen patients accepted at first.

Those accepted into the program had to follow strict protocols. All patients in the program received 300 low-potency marijuana cigarettes per month, or about 10.75 ounces (300 grams). The marijuana used in the program was grown at the University of Mississippi, which could provide patients with marijuana that was pesticide-free and of a standard potency. The Research Triangle Institute in North Carolina was allocated $62,000 a year from the federal government to roll and package the marijuana cigarettes and ship them to the patients' doctors and pharmacists. All of the patients in the program were provided with a document from the FDA that granted them permission to use the marijuana.

Today, the program is administered by the National Institute on Drug Abuse (NIDA). Between 1976 and 1988, there were only about six patients who qualified for the CIND program. By 1989, largely because of the HIV/AIDS epidemic and patients seeking to relieve nausea, the FDA became overwhelmed with applications. President Bush closed the program in 1992, claiming that it sent the wrong message and contradicted the position of the administration concerning illicit drug use. Efforts to reinstate the program in 1994 during the Clinton administration failed. In a court brief, Clinton's Justice Department acknowledged that the program's use of medical marijuana "was bad public policy." As of 2003, the program remained closed to new patients. While at one time the program had 30 patients, at this time, there are only four surviving patients who remain in the program.[4]

Since this time, marijuana use has continued to become more popular among many age groups and populations. Despite the federal government's "War on Drugs," which has included eradicative efforts, increased enforcement of drug trafficking laws, and education/prevention programs, the production and use of the drug has only continued to grow.

Marijuana

Marijuana, or **cannabis**, is a flowering plant that is grown for its strong fibers, but is recognized more for its psychoactive qualities. There are two primary types of cannabis plants. One is *Cannabis sativa*. This plant typically grows to a height of 12 to 16 feet and has long stalks, sparse foliage, and slender leaves. These plants are usually grown for industrial purposes, particularly for fiber and textile use. The second type of cannabis is the *Cannabis indica*, which originated in India. This plant usually grows to a height of four to five feet and has many more, and larger, leaves. This plant contains more **cannabinoids** than the sativa plants, which are the chemicals that have psychoactive properties. Another drug that comes from the cannabis plant is hash, a more powerful drug than marijuana. It is described in Table 6.3.

When a person smokes marijuana, they smoke the leaves and flowering tops (buds) of the plant. The plant material is harvested, dried, and then rolled into cigarette papers to form a "joint." The dried leaves can also be placed in a pipe or bong and smoked. It can also be brewed into a tea, or eaten in cookies, brownies, or other edible items.

Marijuana leaves have about 60 different chemical compounds (called cannabinoids) in them. The primary active ingredient in marijuana is delta-9-tetrahydrocannabinol (THC). **THC** has psychoactive effects and can give users altered sensations and perceptions. For that reason, marijuana is sometimes categorized as a hallucinogenic drug.

The concentration of THC in marijuana is defined as percentage of THC per dry weight of material. In general, the concentrations of THC in plants have increased over the past 30 years. In 1974, the average content of THC in marijuana was less than 1 percent; in the 1990s, the THC concentration averaged 1–5 percent for marijuana, 5–15 percent for hashish, and 20 percent for hashish oil. In 2012, THC concentrations averaged nearly 15 percent, even as much as 25 percent for marijuana. Since many factors can affect potency of the drug, the strength of marijuana sold on the black market can vary considerably.[5]

The effect of the THC on a user will partly depend on how the user ingests the drug, the amount ingested, and characteristics of the individual. When the user smokes marijuana, the THC enters the bloodstream much more quickly than if the drug is consumed through an edible (a food or a drink). The drug is absorbed much more quickly through the lungs as opposed to through the digestive system. Smoking the drug produces a more intense feeling of being high, whereas eating the plant provides a more subtle effect. The duration of the effect is also quite different. If marijuana is smoked, the effects last between 1 and 3 hours; if it is consumed through an edible, the effects will last up to four hours.[6]

Lower doses of THC can produce feelings of relaxation, euphoria, hunger, enjoyment, relief of pain, heightened sensations, altered perceptions, and nausea relief. It can also result in relaxed inhibitions, impaired motor coordination, lack of concentration, dulling of attention spans, and altered perception of time and space. When a user feels these symptoms, it is referred to as being "high." In high doses, or with prolonged use, the THC in marijuana can produce hallucinations and paranoia. Users may also experience psychosis, image distortion, learning and memory impairment, and mood swings. Effects on learning and memory are particularly persistent among those users who began using in adolescence.[7]

Many experts categorize marijuana as a "soft" drug, because it is not a highly addictive drug. But this is debated. Now several strains of marijuana are being bred with higher levels of THC. Other types of marijuana, especially hashish and hash oil, can be very potent and cause long-term harm to the user.

Many studies show that marijuana is not addictive, but this is in question. Some heavy users report feeling withdrawal symptoms if they stop using the drug. The symptoms include restlessness, irritability, insomnia, decreased appetite, and anxiety. According to some statistics, 10 percent of the 25 million Americans who use marijuana are addicted and experience withdrawal symptoms.

Some researchers and physicians have expressed a concern about the short- and long-term effects of marijuana drug on a user's mind and body, particularly young users. The effect that smoking marijuana has on a person's lungs, or the presence of cancer-causing agents in marijuana leaves, is unknown. At this point, the long-term effect of smoking marijuana on the human brain is also unclear. These concerns become even more critical as the level of THC has increased in most strains of marijuana that is available to users. One concern is that these stronger strains of cannabis may cause more people to be addicted to the drug. Another concern relates to the increased effects the drug will have on the user, particularly novice users or young users.

Marijuana is currently categorized as a Schedule I drug in the Controlled Substances Act. Thus, according to the US federal government, THC has no medicinal value and a high potential for abuse. It is estimated that the global consumption of cannabis has remained stable in the past few years, with some 3.8 percent of the global population reporting the use of cannabis in the past year in 2014. The main production and consumption regions are the Americas, followed by Africa.[8]

Depending on its source, method of administration, or other factors, marijuana goes by a wide range of street names. Some include Aunt Mary, boom, bud, dope, gangster, ganja, grass, grifa, hemp, herb, hydro, joint, kif, Mary Jane, MJ, mota, pot, reefer, roach, sinsemilla, skunk, smoke, Thai sticks, weed, widow, and yerba.

Table 6.3 Hashish (Hash) and Hash Oil

Hashish, also called **hash**, is a powerful drug that comes from the cannabis plant. It contains a high concentration of THC levels. Hashish oil also comes from the cannabis plant and is extracted from the plant by use of a solvent.

After the cannabis plant matures and produces a flower, small projections called trichomes that are rich in resinous hashish grow out of the plant. To remove the trichomes from the plant, the flowers can be forced through a sieve in a process referred to as sieving. When this process is completed, the resulting powder, called kief, is gathered and heated so it can be pressed into blocks of hashish. Another method to remove the trichomes from the plant is to immerse the flowers in ice water. Another popular means of collecting the resin from the trichomes is to use a chemical method. No matter the method used, the resulting substance formed is the hash resin, sometimes referred to as honey oil or hash oil. The purity of the drug is important. If small pieces of the flower remain in the final product, it will affect the purity, and in turn the quality, of the drug.

The final hashish product can be crumbled and smoked in a pipe, hookah, or bong. The hash can also be baked into foods such as brownies or cookies to make an edible. When ingested in any of these methods, the hash can have various effects on users, including euphoria, relaxed inhibitions, increased appetite, disoriented behavior, altered coordination of reflexes, and altered perception of time and distance. The effects of hash last between 2 and 4 hours.

Fresh hash is soft and pliable. As it ages, some of the essential oils evaporate and the hash becomes hard and loses potency. Much of the hash that is smuggled into the US is quite old before it is bought by an average user. By then, the drug may not have the intended effect. For this reason, many covert grow operations have popped up across the US with the goal of cultivating high-grade hashish.

The THC content of hash oil is upwards of 15 percent, as compared to 5 percent for marijuana. The color of the hash oil will vary depending on the type of solvent used to extract it from the cannabis plant. Some users place a drop of the oil on regular (tobacco) cigarettes as a way to smoke the THC in a similar way to smoking a marijuana joint.

Although a great deal of marijuana is from North and South America, most of the hash imported into the US comes from the Middle East, North Africa, Pakistan, Afghanistan, and Morocco.

Hashish and hash oil are Category I (Schedule I) drugs under the Controlled Substances Act, meaning that the federal government has decided they have no medical value and are highly addictive and therefore can be easily abused. Despite the connotation that they have no recognized medical purpose, many people believe that hash and hash oil can reduce nausea and vomiting. Many cancer patients choose to use the drugs illegally for this reason. A patient who overdoses on hashish can experience excessive fatigue, hallucinations, paranoia, or other symptoms of psychosis. A person suffering from hash withdrawal may have feelings of insomnia, hyperactivity, and decreased appetite.

Hash has many street names, such as boom, chronic, and gangster.

Testing

Many jobs require their employees remain drug-free and demand random drug testing to ensure this. It is possible to drug test a person to determine if they have been using marijuana. THC is stored by the body in fatty tissue. The THC is slowly released into the bloodstream for up to several weeks after marijuana is used. For users who are heavy or regular users and are physically inactive, THC may accumulate in fatty tissues at a quicker pace than it can be eliminated by the body. This means that those individuals will test positive for the presence of marijuana for a longer period after use than other users who may be more physically fit. Also, those users who have a high percentage of body fat in relation to total body mass are more likely to test positive for longer periods of time after use. Elevated levels of urinary metabolites are present within hours of using marijuana. They remain detectable for 3–10 days after a user smokes the drug.

A new product, the THC One Step Marijuana Test Strip can be used to test for cannabis use. This product is recommended by the US Substance Abuse and Mental Health Services Administration. This is a rapid urine screening test that tests for elevated levels of marijuana in the employee's urine.

Legalization of Marijuana

About 21 states and the District of Columbia have either passed a law that legalizes marijuana in some way or have had voters approve a referendum.

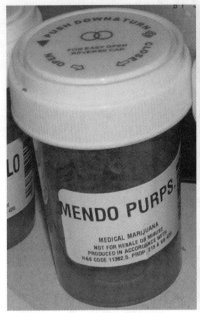 

Medical Cannabis by Coaster420 via wikimedia commons

Some states have legalized the drug for recreational use, but most states have laws only allowing for medical use of marijuana. The state laws are each different, but in general they allow a resident to possess a small amount of the drug, either in leaf form or as an edible. Some states allow residents to grow their own plants, but the number of plants permitted varies by state.

The potential monetary benefit for federal, state, and local governments is a major argument in favor of legalization of marijuana. It is estimated that marijuana sales could top $10 billion in a few years. The market for the drug and paraphernalia could have a major boost on the economy of a state or local government. Taxes on the sales of marijuana can be used for a variety of different items or events in the state and could help pay off deficits that many states are facing.

Medical Marijuana

For centuries, people from all parts of the globe have used marijuana for medical reasons. In China, marijuana was used to treat vomiting, diarrhea, dysentery, and loss of appetite. Greeks relied on marijuana to relieve inflammation, treat ear aches, stop nose bleeds, and treat tapeworms. Egyptians sought out marijuana to treat gout, rheumatism, foot pain, and hemorrhoids. Those living in Africa used marijuana if they had a snake bite, were suffering pains because of child birth, or had malaria, blood poisoning, anthrax, or asthma. Romans also used marijuana for these or similar ailments.

In the US, it was common to use marijuana for medical reasons through the nineteenth century. It was used as a pain reliever until the invention of aspirin. Some patent medicines during this time contained marijuana but it was a small percentage compared to the ones that contained opium or cocaine. This practice changed over time, beginning with the Marihuana Tax Act of 1937.

In recent years, the medical benefits of marijuana use are again being recognized. Marijuana is used to help patients cope with a multitude of ailments. It is used by those suffering from AIDS (and especially the "wasting syndrome" that is characterized by extreme weight loss), alcohol withdrawal, Alzheimer's disease, anorexia, cancer, Crohn's disease, depression, diabetes, fibromyalgia, glaucoma, high blood pressure, insomnia, migraines, multiple sclerosis, nausea, vomiting, pain, convulsions and seizures, and many other ailments.

Those who use marijuana for medical reasons typically do not experience the "high" that is associated with marijuana use. The chemical in marijuana that is responsible for the euphoric feeling that users experience is THC, but there are other chemicals in marijuana that are responsible for the medical effects that the drug has on patients. The primary one is cannabidiol (CBD). This does not have psychoactive properties and does not cause feelings of being "high." However, it is thought to be responsible for the medical impact attributed to marijuana. People who use marijuana for medical reasons will use strains of the plant that have very little THC but high amounts of CBD. This way, they will achieve the medical benefits of the drug without the psychoactive effects.[9]

A synthetic form of THC has been developed and has been used on some patients who are reluctant to use marijuana. Marinol is the brand name for a synthetic form of THC, dronabinol. Some patients report that the synthetic THC does not have the same effects as natural, smoked marijuana, and it takes longer to have an effect. Other patients claim that when they use Marinol, they get "high," as they do when they smoke the drug.

Many state officials have supported the legalization of medical marijuana, and multiple states have passed laws to allow residents to use marijuana under certain circumstances. Each state law is different. Some require that a possible user have a written prescription from a doctor before they can purchase or use marijuana. In some states, users must carry a "marijuana ID card" to purchase marijuana. Some states limit the amount a user may possess, transport, or grow. States have created different methods for dispensing the drug, with some allowing patients to grow their own.

In 1996, California became the first state to pass a bill to legalize medical marijuana. Voters in that state passed **Proposition 215**, the Compassionate Use Act. Under the law, residents can possess and cultivate marijuana for medical purposes if they have a doctor's recommendation. Since then, more states and the District of Columbia have passed laws allowing for medical marijuana. Others states are considering similar laws.

The international community has been active in the debate on marijuana policy. The United Nations Single Convention on Narcotic Drugs labelled marijuana as a Schedule IV drug so that each country can choose to allow research on marijuana's potential as a drug. Marijuana has been legalized in many countries, such as Canada in 2000. Canadians can legally use marijuana if they have been diagnosed as having certain conditions. It can also be used for end-of-life care. Marijuana is distributed by the government, but "compassion clubs" have opened that provide an alternative method of distribution for patients. Some patients are permitted to grow their own marijuana but must be approved by government officials.

Marijuana advocates in the US have urged Congress to reschedule marijuana based on studies that show the medical benefits of the plant. While many states have passed laws that allow for the medical use of marijuana, it remains illegal under federal law. At this point, the marijuana businesses that have developed around the country are in violation of the law and can be closed at any time and the owners and employees charged with federal crimes.

Most public opinion polls indicate that Americans support legalization of medical marijuana. A poll taken in 2013 showed that 77% of respondents agreed that marijuana has at least some legitimate medical uses. The age group that was the most supportive was those between 18 to 29 years.[10]

Medical Marijuana: Arguments in Support

The use of marijuana for medical purposes is becoming more popular, despite the federal government's decision that there is no medical benefit of the drug. Many medical professionals believe that the drug has significant medical value in many ways but others do not.

Marijuana has been used to relieve pain and reduce the symptoms associated with many different diseases and the side effects of treatment. Cancer patients have used marijuana for relief from the pain, nausea, and loss of appetite that can be caused by treatment. Patients with AIDS have used THC to help with wasting syndrome or cachexia (extreme weight loss). It helps to control seizures for those with epilepsy and the intraocular eye pressure that results from glaucoma. It helps people suffering from migraines, seizures, Tourette Syndrome, high blood pressure, and insomnia.[11]

As an industry, marijuana is highly regulated. There are a limited number of licenses that are granted, limiting the number of plants that will be grown. The plants are tested for mold, insects, and pesticides to ensure the product is safe for consumption. Every plant is tracked so no product is "skimmed" or taken illegally. The industry is taking steps to ensure that young people do not have access to the drug, and that it is being used safely by adults.

Additionally, regulation of the product will ensure a safer product with less chance for adulterants to be added to the drug, or for pesticides to be present. The product will be a consistent strength over time. From a market perspective, legalizing the sale of marijuana and taxing it will mean millions for the state's budget.

Medical Marijuana: Arguments Against

Some argue that marijuana should remain illegal. They claim that it has dangerous health consequences, many of which are still unknown. They argue that legalizing the drug will increase its use among adolescents, whose developing brains should not be exposed to psychoactive drugs. Not only will the drug be more readily available but it is also sending the message that the drug is safe and fine to use, when this has not been scientifically proven.

Critics also fear that marijuana is a gateway drug to more dangerous substances. Many studies have shown that marijuana does not have a causal relationship with other drug use (i.e., it does not cause other drug use). Instead, they have concluded that marijuana is the first drug in a progression of drug use for many people who already have the risk factors associated with drug use. In many cases, marijuana is the third drug, after alcohol and cigarettes.

Not only will legalizing marijuana lead to people using the drug more, but it will lead to other drugs being made legal. Once the door has been opened to legalizing marijuana, people will discover that the benefits outweigh the harms, and they will be more accepting of other drug use.

While some people argue that the legalization of the drug will bring an end to the black market, or underground, illegal sales of marijuana, others argue this will not happen. In fact, they argue, it will only change the nature of the black market sales of marijuana and other illicit drugs. They argue that gang rivalries will re-appear or become worse as there is more competition. Gangs that previously relied on marijuana as income have to look to other markets, for example to crack cocaine.

Recreational Marijuana

In November 2012, the states of Washington and Colorado became the first to legalize recreational marijuana. Under the new laws, residents of those states (and those visiting the states) who are over 21 can purchase, possess, and use the drug in a limited quantity. The laws were passed by voters as opposed to being passed by the state legislature. The Colorado law became effective in January 2014. Now, licensed shops can sell up to an ounce of marijuana over the counter to anyone over the age of 21 without a physician's recommendation.[12]

In July 2013, Colorado officials announced the rules by which recreational marijuana will be sold. All sales will be regulated by the state's Revenue Department. Moreover, the marijuana must be labeled to include the product's potency (the amount of THC in the product); instructions on how to properly use the product; a complete list of nonorganic pesticides, fungicides, and herbicides used during cultivation of the product; and more.[13] The marijuana sales will be taxed, and the money used for education programs and to regulate the industry.[14]

According to the rules, all marijuana products sold under the new law must contain these warning statements:

- "There may be health risks associated with the consumption of this product."
- "This product is intended for use by adults 21 years and older. Keep out of the reach of children."
- "This product is unlawful outside the State of Colorado."
- "This product is infused with Retail Marijuana."
- "This product was produced without regulatory oversight for health, safety, or efficacy."
- "The intoxicating effects of this product may be delayed by two or more hours."

Colorado: A Case Study

In the 2000 election, voters in Colorado voted in **Amendment 20** that changed the state constitution to legalize medical marijuana. The new law allowed qualifying patients or their caregivers to legally possess up to six marijuana plants or two ounces of useable marijuana for medical reasons. In 2012, Colorado voters again opted to change the state constitution and passed another ballot initiative, **Amendment 64**. This initiative allowed for the recreational cultivation and use of marijuana by those who were 21 or older.

Under the initiative, as of January 1, 2014, marijuana could be legally sold and used for recreational purposes. The users must be 21 years of age or older and cannot use the drug in a public place. Users can grow their own marijuana, up to six plants per adult, but the plants must be grown in an enclosed, locked space. No more than three plants can be in the flowering stage at one time. If a person grows marijuana plants, they are strictly prohibited from selling it to another person. If a person wants to grow the drug for retail sale, they must be given a license from the state. All growers and sellers must keep track of all marijuana that is purchased and sold and then file that information with the state each month. Anyone visiting Colorado may purchase and use the drug while in the state but cannot transport it to another state.

After the voters passed the new law, it was necessary for the governor, John Hickenlooper, and the state legislature to change the state laws to reflect the vote. They also needed to create policies to outline how sales of recreational marijuana would be implemented. Governor Hickenlooper created a Task Force on the Implementation of Amendment 64. The task force issued a report in March 2013, which the listed 58 recommendations regarding the process by which recreational marijuana should be legally grown, sold, and taxed. The committee wanted to make sure that the availability and consumption of marijuana would be limited to those over 21 years of age, that young people would be prohibited access to the drug, and that an appropriate tax structure for marijuana sales be set up.

The state also set up a Marijuana Enforcement Division, found within the state's Department of Revenue. The new agency was given the job of enforcing the new laws, granting licenses to those who wanted to grow or sell either medical or recreational marijuana, and conducting background checks for those who grow or sell marijuana. The mission statement of the agency is simple: "Our mission is to responsibly administer and enforce medical and retail marijuana laws and regulation in a fair and equitable manner by implementing efficient and effective fiscal management policies, operable enforcement strategies and collaborative partnerships with stakeholders that establish public trust and value in the agency."[15]

New Businesses

With passage of legalized marijuana, a new market for products and services emerged and new businesses surfaced. There has been an explosion of companies pertaining to the drug, making marijuana one of the fastest-growing and most lucrative industries in Colorado. It has been estimated that the value of the cannabis market is approximately $1.53 billion, and projections place of value for the five-year national market potential at $10.2 billion.[16] Some estimate that there are around 10,000 people directly employed in the marijuana business.[17] This expansion of marijuana companies has been called the "**green rush.**"

The new businesses run the gamut. Many of the new businesses are involved with growing the plant. Hundreds of business opportunities surround the cultivation process, from selling seeds and enriched soil, specialized growing lights, containers for holding and transporting the drug, and warehouse space (which now costs up to four times as much as it did before the law was passed). Once the plant has matured, it needs to be harvested, processed, and prepared for sale. This is done by companies who train bud trimmers. The material must then be packaged and labeled for sale and then marketed to buyers, which is a whole separate business opportunity. The product needs to be delivered to retail outlets using a transportation system that meets requirements set forth by the law.[18] Once in the stores, the marijuana is sold by bud tenders who help customers choose the marijuana that is best for their needs. Stores that sell foods infused with marijuana (chocolates, gummies, cookies, pies, marinara sauce, oils, pizza, and soda) have also opened. Each of these steps in the process requires businesses with trained personnel who have become experts at what they do.

Tax Revenues

One of the arguments made in favor of legalizing marijuana was the tax revenue to be made from the sale of the drug. It is clear that many residents of Colorado want to use the drug legally. It was estimated that the total demand for marijuana by residents of Colorado was approximately 121.4 metric tons, and the demand for marijuana by visitors to the state was estimated to be approximately 8.9 metric tons. In total, this means that there is an estimated demand for marijuana in Colorado of 130.3 metric tons each year. It is clear that a tax on this product could potentially make millions for the state.[19]

Colorado voters approved a tax structure for recreational marijuana that was called Proposition AA. Under the plan, recreational marijuana would have a 10% state sales tax imposed, which was in addition to the existing 2.9% state sales tax. There would also be an excise tax of 15% on sales, which would be used to fund public school construction projects. The excise tax would be imposed on the first sale of marijuana from a cultivation facility to a retail store or to a product manufacturing facility. There would be no excise tax on medical marijuana.[20]

Table 6.4 Projected Marijuana Revenue

	Recreational Marijuana Sales		Medical Marijuana Sales	
	FY 2013–14	FY 2014–15	FY 2013–14	FY 2014–15
2.9% Sales Tax	$5,624,900	$17,770,793	$10,344,290	$10,001,306
10% Additional Sales Tax (not including 15% local share)	$16,486,777	$52,086,807		
15% Excise Tax	$11,422,770	$45,958,948		
Fees	$1,688,663	$1,962,413	$4,977,926	$5,682,787
Other	$54,141	$68,696	$77,876	$112,396
Total	$35,277,251	$117,847,657	$15,400,092	$15,796,489

Prior to the implementation of the law in January 2014, the Governor's Task Force predicted potential revenue that would be made from recreational and medical marijuana sales. Table 6.4 shows these predictions.

Once the sale of recreational marijuana began in Colorado, it was apparent that the state would make much more in revenue than they predicted. Data showed that around $14.02 million worth of recreational marijuana was sold in the first month it was legal and the state made roughly $2 million in marijuana taxes.[21] Table 6.5 shows the sales tax revenues from medical and recreational marijuana in 2015. According to Governor Hickenlooper, the tax revenue from the legal marijuana market far exceeded the state's predictions.[22]

Spending

Once the tax funds were collected by the state, officials had to decide how to spend the larger-than-expected pools of money. By law, the first $40 million of the excise tax had to be spent on school construction. The remainder could be spent by state lawmakers. The revenue collected from the new tax was placed into the state's General Fund, then transferred to a "Marijuana Tax Cash Fund" that paid for enforcing laws pertaining to the recreational marijuana industry. Some of the money (15%) was distributed to local governments in areas where there were retail marijuana sales in a program called the "**marijuana rebate**."[23]

In February 2014, Governor Hickenlooper announced his plans for spending the additional revenue. He proposed spending $45.5 million for youth marijuana

Table 6.5 2015 Colorado Marijuana Taxes

January	$7,705,502
February	$7,834,860
March	$8,962,612
April	$9,578,166
May	$10,270,699
June	$9,722,660
July	$11,608,684
August	$11,963,123
September	$10,408,030
October	$10,068,491
November	$10,068,491
December	$10,568,290

Source: Colorado Department of Revenue; Prepared by Office of Research and Analysis, "State of Colorado, Marijuana Taxes, Licenses, and Fees Transfers and Distribution," https://www.colorado.gov/pacific/revenue/marijuana-tax-data-archive.

use prevention and deterrence programs; $40.4 million for substance abuse treatment programs; $12.4 million for public health initiatives; $29 million on enforcement; $1.8 million on regulatory oversight; and $200,000 on statewide coordination efforts.[24] The governor also proposed a new, three-year media campaign to educate citizens on the health risks associated with marijuana use. The cost of this program was estimated to be $5.8 million. Also proposed by the governor was a media campaign called "Drive high, Get a DUI." To implement this, the state's Department of Transportation would receive $1.9 million.[25]

In addition to the governor's requests, state departments and agencies were asked to request money from the Marijuana Cash Fund for different programs. These are described in Table 6.6.

Table 6.6 Department and Agency Requests

- Department of Public Safety: $373,667 to gather and analyze information on the illegal production, sale, and distribution of marijuana and to create a framework to help identify threats to public safety related to illegal drug activity.

- Department of Education: $11 million for mental health and substance abuse prevention programs in public schools and $6 million for additional school resource officers.
- Governor's Office: $190,097 to establish a Drug Policy Office to coordinate the state's public health response to marijuana use.
- Department of Health Care Policy and Financing: $42.3 million for an enhanced substance use disorder program to provide inpatient/residential treatment for those who use medical marijuana; also $13 million for school-based prevention and early intervention programs for marijuana substance use and disorder services in schools.
- Department of Human Services: $32.2 million for substance abuse service initiatives; $10 million to fund prevention programs for youth; $7 million for additional beds in the Intensive Residential Treatment for Substance Use Disorders to treat marijuana misuse; $6 million for the Collaborative Management Program; $5 million for the Tony Grampsas Program, for grants that target the prevention of marijuana use; and $4.1 million for the Colorado Access to Recovery Program that provides community support for people leaving substance abuse programs.
- Department of Law: $456,760 to develop experts on state and local marijuana retail regulations who would then train regulators and peace officers.
- Department of Public Health and Environment: $8.7 million for five health initiatives, including a three-year statewide marijuana education campaign and development of a website to educate residents on the impact of marijuana; development of a registry to collect data on drivers suspected of driving under the influence; creation of a Healthy Kids Colorado Survey to examines the relationships between marijuana use and school performance; a program to monitor marijuana-related health issues through the state; development of a project to determine the correlation between marijuana use during pregnancy and birth defects.
- Department of Revenue: $1,840,000 for programming required for retail marijuana sales and excise taxes.

> • Department of Transportation: $1,875,000 to fund the "Drive High,
>   Get a DUI" campaign for marijuana-impaired driving awareness.
>
> Source: State of Colorado, Office of the Governor, "Governor John Hickenlooper's
> Budget Speech."

Banking Concerns

New marijuana businesses have found it difficult to open and maintain bank accounts because the industry revolves around an illegal endeavor. To some, this is the biggest challenge facing the industry. The problem stems from a law passed in 1970 called the **Bank Secrecy Act**. The law requires bank officials to report large deposits of cash that may be linked to illegal activity, including drugs. Any bank that accepts a large cash deposit that could be from illegal activity may be charged with money laundering and they could be criminally punished and lose their banking license. Since these businesses are making a profit based on activities that are illegal under federal law, most banks will not allow marijuana business owners to open accounts, nor will they approve start-up loans.[26] Because of this, the marijuana industry is largely an all-cash business. Business owners have no place to put their profits and must hold cash in safes in their homes or offices, posing an increased safety risk.

In response, the Obama administration requested that new rules be developed for bankers that would permit them to legally accept deposits from legal marijuana businesses in Colorado. On February 14, 2014, the Financial Crimes Enforcement Network ("FinCEN"), part of the US Department of the Treasury, issued a document to help guide financial institutions trying to provide services to businesses in the marijuana industry while still following federal law. According to the new rules, any bank doing business with a marijuana business must prove, among other things, that actions are being taken to prevent children from having access to marijuana, that the marijuana is not transported to another state, that the business owner has no ties to a drug cartel, and that the drug is not intended for use on federal property. Even given these clarifications, banking officials are still hesitant to work with marijuana businesses. They report that it is very difficult for banks to ensure that these rules are being followed and guarantee these things will not occur.

Federalization

Another concern for emerging marijuana businesses is that all of the state laws that allow for legal marijuana use are each at odds with federal laws that ban such behaviors. The state laws violate the Federal Controlled Substances Act, which prohibits the dispensation and possession of marijuana at all times.[27] This means that the state laws are in violation of federal laws. When there is a discrepancy between state and federal law, the federal law supersedes state law. In essence, the state laws permitting marijuana use can, at any time, be ruled unconstitutional. Moreover, at any time, federal government agents (e.g., ATF or FBI agents) can raid grow sites, dispensaries, stores, and retail markets to arrest those who are growing, transporting, dispensing, prescribing, selling, or possessing marijuana and charge them with federal offenses.

The US Supreme Court has reviewed the state laws on marijuana to evaluate their constitutionality. One of those cases was heard in 2005 when the Court heard the case of *Gonzalez v. Raich*. The justices decided that federal law supersedes state law, reinforcing the possibility that law enforcement could arrest and prosecute those involved in the marijuana market in some way.

Concerns that marijuana businesses would be raided in those states that have legalized the drug were addressed by President Obama, who indicated that the federal government will support the decision of the voters and not challenge state laws. Fears of federal action were further diminished in 2009 when then-Attorney General Eric Holder indicated that he would not spend federal resources to enforce federal laws against individuals in states that allow for marijuana use. Fears were diminished even further in August 2013, when a memo written by US Deputy Attorney General James Cole was published. In the memo, entitled "Guidance Regarding Marijuana Enforcement," he announced that federal drug enforcement agencies were unlikely to obstruct the implementation of the new laws in Colorado and Washington if state officials ensured it met certain standards. They announced that as long as the state laws in these states prevented the use of marijuana by minors, stopped marijuana being taken to other states, inhibited the presence of organized crime, and averted drugged driving and other negative effects on public health, they would allow the law to be implemented. Officials in both states have paid close attention to enacting policies that fit into the standards.[28]

It should be stressed that even though President Obama is not enforcing federal drug laws in those states, a future presidential administration could choose to change this enforcement approach. While marijuana businesses are being allowed to thrive under the Obama administration, this could change if a new president chooses. Marijuana remains illegal under federal law, despite state laws and referendums approving its sale for either medical use or recreation. Any marijuana-related business that is currently operating in any state is violating federal law and could be raided by the Drug Enforcement Administration and shut down at any time. The owners and employees could be punished by fines and imprisonment and their property (homes, cars, bank accounts) seized by the federal government. Until the Congress acts to change existing laws, all marijuana-related businesses and employees are at risk of government action and criminal charges.

The federalism question leads to other glitches when it comes to marijuana-business owners. Like banking officials in Colorado, many attorneys refuse to get involved in anything having to do with legalized marijuana, including representing businesses and owners/operators of any business that is involved in the industry. Many lawyers fear that they could be prosecuted for either helping a client to break federal law or conspiring to break a federal law. If this were to happen, the lawyer could then be disbarred from the profession.[29] Similarly, many banks still will not open accounts for business owners/operators of marijuana businesses.

Conclusion

Marijuana is a naturally occurring plant with psychoactive components that had been used legally for many years in the US before being made illegal by Congress. While it remains illegal under federal law, many states have new policies that allow for either medical or recreational marijuana, or both. The long-term effects of marijuana use are still unknown so there are many critics of these new state laws. Nonetheless, many people find relief for their medical conditions by using the drug, and many others enjoy the euphoric and relaxing feeling that occurs when the drug is ingested. There is no doubt that marijuana will continue to be used for many years in the future, whether legal or illegal.

Important Terms

Amendment 20
Amendment 64
Bank Secrecy Act
Cannabinoids
Cannabis

Compassionate Investigational New
Drug Program
Green Rush
Hashish/Hash
Hemp

Marihuana Tax Act   Proposition 215
Marijuana   THC
Marijuana Rebate

Review Questions

1. Write a short summary of the history of marijuana use in the US.

2. What are some arguments in favor of marijuana legalization? What are the opposing arguments?

3. What are some of the effects a user of marijuana may feel?

4. Why is the "federalization" question critical when it comes to marijuana legalization?

5. What happened in Colorado after marijuana was legalized there? Would other states have the same experiences?

Endnotes

1. Marion, Nancy E. 2014. *The Medical Marijuana Maze.* Durham, NC: Carolina Academic Press.

2. Califano, Joseph A., Jr. 2007. *High Society: How Substance Abuse Ravages America and What to Do About It.* New York: Perseus Books.

3. Davenport-Hines, Richard. 2001. *The Pursuit of Oblivion: A Global History of Narcotics, 1500–2000.* London: Weidenfeld & Nicolson; Earlywine, Mitch. 2002. *Understanding Marijuana: A New Look at the Scientific Evidence.* Oxford: Oxford University Press.

4. Gerber, Rudy. 2004. *Legalizing Marijuana: Drug Policy Reform and Prohibition Politics.* Westport, CT: Praeger; Kreit, Alex. 2003. "The Future of Medical Marijuana: Should the States Grow Their Own?" *University of Pennsylvania Law Review* 151(5): 1787–826.

5. "Marijuana Far More Potent than it Used to Be, Tests Find." March 23, 2015. CBS News. http://www.cbsnews.com/news/marijuana-far-more-potent-than-it-used-to-be-tests-find/; Brangham, William. April 2, 2014. Is Pot Getting More Potent? PBS Newshour. http://www.pbs.org/newshour/updates/pot-getting-potent/; Cabrera, Ann. October 21, 2016. Colorado marijuana's potency getting 'higher.' CNN. http://www.cnn.com/2016/10/21/health/colorado-marijuana-potency-above-national-average/index.html.

6. National Highway Traffic Safety Administration. 2013. "Drugs and Human Performance Fact Sheets: Cannabis/Marijuana (Δ9-Tetrahydrocannabinol, THC)." http://www.nhtsa.gov/people/injury/research/job185drugs/cannabis.htm.

7. National Institute on Drug Abuse. 2012a. "DrugFacts: Marijuana." http://www.drugabuse.gov/publications/drugfacts/marijuana; National Institute on Drug Abuse. 2012b. "Marijuana Abuse: How Does Marijuana Produce Its Effects?" http://www.drugabuse.gov/publications/marijuana-abuse/how-does-marijuana-produce-its-effects.

8. United Nations Office on Drugs and Crime. 2016. World Drug Report. https://www.unodc.org/wdr2016/en/cannabis.html.

9. Hoffman, John, and Susan Froemke, eds. 2007. *Addiction: Why Can't They Just Stop?* New York: Rodale.

10. "Majority Now Supports Legalizing Marijuana." April 4, 2013. Pew Research Center for the People and the Press. http://www.peopole-press.org2013/04/04/majority-now-supports-legalizing-marijuana.

11. Meyer, Robert J. 2014. "Potential Merits of Cannabinoids for Medical Uses." US Food and Drug Administration, US Department of Health and Human Services. http://www.fda.gov/NewsEvents/Testimony/ucm114741.htm.

12. Coffman, Keith. May 28, 2013. "Colorado Governor Signs Recreational Marijuana Regulations into Law." Reuters. http://www.reuters.com/article/2013/05/29/us-usa-colorado-marijuana-idUSBRE94S03Q20130529.

13. Ferner, Matt. July 1, 2013. "Rules for Legal Recreational Marijuana Sales Announced in Colorado." *Huffington Post.* http://www.huffingtonpost.com/2013/07/01/marijuana-legalization_n_3529986.html.

14. Paulson, Amanda. December 22, 2013. "Legal Pot Is Imminent in Colorado and Washington. Are They Ready?" *Christian Science Monitor.* http://www.csmonitor.com/USA/Society/2013/1222/Legal-pot-is-imminent-in-Colorado-and-Washington.-Are-they-ready.

15. Colorado Department of Revenue. 2015. "Stakeholders—Marijuana Enforcement." https://www.colorado.gov/pacific/enforcement/stakeholders-marijuana-enforcement.

16. "Cannabis Industry Creates Rise in New Markets.: 2014, January 24. PR.com. http://www.pr.com/press-release/538773; O'Connor, Amy. 2014, October 2. "Marijuana Insurance Industry: How High Can It Go?" *Insurance Journal.* http://www.insurancejournal.com/news/national/2014/10/01/342142.htm.

17. Lopez, German. 2014, May 20. "Legal Marijuana Created Thousands of Jobs in Colorado." *Vox.* http://www.vox.com/2014/5/20/5734394/legal-marijuana-created-thousands-of-jobs.

18. Huff, Ethan A. 2013, June 24. "New Wave of Business Opportunities Involving Medicinal, Nutritional Marijuana Sweeps Colorado." http://www.naturalnews.com/040920_marijuana_business_opportunities_Colorado.htm.

19. Light, Miles K., Adam Orens, Brian Lewandowski, and Todd Pickton. 2014. Colorado Department of Revenue and the Marijuana Policy Group. "Market Size and Demand for Marijuana in Colorado." http://www.colorado.gov/cs/.

20. Colorado Department of Revenue, Taxation Division, "Marijuana Taxes." https://www.colorado.gov/pacific/tax/marijuana-taxes-file).

21. Associated Press. 2014, March 10. "Colorado Marijuana Taxes Net State $2 Million." Fox News. http://www.foxnews.com/us/2014/03/10/colorado-marijuana-taxes-net-state-2-million.

22. Wyatt, Kristen. 2014, February 19. "Governor: Colorado Pot Market Exceeds Tax Hopes." *Denver Post.* http://www.denverpost.com/marijuana/ci_25180402/colorado-governor-reveals-pot-tax.

23. Colorado Office of State Planning and Budgeting. 2014, September. "The Colorado Economic Outlook: Economic and Fiscal Review." http://www.colorado.gov/cs/Satellite/OSPB/GOVR/1218709343298.

24. Associated Press. 2014, February 19. "Colorado Governor Reveals Plan to Spend

Marijuana Tax Revenue." Fox News. http://www.foxnews.com/politics/2014/02/19colorado-governor-reveals-plan-to-spend.

25. Associated Press. 2014, March 10. "Colorado Marijuana Taxes Net State $2 Million." Fox News. http://www.foxnews.com/us/2014/03/10/colorado-marijuana-taxes-net-state-2-million.

26. Wells, Jane. 2013, December 16. "Marijuana Related Business Sees Growth as Pot Legalization Spreads." NBC News. http://www.nbcnews.com/business/consumer/-marijuana-related-business-sees-growth-pot-legalization-spreads-f2D11750342.

27. Goodnough, A., and K. Zezima. 2011. "An Alarming New Stimulant, Legal in Many States." *New York Times*. http://www.nytimes.com/2011/07/17/us/17salts.html; Hoffmann, D. E., and E. Weber. 2010. "Medical Marijuana and the Law." *New England Journal of Medicine* 362: 1453–57.

28. Knickerbocker, Brad. August 29, 2013. "Colorado Marijuana Law: Obama Administration Backs Off." *Christian Science Monitor*. http://www.csmonitor.com/USA/Justice/2013/0829/Colorado-marijuana-law-Obama-administration-backs-off-video.

29. Steinmetz, Katy. December 23, 2013. "Why Some Lawyers Won't Work for Colorado Marijuana Businesses." *Time*. http://nation.time.com/2013/12/23/why-some-lawyers-wont-work-for-colorado-marijuana-businesses/#ixzz2oP9qMoKA.

Chapter 7

The Politics of Drugs: Presidents

Chapter Objective: This chapter provides the reader with a description the policies chosen by US presidents to reduce illicit drug use in the nation. It also includes various commissions set up to advise the president as well as reports issued.

Introduction

Drug policies have become political issues that are frequently debated by all types of political officials. Drugs were not a major concern on the political scene until the 1910s, with the push for Prohibition and its eventual passage. This was not a popular law and it was eventually repealed. After this, there was a long period when there was minimal attention given to the problems of drug use.

This changed in the 1960s and early 1970s. President Nixon declared drug abuse to be "public enemy number one in the United States."[1] His 1971 statement became the basis of the federal government's drug policy from then on, and most states followed suit. Many pieces of legislation were passed to limit the availability and use of narcotic drugs, the most influential being the Controlled Substances Act (CSA) that was passed in 1970. This law categorized different drugs according to their potential for abuse and then prescribed penalties for their distribution and use. In 1973, Nixon created a new agency, the DEA, which was responsible for enforcing the nation's anti-drug laws. More legislation was passed and more agencies were created over time that furthered the nation's War on Drugs.

Criticism of the War on Drugs has been made apparent and many people today believe that the war has been lost. The federal government has spent

Abraham Lincoln from the United States Library of Congress's Prints and Photographs division.

hundreds of billions of dollars to regulate illegal drug use but demand for these drugs, and their availability, remains high. Opponents point out similarities between the Drug War and Prohibition, which banned alcohol but quickly failed, causing more crime in most major cities.

As leader of the country, the president directs policies for drug control. The president can choose to focus more on increasing punishments for offenders, on providing treatment for addicts, or a combination of both. Since the 1950s, each president has discussed their plans to reduce drug use. This chapter is a review of presidential actions related to illicit drugs, as well as the creation of advisory agencies developed to provide counsel and recommendations to the president.

Early Presidential Action: Abraham Lincoln

The political debate about drugs can be traced as far back as President Lincoln, who served in the White House from 1861–1865. Lincoln himself abstained from alcohol and supported the temperance movement. He expressed his support of the temperance followers on February 22, 1842, in a speech referred to as the "Temperance Address." He made it clear in the speech that while he supported temperance, he did not stand behind the extreme tactics used by some members of the temperance movement. He also explained that people choose to drink because their friends do, and that nondrinkers can help those who drink change their behavior through friendly support.[2] His speech is detailed in Box 7.1.

Table 7.1 President Lincoln's Speech on Temperance

And again, it is so common and so easy to ascribe motives to men of these classes, other than those they profess to act upon. The preacher, it is said, advocates temperance because he is a fanatic, and desires a union of the Church and State; the lawyer, from his pride and vanity of hearing himself speak; and the hired agent, for his salary. But when one, who has long been known as a victim of intemperance bursts the fetters that have bound him, and appears before his neighbors "clothed, and in his right mind," a redeemed specimen of long-lost humanity, and stands up with tears of joy trembling in his eyes, to tell of the miseries once endured, now to be endured no more forever; of his once naked and starving children, now clad and fed comfortably; of a wife long weighed down with woe, weeping, and a broken heart, now restored to health, happiness, and a renewed affection; and how easily it is all done, once it is resolved to be done; how simple his language, there is a logic, and an eloquence in it, that few, with human feelings, can resist. They cannot say that he desires a union of church and state, for he is not a church member; they cannot say he is vain of hearing himself speak, for his whole demeanor shows he would gladly avoid speaking at all; they cannot say he speaks for pay for he receives none, and asks for none. Nor can his sincerity in any way be doubted; or his sympathy for those he would persuade to imitate his example be denied.

There is some evidence that Lincoln said the following about the temperance movement in a speech on December 18, 1840, to the Illinois House of Representatives. However, there is great debate as to whether this is an accurate record of what was actually said that day.

Prohibition will work great injury to the cause of temperance. It is a species of intemperance within itself, for it goes beyond the bounds of reason in that it attempts to control a man's appetite by legislation, and makes a crime out of things that are not crimes. A Prohibition law strikes a blow at the very principles upon which our government was founded.

Source: Roy P. Basler, editor. 1953. *Collected Works of Abraham Lincoln.* New Brunswick, NJ, Rutgers Univ. Press

Modern Presidential Debate and Action

Every president from Truman to Obama has talked about drug and drug abuse and supported various anti-drug policies. Some presidents take a more conservative approach to their anti-drug tactics and support increased penalties for drug offenses whereas others lean more toward treatment and rehabilitation of offenders. In the end, no president has been effective in reducing drug use in the US.

Dwight D. Eisenhower (1890–1969)

Dwight D. Eisenhower served as president from 1953 to 1961. The Eisenhower administration took a strong stance with its anti-drug policies. Eisenhower signed amendments to the Boggs Act into law and then, in 1956, he signed the Narcotic Control Act that increased the mandatory minimum sentencing policy that was first established in the Boggs Act. The new law also created the death penalty for certain drug offenses. At the same time, Eisenhower supported treatment programs for those addicted to drugs. He signed H.R. 3307 (PL 83-76) in 1953 to ensure the availability of treatment programs for regular narcotics users who lived in the District of Columbia. This was the first law to make treatment an option for addicts rather than a reliance on prison sentences. Eisenhower was certain that this law would address the problem of drug addiction in the US.

In 1954, Eisenhower called for a special committee that would establish a new war on narcotic addiction at the local, national, and international level. The committee members were asked to examine the current policies geared toward fighting drugs and then to recommend new solutions that would lead to a more effective national anti-drug campaign. The committee's work included a national survey to learn more about the problem of addiction. The final report of the committee was made public in February 1956. The report called for increased cooperation between federal and state agencies, more treatment resources, the ability to commit addicts to hospitals for treatment, and harsher penalties for non-using drug sellers. The committee also made it clear that the problem of addiction among youth appeared to be exaggerated.

During the Eisenhower presidency, the number of people using illegal drugs remained relatively low. However, there was an increase in the use of amphetamines, barbiturates, and heroin. Eisenhower relied on new legislation with tough sentences to reduce drug use. He set the penalties for illegal drugs very high, hoping that it would deter potential users from consuming drugs.[3]

John F. Kennedy (1917–1963)

John F. Kennedy was the president from 1961 until his assassination in 1963. During his campaign for the presidency, Kennedy promised to take action on the issue of drug use. In his 1962 State of the Union Address, Kennedy discussed the problem of illicit drug use and called for government action on it. In September of 1962, Kennedy convened a **White House Conference on Narcotics and Drug Abuse.** The conference was two days long and attended by a wide range of people, from law enforcement professionals to elected politicians and doctors. It quickly became clear that the attendees, experts in their fields, knew little about illicit narcotics and the drug trade, the effects of drug use on the body, or even why people use drugs.

Kennedy also appointed a **President's Advisory Commission on Narcotics and Drug Abuse** in 1963, through Executive Order 11076. The commission studied illicit narcotics use, including any existing research (of which there was little), possible effects, likelihood of addiction, and treatment options. The final report had not been released to the public when Kennedy was assassinated.[4]

Lyndon B. Johnson (1908–1973)

Lyndon B. Johnson was president from 1963 to 1969, serving after Kennedy was assassinated. During this administration, there was more public drug use by young people and concern about drug use was increasing. Partly based on the final report of the Prettyman Commission, Johnson asked Congress to pass a bill that would set tighter controls and record keeping over the production and distribution of amphetamines, barbiturates, and other psychoactive drugs that had not been included in earlier legislation. Congress agreed, and the resulting law was the Drug Abuse Control Amendments of 1965. The new law also included provisions to deter the diversion of depressant and stimulant drugs from legal channels and into the illicit market.

On July 15, 1964, Johnson gave a speech on narcotic and drug abuse around the country. In it, he said that "narcotic and other drug abuse [was] inflicting upon parts of the country enormous damage in human suffering, crime, and economic loss through thievery. The Federal Government, being responsible for the regulation of foreign and interstate commerce, bears a major responsibility in respect to the illegal traffic in drugs and the consequences of that traffic." Johnson wanted "the full power of the Federal Government to be brought to bear upon three objectives: (1) the destruction of the illegal traffic in drugs, (2) the prevention of drug abuse, and (3) the cure and rehabilitation of victims of this traffic."[5]

One year later, Johnson gave another speech on drug abuse, this time about the 1965 Drug Abuse Control Amendments bill. Johnson praised Congress for the new law, saying it would prevent the abuse and trafficking of prescription drug, including sedatives and stimulants. As a way to ensure the new provisions were implemented, Johnson created the Bureau of Drug Abuse Control (BDAC).[6]

Congress supported Johnson's approach to drug rehabilitation for drug offenders and in 1966 passed the Narcotics Addict Rehabilitation Act that provided rehabilitation for addicts and increased research about drug use and treatment. In support of the bill, Johnson created the President's Commission on Law Enforcement and Administration of Justice to "undertake a comprehensive study of the nation's crime problem to provide recommendations to coordinate its eradication on all fronts."[7]

Early in 1968, Johnson proposed a plan to reorganize the federal agencies that played a role in drug enforcement. In an odd twist, he proposed eliminating the BDAC and the Federal Bureau of Narcotics. In their place would be a Bureau of Narcotics and Dangerous Drugs that would be housed in the Department of Justice. This gave the Justice Department a critical role in the enforcement of federal drug abuse laws. During his 1968 State of the Union Address, Johnson again spoke about issues relating to drug use and control. He proposed a new law to increase penalties for trafficking in LSD and other dangerous drugs. He also sought stricter enforcement of existing drug laws, which he estimated could be accomplished by hiring 30 percent more federal drug and narcotics control agents.[8]

In addition to these items, the president felt it was essential to give more attention to educating people about the dangers of drug abuse. Johnson believed education was essential in the fight against drug abuse and especially in deterring young Americans from becoming drug abusers. He also wanted to find a way that former drug abusers could be reintegrated into the community. Johnson wanted to find ways to help communities understand and support the process of allowing former addicts to become functioning members of society, thereby reducing the likelihood of returning to abusing drugs.[9]

Richard M. Nixon (1913–1994)

Richard M. Nixon, the self-proclaimed "law-and-order president," believed drug abuse to be a sickness instead of a crime. He was the first president to focus on treatment and reducing demand over punishing offenders. However, illegal drug use did not wane during his first term and so it became one of the major issues of the 1968 presidential campaign. Nixon changed his policies on drug abuse in his reelection bid, moving toward tougher policies on drug users.

Throughout the Nixon administration, the number of people abusing marijuana and methadone was increasing. Nixon proposed a new agency that would centralize all federal agencies and efforts for drug treatment, rehabilitation, education, prevention, training, and research into one. The agency was the Special Action Office for Drug Abuse Prevention (SAODAP). Nixon appointed Dr. Jerome Jaffe to be a special consultant for narcotics and dangerous drugs and to propose ways to increase treatment for those on methadone. When Jaffe began the task in 1971, there were 135 federally funded drug-treatment programs for people on methadone. In a year and a half, that number had increased to 394. The number of people in treatment programs increased from 20,000 to 60,000. One of the areas of concern was servicemen and women returning from Vietnam who were addicted to drugs. Jaffe had programs to identify those individuals and provide them with treatment options. Despite these programs, the use of methadone continued to increase and Jaffe resigned in 1973.[10]

A second concern that rose during Nixon's tenure was marijuana. During his presidency, the National Commission on Marihuana and Drug Abuse (the Shaffer Commission) recommended that marijuana use be decriminalized as the use of marijuana did not cause a person to become violent, nor was it an addictive drug. Nixon did not agree with this finding and continued to maintain that marijuana was a dangerous drug.

Nixon took an international focus to the drug problem and met with leaders of other countries, particularly President Diaz Ordaz of Mexico, to seek their help in stopping drug trafficking into the US. Nixon also sought to increase punishments for drug traffickers.[11]

In the spring of 1973, Nixon announced Reorganization Plan No 2. In it, he called for "an all-out global war on the drug menace."[12] He combined the anti-drug responsibilities of other agencies, including the Office of Drug Abuse Law Enforcement and the Office of National Narcotics Intelligence, into a new agency he called the Drug Enforcement Administration (DEA). It was thought that the merger would allow the agency to be more consistent and effective in fighting drugs from one place rather than having many agencies attacking the problem from different perspectives.

Gerald R. Ford (1913–2006)

Gerald R. Ford was president of the US from 1974 until 1977. During his short administration, the problem of illicit drug use received attention from the president. In a 1976 speech, Ford said that "drug abuse is one of the most serious and tragic problems in this country. Its cost to the Nation in terms of ruined lives, broken homes, and divided communities is staggering. In addition to this toll, it is a major cause of crime."[13]

Ford continued the interdiction strategy that was the focus of the Nixon administration. The US and Mexico began using the herbicide paraquat to eradicate the marijuana crop in Mexico. Because paraquat did not destroy the plant, the plants were still harvested and trafficked into the US. Many marijuana users in the US were sickened, and many others were deterred from using the drug. Thus, use rates declined.

Ford did not back the creation of an executive-level office for drug abuse prevention. When Congress passed an amendment that created a new agency they called the Office of Drug Abuse Policy (ODAP), he did not hire any staff to run it. Eventually, the agency came into being in 1977 under the next president, President Carter.

In 1974, Ford signed H.R. 9456, the Alcohol and Drug Abuse Education Act Amendments. That same year he designated October 20 through October 26 to be "Drug Abuse Prevention Week." In doing this, Ford sought to spur local leaders and communities into action in the fight against drug abuse.[14]

James E. "Jimmy" Carter (1924–)

James E. "Jimmy" Carter, a Democrat, served as president of the US from 1977 to 1981. During his administration, the use of cocaine and marijuana were growing as many users saw no harm that resulted from using these drugs. At the same time, the federal government's anti-drug policy was changing. Carter softened the government's position on marijuana and cocaine. Dr. Peter Bourne, the director of the Office of Drug Abuse Policy, described cocaine as one of the most benign illicit drugs being used and that a case could be made for legalizing it. He called marijuana short acting and not physically addictive, and noted that cocaine was used by people in all socioeconomic levels.[15]

Carter also cut back on international operations for reducing drug trafficking. In 1979, there was evidence that heroin was being trafficked into the US from Afghanistan, causing more Americans to be addicted to the drug. Some critics of Carter's policies pointed out that the global heroin supply could be traced largely to the failure of the DEA to interdict the drugs. Some critics went so far as to allege that the CIA had promoted drug use in the United States by helping allies in Southeast Asia and Afghanistan who were involved in international drug trafficking.[16]

Ronald W. Reagan (1911–2004)

Ronald W. Reagan was president from 1981–1989. He believed that illicit drugs was one of the most serious problems facing the nation and promised to crack down on the production, trafficking, and use of these substances, promising a "War on Drugs," a term first used by Richard Nixon. On October 14, 1982, Reagan stated that illicit drugs were a threat to the national security of the US.[17] In his fight against drugs, Reagan took both a domestic and international approach.[18]

Domestically, Reagan supported law enforcement's battle against drugs. He hired new federal drug law enforcement agents to investigate drug offenders and established drug task forces in major cities. Reagan asked the Department of Defense to provide training, intelligence, and equipment to law enforcement agencies when they investigated drug traffickers. Reagan also allowed members of the Army, Navy, Air Force, and Marines to operate military equipment for civilian law enforcement agencies who were carrying out drug-related operations.

Reagan worked with Congress to develop new policies that increased punishments for drug offenses. The Controlled Substances Registration Protection Act increased penalties for stealing prescription drugs from pharmacies. The Bail Reform Act made it more difficult for individuals accused of breaking drug laws to get out on bail. The Comprehensive Crime Control Act again strengthened the interdiction efforts of drug law enforcement. Reagan then added more federal prosecutors to prosecute people who violated these laws and provided more money for building new prisons to house offenders convicted of drug-related crimes. At the same time, Reagan also focused just as much attention on treatment options for addicts.

In particular, Reagan targeted the growing drug trade in the Miami area, creating a new task force led by Vice President George H. W. Bush to address the problem in 1982. Reagan sent federal law enforcement agents to South Florida, bolstering the presence of the Federal Bureau of Investigation, the Customs Service, the Bureau of Alcohol, Tobacco and Firearms, and the Internal Revenue Service in order to investigate drug-related crimes, stop the proliferation of weapons in the drug trade, and crack down on money laundering operations.

To provide better coordination for all of these new programs, in 1988 Reagan created the Office of National Drug Control Policy to coordinate drug-related legislative, security, diplomatic, research, and health policy throughout the government. He also made the FBI the lead agency for drug enforcement and investigations.

Reagan increased the budgets for drug control dramatically, as funding for drug law-related programs nearly doubled between 1981 and 1986. Reagan allocated billions of additional dollars to fight drug abuse and trafficking, and stiffening penalties for drug law offenses by overseeing the passage of the Anti-Drug Abuse Acts of 1986 and 1988. In addition to the domestic anti-drug policies, Reagan also took international efforts to crack down on drug production and smuggling and cut off supplies of illicit drugs coming into the country. In 1981, he authorized intelligence agencies to investigate and take an active role in breaking up international drug rings.

Overall, the presidency of Ronald Reagan saw the War on Drugs reach new heights, as the government toughened laws and increased expenditures in order to crack down on drug use. Though there was new legislation that expanded treatment options for addicts, Reagan's approach to drug control was a tough, law-and-order approach.[19]

In 1988, President Reagan began what he termed the Zero Tolerance Policy Program as a way to reduce the supply of illegal drugs that were regularly being smuggled into the US. This policy required law enforcement to investigate both casual and heavy drug users. Federal officials were also required to seize vessels that had any amount of an illegal substance on board if it was within a 12-mile radius of the US coast. Critics of the new policy alleged that the program was unfair and within two months, the Reagan administration began to back off of the zero tolerance standard.[20]

George H. W. Bush (1924–)

George H. W. Bush was president of the US from 1989 to 1993. For the most part, Bush continued Reagan's tough policies on illicit drugs. These policies reflected the public's opinion at the time, which sought tougher policies on illegal drugs and drug-related violence that was prevalent in many cities.

Bush took an international approach to controlling drugs. He asked Congress to give more military and economic assistance to Andean countries as a way to reduce the traffic of cocaine into the US. This program, called the "Andean Strategy," required the US to provide military assistance to the source countries of Peru, Colombia, and Bolivia. Prior to the initiative, US assistance to these countries was about $40 to $50 million, but after the plan was approved, expenditures by the US on anti-drug expenditures for South American countries increased sevenfold from fiscal year 1989 to 1991. In exchange for US support, leaders from the Andean countries agreed to cooperate and increase anti-drug efforts in their countries. They requested that Bush create new employment opportunities for farmers and workers who would be displaced from growing and producing cocaine.[21]

Bush ordered special forces units (particularly the Green Berets) to enter into countries like Peru and Colombia to arrest drug dealers and other criminals. This was despite opposition from military leaders and without the consent of the host countries.[22]

William J. "Bill" Clinton (1946–)

William J. "Bill" Clinton was the US president from 1993 to 2001. During the 1992 presidential election, Clinton promised to change US policy, promising to combine tough law enforcement with more treatment and prevention programs. As president, Clinton had an active agenda for the problems related to illicit drugs.

Funding for drug interdiction declined during Clinton's first term of office—from about $1 billion to $569 million. This meant that there were fewer activities devoted to drug interdiction. Cocaine seizures dropped from 70,336 kilograms in 1992 to 37,181 in 1995.

Clinton continued to seek a military solution to the drug problem. Clinton promised to give $75 million worth of helicopters, planes, arms, and other military equipment to the governments of Colombia, Peru, Bolivia, Venezuela, and the Caribbean region, a strong indication that it was going to be the Drug War as usual if Clinton were reelected.[23]

Clinton supported the National Youth Anti-Drug Media Campaign that began in 1998. This was a government-funded program that targeted drug use among youth. It involved using ads on television, radio, and other locations that would reach out to youth and send messages about the dangers of drug use. It also was aimed at parents and other adults as a way to encourage them to take actions to reduce drug abuse. Later analysis of the program showed that it was not successful.[24]

George W. Bush (1946–)

George W. Bush, who served as president from 2001–2009, had a comprehensive approach to illicit drug use in the country. He described his anti-drug agenda in a speech in which he introduced John P. Walters to be the next drug czar, making it very clear that the legalization of drugs would be catastrophic. Bush noted that illegal drug use costs the country over $100 billion every year from lost productivity, but it also caused deaths, destroyed families, ruins educational and job opportunities, and causes increased healthcare costs.[25]

Bush's approach to anti-drug efforts included many facets. One was working with other nations to eradicate drugs at the source and stop the flow of drugs into the US. Bush continued to cooperate with leaders of other countries to limit drug trafficking. He had meetings with Vicente Fox of Mexico, the leaders of the Andean countries (Colombia, Peru, and Ecuador), and leaders from the Caribbean.[26]

Bush admitted that the most effective method for reducing drug use in America is to reduce the demand for drugs. He focused a great deal of energy on preventing children from using drugs. For example, he supported the Drug Abuse Resistance Education program (DARE) to education children about the dangers of drugs. He declared one day in April of every year in his presidency to be National DARE Day to bring attention to this cause.[27] He also supported drug testing of children in schools.

In conjunction with this, Bush believed that families could help in keeping children drug-free. Bush proposed creating a Parent Drug Corps to provide support to educate and train parents in effective drug prevention. He also sought an increase in federal funding to help fund drug-free communities programs.

Understanding that many inmates in our prisons and jails had committed their offenses because of addiction to drugs and alcohol, Bush provided funds for drug testing programs for inmates, probationers, and parolees. For those users who were addicted to drugs, Bush proposed funding for programs that sought to close the "treatment gap" for those who sought treatment but were not unable to receive it. Bush also reserved additional money to fund treatment programs for addicts in states, and also for programs that incorporated faith-based elements into their programs. Because drug courts also provide treatment for some offenders, Bush increased funding for state drug courts.

In an effort to increase people's understanding of drug use, Bush increased the funding for the National Institute on Drug Abuse and the National Institute on Alcohol Abuse and Alcoholism. This way, experts could learn more about the causes of drug use and the best treatment methods.[28]

Bush made it clear that athletes who used performance-enhancing steroids did not serve as a good role model for children, and called on athletes and team owners to eliminate steroid use in sports.

Barack H. Obama (1961–)

President **Barack H. Obama** was candid that he used drugs as a young man. He admitted the he used marijuana and "maybe a little blow" (cocaine) while he was in high school during the 1970s. As president, Obama has sought to change the government's War on Drugs by treating drug abuse as a public health issue rather than a crime. According to his National Drug Control Strategy, President Obama promised to reduce drug use by 15 percent by 2015. In fact, he called the War on Drugs "an utter failure."

Obama supported changing the mandatory minimum sentences for drug offenders that would lower the mandatory prison sentences for "low-level, nonviolent drug offenders who have no ties to large-scale organizations, gangs or cartels." Instead, these nonviolent offenders would receive sentences that relied on drug treatment and community services, as they are "better suited to their individual conduct." Obama also ordered federal prosecutors to back away from prosecuting individual, recreational users of certain drugs. Thus, the new sentencing structure includes less severe punishments for recreational drug users.

Obama has also expressed concerns about the discrimination that exists in sentencing for drugs, and he often mentioned the inequitable sentencing policies between crack and powder cocaine. This difference was reduced by the Fair Sentencing Act of 2010. Obama took action to help federal inmates who had been convicted of charges relating to crack cocaine in December 2013, when he commuted the sentences of eight federal inmates who had been convicted of charges related to crack cocaine. All of the offenders had been in prison for at least 15 years. Six had received life sentences. Obama said that these inmates would have received shorter sentences had they been sentenced under current drug laws.[29]

Obama sought to ensure that drug addicts and abusers can get treatment. He has stressed that treatment options are available for addicts through his Affordable Care Act. Under the act, insurance companies would be required to cover treatment for substance abuse just as they would for any other chronic disease. It also expands treatment and reentry services for those individuals who are incarcerated.

In the 2013 National Drug Control Strategy, the administration stated that there is a need for a more thorough and scientific understanding of addiction. In general, the strategy promotes national and community-based anti-drug use programs that are intended to prevent substance use in schools, on college campuses, and in the workplace. The expansion of specialized drug courts was suggested whereby nonviolent, first-time offenders are diverted into treatment instead of prison. Obama's strategy also indicates the need for expanding drug prevention and treatment on a global level. He has also proposed promoting alternative crops for farmers in those areas of the world that are known for producing drugs and expanding and modernizing law enforcement capabilities on the international scene.[30]

The Obama administration's position on the legalization of marijuana changed during his presidency. In a report issued in 2010, the Office of National Drug Control Policy argued against legalizing marijuana based on a report from the RAND Corporation in which legalized marijuana was linked with decreasing prices and increased use.[31] The report argued that the potential societal costs from legalized marijuana would be higher than any potential tax revenues that could be generated from it. Moreover, the increased use of the drug and the potential for increased harm would, in the long run, create more of a burden on the criminal justice system.

However, in the later years of his presidency, the Obama administration has backed off of strict enforcement of marijuana laws after many states passed laws allowing for both medical and recreational use. The administration announced an ending to what they called "marijuana prohibition." The Justice Department has decided not to pursue those states that have legalized marijuana and have announced that they will not arrest users and sellers, nor will they raid stores and distribution sites. To that effect, the Justice Department sent a four-page memorandum to federal prosecutors across the United States in which they outlined eight priority areas that should be enforced. In other words, the attorneys were encouraged to bring charges only in these eight areas. The eight areas include distribution of marijuana to minors, if marijuana revenue is being displaced to criminal enterprises, trafficking across state boundaries, and growing marijuana on public land. However, if states are unable to control the use of the drug, the federal government has reserved the right to step in and take control.[32]

Committees, Commissions, and Conferences

Some presidents have called for commissions and conferences, or special meetings, as a way to bring together experts in the field and learn more about drug use. In some cases, these conferences resulted in recommendations for new policies that were turned into law. Below is a description of some of these conference events and commissions.

1918: Special Narcotic Committee

The **Special Narcotic Committee** (SNC) was formed by the Treasury Department in 1918 to study the emerging problems of narcotics control and to make recommendations for new laws. The committee found that narcotic drug use actually increased after the Harrison Narcotics Act was passed in 1914 and so they proposed a new law that tightened the government's restrictions over narcotics. The new law created an extra tax of one cent per ounce of narcotics a person possessed. This meant that a person who possessed narcotics but did not have a tax stamp could be charged with illegal possession of the drug (unless they had a doctor's prescription).

Other findings by the SNC showed that there were over 1 million drug addicts in the country, that the country's per capita consumption of opium was higher than in any other industrialized nation, and those numbers would probably grow. The information in the report clearly showed a need for more government action to provide treatment for addicts who might become violent without medical care.

In the end, the SNC was short lived but had a lasting impact on drug policy in the US. It served to spread fear about narcotics addiction, and about drug users and traffickers.[33]

1962: White House Conference on Narcotics and Drug Abuse

The White House held a conference to discover more about narcotics and drug abuse in the country. Held in September 1962, this conference lasted two days and was attended by about 500 people with different backgrounds including police, psychiatrists, and government officials. In the end, the meeting showed how little officials knew about narcotics and drug abuse. Based on that, President Kennedy appointed an official President's Advisory Commission on Narcotics and Drug Abuse.[34]

1963: President's Advisory Commission on Narcotic and Drug Abuse

Through Executive Order 11076, issued on January 15, 1963, President Kennedy established the President's Advisory Commission on Narcotic and Drug Abuse.[35] The commission was composed of seven members who were not members of the federal government, each of whom was appointed by the president. The committee members were given the task of making recommendations for legislation that would have the goal of preventing the abuse of both narcotic and nonnarcotic drugs (mostly barbiturates and amphetamines) by Americans. They were also to recommend new ways to provide rehabilitation and treatment for habitual drug users, and how to improve law enforcement programs related to narcotic drugs.

The final report, released in January 1964, included many recommendations from the committee. The commission members thought that severe penalties for the use of narcotics did not deter illicit traffic in narcotics and marijuana. Instead, they wanted to see drug users receive rehabilitative services. Therefore, one of the recommendations called for a federal civil commitment statute to allow for treatment of users and less reliance on mandatory minimum penalties. At the same time, the group recommended that illegal drug trafficking should receive more attention from the federal government, that the federal government should have the power and the responsibility to prevent the importation, manufacture, and transfer of illegal narcotic drugs in a more coordinated approach. They recommended that the Federal Bureau of Narcotics be dissolved. Finally, the group recommended that the public be more educated about the effects of narcotics and the potential for harm that could result from drug use.[36] In the end, the commission brought more attention to the problem of illicit drug use, but they were also able to refocus the nation's drug policy from punishment to rehabilitation.[37]

1970: Commission on Marihuana and Drug Abuse

When President Nixon signed the Comprehensive Drug Abuse Prevention and Control Act of 1970 (the CSA), he established the **Commission on Marihuana and Drug Abuse** (or the Shafer Commission). The commission was asked to recommend how to improve federal policy toward marijuana. The commission members carried out a comprehensive analysis of the drug by studying patterns of marijuana use and the possible addictive properties of the drug. They also examined the relationship between marijuana and violent behavior.

In 1972, the commission released issued its first report, entitled *Marihuana: A Signal of Misunderstanding*. The committee members admitted that marijuana had not been tested thoroughly and that the effects of using the drug were not understood. They estimated that a large portion of the adult population had used the drug, many out of curiosity, but a very small portion of it used it regularly. The report challenged the government's policy toward marijuana. They wrote that while previous reports described users as aggressive, irresponsible, mentally ill, and dangerous, they found that users are more likely to be passive, lethargic, and timid. They also noted that there has been no definite correlation between marijuana use and brain damage, violence, or crime. Instead, the committee acknowledged that there was a great deal of misinformation about marijuana, much of it from an intense media campaign.

The committee recommended that marijuana use be discouraged and that the government decriminalize simple possession of the drug. They recommended that penalties for nonprofit distribution of marijuana be removed as it does not create a danger to the safety of the public. The commission concluded that marijuana should be classified as a Schedule II drug.

The Nixon administration did not agree with the recommendations of the committee and ignored their conclusions. Nixon went so far as to denounce the commission prior to the final report. The commission was disbanded by President Nixon in 1973.[38]

1987: White House Conference for a Drug-Free America

In 1987, President Reagan sponsored a **White House Conference for a Drug-Free America** as a way for experts in issues relating to drug abuse education, from both the public and private sectors, to discuss drug abuse education, prevention, and treatment, and the production, trafficking, and distribution of illicit drugs. The conference gave attendees the opportunity to share information about drug abuse—what programs had been tried and how effective they were. The conference also served to increase the public's attention to different drug abuse education policies that have been successful, as well as various treatment methods that have shown promise. The role that parents and other family members play in drug abuse patterns was also a topic of discussion. Other areas of concern to those attending the conference were the circumstances that contributed to youth drug use.

Department heads of the appropriate departments attended the conference, as did the heads of military departments, relevant federal, state, and local officials, and private entities who were experts in some area of drug abuse. The goal was to make recommendations for new laws and actions to combat some of the issues raised during the conference.[39]

1987: National Drug Policy Board

The **National Drug Policy Board** was created on March 26, 1987, by President Reagan through Executive Order 12590. The board members were asked to create a National Drug Policy that would reduce the availability and use of illegal drugs in the US. Their plan was to include international approaches and new strategies for law enforcement, alongside new policies for drug prevention, education, treatment, and rehabilitation. Another task for the board was to find a way to collect information concerning patterns of drug use across the country and to support additional research. The board was asked to provide advice to the president and to Congress on policies that should be implemented to reduce illicit drug use and abuse.

The board was also given the responsibility to coordinate all groups and agencies that had a role in fighting illicit drug use. To do this, the board was asked to establish a Drug Enforcement Coordinating Group and a Drug Abuse Prevention and Health Coordinating Group, the members of which were to be designated by the chairman of the board. According to Reagan's executive order, the board was to be comprised of key cabinet members, such as the attorney general and the Secretaries of State, Treasury, Defense, and Health and Human Services, among others.[40]

1989: President's Drug Advisory Council

In 1989, President Bush created the **President's Drug Advisory Council** through Executive Order 12696. This council was given the task of making drug use "socially unacceptable" through a process called "denormalization." The members of the committee were to come up with ways to explain the National Drug Control Strategy to citizens. They could do this by working with the media, but also by sponsoring forums and seminars. In 1991 Bush extended the council through Executive Order 12755 until 1993.[41]

Reports

In addition to creating advisory commissions, presidents also request reports that can serve as advisory statements. Two of those reports are described below.

1964: Surgeon General's Reports on Tobacco

In 1964, the US Surgeon General published the first of what would become an annual report on tobacco use. The first report, entitled *Smoking and Health*, was a groundbreaking document that was based on many years of research. Over 7,000 articles about smoking, health, and disease were reviewed in the preparation of the document. The final report concluded that there were multiple health effects that were caused by smoking tobacco, including lung and laryngeal cancer, chronic bronchitis, emphysema, and coronary artery disease.

In response to these findings, the committee concluded that smoking tobacco was such a health hazard that some kind of action should be taken but it did not define what that action should be. The report was a serious blow to the tobacco industry. Similar reports that were issued almost every year after this one made similar conclusions about the effects of smoking.[42]

2001: National Research Council Report on Drug Enforcement Activities

In 2001, the National Research Council filed a report criticizing the government's War on Drugs. According to the report, the federal government spent about $12 billion per year to fund drug-enforcement programs, but there was little evidence to show that the programs solved the problem. The chairman of the committee noted that it was unacceptable that the government should spend such a high amount to fund the programs without evidence that they worked. Further, the council argued that the nation's drug enforcement measures are not based on scientific principles. There is not a clear understanding of how the drug markets operate, why people begin to use drugs, why they continue to use them, or how to help people refrain from using them. The full report was entitled "Informing America's Policy on Illegal Drugs: What We Don't Know Keeps Hurting Us."[43]

Conclusion

Presidents have great power to direct the nation's policies. This is certainly true with drug control. Beginning with President Eisenhower, the nation's leaders have each addressed illicit drugs and come up with different solutions. They are not always popular ideas, but they offer at least some policy options that will help reduce drug use in the nation. Simply by talking about the problem in various settings, the presidents are making people aware of the seriousness of the issue and the need to continue anti-drug efforts.

Important Terms

Abraham Lincoln
Barack H. Obama
Commission on Marihuana and
    Drug Abuse
Dwight D. Eisenhower

George H. W. Bush
George W. Bush
Gerald R. Ford
James E. "Jimmy" Carter
John F. Kennedy

Lyndon B. Johnson
National Drug Policy Board
National Research Council Report
on Drug Enforcement Activities
President's Advisory Commission
on Narcotic and Drug Abuse
President's Drug Advisory Council
Richard M. Nixon
Ronald W. Reagan

Special Narcotic Committee
Surgeon General's Reports on
    Tobacco
White House Conference for a
    Drug-Free America
White House Conference on
    Narcotics and Drug Abuse
William J. "Bill" Clinton

Review Questions

1. How have different presidents suggested we address drug use? Is there a difference between Republican and Democratic presidents?

2. Describe the different conferences that have been arranged to learn more about drug use. What were the conclusions of these events?

3. There were two reports described in this chapter that made recommendations on drug use. What were they and what were the conclusions made in the report?

4. If you became president of the US, what anti-drug policies would you support?

Endnotes

1. Nixon, Richard M. June 7, 1971. "Remarks about an Intensified Program for Drug Abuse Prevention and Control." Online by Gerhard Peters and John T. Woolley. *The American Presidency Project.* http://www.presidency.ucsb.edu/ws/?pid=3047.

2. Lincoln, Abraham. 1842. "Temperance Address." Abraham Lincoln Online. http://www.abrahamlincolnonline.org/lincoln/speeches/temperance.htm; Morel, Lucas E. 1999. "Lincoln Among the Reformers: Tempering the Temperance Movement." *Journal of the Abraham Lincoln Association* 20(1) (Winter). http://quod.lib.umich.edu/j/jala/2629860.0020.103/—lincoln-among-the-reformers-tempering-the-temperance?rgn=main;view=fulltext; Thompson, David DeCamp. 1901. *Abraham Lincoln and Temperance.* Chicago: Jennings and Pye; Wilson, Samuel. 2009. *Abraham Lincoln: An Apostle of Temperance and Prohibition.* Washington, DC: Library of Congress.

3. Eisenhower, Dwight D. November 27, 1954. "Letter to Heads of Departments Constituting the Interdepartmental Committee on Narcotics." Online by Gerhard Peters and John T. Woolley, *The American Presidency Project.* http://www.presidency.ucsb.edu/ws/?pid=10145; Shaffer, H. B. 1956. *Control of Drug Addiction.* Washington, DC: CQ Press. http://library.cqpress.com.

4. Kennedy, John F. January 11, 1962. "Annual Message to the Congress on the State of the Union." Online by Gerhard Peters and John T. Woolley. *American Presidency Project.* http://www.presidency.ucsb.edu/ws/?pid=9082; Kennedy, John F. September 27, 1962. "Remarks to the White House Conference on Narcotic and Drug Abuse." Online by Gerhard Peters and John T. Woolley. *American Presidency Project.* http://www.presidency.ucsb.edu/ws/?pid=8905; Kennedy, John F. May 29, 1962. "Statement by the President Announcing a Forthcoming White House Conference on Narcotics." Online by Gerhard Peters and John T. Woolley. *American Presidency Project.* http://www.presidency.ucsb.edu/ws/?pid=8686; Kennedy, John F. April 4, 1963. "Letter to the Chairman in Response to the Interim Report of the President's Advisory Commission on Narcotic and Drug Abuse." Online by Gerhard Peters and John T. Woolley. *American Presidency Project.* http://www.presidency.ucsb.edu/ws/?pid=9140.

5. Lyndon B. Johnson. July 15, 1964. "Statement by the President on Narcotic and Drug Abuse." Online by Gerhard Peters and John T. Woolley. *The American Presidency Project.* http://www.presidency.ucsb.edu/ws/?pid=26374.

6. Lyndon B. Johnson. July 15, 1965. "Remarks at the Signing of the Drug Abuse Control Amendments Bill." Online by Gerhard Peters and John T. Woolley. *The American Presidency Project.* http://www.presidency.ucsb.edu/ws/?pid=27087.

7. President's Commission on Organized Crime. 1986. "America's Habit: Drug Trafficking and Organized Crime." 220.

8. Lyndon B. Johnson. January 17, 1968. "Annual Message to the Congress on the State of the Union." Online by Gerhard Peters and John T. Woolley. *The American Presidency Project.* http://www.presidency.ucsb.edu/ws/?pid=28738.

9. Johnson, Lyndon B. July 15, 1964. "Statement by the President on Narcotic and Drug Abuse." Online by Gerhard Peters and John T. Woolley. *American Presidency Project.* http://www.presidency.ucsb.edu/ws/?pid=26374; Johnson, Lyndon B. July 15, 1965. "Remarks at the Signing of the Drug Abuse Control Amendments Bill." Online by Gerhard Peters and John T. Woolley. *American Presidency Project.* http://www.presidency.ucsb.edu/ws/?pid=27087; Johnson, Lyndon B. January 10, 1967. "State of the Union Address." http://www2.hn.psu.edu/faculty/jmanis/poldocs/uspressu/SUaddressLBJohnson.pdf; Johnson, Lyndon B. April 29, 1968. "Remarks Upon Accepting an Award from the International Narcotics Enforcement Officers Association." Online by Gerhard Peters and John T. Woolley. *American Presidency Project.* http://www.presidency.ucsb.edu/ws/?pid=28824; President's Commission on Organized Crime. 1986. "America's Habit: Drug Trafficking and Organized Crime."

10. Nixon, Richard M. June 17, 1971. "Special Message to the Congress on Drug Abuse Prevention and Control." Online by Gerhard Peters and John T. Woolley. *American Presidency Project.* http://www.presidency.ucsb.edu/ws/?pid=3048; Nixon, Richard M. January 28, 1972. "Statement on Establishing the Office for Drug Abuse in Law Enforcement." Online by Gerhard Peters and John T. Woolley. *American Presidency Project.* http://www.presidency.ucsb.edu/ws/?pid=3552.

11. Nixon, Richard. July 14, 1969. "Special Message to the Congress on Control of Narcotics and Dangerous Drugs." Online by Gerhard Peters and John T. Woolley. *American Presidency Project.* http://www.presidency.ucsb.edu/ws/?pid=2126; Nixon, Richard. August 21, 1970. "Joint Statement Following Discussions with President Diaz Ordaz of Mexico." Online by Gerhard Peters and John T. Woolley. *American Presidency Project.* http://www.presidency.ucsb.edu/ws/?pid=2640; Nixon, Richard. March 15, 1973. "The President's News Conference." Online by Gerhard Peters and John T. Woolley. *American Presidency Project.*

http://www.presidency.ucsb.edu/ws/?pid=4142; Nixon, Richard. March 10, 1973. "Radio Address about the State of the Union Message on Law Enforcement and Drug Abuse Prevention." Online by Gerhard Peters and John T. Woolley. *American Presidency Project.* http://www.presidency.ucsb.edu/ws/?pid=4135; Nixon, Richard M. March 14, 1973. "State of the Union Message to the Congress on Law Enforcement and Drug Abuse Prevention." Online by Gerhard Peters and John T. Woolley. *American Presidency Project.* http://www.presidency.ucsb.edu/ws/?pid=4140.

12. Nixon, Richard. March 28, 1973. "Message to the Congress Transmitting Reorganization Plan 2 of 1973 Establishing the Drug Enforcement Administration." Online by Gerhard Peters and John T. Woolley. *The American Presidency Project.* http://www.presidency.ucsb.edu/ws/?pid=4159.

13. Ford, Gerald. April 1976. *Gerald R. Ford's Special Message to the Congress on Drug Abuse.* Speech Presented at the White House. http://www.fordlibrarymuseum.gov/library/speeches/760368.htm.

14. Ford, Gerald. 1974. *Proclamation 4328 Drug Abuse Prevention Week, 1974.* http://www.presidency.ucsb.edu/ws/index.php?pid=23880; "Gerald Ford on Drugs." July 11, 2013. *On the Issues: Every Political Leader on Every Issue.* http://www.ontheissues.org/celeb/Gerald_Ford_Drugs.htm; President's Commission on Organized Crime. 1986. *America's Habit: Drug Trafficking and Organized Crime.*

15. Carter, Jimmy. August 2, 1977. "Drug Abuse Message to the Congress." Online by Gerhard Peters and John T. Woolley. *The American Presidency Project.* http://www.presidency.ucsb.edu/ws/?pid=7908; Carter, Jimmy. 1977. "Rethinking the War on Drugs." New York: Encyclopedia Americana/CBS News Audio Resource Library #08773; Carter, Jimmy. June 16, 2011. "Call off the Global Drug War." *New York Times.* http://www.nytimes.com/2011/06/17/opinion/17carter.html?_r=0.

16. De Grazia, Jessica. 1991. *DEA: The War Against Drugs.* London: BBC Books; McCoy, Alfred W., and Alan A. Block. 1992. "U.S. Narcotics Policy: An Anatomy of Failure." In *War on Drugs: Studies in the Failure of U.S. Narcotics Policy.* Boulder, CO: Westview Press; Morgan, H. Wayne. 1981. *Drugs in America: A Social History, 1800–1980.* Syracuse, NY: Syracuse University Press; President's Commission on Organized Crime. 1986. *America's Habit: Drug Trafficking and Organized Crime.* Shaffer Library of Drug Policy, http://www.druglibrary.org/schaffer/GovPubs/amhab/amhabc3.htm.

17. Reagan, Ronald. 1982. "Radio Address to the Nation on the Federal Drug Policy." http://www.presidency.ucsb.edu/ws/?pid=43085#axzz2iZ84KMbF.

18. Glass, Andrew. October 14, 1982. "Reagan Declares 'War on Drugs,'" *Politico.* http://www.politico.com/news/stories/1010/43552.html.

19. Davenport-Hines, Richard. 2001. *The Pursuit of Oblivion: A Global History of Narcotics, 1500–2000.* London: Weidenfeld & Nicolson; Reagan, Ronald. 1996. *The Uncommon Wisdom of Ronald Reagan: A Portrait in His Words.* Boston: Little, Brown and Company.

20. Cooper, Mary H. 1990. *The Business of Drugs.* Washington, DC: Congressional Quarterly.

21. Bagley, Bruce. 1989–1990. "Dateline Drug Wars Colombia: The Wrong Strategy." *Foreign Affairs* (Winter): 54; Bagley, Bruce M. 1996. *The Drug War in Colombia.* Wilmington, DE: Scholarly Resources; Podesta, Don, and Douglas Farah. March 27, 1993. "Drug Policing in the Andes." *Washington Post.*

22. Isenberg, David. July 7, 1990. "Military Options in the War on Drugs." *USA Today*; Isikoff, Michael. September 16, 1993. "U.S. Considers Shift in Drug War." *Washington Post*;

Klare, Michael T. January 1990. "Fighting Drugs with the Military." *Nation*.

23. "Clinton Pushing Anti-Drug Plan." December 2, 1992. *Miami Herald*. International Satellite Edition; "New Drug Strategy Needed." November 18–24, 1996. *Colombia Post*; Teaster, Joseph A. October 31, 1993. "Exiting Drug War Chief Warns of Cartels." *New York Times*; US General Accounting Office. 1996. *Drug Control: U.S. Interdiction Efforts in Caribbean Decline*; Wren, Christopher. February 21, 1994. *New International Drug Strategy Needed to Combat Drugs*. United States Department of State Dispatch; York, Byron. February 1994. "Clinton's Phony War." *American Spectator*.

24. Anti-Drug Media Campaign. http://www.whitehouse.gov/ondcp/anti-drug-media-campaign; Carpenter, C. S., and C. Pechmann. 2011. "Exposure to the Above the Influence Antidrug Advertisements and Adolescent Marijuana Use in the United States, 2006–2008." *American Journal of Public Health* 101(5): 948–54; Fishbein, Martin, Kathleen Hall-Jamieson, Eric Zimmer, Ina von Haeften, and Robin Nabi. 2002. "Avoiding the Boomerang: Testing the Relative Effectiveness of Antidrug Public Service Announcements Before a National Campaign." *American Journal of Public Health* 92(2): 238–45; Library of Congress, Congressional Research Service. 2009. "The War on Drugs: The National Youth Anti-Drug Media Campaign"; Office of National Drug Control Policy. 2010. "National Youth Anti-Drug Media Campaign." Washington, DC: Office of National Drug Control Policy, Executive Office of the President; Palmgreen, P., E. P. Lorch, M. T. Stephenson, R. H. Hoyle, and L. Donohew. 2007. "Effects of the Office of National Drug Control Policy's Marijuana Initiative Campaign on High-Sensation-Seeking Adolescents." *American Journal of Public Health* 97(9): 1644–49; Rich, Frank. July 15, 1998. "Just Say $1 Billion." *New York Times*. http://www.nytimes.com/1998/07/15/opinion/journal-just-say-1-billion.html?ref=frankrich; US Government Accountability Office. 2006. "ONDCP Media Campaign: Contractor's National Evaluation Did Not Find That the Youth Anti-Drug Media Campaign Was Effective in Reducing Youth Drug Use." Washington, DC: US Government Accountability Office.

25. Bush, George W. May 10, 2001. "Remarks Announcing the Nomination of John P. Walters to Be Director of the Office of National Drug Control Policy." Online by Gerhard Peters and John T. Woolley. *The American Presidency Project*. http://www.presidency.ucsb.edu/ws/?pid=45600.

26. Bush, George W. January 20, 2004. "Address Before a Joint Session of the Congress on the State of the Union." Online by Gerhard Peters and John T. Woolley, *The American Presidency Project*. http://www.presidency.ucsb.edu/ws/?pid=29646; Bush, George W. April 21, 2001. "Remarks at the Summit of the Americas Working Session in Quebec City." Online by Gerhard Peters and John T. Woolley. *The American Presidency Project*. http://www.presidency.ucsb.edu/ws/?pid=45633.

27. Bush, George W. April 10, 2001. "Proclamation 7425—National D.A.R.E. Day, 2001." Online by Gerhard Peters and John T. Woolley. *The American Presidency Project*. http://www.presidency.ucsb.edu/ws/?pid=61722.

28. Bush, George W. November 9, 2001. "Proclamation 7496—National Alcohol and Drug Addiction Recovery Month." Online by Gerhard Peters and John T. Woolley. *The American Presidency Project*. http://www.presidency.ucsb.edu/ws/?pid=61793.

29. Bruce, Mary. December 19, 2013. "Obama Commutes Eight 'Unduly Harsh' Crack Cocaine Sentences." *ABC News*. http://abcnews.go.com/blogs/politics/2013/12/obama-commutes-eight-unduly-harsh-crack-cocaine-sentences/; Dwyer, Devin. August 12, 2013. "Obama's Own Drug Use a Backdrop to More Lenient Sentences." *ABC News*. http://abcnewsgo.com/blogs/politics/2013/08/obamas-own-drug-use-a-backdrop-to-more-lenient--

sentences/; Savage, Charlie. December 19, 2013. "Obama Commutes Sentences for 8 in Crack Cocaine Cases." *New York Times*. http://www.nytimes.com/2013/12/20/us/obama-commuting-sentences-in-crack-cocaine-cases.html?pagewanted=all&_r=0.

30. Office of National Drug Control Policy, Office of Public Affairs. 2013. "Fact Sheet: A 21st Century Drug Policy." http://www.whitehouse.gov/sites/default/files/ondcp/policy-and-research/2013_strategy_fact_sheet.pdf.

31. Office of National Drug Control Policy. 2010. "Marijuana Legalization." http://www.whitehouse.gov/ondcp-fact-sheets/marijuana-legalization.

32. Ingram, David. August 29, 2013. "U.S. Allows States to Legalize Recreational Marijuana within Limits." *Reuters*. http://www.reuters.com/article/2013/08/29/us-usa-crime-marijuana-idUSBRE97S0YW20130829; Office of National Drug Control Policy. 2010. "Marijuana Legalization." http://www.whitehouse.gov/ondcp-fact-sheets/marijuana-legalization.

33. Acker, Caroline Jean. 2002. *Creating the American Junkie: Addiction Research in the Classic Era of Narcotic Control*. Baltimore: Johns Hopkins University Press; "More than 1,000,000 Drug Users in U.S." June 13, 1919. *New York Times*; Musto, David F. 1987. *The American Disease: Origins of Narcotic Control*. Expanded Edition. New York: Oxford University Press.

34. Jonnes, Jill. 1996. *Hep-Cats, Narcs and Pipe Dreams*. New York: Scribner; President's Commission on Organized Crime. 1986. *America's Habit: Drug Trafficking and Organized Crime*.

35. Federal Register. 1963; *Congress and the Nation*. 1965, 1194; President's Drug Advisory Council, Executive Office of the President of the United States, 1963.

36. *Congress and the Nation*. 1965, 1194; President's Drug Advisory Council, Executive Office of the President of the United States, 1963; "Executive Orders Disposition Tables John. F. Kennedy—1963." National Archives. Federal Register. 28 FR 477. http://www.archives.gov/federal-register/executive-orders/1963-kennedy.html; "President's Advisory Commission on Narcotic and Drug Abuse: Final Report." 1963. President's Drug Advisory Council, Executive Office of the President of the United States of America. *National Criminal Justice Reference Service*. https://www.ncjrs.gov/App/Publications/abstract.aspx?ID=164685; "Narcotics, 1945–1964 Legislative Overview." 1965. *Congress and the Nation*, 1945–1964, vol. 1, 1193–94. Washington, DC: CQ Press, 1965. http://library.cqpress.com/catn/catn45-4-18126–975530; Johnson, Lyndon B. 1964. "Statement by the President on Narcotic and Drug Abuse." Online by Gerhard T. Peters and John T. Wooley. *American Presidency Project*. http://www.presidency.ucsb.edu/ws/?pid=26374.

37. Johnson, Lyndon B. January 28, 1964. "Letter to Judge Prettyman in Response to Report of the President's Advisory Commission on Narcotic and Drug Abuse." Online by Gerhard Peters and John T. Woolley. *American Presidency Project*. http://www.presidency.ucsb.edu/ws/?pid=26042; Johnson, Lyndon B. July 15, 1964. "Statement by the President on Narcotic and Drug Abuse" Online by Gerhard Peters and John T. Woolley. *American Presidency Project*. http://www.presidency.ucsb.edu/ws/?pid=26374; Johnson, Lyndon B. March 8, 1965. "Special Message to the Congress on Law Enforcement and the Administration of Justice." Online by Gerhard Peters and John T. Woolley. *American Presidency Project*. http://www.presidency.ucsb.edu/ws/?pid=26800; Kennedy, John F. January 15, 1963. "Executive Order 11076." Online by Gerhard Peters and John T. Woolley. *American Presidency Project*. http://www.presidency.ucsb.edu/ws/?pid=59015; President's Drug Advisory Council, Executive Office of the President. 1963. "President's Advisory Commission

on Narcotic and Drug Abuse: Final Report."

38. "Comprehensive Drug Control Bill Cleared by Congress." 1971. In *CQ Almanac 1970*, 26th ed., 03-531-03-539. Washington, DC: Congressional Quarterly. http://library. cqpress.com/cqalmanac/cqal70-1293935; National Commission on Marihuana and Drug Use. 1972. *Marihuana: A Signal of Misunderstanding*. Washington, DC: US Government Printing Office. http://www.druglibrary.org/schaffer/library/studies/nc/ncmenu.htm; Nixon, Richard. May 1, 1971. "The President's News Conference." Online by Gerhard Peters and John T. Woolley. *The American Presidency Project*. http://www.presidency.ucsb.edu/ws/?pid= 2995; Nixon, Richard. June 17, 1971. "Remarks About an Intensified Program for Drug Abuse Prevention and Control." Online by Gerhard Peters and John T. Woolley. *The American Presidency Project*. http://www.presidency.ucsb.edu/ws/?pid=3047; Nixon Presidential Library and Museum. "FG 308 (Commission on Marihuana and Drug Abuse)." http://www.nixonlibrary.org/forresearchers/find/textual/central/subject/FG308.php; NORML. March 21, 2002. "Nixon Commission Report Advising Decriminalization of Marijuana Celebrates 30th Anniversary." http://www.norml.org/news/2002/03/21/nixon-commission-report-advising-decriminalization-of-marijuana-celebrates-30th-anniversary; NORML. March 22, 2007. "National Commission on Marihuana Celebrates 35th Anniversary." http:// norml.org/news/2007/03/22/national-commission-on-marihuana-celebrates-35th-anniversary; NORML. March 21, 2012. "Forty Years Ago This Week: National Commission on Marihuana Recommends Decriminalizing Cannabis." http://www.norml.org/news/2012/03/21/ forty-years-ago-this-week-national-commission-on-marihuana-recommends-decriminalizing-cannabis; Sterling, Eric A. March 21, 2013. "Shafer Commission Report on Marijuana and Drugs, Issued 40 Years Ago Today, Was Ahead of Its Time" *Huff Post Politics*. http:// www.huffingtonpost.com/eric-e-sterling/shafer-commission-report-b-2925777.html?.

39. US White House, Office of the President. May 5, 1987. "Executive Order 12595— White House Conference for a Drug Free America." http://www.reagan.utexas.edu/archives/ speeches/1987/050587e.htm.

40. Reagan, Ronald. March 26, 1987. "Executive Order 12590—National Drug Policy Board." Online by Gerhard Peters and John T. Woolley. *American Presidency Project*. http:// www.presidency.ucsb.edu/ws/?pid=34026; Reagan, Ronald. October 3, 1988. "Remarks to the National Drug Policy Board." Online by Gerhard Peters and John T. Woolley. *American Presidency Project*. http://www.presidency.ucsb.edu/ws/?pid=34956.

41. Bush, G. H. W. November 13, 1989. "Executive Order No. 12696 President's Drug Advisory Council." Online by Gerhard Peters and John T. Woolley. *American Presidency Project*. http://www.presidency.ucsb.edu/ws/?pid=23542#axzz2i0WrRVB0; Bush, G. H. W. July 22, 1992. "Remarks to the President's Drug Advisory Council." Online by Gerhard Peters and John T. Woolley. *American Presidency Project*. http://www.presidency.ucsb.edu/ws/ ?pid=21252#ixzz2i0kJwMUX; Bush, G. H. W. March 18, 1991. "Executive Order No. 12756 Continuance of the President's Drug Advisory Council." Online by Gerhard Peters and John T. Woolley. *American Presidency Project*. http://www.presidency.ucsb.edu/ws/?pid= 23595#ixzz2i0pRvhuI; "President Names 27 to Newly Created Advisory Council on Drugs." November 14, 1989. *New York Times*. http://www.nytimes.com/1989/11/14/us/president-names-27-to-newly-created-advisory-council-on-drugs.html.

42. Brandt, Allan M. 2007. *The Cigarette Century: The Rise, Fall, and Deadly Persistence of the Product That Defined America*. New York: Basic Books; Cordry, Harold V. 2001. *Tobacco: A Reference Handbook*. Santa Barbara, CA: ABC-CLIO; US Public Health Services. Office of the Surgeon General. 1988. *The Health Consequences of Smoking—Nicotine Ad-*

diction: A Report of the Surgeon General. http://profiles.nlm.nih.gov/NN/B/B/Z/D/_/nnb bzd.pdf; US Surgeon General's Advisory Committee on Smoking and Health. 1964. *Smoking and Health: Report of the Advisory Committee to the Surgeon General of the Public Health Service.* http://profiles.nlm.nih.gov/NN/B/B/M/Q/_/nnbbmq.pdf.

43. Manski, Charles F., John V. Pepper, and Carol V. Petrie. 2013. "What We Don't Know Keeps Hurting Us." Washington, DC: National Academies. http://www.nap.edu/openbook.php?record_id=10021; National Academy of Sciences. "Data Sorely Lacking on Effectiveness of Nation's Drug-Enforcement Programs." http://www8.nationalacademies.org/onpinews/newsitem.aspx?RecordID=10021.

Chapter 8

The Politics of Drug Use: Agencies and Interest Groups

Chapter Objective: The focus of this chapter is on the bureaucracies that have been created to either advise the president on drug use policy, or to carry out the policies passed by Congress. Also in this chapter is a review of some interest groups that are involved in influencing the government's response to the public's continued use of illicit drugs.

Introduction

There have been many agencies set up to address problems related to drug use and abuse. Some have been short-lived, whereas others have been long-term; some have had a very narrow focus and others have a larger focus. Nonetheless, they have each played a role in the political debate about drugs and had some influence on the drug policy carried out at that time. This chapter provides information on the different agencies and bureaucracies that have played, or currently play, a role in the country's drug policies.

Agencies

1938: *Food and Drug Administration*

One of the earliest agencies to play a role in the nation's drug policy was the Food and Drug Administration (FDA), which was originally created in 1862 as the Department of Chemistry. The FDA is the federal agency that ensures that the medicines people take are safe. In the beginning, this agency was responsible for regulating the safety of food, but their oversight of drugs (patent medicines, prescription drugs, and narcotics) and then tobacco became a greater concern in later years.

The Food, Drug, and Cosmetic Act passed in 1938, which increased the FDA's power to regulate drugs. Drug manufacturers had to prove to the FDA that their drugs were safe for consumers, and all drugs had to be labeled with directions for safe use. From 1940 through the 1960s, the illegal sale and use of amphetamines and barbiturates was a primary concern of the FDA. To aid in this work, Congress granted the FDA increased authority over drugs when they passed the 1965 Drug Abuse Control Amendments.

In the mid-1990s, the FDA began to regulate tobacco products. The commissioner of the FDA at the time, David Kessler, argued that such regulation would be warranted if cigarettes were viewed as nicotine-delivery devices. With the approval of President Clinton, Kessler relied on the Food, Drug, and Cosmetic Act to define cigarettes as a method to deliver drugs, thereby giving the FDA the ability to regulate all products that contain nicotine. They also now regulate advertising and sale of tobacco products to minors.

The tobacco industry responded by suing the FDA, claiming that cigarettes did not fit the Food, Drug, and Cosmetic Act's definition of a drug or drug-delivery device. The Supreme Court agreed with the tobacco industry, deciding in a 5–4 decision that the FDA did not have the jurisdiction to regulate tobacco products. However, the FDA regained control over tobacco after Congress passed the Family Smoking Prevention and Tobacco Control Act in 2009.[1]

Today the FDA is housed within the Department of Health and Human Services and is one of the largest organizations in government. It regulates the safety, effectiveness, quality, and labeling of both prescription and nonprescription (over-the-counter) medications and drugs and their manufacturing standards.[2]

1919: Prohibition Unit

The **Prohibition Unit**, formed in 1919 and later renamed the Prohibition Bureau in 1927, was the federal agency that enforced the nation's laws on Prohibition and the Volstead Act when alcohol use was illegal from 1919 until 1933. The Narcotics Division of the Prohibition Unit enforced provisions of the Harrison Narcotics Act until 1930. While the Prohibition Unit struggled to enforce the law on alcohol, its Narcotics Division was successful in enforcing the nation's drug laws.

Prohibition agents were given the authority to seize and sell any vehicles that were used to transport illegal liquor and could close any establishment that was used to manufacture or sell illegal alcohol. They could also arrest any-one who was manufacturing, transporting, or using alcohol. Anyone taken into custody could be fined up to $1,000 and sent to jail for six months. Those who violated the Harrison Act could be tracked by the Narcotic Division. This included people who used illegal drugs, drug dealers, and physicians who pre-scribed opiates.

The Prohibition Unit was underfunded, understaffed, in some cases uneth-ical, and faced a public that did not support the law they were tasked with en-forcing. Prohibition was repealed in 1933, and the Prohibition Bureau was subsequently shut down. In 1930, the job of enforcing laws concerning alcohol was given to the Bureau of Alcohol, Tobacco and Firearms, and enforcement of federal drug laws was given to a new federal agency, the Federal Bureau of Narcotics.[3]

1930: Federal Bureau of Narcotics (FBN)

The **Federal Bureau of Narcotics** (FBN) was created in 1930 to enforce the nation's narcotics laws, and they did so until 1968. The head of the FBN was Harry J. Anslinger. FBN agents spent most of their time focused on those who were using drugs recreationally and those who were trafficking in illicit drugs. The primary focus of the FBN was to cut off the illicit drug traffic coming into the US, as well as the trafficking of controlled substances within the US. Because of inadequate funding, agents did not arrest any major smugglers and there were calls for it to be broken up. But it was given new responsibilities when the Marijuana Tax Act was passed in 1937.

During World War II, drug smuggling and use decreased as drug trade routes were interrupted. When the war ended in 1945, Anslinger predicted that drug smuggling would resume as the trade routes opened again, and so he sought new laws that would impose mandatory minimum sentences for individuals con-victed of violating a federal drug law. Congress agreed with Anslinger and passed the Boggs Act in 1951. The act was intended to be a deterrent for drug users and dealers, as it required that judges impose specific sentences on offenders.

The FBN came under criticism for intimidating physicians and others in the medical field and for their tough, anti-crime policies. Anslinger retired in 1962 and in 1963, a report from the Presidential Commission on Narcotic and Drug Abuse recommended that mandatory minimum sentences be less-ened and that the FBN be abolished. In 1968, the FBN was merged with the Bureau of Drug Abuse Control, renamed the Bureau of Narcotics and Dan-gerous Drugs, and transferred from the Treasury Department to the Justice Department.[4]

U.S. ATF Alcohol Tobacco and Firearm dept building by blvdone via fotolia.com.

1920s: Bureau of Alcohol, Tobacco, Firearms and Explosives (ATF)

When the Prohibition Unit dissolved, their responsibilities were given to the **Bureau of Alcohol, Tobacco, and Firearms** (BATF). The BATF (now BAFTE with the addition of explosives) is a federal law enforcement organization located in the Department of Justice that is responsible for enforcing laws related to alcohol and tobacco products. When first created, the ATF had the authority to regulate the permitting, labeling, and marketing of tobacco and alcohol. However, in the Homeland Security Act of 2002, those responsibilities were placed in the newly created Alcohol and Tobacco Tax and Trade Bureau (TTB). The ATF no longer regulates the alcohol or tobacco industries, but instead focuses on illegal smuggling and trafficking of alcohol and tobacco.[5]

1933: Federal Alcohol Control Administration (FACA) and Federal Alcohol Administration (FAA)

When Prohibition was repealed in 1933, President Roosevelt issued Executive Order 6474 that established the **Federal Alcohol Control Adminis-**

tration (FACA). He asked this agency to oversee the growing legal alcohol industry. FACA was intended to provide guidance and assistance to those who owned and operated wineries and distilleries. In 1935, the Supreme Court decided the case of *Schechter Poultry Co v. United States*, in which they deemed the FACA to be unconstitutional. The FACA was disbanded and replaced with the Federal Alcohol Administration (FAA) within the Treasury Department. It was given the task of collecting data, establishing license and permit requirements, and defining regulations to help ensure that there was an open and fair marketplace for the legitimate alcohol industry. In 1940, the FAA merged with the Alcohol Tax Unit.

According to laws passed at the time, alcohol importers, producers, wholesalers, state agencies, and individuals had to have a permit before being able to distribute alcohol. In addition, these individuals could not have a felony conviction on their record within the five years prior to the application date, nor could they have a misdemeanor conviction relating to a federal liquor law within the previous three years. The FAA was the agency that approved these permits or revoked them as needed. Those people who were not likely to operate a business legally could be prohibited from entering into the business. Another responsibility of the FAA was to ensure that products were labeled lawfully and that advertising of alcohol beverages provide adequate information to the consumer about the product. It was illegal to have misleading labels or deceptive advertising.

Today, measures of the FAA Act are carried out under the Bureau of Alcohol, Tobacco, and Firearms.[6]

1946: Centers for Disease Control and Prevention (CDC)

Founded in 1946, the **Centers for Disease Control and Prevention** (CDC) was established to be the "nation's health protection agency." It a federal agency within the Department of Health and Human Services and is one of the best known National Public Health Institutes. The agency works to protect public health and safety by preventing disease, injury, and disability.

The CDC plays a major role in the fight against drug abuse. The primary federal organization to limit tobacco use is the Office on Smoking and Health. Established in 1965, the agency develops policies aimed at reducing deaths and diseases that result from tobacco use. The CDC also has created programs that attack excessive alcohol use.

Another program in the CDC spotlights illicit drug use. Here, the goal is to educate the public about the dangers and consequences of illegal drugs. They carry out research on the link between drug use, the brain, and behavior.

They track trends in drug use and patterns of drug use over time. For anyone who has become addicted to drugs, the CDC helps with treatment options.

One of their primary target audiences when it comes to drugs and drug use is youth. According to the CDC, alcohol and drug use among youth is a serious public health problem. They work to develop programs to prevent this behavior. They also monitor behaviors that contribute to deaths of young adults in their Youth Risk Behavior Surveillance System. Some of these behaviors are alcohol, tobacco, and other drug use.[7]

1965: Bureau of Drug Abuse Control

The **Bureau of Drug Abuse Control** (BDAC) was established in December 1965, by President Johnson. Originally housed within the Food and Drug Administration, the new agency was given the task of implementing the Drug Abuse Control Amendments Act also passed in 1965. The first director of the agency was John Finlator, who publicly supported the policy of putting marijuana smokers in prison (even though he did not personally support that idea). To increase the public's support for his anti-drug campaign, Finlator invited Elvis Presley to the White House and arranged for Presley to receive a badge to give him "consultant" credentials.

The BDAC was responsible for enforcing the laws on depressants, stimulants, and hallucinogens that were used most frequently by the emerging "counterculture." In 1968, the BDAC merged with the Federal Bureau of Narcotics to create the **Bureau of Narcotics and Dangerous Drugs** (BNDD).[8]

After he retired, Finlator wrote a book entitled *Drugged Nation: A Narc's Story*. He also worked for the National Organization for Reform of Marijuana Laws (NORML), a group that advocated the decriminalization of marijuana.

1968: Bureau of Narcotics and Dangerous Drugs (BNDD)

In 1968, President Johnson consolidated two existing agencies to create the new Bureau of Narcotics and Dangerous Drugs that would be housed in the Department of Justice. To create the new agency, Johnson consolidated the Federal Bureau of Narcotics (FBN) from the Department of the Treasury and the Bureau of Drug Abuse Control (BDAC) from the Food and Drug Administration. Johnson gave the BNDD the task of controlling stimulants such as methamphetamines and hallucinogens.

The director of the BNDD was John Ingersoll, a police official from California. He served in that position from the time the agency was created until the agency was eliminated. The BNDD placed attention on international and interstate trafficking of drugs. The agency also provided training programs for local law enforcement so they could more effectively enforce drug laws. A critical role of the BNDD was to oversee people who registered with the government as distributors of marijuana.

The BNDD faced many critics who pointed out that drug use increased during its existence, especially by young people. The agency was abolished in 1973 by President Nixon when he created the Drug Enforcement Administration (DEA).[9]

1970: National Institute on Alcohol Abuse and Alcoholism (NIAAA)

The **National Institute on Alcohol Abuse and Alcoholism** (NIAAA) was formed in 1970 when President Nixon signed the Comprehensive Alcohol Abuse and Alcoholism Prevention, Treatment and Rehabilitation Act. The agency was the first one to focus on alcohol use since the Prohibition Bureau. The agency funded and carried out research on alcohol use based on the perception that alcoholism is a public health issue and those who are addicted to alcohol need medical treatment.

After receiving complaints about how the NIAA was funding research, the agency was reorganized by President Reagan in 1981. It was moved to the National Institutes of Health, along with other organizations like the Alcohol, Drug Abuse, and Mental Health Administration and the National Institute on Drug Abuse. The reorganization made the NIAAA into a research organization.[10]

1972: Office for Drug Abuse Law Enforcement (ODALE)

During the 1970s, many people wanted to see the government pass stricter policies to crack down on drug use and trafficking. President Nixon established the **Office for Drug Abuse Law Enforcement** (ODALE) on January 28, 1972, through Executive Order 11641. The new office was placed in the Department of Justice. The purpose of ODALE was to remove drug traffickers from the streets. Employees in the program were to cooperate with regional offices and special grand juries to collect and review information about drug traffickers, and then assist local agencies to detect, arrest, and prosecute heroin traffickers more efficiently.

The goal behind these programs supported Nixon's overall approach to the drug menace—that the federal drug programs be balanced and comprehensive.

He sought ways to fight against those who were trafficking the drugs, and at the same time help those who have been victimized by drugs and protect those who have not yet been threatened by drugs. He wanted law enforcement to stop anyone who might profit from drugs. At the same time, Nixon though it was important to have quality treatment facilities for those addicts who sought treatment.

Despite Nixon's attempts to coordinate the different agencies, the organizations did not communicate well with the others. ODALE was eventually consolidated with other federal anti-drug agencies (the Bureau of Narcotics and Dangerous Drugs, the Office of National Narcotics Intelligence, and the Customs Service Investigation Unit) to become the Drug Enforcement Administration. Another agency created was the Office of National Narcotics Intelligence, which was responsible for collecting, analyzing, and identifying drug intelligence.[11]

1973: Drug Enforcement Administration (DEA)

The **Drug Enforcement Agency** (DEA) was created in 1973 when President Nixon reorganized existing agencies that enforced drug laws in some way. Through Reorganization Plan Number 2, he proposed a single federal agency to coordinate the government's drug control efforts and made it official in an executive order. The new organization, the **DEA**, was tasked with coordinating all federal drug control efforts. In the early 1980s, the DEA began working under the FBI.

The DEA has become the federal agency that enforces the nation's drug laws. Agents often cooperate with local law enforcement agencies to exchange intelligence and expertise to investigate and prosecute people who have violated federal drug laws. They can seize assets from criminals if they are related to drug trafficking. The DEA also cooperates with international offices through its field offices in 63 countries to coordinate transnational drug control efforts. They oversee the Department of Justice's Asset Forfeiture Program, which confiscates the money and property of major drug traffickers. It uses aircraft to track smuggling operations. It oversees crop eradication programs both domestically and in foreign countries. They help ensure that substances produced for legitimate medical purposes are not diverted to the black market. The DEA has a laboratory to test seized samples and build cases against major drug traffickers. The DEA also has agents who serve as Demand Reduction Coordinators, who work with community leaders, organizations, and the general public to help educate the public on the dangers of illicit drug use.[12]

1974: National Institute on Drug Abuse (NIDA)

The **National Institute on Drug Abuse** (NIDA) is the federal agency that oversees the government's research on drug abuse and addiction. NIDA's mission is to advance knowledge on addiction and drug abuse. Their research focuses on gaining a deeper understanding of how drugs affect a user's brain and body. They also work to develop and test alternative approaches for treatment and prevention.

In 1975, NIDA began the Monitoring the Future Survey and the Research Monograph Series. The Monitoring the Future Survey is a questionnaire of high school seniors that measures levels of nonmedical drug use and attitudes towards it. The Research Monograph Series is comprised of publications supported by NIDA and used to educate the public about addiction, treatment, and prevention. In 1976, NIDA instituted the Community Epidemiology Work Group, which provided an opportunity for local and state representatives to meet with NIDA staff to exchange information on drug abuse trends in their communities and identify at-risk populations. In the 1980s, NIDA conducted research into IV drug use and HIV, as well as the link between them. In 1999 it created the Transdisciplinary Tobacco Use Research Centers to study tobacco addiction.[13]

1982: Organized Crime Drug Enforcement Task Forces Program

In 1982, the **Organized Crime Drug Enforcement Task Forces Program** (OCDETF) was established. The goal of this agency was to attack organized drug traffickers by disrupting their organizations and thus their drug operations. The OCDETF brought together many different agencies that each had the goal of reducing drug-related crime, such as federal and state law enforcement personnel from major cities around the country. These agencies collected and shared intelligence on trafficking organizations, using that information to go after organized traffickers. This approach created a national, coordinated attack against drug traffickers.[14]

1983: National Narcotics Border Interdiction System (NNBIS)

Established in 1983 by President Reagan, the **National Narcotics Border Interdiction System** brought together 13 different task forces that included many officials from both federal and state agencies. The personnel monitored suspected drug smuggling activity that began outside of the US. Officials would then use that information to arrest those involved and seize the contraband as a way to stop the flow of drugs into the US. The NNBIS would work closely with the Drug Enforcement Administration (DEA) and the Department of Justice.

In 1984, the NNBIS was criticized after the head of the DEA, Frances Mullen Jr., claimed that the NNBIS may have hindered the DEA from being more effective. More criticism was heard in 1985, after the General Accountability Office announced that the NNBIS was largely ineffective in halting drug traffickers.[15]

1988: Office of National Drug Control Policy (ONDCP)

Created by the Anti-Drug Abuse Act of 1988, the **Office of National Drug Control Policy** (ONDCP) is an agency housed within the Executive Office of the President that oversees the government's anti-drug plan. Specifically, the office helps to create the country's priorities on drug control and then seeks to develop and implement the strategies. They also work with federal, state, and local agencies to coordinate policies and actions to fight drug abuse.

The law mandated three positions, including the director (more commonly known as the "Drug Czar"), the deputy director for demand reduction and the deputy director for supply reduction. Two new offices were also created: The Office for Demand Reduction that helps to coordinate prevention, treatment, and recovery policies for federal agencies and the Office of Supply Reduction that coordinates the international policies.

Each year, the ONDCP publishes the National Drug Control Strategy, a document that outlines the administration's priorities and goals for drug reduction, as required by the Anti-Drug Abuse Act of 1988. The report must be research-based and comprehensive. It provides a plan to reduce illicit drug use and availability in the United States, along with plans to reduce the manufacture and distribution of illicit drugs and the crime and violence associated with them. Another goal is to reduce the health consequences that result from the use of illicit drugs. There are both domestic and international components in the report, as well as federal, state, and local plans. It also contains components of drug treatment, prevention, and interdiction.[16] For example, a report issued by the Obama administration in 2013 has included goals that should be met by 2015. They are outlined in Table 8.1.

> ## Table 8.1 2013 Drug Control Strategy Goals
>
> **Goal 1:** Curtail illicit drug consumption in America.
>
> 1a. Decrease the 30-day prevalence of drug use among 12–17-year-olds by 15 percent.
>
> 1b. Decrease the lifetime prevalence of 8th graders who have used drugs, alcohol, or tobacco by 15 percent.
>
> 1c. Decrease the 30-day prevalence of drug use among young adults aged 18–25 by 10 percent.
>
> 1d. Reduce the number of chronic drug users by 15 percent.
>
> **Goal 2:** Improve the public health and public safety of the American people by reducing the consequences of drug abuse.
>
> 2a. Reduce drug-induced deaths by 15 percent.
>
> 2b. Reduce drug-related morbidity by 15 percent.
>
> 2c. Reduce the prevalence of drugged driving by 10 percent.

The 2013 Report includes four supplemental strategies: the Prescription Drug Abuse Action Plan, Increasing Security along the Southwest Border, Strategy to Combat Transnational Organized Crime, and National Northern Border Counternarcotics Strategy. These individual plans provide more details of the strategies ONDCP has developed to control drug abuse.

In addition to the National Drug Control Strategy, the ONDCP manages three critical drug control programs. The first is the High Intensity Drug Trafficking Area Program (HIDTA); the second is the National Youth Anti-Drug Media Campaign (Media Campaign); and the third is the Drug-Free Communities Program (DFC).

The first of the programs, HIDTA, identifies regions of the country that experience the most drug trafficking. Law enforcement in these areas are encouraged to cooperate and share intelligence. The second program, the Media Campaign, is an attempt to educate youth about the dangers of drug use by the use of both traditional and social media. The slogan, "Above the Influence," has a large presence in social media. The third program, the DFC, provides funding to community organizations that seek to reduce drug use by youth in their neighborhoods.[17]

In 1998, the Office of National Drug Control Policy Reauthorization Act was passed by Congress. This law expanded the duties of the organization and required that the agency develop a long-term drug control policy, among other things. The agency was again reauthorized in the Office of National Drug Control Policy Reauthorization Act of 2006. In this law, the position of the US interdiction coordinator and the Interdiction Committee were created.[18]

Since its creation, the ONDCP has come under criticism. One of those criticisms has to do with their budgets. The majority of the agency budget is spent on drug interdiction and law enforcement programs. Many critics point out that the majority of the money should be spent on treatment and recovery programs for users and addicts. The ONDCP also came under criticism for paying television programs to include anti-drug messages. The FCC investigated these allegations and found that officials at the ONDCP reviewed scripts of popular television shows before they were aired and that the ONDCP had even paid television officials to edit scripts that were considered to be pro-drug.

Since its inception, the ONDCP has had six directors, known as "drug czars." These leaders are nominated by the president but must have the approval of the Senate. The drug czar is responsible for implementing the National Drug Control Strategy. A list of the drug czars is listed in Table 8.2.

Table 8.2 ONDCP Drug Czars

William Bennett (George H. W. Bush): 1989 to 1991: Bennett was a conservative Republican who served as the secretary of education prior to being the drug czar. He was vehemently opposed to legalizing drugs, claiming that legalizing drugs would allow more drugs to end up in the hands of children.

Bob Martinez (George H. W. Bush): 1991 to 1993: The former governor of Florida supported a program to eradicate poppies in Mexico and Colombia as a way to reduce cultivation of the drug. Martinez sought to create a "most wanted" list for drug trafficking organizations, and sought to require states to match any federal funding for drug-education programs.

Lee Brown (Bill Clinton): 1993 to 1995: Brown was the first Democratic drug czar. Brown supported the High Intensity Drug Trafficking Area teams and increased the investigation of the role of the Colombian Cali drug trafficking cartel. The aggressive investigation under Brown resulted in the indictment of that cartel's leaders and their lawyers who aided criminal drug activities across the United States.

Barry McCaffrey (Bill Clinton): 1996 to 2001: McCaffrey received praise for improving the efficiency of the ONDCP, and often showed his support for demand reduction programs (however, spending for both demand reduction and supply reduction both decreased under McCaffrey). McCaffrey tended to focus more on an international approach to drug control policy, in particular international law enforcement and interdiction programs. He supported methadone maintenance programs, but not the push toward legalizing marijuana.

John P. Walters (George W. Bush): 2001 to 2009: A conservative Republican, Walters called medical marijuana "medical crack" and opposed legalization of marijuana or any drug. He fought against prescription drug addictions and worked to counter narcoterrorism in Colombia, Mexico, and Afghanistan. Since leaving office, Walters has written a book in which he posits that the "moral poverty" of today's youth is the cause of increased crime and drug abuse.

Gil Kerlikowske (Barack Obama): May 2009 to March 2014: Kerlikowske was the police chief of Seattle prior to his taking office. He made it clear that he opposed the legalization of marijuana or other drugs. He has also indicated that the focus of the Obama administration's drug policy would be on treatment of offenders as the best way to reduce drug use.

Michael P. Botticelli (Barack Obama): March 2014–present: Botticelli was an administrator at Brandeis University in Massachusetts when he was arrested for causing an accident on the Massachusetts Turnpike while driving drunk. He was sentenced to an outpatient treatment program, and upon completion of the program he worked for 10 years as the director of the Bureau of Substance Abuse Services in Massachusetts. He then served as the deputy director of the Office of National Drug Control Policy with Gil Kerlikowske. Botticelli was sworn in as the nation's drug czar in November in 2015 after serving as acting director.

Sources: Nancy Marion, 2015. "Drug Czar" in Nancy E. Marion and Willard M. Oliver, eds. Drugs in American Society. Santa Barbara, CA: ABC-CLIO, pp. 290–292; Office of National Drug Control Policy, "Michael Botticelli" https://www.whitehouse.gov/ondcp/botticelli-bio.

1992: Substance Abuse and Mental Health Services Administration (SAMHSA)

The **Substance Abuse and Mental Health Services Administration** (SAMHSA), a federal agency housed in the US Department of Health and

Human Services, funds research and other programs that help individuals with substance abuse problems. The agency was created in 1992 after a reorganization of mental health and substance abuse agencies.

The organization seeks to make more programs available to those who need them. To do this, four primary programs have been initiated. These include the Center for Mental Health Services, the Center for Substance Abuse Prevention, the Center for Substance Abuse Treatment, and the Office of Applied Studies. Other major programs include National Survey on Drug Use and Health, the Drug Abuse Warning Network, and the Drug and Alcohol Services Information System.[19] Today, SAMHSA oversees a survey of people aged 12 and older across the US as a way to know more about trends in substance abuse and provide information about the use of illicit drugs, alcohol, and tobacco.

1992: Center for Substance Abuse Prevention

The **Center for Substance Abuse Prevention** (CSAP) is a federal agency housed within the Department of Health and Human Services and the Substance Abuse and Mental Health Services Administration. CSAP was originally established in 1992 after other offices were reorganized. The mission of the new agency was to reduce the use of illegal substances and the abuse of legal ones.

CSAP coordinates its activities with other drug prevention agencies at the federal, state, and local levels. They also work with both public and private organizations. No matter the agency, CSAP works to develop comprehensive drug abuse prevention programs. They work to develop effective policies, programs, and services to prevent the use of illegal drug use, prescription drug misuse and abuse, and alcohol and tobacco use by young people.

CSAP has developed six strategies. They are: (1) to disseminate information about the dangers of drug use; (2) to increase prevention education; (3) to develop alternative activities (activities that do not revolve around the use of drugs); (4) to encourage community-based prevention and treatment services; (5) to create environmental policies (i.e., community standards, codes that influence the prevalence and use of drugs); and (6) to increase problem identification and referral.[20]

US Coast Guard

The US Coast Guard is one element of the five armed forces in the US. The agency is located within the Department of Homeland Security. The personnel

Customs officers are participating in a training for drugs detec by Belish via fotolia.com.

oversee the country's maritime interests, and as such has been given the authority to oversee rivers, ports, and seas.

Another responsibility of the Coast Guard is found in its role as a federal law enforcement agency. This responsibility can be traced back to 1790 when President George Washington authorized ten vessels to enforce federal laws on smuggling. Today, the Coast Guard still does this. As an example of their success, in 2012, the Coast Guard seized 107 metric tons of cocaine that was being smuggled into the US.[21]

US Customs and Border Protection

The US Customs and Border Protection (CBP) is a large part of the Department of Homeland Security. Agents in CBP protect the country's borders from terrorists and smugglers. One of their tasks is to prevent the importation of drugs into the US through ports, airports, and land borders. CBP agents inspect goods coming into the US to interdict smuggled drugs, and then seizes them in an attempt to reduce the supply of drugs. The CBP also works with law enforcement in other countries in cooperative efforts to reduce the flow of drugs between nations.

The success of CBP is clear. In 2012, agents seized over 200,000 pounds of cocaine, 4,000 pounds of heroin, and almost 4 million pounds of marijuana.[22]

US Immigration and Customs Enforcement (ICE)

As part of the Department of Homeland Security, the US Immigration and Customs Enforcement (ICE) is responsible for violations of customs, trade, and immigration policies. ICE agents investigate crimes involving narcotics smuggling into the US.

As part of their role in preventing drug smuggling, ICE agents participate in high-intensity drug trafficking area task forces. These are organizations made up of local, state, and federal law enforcement agents who work to combat drug trafficking in major cities in the US. Agents also participate in organized crime drug enforcement task forces to investigate instances of large drug-trafficking and money-laundering organizations.[23]

Interest Groups

Interest groups are composed of individuals who seek to influence government action or policy in a particular area. Since most citizens are unable to speak to members of Congress regularly, they join an interest group that will represent them in the political process. Each interest group has a variety of methods to affect policy. They can seek out media coverage to increase public awareness, or they can meet individually with members of Congress and try to convince them to support a policy or support a particular point of view. They can get involved in elections through fundraising events, or provide expertise and information to Congress. All of this is done to have an impact on the policies that are passed and implemented.

Some interest groups that have been active in the legislative process regarding drug use and abuse include Common Sense for Drug Policy, Drug Policy Alliance Network, Drug Watch International, Drug-Free America Foundation, Families Against Mandatory Minimums, the Tobacco Institute, Mothers Against Drunk Driving, Students Against Destructive Decisions, the American Society of Addiction Medicine, National Council on Alcoholism and Drug Dependence, and the National Organization for the Reform of Marijuana Laws.

Common Sense for Drug Policy

Common Sense for Drug Policy (CSDP) was established in 1995 as a nonprofit organization concerned with the nation's drug policies. Members of the organization feel that policies such as asset forfeiture and mandatory sentences are not fair and should be repealed or rewritten. The group also supports "harm reduction" policies that are intended to reduce potential harms that are caused by federal drug policies. This includes needle exchange programs that reduce the spread of diseases. Other proposals from CSDP include decriminalization of hard drugs and regulating marijuana in a similar fashion to alcohol.[24]

National Organization for the Reform of Marijuana Laws (NORML)

The **National Organization for the Reform of Marijuana Laws** (NORML) is a nonprofit advocacy group that lobbies to change the legal status of marijuana in the US. It is the oldest and largest organization advocating for the reform of the nation's marijuana laws.

NORML was founded in 1970 by Keith Stroup and was initially funded by Hugh Hefner, the founder and publisher of *Playboy* magazine. An unusual group of people started the organization, including hippies, civic leaders, and lawyers. Some used marijuana regularly and others only occasionally, but they all believed that the nation's marijuana laws were too strict. NORML was not successful in changing legislation in the national arena, so they focused on states. Members of NORML would advise state legislators on marijuana legislation. They advised them on what strategies would be effective, what expert witnesses would testify. They even, at times, paid outside witnesses to travel to states to testify. NORML also began an extensive legal program to assist defendants in court and challenges to the constitutionality of federal marijuana laws.[25]

Today, NORML continues to advocate for marijuana law reform at both the state and federal level. It does not advocate for marijuana use, nor does it believe marijuana should be completely unregulated. Instead, the group supports laws that remove criminal penalties for private possession of the drug, and wants people to be allowed to grow the plant for personal use and casual nonprofit transfers of small amounts of the drug. It supports a controlled market for marijuana, where consumers could purchase it from safe, legal, and regulated sources.

A new group within NORML is the Women's Alliance, made up of women who support decriminalizing marijuana. This organization was created in 2010 and is a nonpartisan group of educated, prominent, successful women who believe that marijuana should be legalized. They believe that its illegality undermines the family, sends a mixed message to young people, and is not in line with the principles of states' rights. They help to educate others about marijuana, and have a core group of speakers who are available to meet with the public and the media to discuss marijuana legalization.

One of the positions taken by the Women's Alliance is that the laws prohibiting marijuana are failing, wasting billions of dollars each year. Moreover, the prohibition of marijuana violates states' rights by taking away their right to choose the legal status of the drug. It also expands the reach of government into the lives of law-abiding citizens. They support more research about medical marijuana.

Another group found within NORML is the NORML Foundation. This is a 501(c)3 nonprofit organization was founded in 1997 to educate the public about marijuana. They do this through weekly press releases to the media and a regular newsletter. They also work to assist victims of the current laws. Any donations made to the foundation are tax deductible.[26]

Tobacco Institute

Following early reports in the 1940s that tobacco use might have a strong relation to lung cancer, various tobacco companies met at the Plaza Hotel of New York City in December 1953 and formed two new organizations: the Tobacco Institute Research Committee (later the Council for Tobacco Research) and the **Tobacco Institute**. While the first agency published research studies contesting findings about the negative effects of smoking, the second would act as a public relations organization. They issued pamphlets, letters to newspaper editors, magazine articles, newsletters, advertisements, and white papers that attempted to counteract the negative research on the effects of using tobacco. On occasion, it paid scientists for favorable medical journal articles and letters to the press. In one instance, the Tobacco Institute paid $156,000 to 13 scientists to counter studies, including a 1993 Environmental Protection Agency report that indicated that secondhand smoke related to increased rates of lung cancer.

The institute also gathered intelligence for the industry regarding public attitudes towards smoking. It then used that information to formulate legislative strategies for its own lobbyists to use against efforts inimical to tobacco company interests.

The Tobacco Institute was active well into the 1990s. After the attorneys general from many states brought lawsuits against the tobacco companies for increased Medicaid costs from smoking-related disease, limitations on industry lobbying were included in settlement demands. The Tobacco Institute was discontinued as part of the Tobacco Master Settlement Agreement in 1998.[27]

Students Against Destructive Decisions (SADD)

Students Against Destructive Decisions (SADD, originally known as Students Against Driving Drunk) began in 1981 after two teenagers died in separate alcohol-related accidents during one week in Wayland, Massachusetts. In SADD, young people and their parents sign a contract in which the youth pledges to making safe decisions, particularly with regard to drinking and driving. A student who signs the contract agrees to call home for advice and/or transportation, at any hour and from any place, if they have been drinking alcohol, or their friend or date who is driving has been drinking alcohol. In turn, the parents also pledge to either pick up their child, no questions asked, from any place and at any hour, or pay for a taxi to bring their child home. Parents must also promise to seek safe transportation home if they have had too much to drink.[28] SADD has approximately 10,000 chapters in middle schools, high schools, and colleges around the country.

Drug Policy Alliance Network

The **Drug Policy Alliance Network** is one of America's leading organizations that advocates for changes in US drug policy. The group maintains that current policies are rooted in outdated punitive approaches, and these should be replaced by policies that are grounded in science, concerns over health, and a respect for human rights. The agency was formed in 2000 when two organizations that worked for drug policy reform—the Drug Policy Foundation, and the Lindesmith Center—merged.

The Drug Policy Alliance Network maintains that drug abuse is problematic, but past punitive policies and zero tolerance approaches have only lead to thousands of people being incarcerated, leading to even more disastrous results. Instead, the network promotes policies that decrease the harms of both drug abuse and drug prohibition. The membership campaigns for solutions to the drug problem that increase safety for both the user and society, while at the same time maintaining individual rights and liberties.

The network is a funding source that allocates funds for many projects, both nationally and at the state level. One of its more popular programs is Safety First, a way to increase information about drugs and laws to parents and youth. Another key agency in the network is the Office of National Affairs, located in Washington, DC, also with state offices around the US. This branch of the network lobbies to promote programs for treatment of drug offenders as opposed to incarceration, especially for nonviolent offenders.[29]

Families Against Mandatory Minimums (FAMM)

Families Against Mandatory Minimums (FAMM) is a nonprofit, nonpartisan organization that challenges the mandatory sentencing laws that have been passed on both the federal and state levels. Instead, FAMM supports a sentencing structure that can be individualized to the offender and the offense, thereby being more humane and fair. The organization was started by Julia Stewart, a former employee of the Cato Institute in Washington, DC, but now has members from a wide variety of individuals who are concerned with abuses related to sentencing structures that are used to punish those who have been convicted of drug charges. Many of the members are inmates in federal and state institutions. The group's mission is to be a "national voice for fair and proportionate sentencing laws. We shine a light on the human face of sentencing, advocate for state and federal sentencing reform, and mobilize thousands of individuals and families whose lives are adversely impacted by unjust sentencing laws."[30]

Drug-Free America Foundation

The **Drug-Free America Foundation**, Inc., (DFAF) is a conservative, nonprofit organization that seeks to develop policies, both national and international, that reduce the use of, and addiction to, illegal drugs. The organization was founded in 1976 and works to defeat any ballot initiatives that are intended to legalize drugs in any way, or those that propose a reduction in penalties associated with the illegal possession of drugs. The group also encourages all citizens to remain drug-free, including in their homes, schools, workplaces, and communities. They advocate for abstinence-based drug education in schools and support law enforcement and drug interdiction efforts. Cooperation between national and international leaders is essential in the development of policies to reduce drug use.

DFAF has six divisions, each with its own purpose. They are:

1. The Institute on Global Drug Policy: Comprised of physicians, scientists, attorneys, and drug experts who seek to pass policies that will reduce the use of illicit drugs and the mis-use of legal drugs and alcohol.
2. The International Scientific and Medical Forum on Drug Abuse. A group of leading researchers on drug issues who try to dispel myths about current controversies in the public arena.
3. The International Task Force on Strategic Drug Policy: Comprised of leaders who advocate for policies based on reducing the demand for drugs. They also support increased communication between organizations seeking to reduce drug use.

4. The Drug Prevention Network of the Americas: Made up of private organizations from North, Central, and South America who seek to exchange information on demand reduction programs. Their goal is to develop strong links between agencies and reduce drug abuse.
5. Students Taking Action Not Drugs: A student-based movement seeking to educate others about drugs with accurate, scientifically based information.
6. National Drug-Free Workplace Alliance: Members of this group recognize the importance of preventing drug use in the workplace.[31]

Mothers Against Drunk Driving (MADD)

Mothers Against Drunk Driving (MADD) (originally known as Mothers Against Drunk Drivers) is a nonprofit organization whose mission is to stop drunk driving, support victims affected by it, and prevent underage drinking. MADD began as a handful of mothers who were dedicated to fighting drunk driving but has grown into one of the nation's most prominent anti-drunk driving organizations.

MADD was founded by Candy Lightner in May 1980 after her thirteen-year-old daughter was killed by a drunk driver in a hit-and-run accident. Cari Lightner was walking on the sidewalk to a church carnival in Fair Oaks, California, when she was struck from behind by a repeat drunk driving offender. The driver had a blood-alcohol content of 0.20 at the time of the incident. He also had numerous prior drunk driving convictions, including one just two days before the accident. He was out on bail at the time of the fatal crash. The driver received a sentence of two years for killing Cari. Enraged by the light punishment, Candy Lightner incorporated MADD to empower victims of drunk driving to prevent similar incidents.

Lightner and MADD initially attempted to persuade government officials to pass tougher driving while intoxicated (DWI) legislation. Because public awareness of the dangers of drunk driving were limited at the time, MADD failed to effect legislative change. But Lightner and the organization received enough media attention to increase awareness of the problem. On the state level, MADD was able to bring about some change. The governor of California created the Governor's Task Force on Drinking-Driving. On the federal level, MADD became more recognized and was able to increase awareness of the serious consequences of drunk driving. The Presidential Commission on Drunk Driving was formed in 1982, and a bill that gave states federal highway funds for anti drunk driving efforts was passed. In 1984, Congress passed the

National Minimum Drinking Age Act that threatened to withhold highway funds to those states that did not raise the drinking age to 21.

In the 1990s, MADD changed its mission statement to include the prevention of underage drinking. MADD lobbied for a "zero tolerance" policy that would make any measurable amount of alcohol in the system of a driver under the age of 21 illegal. The membership also called on the Office of National Drug Control Policy to declare alcohol as the nation's top drug problem affecting youth. This would force the office to set aside a drug education funds for alcohol education.

For drivers who are of legal drinking age, MADD has programs to encourage more responsible alcohol consumption. One of those is the "designated driver" program, whereby one individual is chosen from a group of drinkers as the person who will remain sober and drive others home. MADD also continues to promote awareness of the dangers of driving while under the influence through public service announcements.[32]

American Society of Addiction Medicine (ASAM)

The **American Society of Addiction Medicine** (ASAM) is a nonprofit organization made up of physicians who treat patients with addiction problems. ASAM's mission is to increase the accessibility and quality of treatment for addiction. They also seek to educate physicians and other healthcare providers on issues pertaining to addiction and support research of addiction. They would like to establish addiction medicine as a specialty within the medical field. The organization exists on both the national and state levels.

The premise of the organization is that addiction is a chronic disease that often involves cycles of relapse and remission. Without treatment or recovery, addiction can be progressive and can cause disability or premature death. The group advocates for alcoholism to be recognized as a medical disorder by physicians, health insurers, healthcare organizations, and policymakers. This would widen a patient's access to treatment options.[33]

National Council on Alcoholism and Drug Dependence (NCADD)

The **National Council on Alcoholism and Drug Dependence** (NCADD) is the largest public health advocacy group in the US on problems related to alcoholism and drug use. NCADD was founded in 1944 and originally called the National Committee for Education on Alcoholism (NCEA). Today it covers two broad areas, alcohol and drug abuse. The drug section includes prescribed, non-prescribed, and hard drugs. NCADD offers its services to parents, youth, and addicts recovering from drug abuse. NCADD therefore provides preventive and treatment services.[34]

Drug Watch International

Drug Watch International (DWI) was founded in Chicago on September 14, 1991, to support those who seek to live a drug-free lifestyle. DWI members believe that preventing drug abuse is the most effective, humane, and cost effective way to address the consequences of illegal, harmful, and mind-altering drugs in our society. They believe that the best way to address the problem is through drug prevention, and it should be reinforced, enhanced, and expanded in all nations. To do this, societal norms need to be developed that support drug-free attitudes and acceptance of drugs and their destructive behavior need to be abolished. Their goals are outlined in Table 8.3.

The organization is a nonprofit organization that is made up of volunteers from the US and other nations. It stresses the importance of prevention, education, research, intervention, treatment, law enforcement, and interdiction. The DWI disseminates drug research by publishing articles on a variety of topics including medical marijuana, methamphetamine use, and marijuana use by teenagers. The organization also includes representatives from international, national, and state prevention and treatment organizations.

The goal of the DWI is to disseminate current information and factual research to the public and the media, and to those who support drug legalization. The mission statement for the DWI is the following: "The illegal or harmful use of psychoactive or addictive drugs is a major threat to all world communities and to future generations. Drug Watch International is a network of prevention experts and community volunteers from a wide range of professions whose mission is to help assure a healthier and safer world through drug prevention efforts by: providing accurate information on both illicit and harmful psychoactive substances; promoting sound drug policies based on scientific research; and opposing efforts to legalize or decriminalize drugs."[35]

A component of DWI is the International Drug Strategy Institute, a bipartisan group of professionals that includes physicians, attorneys, educators, law enforcement personnel, and drug prevention specialists who provide expertise on national and international drug research. The institute pursues innovative research and public policy related to drug issues.

Table 8.3 DWI Goals

Support clear messages and standards of no illegal use of alcohol, tobacco, and other drugs, (including "no use" under legal age) and no abuse of legal drugs or substances for adults or youth.

Support comprehensive and coordinated approaches that include prevention, education, law enforcement, research, and treatment in addressing issues regarding alcohol, tobacco, and other drugs.

Support strong laws and meaningful legal penalties that hold users and dealers accountable for their actions.

Support the requirement that any medical use of psychoactive or addictive drugs meet the current criteria required of all other therapeutic drugs.

Support adherence to the scientific research standards and ethics that are prescribed by the world scientific community and professional associations in conducting studies and reviews on alcohol, tobacco, and other drugs (without exception of illicit drugs).

Support efforts to prevent availability and use of drugs, and oppose policies and programs that accept drug use based erroneously on reduction or minimization of harm.

Support international treaties and agreements, including international sanctions and penalties against drug trafficking, and oppose attempts to weaken international drug policies and laws.

Support efforts to halt the legalization/decriminalization of drugs.

Support the freedom and rights of individuals without jeopardizing the stability, health, and welfare of society.

Source: "Principles" Drug Watch International. http://www.drugwatch.org/about/mission-philosophy-principles.html.

Conclusion

Drugs and drug policies are very controversial issues in the political arena. Since there seems to be no single solution to the problems associated with drug use, there is great debate about what the policies regarding drugs ought to be. Over the years, politicians have passed new laws, created agencies, and established new approaches to anti-drug strategies. The debate over drug policies will undoubtedly continue in the future as society attempts to understand drug abuse and find a resolution to this problem.

Important Terms

American Society of Addiction Medicine

Bureau of Alcohol, Tobacco and Firearms

Bureau of Drug Abuse Control

Bureau of Narcotics and Dangerous Drugs

Center for Substance Abuse Prevention

Centers for Disease Control and Prevention

Common Sense for Drug Policy

Drug Enforcement Administration

Drug Policy Alliance Network

Drug Watch International

Drug-Free America Foundation

Families Against Mandatory Minimums

Federal Alcohol Control Administration

Federal Bureau of Narcotics

Food and Drug Administration

Mothers Against Drunk Driving

National Council on Alcoholism and Drug Dependence

National Institute on Alcohol Abuse and Alcoholism

National Institute on Drug Abuse

National Narcotics Border Interdiction System

National Organization for the Reform of Marijuana Laws

Office for Drug Abuse Law Enforcement

Office of National Drug Control Policy

Organized Crime Drug Enforcement Task Forces Program

Prohibition Unit

Students Against Destructive Decisions

Substance Abuse and Mental Health Services Administration (SAMHSA)

Tobacco Institute

US Coast Guard

US Customs and Border Protection

US Immigration and Customs Enforcement

Review Questions

1. Describe some agencies that have been created to help deter drug use and abuse in the US. Have they been effective?

2. What role do advisory groups have on national anti-drug policy?

3. What are some interest groups that play a role in drug policy?

4. Should we continue the War on Drugs?

Endnotes

1. CNN.com. 2009. "House Passes Bill Giving FDA Power over Tobacco Ads, Sales." http://www.cnn.com/2009/POLITICS/04/02/tobacco.regulation/index.html.

2. Cordry, Harold V. 2001. *Tobacco: A Reference Handbook.* Santa Barbara, CA: ABC-CLIO; Swann, John P. "History of the FDA." http://www.fda.gov/oc/history/historyoffda/default.htm; US Food and Drug Administration. http://www.fda.gov/.

3. Kyvig, David E. 2000. *Repealing National Prohibition.* 2nd ed. Kent, OH: Kent State University Press; Musto, David F. 1987. *The American Disease: Origins of Narcotic Control.* Expanded Edition. New York: Oxford University Press; Pegram, Thomas P. 1998. *Battling Demon Rum: The Struggle for a Dry America, 1800–1933.* Chicago: Ivan R. Dee.

4. McWilliams, John C. 1990. *The Protectors: Harry J. Anslinger and the Federal Bureau of Narcotics, 1930–1962.* Newark: University of Delaware Press; Musto, David F. 1987. *The American Disease: Origins of Narcotic Control.* Expanded Edition. New York: Oxford University Press.

5. Bureau of Alcohol, Tobacco and Firearms. 1998. *An Introduction to the Bureau of Alcohol, Tobacco, and Firearms and the Regulated Industries.* Washington, DC: US Department of the Treasury; Bureau of Alcohol, Tobacco and Firearms. http://www.atf.gov/; Bureau of Alcohol, Tobacco and Firearms. USA.gov. http://www.usa.gov/directory/federal/alcohol-tobacco-firearms-and-explosives-bureau.shtml; Moore, James. 1997. *Very Special Agents: The Inside Story of America's Most Controversial Law Enforcement Agency—the Bureau of Alcohol, Tobacco, and Firearms.* New York: Pocket Books; Vizzard, William J. 1997. *In the Cross Fire: A Political History of the Bureau of Alcohol, Tobacco and Firearms.* Boulder, CO: Lynne Rienner.

6. Cornell University Law School. Federal Alcohol Administration Act. http://www.law.cornell.edu/uscode/text/27/chapter-8; Executive Order No. 6474, Creation of the Federal Alcohol Control Administration. December 1933. http://www.presidency.ucsb.edu/ws/?pid=14569; Federal Alcohol Control Administration. 1935. "Legislative History of the Federal Alcohol Administration Act." http://archive.org/stream/legislativehisto00unit/legislativehisto00unit_djvu.txt; US Department of the Treasury, Alcohol and Tobacco Tax and Trade Bureau. 2013. Federal Alcohol Administration Act of 1935 Historical Background. http://www.ttb.gov/trade_practices/historical_bg.shtml.

7. Centers for Disease Control and Prevention. 2012. "CDC Overview." http://www.cdc.gov/24–7/local/documents/2315501–1_CongressionalFactsheet_Final508.pdf; Centers for Disease Control and Prevention. 2002. "Office of Smoking and Health." http://www.cdc.gov/tobacco/osh/index.htm; Friede, Andrew, Patrick W. O'Carroll, Ray M. Nicola, Mark W. Oberle, and Steven M. Teutsch. 1997. *CDC Prevention Guidelines: A Guide for Action.* Baltimore: Williams and Wilkins; US General Accounting Office. 2004. "Centers for Disease Control and Prevention: Agency Leadership Taking Steps to Improve Management and Planning, but Challenges Remain." Washington, DC: US General Accounting Office; US Government Accountability Office. 2008. "Centers for Disease Control and Prevention: Changes in Obligations and Activities Before and After FY 2005 Budget Reorganization."

Washington, DC: GPO.

8. Finlator, John. 1973. *Drugged Nation: A Narc's Story*. New York: Simon and Schuster; Lohmann, Joseph D., and Robert M. Carter. 1965. "A University Training Program for Agents of the Bureau of Drug Abuse Control." *Journal of Criminal Law, Criminology and Police Science* 57(4): 526–530; "Narcotics Bureau Official John Finlator Dies." August 19, 1990. *Washington Post*. http://www.highbeam.com/doc/1P2–1143269.html; President's Commission on Organized Crime. 1986. *America's Habit: Drug Trafficking and Organized Crime*; US Bureau of Drug Abuse Control. 1967. "BDAC: A Review." Washington, DC: US Department of Health, Education and Welfare, Food and Drug Administration; US Bureau of Drug Abuse Control. *Fact Sheet*. Washington, DC: GPO; US Department of Justice. March 20, 1968. "Statement by Attorney General Ramsey Clark." http://www.justice.gov/ag/aghistory/clark/1968/03–20–1968.pdf.

9. Epstein, Edward J. "Agency of Fear: Opiates and Political Power in America." Schaffer Library of Drug Policy. http://druglibrary.org/schaffer/history/aof/aof11.html; Frydl, Kathleen J. 2013. *The Drug Wars in America, 1940–1973*. Cambridge: Cambridge University Press; Johnson, Lyndon B. February 7, 1968. "Special Message to the Congress Transmitting Reorganization Plan 1 of 1968 Relating to Narcotics and Drug Abuse Control." Online by Gerhard Peters and John T. Woolley. *American Presidency Project*. http://www.presidency.ucsb.edu/ws/?pid=29249.

10. National Institute on Alcohol Abuse and Alcoholism. "About NIAA." http://www.niaaa.nih.gov/AboutNIAAA/; National Institute on Alcohol Abuse and Alcoholism. "Research." http://www.niaaa.nih.gov/research; Nixon, Richard. May 14, 1974. "Remarks on Signing Two Bills Providing for Drug and Alcohol Abuse Prevention." Online by Gerhard Peters and John T. Woolley. *American Presidency Project*. http://www.presidency.ucsb.edu/ws/?pid=4207; Warren, Kenneth R., and Brenda G. Hewitt, "NIAAA: Advancing Alcohol Research for 40 Years." National Institute on Alcohol Abuse and Alcoholism. http://pubs.niaaa.nih.gov/publications/arh40/5–17.htm.

11. Bertram, Eva, Kenneth Sharpe, and Peter Anders. 1996. *Drug War Politics: The Price of Denial*. Berkeley: University of California Press; Nixon, Richard M. January 28, 1972. "Statement on Establishing the Office for Drug Abuse in Law Enforcement." Online by Gerhard Peters and John T. Woolley. *American Presidency Project*. http://www.presidency.ucsb.edu/ws/?pid=3552; Russell, Jesse, and Ronald Cohn. 2012. *Office of Drug Abuse Law Enforcement*. Key Biscayne, FL: Bookvika.

12. Drug Enforcement Administration. 2008. "DEA History in Depth." http://www.usdoj.gov/dea/history.htm; US Department of Justice. 2009. "DEA Mission Statement." http://www.usdoj.gov/dea/agency/mission.htm; US Department of Justice. 2009. "Programs and Operations." http://www.usdoj.gov/dea/programs/progs.htm.

13. National Institute on Drug Abuse. "Important Events in NIDA History." http://www.nih.gov/about/almanac/archive/1999/organization/nida/history.html; National Institutes of Health. "The NIH Almanac." http://www.nih.gov/about/almanac/organization/NIDA.htm.

14. US Department of Justice. "Organized Crime Drug Enforcement Task Forces." http://www.justice.gov/criminal/taskforces/ocdetf.html.

15. Brinkley, Joel. May 13, 1984. "Director of Federal Drug Agency Calls Reagan Program 'Liability.'" *New York Times*. http://www.nytimes.com/1984/05/13/us/director-of-federal-drug-agency-calls-reagan-program-liability.html; Cooper, Mary H. 1990. *The Business of Drugs*. Washington, DC: Congressional Quarterly; Gibson, William E. July 19, 1985. "Drug Task Forces Called a Failure." *Sun Sentinel*. http://articles.sun-sentinel.com/

1985–07–19/news/8501290983_1_anti-drug-agencies-border-system-gao; National Narcotics Border Interdiction System. http://www.reagan.utexas.edu/archives/speeches/1983/32383c.htm; US Government Accountability Office. 1984. "Justice and Law Enforcement: The Role of the National Narcotics Border Interdiction System in Coordinating Federal Drug Interdiction Efforts." http://www.gao.gov/products/123698.

16. Office of National Drug Control Policy. http://www.whitehouse.drug.policy.gov/; Office of National Drug Control Policy. "The 2013 National Drug Control Strategy." http://www.whitehouse.gov/ondcp/2013-national-drug-control-strategy; Office of National Drug Control Policy. "The 2013 National Drug Control Strategy–Full Strategy." http://www.white house.gov//sites/default/files/ondcp/policy-and-research/ndcs_2013.pdf.

17. Office of National Drug Control Policy. "About." http://www.whitehousedrugpolicy.gov/about/index.html; USA.gov. "Office of National Drug Control Policy." http://www.usa.gov/directory/federal/office-of-national-drug-control-policy.shtml.

18. Office of National Drug Control Policy. "Reauthorization Act of 1998." http://www.whitehousedrugpolicy.gov/about/98reauthorization.html; Office of National Drug Control Policy. "The President's National Drug Control Strategy, January 2009." http://www.white housedrugpolicy.gov/publications/policy/ndcs09/index.html; US Congress, House Committee on Energy and Commerce. 2006. "Office of National Drug Control Policy Reauthorization Act of 2005." Washington, DC.

19. Substance Abuse and Mental Health Services Administration. "About." http://www.hhs.gov/samhsa/about/1336.html; Substance Abuse and Mental Health Services Administration. "About Us." http://www.samhsa.gov/About/background.aspx; Substance Abuse and Mental Health Services Administration. 2012. *Results from the 2011 National Survey on Drug Use and Health: Summary of National Findings.* NSDUH Series H-44, HHS Publication No. (SMA) 12-4713. Rockville, MD: Substance Abuse and Mental Health Services Administration.

20. Commonwealth Prevention Alliance. "CSAP Prevention Strategies." http://www.commonwealthpreventionalliance.org/Documents/SAMHSA%20CSAP%206%20Prevention %20Strategies.ppt; SAMHSA. "Center for Substance Abuse Prevention." http://www.beta.samhsa.gov/about-us/who-we-are/offices-centers/csap.

21. United States Coast Guard. "About Us: Overview of the United States Coast Guard." http://www.uscg.mil/; National Archives and Records Service. Office of the Federal Registry. 1997–1998. *The United States Government Manual, 1997–1998.*

22. Customs and Border Protection. "U.S. Border Patrol—Protecting Our Sovereign Borders." www.cbp.gov/xp/cgov/about/history/legacy/bp_historcut.xml. Customs and Border Protection. 2012. "2012 Performance Accountability Review." http://www.cbp.gov/link handler/cgov/newsroom/publications/admin/perform_account_rpt_2013.ctt/perform_account_rpt_2013.pdf; Customs and Border Protection. 2013. "Customs and Border Protection Snapshot." http://www.cbp.gov/linkhandler/cgov/about/accomplish/cbp_snapshot_2013.ctt/cbp_snapshot_2013.pdf; Customs and Border Protection. 2013. "How CBP Combats Narcotics." https://help.cbp.gov/app/answers/detail/a_id/17/~/how-cbp-combats-narcotics; Customs and Border Protection. 2013. "Who We Are." http://www.cbp.gov/xp/cgov/careers/customs_careers/we_are_cbp.xml.

23. Immigration and Customs Enforcement. 2013. "Drug Enforcement Task Forces." http://www.ice.gov/drug-task-force/; Immigration and Customs Enforcement. 2013. "Joint Terrorism Task Force." http://www.ice.gov/jttf/#; Immigration and Customs Enforcement. 2013. "Overview." http://www.ice.gov/about/overview.

24. Common Sense for Drug Policy. http://www.csdp.org.

25. Anderson, Patrick. 1981. *High in America: The True Story behind NORML and the Politics of Marijuana.* New York: Viking Press.

26. More information on NORML and its current activities is available at the group's web site: http://norml.org/index.cfm?Group_ID=3374; National Organization for the Reform of Marijuana Laws. "FAQ's." http://norml.org/index.cfm?Group_ID=3418; "Introduction." http://norml.org/index.cfm?Group_ID=5493; "Medical Use." http://www.norml.org/index.cfm?Group_ID=5441.

27. Greene, B. 2000. "The Tobacco Institute Has Blown Smoke for the Last Time." *Chicago Tribune.* http://articles.chicagotribune.com/2000–07–17/features/0007170003_1_tobacco-companies-williamson-tobacco-corp-big-tobacco; "Tobacco Firms Paid Scientists to Deride Anti-Smoking Studies." August 5, 1998. *Chicago Tribune.* http://articles.chicagotribune.com/1998–08–05/news/9808050211_1_tobacco-industry-tobacco-institute-environmental-protection-agency-report; Tobacco Institute. 1976. *Status Report and Update: Public Relations Strategy of U.S. Tobacco Manufacturers re: Smoking & Health Controversy.* http://legacy.library.ucsf.edu/tid/agu91f00/pdf; Master Settlement Agreement. 1998. http://www.naag.org/backpages/naag/tobacco/msa/msa-pdf/MSA%20with%20Sig%20Pages%20and%20Exhibits.pdf/file_view.

28. Ross, H. Laurence. 1992. *Confronting Drunk Driving: A Social Policy for Saving Lives.* New Haven, CT: Yale University Press; Students Against Destructive Decisions. "History of SADD." http://www.sadd.org/history.htm; _____. "SADD's Mission." http://www.sadd.org/mission.htm.

29. Drug Policy Alliance. "About DPA Network." http://www.drugpolicy.org/about/history/ and http://www.drugpolicy.org/about/.

30. "About FAMM." http://famm.org/about/.; Gill, Molly M. November 24, 2013. "Pardon Humans, Not Just Turkeys." *Huffington Post.* http://www.huffingtonpost.com/molly-m-gill/pardon-humans-not-just-tu_b_4325978.html; Stewart, Julie. 2013. "Family Members Fight for Reform." *Nation* 297(20): 22–27.

31. Drug-Free America Foundation. "About Us." http://www.dfaf.org/content/about-dfaf-inc.

32. Laurence, Michael D., John R. Snortum, and Franklin E. Zimring, eds. 1988. *Social Control of the Drinking Driver.* Chicago: University of Chicago Press; Ross, H. Laurence. 1992. *Confronting Drunk Driving: A Social Policy for Saving Lives.* New Haven, CT: Yale University Press.

33. American Society of Addiction Medicine. "ASAM Mission." http://www.asam.org/about.html; American Society of Addiction Medicine. 1996. "Patient Placement Criteria for the Treatment of Substance-Related Disorders." Chevy Chase, MD: American Society of Addiction Medicine.

34. National Council on Alcoholism and Drug Dependence. "NCADD History and Mission." http://www.ncadd.org/history/index.html.

35. Drug Watch International. http://www.drugwatch.org.

Chapter 9

The Drugs-Crime Link

Chapter Objective: Drug use often leads to crime, but the link between the two behaviors is not always a direct one. This chapter examines the various types of criminal behavior that can result from using illicit substances.

Introduction

The link between drug use and crime is complex. It cannot be said that a person who uses a specific drug (or any drug at all) will commit a specific crime, or even any crime at all. Part of the problem is that drugs affect people in different ways, depending on the purity of the drug used, the amount ingested, or the user's experience in taking the drug. It is therefore impossible to directly link the use of a drug with a particular behavior. Instead, those who abuse drugs may commit crimes after using drugs for other reasons, such as they are more apt to act irrationally as they are not thinking clearly or because they need money to buy more drugs. Thus, it can be said that some users commit crimes indirectly related to their drug use in some way. This chapter will look at the link between crime and drugs to decipher the link between the two phenomena.

The Association between Crime and Drugs

Many people get arrested for drug-related crimes. According to the FBI's 2014 Uniform Crime Report, there were 1,561,231 people arrested for drug abuse violations. In addition, 15.7% of all inmates in state institutions are serving time for drug-related charges, and 50.1% of those in federal institutions are as well.[1] Drug use results in thousands of arrests each year across the US.

Many people become victims of offenders who are using drugs. According to the 2007 National Crime Victimization Survey, in which victims of crime are asked to describe whether their offender had been drinking alcohol or using drugs, about 26 percent of the victims of violence reported that the offender had been using either drugs or alcohol at the time the crime occurred. Between the years of 1995 and 2000, about 41 percent of violent crimes that were committed against college students and 38 percent of violent crimes committed against nonstudents were carried out by a person who was perceived to be using drugs. About 2 out of 5 rapes or sexual assault crimes and about a quarter of all robberies against college students were committed by an offender who was thought to be using drugs.[2]

According to the National Institute on Drug Abuse, there are three categories of drug-related crime. The first is offenses defined by drug possession or sales. These are violations of a law, either federal or state, that prohibits or regulates the possession, distribution, or manufacture of illegal drugs. Examples of these types of crime include drug possession or use, drug cultivation, production of methamphetamine, or illegal drug sales. The second category is those offenses that are directly related to drug use or abuse. These refer to those offenses in which the drug's effects contribute to the offense. Examples are offenses that are motivated by the user's need for money to pay for more drugs and offenses connected to drug distribution such as violent behavior that results from drug use, stealing to get more money to pay for drugs, theft or burglary, or violence committed toward a rival drug dealer. The third category of drug-related offenses are those related to a lifestyle that predisposes the drug abuser to engage in illegal activity. For example, a person may commit a crime because of their association with other offenders or with the illicit drug market. This can be crimes that are part of an overall deviant lifestyle. In some cases, people are exposed to situations that encourage crime. Examples of these crimes are criminal skills learned from other offenders.[3] Each of these categories is described in more detail below.

Offenses Defined by Drug Possession or Sales

There are many crimes that are the result of violating either federal or state laws pertaining to illicit drugs. Some of these include cultivating or manufacturing drugs, transporting drugs, selling/dealing, possession. and trafficking.

Cultivation and Manufacturing

Under state and federal laws (specifically the Controlled Substances Act), manufacturing or cultivating a controlled substance is illegal unless it is being done by a licensed pharmaceutical company (with the exception of marijuana in some states under state law). Some drugs, particularly marijuana, can be grown by a user. This is called **cultivation**. Growing marijuana is relatively easy. The plants thrive in warm climates and mature within a few months. Plants can be grown indoors or outdoors, and there are many resources to help people learn how to grow the plant. Marijuana grow sites have been located in homes, in backyards, or hidden in the woods on private or public land. But if a person is caught doing this, it is called cultivation of a drug and is illegal.

Other drugs, such as methamphetamine, are manufactured or made in a home lab. Bootleg alcohol can be made in a still hidden in the woods. This is also illegal and is considered to be **manufacturing** an illegal drug. Either way, it is prohibited to produce, manufacture, or cultivate controlled drugs. In other words, the manufacturing of a controlled material by a person who does not have a license to do so is illegal.

Manufacturing a drug can be very dangerous (see Table 9.1). There are many chemicals involved in the production process that can either cause an explosion or the fumes of which could be harmful if inhaled by those in proximity to them. At the same time, manufacturing a drug can be a relatively easy process, typically using common ingredients that are readily available. Drug labs can be set up in virtually any place (a home, apartment, trailer, or car), and some can even be mobile as a way to evade authorities.

Under another law, the federal Controlled Substances Analogue Enforcement Act of 1986 (CSEA), it is also illegal to manufacture a "controlled substance analogue."[4] **Analogues** are substances that have a similar chemical structure to a Schedule I or Schedule II drug and are intended to have a similar effect on a user's central nervous system as the scheduled drug. To make an analogue drug, an individual only needs to slightly modify the chemical structure of an existing drug in the smallest way to make a new form of the drug. The new drug can be sold with the appearance of being legal. If caught manufacturing an analogue drug, the offender faces stiff criminal penalties.

Law enforcement agents spend a great amount of time searching for grow sites, labs, or stills and then either uprooting them or dismantling them. Anyone who is the owner or operator of the venture, or any people working there, can be found guilty and punished. Any product will be confiscated and/or destroyed.

A person "manufactures" a drug if they are involved in any step of the production process. So if the police find cannabis seeds, heat lamps, and plants in a home, the owners could be charged with manufacturing an illicit drug. Similarly, if a person has precursor chemicals that are used to make methamphetamine, that also could be considered to be manufacturing. In most cases, drug production is a felony offense. A person found guilty of this crime will face a possible prison term and fines. Another option in some cases may be probation, depending on the amount of drug found or the past criminal history of the offender. If the manufacturing site is near a school or other drug-free zone, the penalty may be doubled.

Table 9.1 Meth Labs

One drug that is commonly manufactured by individuals in most states is methamphetamine because it is easy to make and uses ingredients that are readily available. Plus, the drug is easy to sell and profitable. Places where meth is made are referred to as meth labs. Meth labs contain the equipment and the chemicals needed to produce the drug (called "cooking").

The first meth labs appeared in California in the 1950s. Other labs were then found in Southwestern states in the 1960s. Today meth labs can be found in every state in the US, in both rural and urban areas. Labs can be set up in homes, apartments, trailers, or campers. Drug cartels have set up super labs that manufacture pounds of the meth at a time that can be imported to the US and sold on the streets.

Making meth is a relatively simple process and the steps are readily available on the Internet. One of the main ingredients is ephedrine or pseudoephedrine, an ingredient in over-the-counter cold and allergy medicine. The other ingredients that are needed to make meth are also readily available and include rubbing alcohol, drain cleaner, lye, and matches. Other materials needed to produce meth are salt, kerosene, and paint thinner.

Meth labs are very dangerous. The chemicals used can ignite or explode if mixed together or not handled properly. There is a constant risk of an explosion or fire in a meth lab. It is not uncommon for meth labs to blow up. This can cause harm to any people inside the lab as well as anyone in the surrounding area.[5]

The chemicals can also cause harm to anyone who is exposed to them. They can cause dizziness, nausea, disorientation, lack of coordination, pulmonary edema, serious respiratory problems, severe chemical burns, shortness of breath, cough, chest pain, and damage to internal organs. Children who are exposed to the chemicals are especially susceptible to the health risks. If they inhale toxic fumes they may experience long-term damage to the brain, liver, kidneys, lungs, and eyes. The chemicals can also cause the child to have learning disabilities or exhibit emotional or behavioral problems.[6]

It can be extremely expensive to clean up a meth lab. The chemicals will become embedded in the walls and carpets and permeate the structure. Families who have unknowingly moved in to a former meth lab often suffer serious health problems such as migraine headaches, respiratory difficulties, skin irritation, and rashes. Long-term exposure to the chemicals is thought to cause cancer.

To combat the problem of meth labs, Congress in 1996 passed the Comprehensive Methamphetamine Control Act. The law mandated that stores keep cold medicines that contain ephedrine behind the counter, and limited sales to three packages per customer. The bill also limited the sales of other ingredients used in meth such as iodine, red phosphorous, and hydrochloric gas.

To an outsider, there are many indicators that a home, apartment, or car (or any other location) is being used as a meth lab. There may be an unusual odor around the home, described by some to be like cat urine. There may also be a chemical smell like ether, ammonia, or acetone. It is common to have a large amount of trash around the location from the ingredients or from processing the chemicals. Containers, duct tape rolls, coffee filters, or small pieces of cloth that are stained red are common. The lab operators will tend to cover any windows.[7] Some meth labs will have many people who come to visit for a short time, as they purchase the drug and leave right away, sometimes at odd times. The occupants of the home may not be overly friendly or may be secretive about what they are doing.

Source: Christie, Les. 2013. "How to Spot a Meth Lab." *CNN Money*, February 12. http://money.cnn.com/2013/02/12/real.estate/meth-lab-house/index.html; U.S. Department of Justice, National Drug Intelligence Center. 2004. "Methamphetamine Laboratory Identification and Hazards: Fast Facts." NDIC Product No. 2004-LO559-001.

Transporting

Transporting drugs from one location to another is illegal (except in some states where marijuana is permitted for some people). Whether it is major trafficking of illicit drugs being smuggled across a border, for example by gangs and Mexican cartels, or simply carrying a small amount to sell in a neighborhood skate park, it is illegal to traffic or transport illegal substances, and people caught doing so face serious penalties. Even the small-time neighborhood dealer can be sent to prison for selling narcotics, as would a major international smuggler. There is often a great deal of violence associated with the drug trade.

Hundreds of pounds of illegal drugs are smuggled into the US each day. There is no end to how the drugs are covertly brought across the border. They

Man with gun approaching drug dealers by Paul Bradbury via istockphoto.com.

are brought into the country by land (car, truck, on foot), air, and sea. Some people swallow the drugs or hide them in their bodies, ship them via boat, or bring them through underground tunnels. Most of the drugs are transported through Mexico, but they also are smuggled from the northern border with Canada, and also through the southern part of the US (e.g., Florida).

Selling and Dealing

It is also illegal to sell a controlled drug to another person, or to buy the drug from another person. It is illegal to obtain a drug without a physician's script that details the specific person who will use the drug and the dosage of the drug (the amount to be taken and during what intervals). It has been deemed against the law, both federally and on the state level, to sell, attempt to sell, or distribute drugs to others without a license. The penalties for drug dealing depend on the drug involved, the amount of the drug, and the offender's prior record. In most cases, drug sales are felony offenses.

In many cases, the punishment for selling drugs is determined in part by the drug involved, the amount of drug involved, and if the defendant had any prior criminal history. In Texas, for example, if a defendant has less than 1 gram of a Penalty Group 1 drug (e.g., cocaine, heroin), a defendant will face a possible punishment of up to 2 years in a facility and a fine of up to $10,000. If the amount is between 1 and 4 grams, the possible imprisonment increases to 2–20 years and a fine of up to $10,000. If the amount increases to 400 grams or more, the punishment could be life in prison or a fine of up to $250,000.

Under federal law (21 U.S.C. 859(a)), if a person is convicted of distribution (selling) a drug to a person under the age of 21 years old and it is their first offense, they will receive a mandatory sentence of one year in prison. The mandatory minimum sentence is also one year for a person convicted of distributing a controlled substance near a school if it is their first offense.

Possession

It is illegal to possess and use illicit drugs. Under federal law, specifically the Controlled Substances Act, "simple possession" is defined as, "knowingly or intentionally … possess[ing] a controlled substance unless such substance was obtained directly, or pursuant to a valid prescription or order, from a practitioner, while acting in the course of his professional practice, or except as otherwise authorized by this subchapter."[8]

Depending on the amount a person has in their possession when arrested, they can be charged with **drug possession** (usually a small amount of the drug)

Arrested by TerryJ via istockphoto.com.

or if it is a large amount, trafficking. It also depends on how the drug is packaged. If the drug is packaged in small doses (small bags, for instance), it can be considered to be packaged for sale to others. A person can be considered to be "using" a drug if they possess an illegal substance that was not prescribed by a physician.

A possession charge (without the intent to sell) is typically a misdemeanor offense. The penalty for a simple possession can be as low as a $100 fine with a few days in jail. All states regulate the possession of controlled dangerous substances. Each state has a different way to define "controlled dangerous substance" and the associated punishment. Table 9.2 gives some examples of state penalties for possession of a controlled substance. A description of how the punishment changes depending on the defendant's prior criminal background is shown in Table 9.3. The punishments rise for the second and third drug possession offenses. Laws also prohibit possessing paraphernalia, including pipes, bongs, or syringes that are used to ingest illicit drugs.

Trafficking

A person found with a certain amount of a drug may be charged with **drug trafficking** (intent to sell). If the amount held is above a legally determined

Table 9.2 State Possession Penalties

California	All drug possession crimes are considered to be infractions, misdemeanors, or felonies. Infractions are the least serious and do not have jail time associated with them; a misdemeanor offense may result in up to one year in jail; felonies could be more.
Colorado	Considers compounds used to manufacture controlled substances to be a controlled substance.
Florida	Does not take into account ownership of a drug; a person will be criminally liable for possession of the substance even if they are not the owner.
Hawaii	All possession crimes are called "promoting." The offense can either be a felony or a misdemeanor.
Louisiana	Divides possession charges into five schedules, from the most dangerous to the least, similar to the federal schedules.
Massachusetts	A person cannot possess a controlled substance without a physician's prescription. The penalty will vary depending on the type of drug.
Ohio	Penalties vary according to type and amount of drug involved.

amount, that person can be charged with trafficking (otherwise it is simply possession). The amount varies by drug. A person does not have to sell the drug—just possess the amount stated in the law. Drug trafficking is regulated by both state laws and federal laws. If the offender crosses state lines to sell the drug or is in multiple states, it could be a federal crime. Another caveat is that if the case were to go to a trial, the prosecutor would have to show that the offender had the intent to possess the drug. So, for example, if a person is driving

Table 9.3 Federal Penalties for Simple Possession of a Controlled Substance (21 U.S.C. 844)

Offense	Possible Fine	Possible Imprisonment
1st	Not less than $1,000	Up to 1 year
2nd	Not less than $2,500	15 days to 2 years
3rd	Not less than $5,000	90 days to 3 years

Source: Brian T. Yeh, January 20, 2015. Drug Offenses: Maximum Fines and Terms of Imprisonment for Violation of the Federal Controlled Substances Act and Related Laws. Congressional Research Service, Report RL30722.

in a rented car and the car is found to have marijuana hidden in it, the defendant may not have the intent to have the drug—they may not have known the drug was even in the car.

A study by the Bureau of Justice Statistics shows that of almost 95,000 drug offenders in federal prison in 2012, almost all (99.5%) were serving time for drug trafficking offenses. Of those offenders, over half (54%) had been charged and convicted for offenses pertaining to cocaine (either powder or crack). The average prison term for federal drug offenders was over 11 years.[9] Most offenders who were convicted of drug trafficking were male (85.5%), with the average age of 35. About half of the offenders were Hispanic (47.9%), followed by black (26.7%), white (22.3%), and other (3.1%).[10]

Under federal law (21 USC §841), mandatory sentences for drug trafficking are required when the offense involves particular amounts of drugs. The mandatory sentences required under the law are detailed in Table 9.4.

Crimes Directly Related to Drug Use or Abuse

The second category of crimes are those committed because of drug use, or those crimes that occur because a person has been using a drug. These include public intoxication, burglary/theft, domestic abuse, drunk driving/drugged driving, and sexual violence.

Public Intoxication

It is illegal to be visibly under the influence of drugs in public. Most people think of being under the influence of alcohol when they hear the term "**public intoxication**," but the term refers to being under the influence of any drug, including cocaine, methamphetamine, or any other substance. A person could be arrested or brought into custody by law enforcement and be charged with public intoxication, or sometimes called "drunk and disorderly." Each state has set a threshold level for intoxication based on a person's **blood-alcohol content** (BAC).

In most cases public intoxication is a misdemeanor crime. Some states also require that prosecutors show that the individual does not appear to be able to take care of themselves in order to be found guilty or poses a threat to others. Public intoxication is typically punished by short jail terms and fines. Sometimes an officer must bring a suspect to a "sobering facility" for up to 72 hours where they remain until they are no longer exhibiting the effects of alcohol consumption.

Table 9.4 Federal Penalties for Trafficking Offenses

Drug	Amount	Fine	Imprisonment
Heroin	1 kilogram or more	$10–50 million	10 years to life
	100–999 grams	$5–$25 million	5–40 years
	Under 100 grams	$1–5 million	Up to 20 years
LSD	10 grams or more	$10–50 million	10 years to life
	1–9 grams	$5–25 million	5–40 years
	Less than 1 gram	$1–5 million	Up to 20 years
Marijuana	1,000 kilograms or more OR 1,000 or more plants	$10–50 million	10 years to life
	100–999 kilograms OR 100–999 plants	$5–25 million	5–40 years
	50–99 kilograms or 50–99 plants	$1–5 million	Up to 20 years
	Under 50 kilograms, 10 kilograms of hashish, 1 kilogram of hashish oil, or 1–49 plants	$250,000–1 million	Up to 5 years
Methamphetamine	50 grams or more	$10–50 million	10 years to life
	5–49 grams	$5–25 million	5–40 years
	Less than 5 grams	$1–5 million	Up to 20 years

Source: Brian T. Yeh, January 20, 2015. Drug Offenses: Maximum Fines and Terms of Imprisonment for Violation of the Federal Controlled Substances Act and Related Laws. Congressional Research Service, Report RL30722.

For some crimes, intoxication is recognized as a defense for criminal behavior, most often for specific-intent crimes. However, this is not always the case, particularly if the person voluntarily ingested the alcohol. Involuntary intoxication can be considered a legal defense, and is often treated similarly to insanity.

It is often the case that those who use drugs commit crimes while under the influence. Drug use often reduces a person's inhibitions, causing them to act in ways they would not normally act. Someone who has been using drugs does not think clearly while experiencing the effects of drugs and does not behave rationally. Some drugs cause the user to be more violent and more aggressive toward others. For example, in many cases, high-dose or frequent users of methamphetamine often exhibit more aggressive and mean behaviors. It is well known that alcohol use is associated with impaired judgment and increased aggression. On the other hand, those who use marijuana typically become more mellow and calm.

Burglary and Theft

Drug users often commit crimes to get more money to buy drugs. According to the Bureau of Justice, 17 percent of state prisoners and 18 percent of federal inmates in 2004 reported that they participated in criminal behavior as a way to get money so they could buy more drugs. This number was down from 2002, when about a quarter of those in local jails admitted that they committed their offenses to get money to buy more drugs.[11]

Statistics from another source show some different patterns. In the 2004 Survey of Inmates in State and Federal Correctional Facilities, it was found that 32 percent of inmates in state prisons and 26 percent of inmates in federal prisons reported that they had committed their offense after taking drugs. Among state inmates, drug offenders (44 percent) and property offenders (39 percent) reported the highest incidence of drug use at the time of the offense. Among federal prisoners, drug offenders (32 percent) and violent offenders (24 percent) were the most likely to report drug use at the time of their crimes.[12]

It is common for addicts to be unemployed since it is difficult for them to maintain a job while addicted. Users will frequently steal from other people or break into homes or businesses, and then sell the stolen goods to get money to buy more drugs.

Domestic Abuse

Use of alcohol and other drugs does not cause domestic violence, but consumption of drugs may impair a person's logic and hinder their ability to consider the possible consequences of his or her actions. Substance abuse often increases the chances that a person will act out in anger or rage. Some people become angry, depressed, or violent when they drink alcohol and they may be likely to take this out on family members or others living in the same home. In fact, about two thirds of victims of domestic violence report that the offender had been drinking at the time the offense occurred.[13]

Drunk Driving and Drugged Driving

A person who has used drugs may choose to operate an automobile, motorcycle, jet-ski, or boat (or any other type of machinery) while under the influence of an illegal substance. If they have consumed alcohol, this is considered **drunk driving**; if they have consumed other drugs, this is called drugged driving. They often feel that they can control a vehicle, but their reflexes and coordination are affected by the drug. Drugs may impair the perception of time and distance in a user who is driving. Some drugs, particularly sedatives, can result in dizziness and drowsiness. Marijuana slows a driver's perception of time, space, and distance. Driving or operating machinery after ingesting a substance poses a danger not only to the driver but also to others.

According to the National Highway Traffic Safety Administration, impaired drivers kill over 16,000 people a year in the US. Between 10 and 22 percent of drivers involved in accidents have been using drugs. Results from a study by the Office of National Drug Control Policy show that about one in eight drivers could test positive for an illicit drug. In 2005, 16,885 people died in alcohol-related motor vehicle crashes, which was 39 percent of all traffic-related deaths in the US. Male drivers are more likely to be impaired than female drivers and younger drivers are more at risk than older drivers.

It is illegal in all states to drive a motor vehicle while under the influence of drugs. When someone does this, they can be charged with "driving under the influence" (DUI), "drugged driving," or "driving while intoxicated" (DWI), depending on the state. In each state, a person convicted of this offense may face serious penalties. The penalties vary from one state to another. Some states have passed laws that prohibit operating a motor vehicle with even a detectable level of a prohibited drug in the bloodstream. Laws in other states define drugged driving as driving when a drug "causes the driver to be impaired."

Legislatures in every state and the District of Columbia have passed laws to define the threshold for driving under the influence of alcohol at 0.08 blood alcohol concentration (BAC). The penalties imposed by states differ, but there is typically some combination of fines, license suspensions, or vehicle forfeiture if the driver is guilty of multiple offenses.

It is relatively easy to determine if a driver is under the influence of alcohol, but it is more difficult to determine if a driver has ingested drugs. There are no easy tests to determine if a person has used another drug and there is no established legal limit for drugs other than alcohol. A driver suspected of using drugs must be evaluated on an individual basis. A blood test may be used to verify what was observed. States may test for different drugs, use different drug test types, or rely on different thresholds for determining if a driver is under the influence.[14]

Sexual Violence

Many sexual crimes are committed while the offender is under the influence of drugs. GHB, or the date rape drug, is commonly used by a sex offender to sedate or subdue a victim and then sexually assault them. This is called an Alcohol/Drug Facilitated Sexual Assault. Those who commit these crimes rely on drugs such as Rohypnol, GHB, and Ketamine (referred to as date rape drugs). When these are consumed, the victim will begin to feel the effects within about 15 minutes. They may also use alcohol, which is the most commonly used substance to subdue a potential victim.[15] Offenders sometimes put alcohol into a nonalcoholic drink. Victims are unaware that they have consumed the alcohol until they feel its effects. It can also be combined with marijuana or cocaine.

Date rape drugs are often mixed with an alcoholic drink. A victim does not know they are ingesting it because the drugs are odorless and tasteless. A victim will quickly become helpless and an easy victim for assault. In some cases, the victim may be sleeping or unconscious during the assault. The next day, the victim often has no memory of the event. They may also feel guilty or blame themselves. The delay in reporting the crime makes it more difficult to charge an offender with wrongdoing.[16]

Even if the drug is ingested voluntarily, a person can still be victimized. Alcohol is often a factor for increased risk for sexual victimization, especially in a college environment where many events involve alcohol consumption. In many cases, the victim knows their attacker and feels comfortable with them. In this case, they may be more inclined to drink to excess and less likely to think about the risk of a sexual assault. If a person has had too much alcohol, they may be unable to respond to unwanted sexual contact.[17]

Lifestyles That Predispose Users to Crime

The third category of crimes that occur because of drug use is related to a lifestyle that predisposes the drug abuser to engage in illegal activity. One of those is gang behavior. Being a member of a gang predisposes a person to a lifestyle where crimes are commonly committed.

Gangs and Drugs

For many years, gangs have been the primary distributor of drugs in large and medium-sized cities and neighborhoods in the US. In 2010, 69% of law enforcement agencies in the US reported the presence of gangs in drug distribution.[18] Some larger gangs can make millions of dollars each month by selling illicit drugs and other activities. Drug trafficking behaviors by gangs is very violent. Gangs rely on intimidation and violence to ensure that members comply with rules and orders and as a way to protect their territory or seek to expand their territory. Gang members often fight with rival gangs and law enforcement, resulting in hostility and brutality. Gang control of the drug market presents a serious threat to the public's safety as many innocent bystanders can be unwittingly injured or killed.

Today's gangs have moved beyond traditional drug distribution and are now involved with smuggling drugs into the US and large-scale trafficking. Gangs smuggle large quantities of marijuana and cocaine, and smaller quantities of heroin, methamphetamine, and ecstasy. Some gangs have developed new ties with rival gangs, and others have established relationships with Mexican Drug Trafficking Organizations (MDTOs) to create drug trafficking networks that smuggle drugs across the border. The Mexican crime groups rely on the gangs to transport and sell the drugs, and the gangs rely on the Mexicans to supply the drug. The gangs are also establishing relationships with organized crime groups to traffic drugs, including Asian gangs, Colombian cartels, Russian gangs, and others.[19] This has also become very violent as gangs seek to protect their territories. They often use high-powered, military-style weapons to further their activities.

Another new trend is for gangs to produce or manufacture illegal drugs. Gangs convert powdered cocaine into crack, and also produce the majority of PCP that is available in the black market. They also make large quantities of methamphetamine sold on the streets.[20]

To fight the gang violence associated with the drug trade, the FBI established a Safe Streets Violent Crime Initiative in 1992. Through this initiative, the FBI is able to provide support to FBI field offices in most major cities in their fight against drug-related gang violence. Law enforcement agencies from the federal, state, and local levels banded together to create the Violent Gang Safe Streets Task Force.[21] The FBI has also created a National Gang Intelligence Center in 2005 to collect intelligence from all levels of law enforcement on the growth, migration, and activities of gangs. They provide this information to law enforcement so they are able to respond strategically.[22]

Asset Forfeiture

If a person is convicted of violating a federal or state drug law, the government can legally seize any property that was either used by the offender to commit the crime or that was purchased with the profits from the crime. This is called **asset forfeiture** and can include houses, cars, boats, weapons, art, or jewelry, among other items. For example, if illicit drugs were transported in an automobile, the car could be seized by the government. If the offender purchased a piece of jewelry with the profits from selling drugs, it could be seized by law enforcement. Any assets seized by law enforcement may be used as evidence in a trial. If the defendant is convicted of the charges, the seizure is considered to be part of the offender's sentence and can be sold to the public.

When any seized property is sold, any profit is placed into the Assets Forfeiture Fund that is held by the US Department of Justice. Any cash that is seized is also put directly into the fund. Any profits made from the sale of seized assets can be used for other projects.[23] When a state or federal agency takes part in the seizure and forfeiture of property, a portion of that profit can be transferred to that agency to be used for law enforcement purposes.[24]

The reasoning behind asset seizure is that it is not fair for those who profit from criminal behavior to be allowed to purchase goods and keep those goods. Nor does it seem fair to most people that offenders should be permitted to save money from their illegal behavior so that they can live off that money after being released from prison. Seizing profits from illegal activity, or the property purchased with profits from illegal acts, prevents a person from profiting. It also helps fund government programs, either education programs or treatment programs for users, and helps pay victims' restitution. Another goal of the asset forfeiture programs is to disrupt or dismantle the offender's organization. Without equipment and money, the offenders are unable to continue their criminal behavior.

The asset forfeiture program has been criticized for being unconstitutional and in violation of the Fifth Amendment's protection against illegal seizure of property without due process of law.[25]

If an individual can prove that the property was not purchased from drug profits, they can keep the property. If this happens, the government is not required to pay for any damage that was done to the property, nor do they have to pay interest for the time it was being held by the government.

Conclusion

Drug use can result in many types of crime, although the link between the two acts is not always clear. Some crimes occur simply because a person chooses to use illegal substances. Crimes such as drug manufacturing, possession, and use itself is against the law, resulting in many arrests each year. Many other crimes that are likely to occur after someone ingests drugs, such as drunk driving or public intoxication, are also committed frequently by drug users. Finally, some users commit drug-related crimes because of their lifestyles, such as membership in a gang. Even though the crime-drug link is not always direct, it is clear that there is a relationship between these two behaviors.

Important Terms

Analogue

Asset Forfeiture

Blood-Alcohol Content (BAC)

Cultivation

Drug Possession

Drug Trafficking

Drunk Driving

Manufacturing

Selling and Dealing

Transporting

Public Intoxication

Review Questions

1. What are the three categories of drug-related crimes and some examples of each?

2. Describe some of the mandatory minimum sentences for drug crimes. Is it fair to have required sentences for these offenses?

3. How is gang membership associated with drug-related crime?

4. What is the asset forfeiture program and how is it useful in the fight against crime?

Endnotes

1. Carson, E. Ann. September 2015. Prisoners in 2014. US Department of Justice, Office of Justice Programs. http://www.bjs.gov/content/pub/pdf/p14.pdf.

2. Duhart, Detis T. 2001. "Violence in the Workplace, 1993–99." US Bureau of Justice Statistics, Office of Justice Programs. NCJ 190076. http://www.bjs.gov/index.cfm?ty= pbdetail&iid=693.

3. National Institute on Drug Abuse. 2014. "Principles of Drug Abuse Treatment for Criminal Justice Populations—A Research Based Guide." https://www.drugabuse.gov/publications/principles-drug-abuse-treatment-criminal-justice-popularions/introduction.

4. 21 U.S.C.

5. US Department of Justice, National Drug Intelligence Center. 2004. "Methamphetamine Laboratory Identification and Hazards: Fast Facts." NDIC Product No. 2004-L0559-001.

6. Easter, Michael Glenn. April 29, 2010. "Are You Living in a Former Meth Lab?" *Scientific American*. http://www.scientificamerican.com/article.cfm?id=former-meth-lab.

7. Christie, Les. February 12, 2013. "How to Spot a Meth Lab." *CNN Money* http://money.cnn.com/2013/02/12/real_estate/meth-lab-house/index.html.

8. 21 U.S.C. §844.

9. Taxy, Sam, Julie Samuels, and William Adams, October 2015. "Drug Offenders in Federal Prison: Estimates of Characteristics Based on Linked Data." US Bureau of Justice Statistics, US Department of Justice. www.bjs.gov/content/pub/pdf/dofp12.pdf.

10. US Sentencing Commission, "Quick Facts: Drug Trafficking Offenses: 2003–2013." http://www.ussc.gov/sites/default/files/pdf/research-and-publications/quick-facts/Quick_Facts_Drug_Trafficking_2013.pdf.

11. James, Doris J., and Jennifer C. Karberg. 2005. "Substance Dependence, Abuse, and Treatment of Jail Inmates, 2002." US Bureau of Justice Statistics, Office of Justice Programs. NCJ 209588. http://www.bjs.gov/index.cfm?ty=pbdetail&iid=1128.

12. Karberg, Jennifer C., and Christopher J. Mumola. 2006. "Drug Use and Dependence, State and Federal Prisoners, 2004." US Bureau of Justice Statistics, Office of Justice Programs. NCJ 213530. http://www.bjs.gov/index.cfm?ty=pbdetail&iid=1095.

13. National Council on Alcoholism and Drug Dependence. June 27, 2015. Alcohol, Drugs and Crime. https://www.ncadd.org/about-addiction/alcohol-drugs-and-crime.

14. US Department of Transportation, National Highway Traffic Safety Administration. 2010. "Drug Involvement of Fatally Injured Drivers." http://www-nrd.nhtsa.dot.gov/Pubs/811415.pdf.

15. Abbey, A., and L. Guy Ortiz. 2008. "Alcohol and Sexual Violence Perpetration." *Applied Research Forum* 5: 1–15.

16. Brecklin, R. L., and E. S. Ullman. 2010. "The Roles of Victim and Offender Substance Use in Sexual Assault Outcomes." *Journal of Interpersonal Violence* 25(8): 1503–22; Centers for Disease Control and Prevention. (n.d.). "Definition of Sexual Violence." http://www.cdc.gov/ViolencePrevention/sexualviolence/definitions.html.

17. McCauley J. L., S. K. Calhoun, and A. C. Gidycz. 2010. "Binge Drinking and Rape: A Prospective Examination of College Women with a History of Previous Sexual Victimization." *Journal of Interpersonal Violence* 25(9): 1655–68. Testa, M. 2004. "The Role of Substance Use in Male-to-Female Physical and Sexual Violence." *Journal of Interpersonal Violence* 19(12): 1494–505.

18. Federal Bureau of Investigation 2012. 2011 National Gang Threat Assessment—Emerging Trends. https://www.fbi.gov/stats-services/publications/2011-national-gang-threat-assessment/2011-national-gang-threat-assessment#currentGang.

19. Federal Bureau of Investigation. 2012. 2011 National Gang Threat Assessment—Emerging Trends. https://www.fbi.gov/stats-services/publications/2011-national-gang-threat-assessment/2011-national-gang-threat-assessment#currentGang.

20. National Drug Intelligence Center. January 2005. "Drugs and Gangs: Fast Facts." https://www.justice.gov/archive/ndic/pubs11/13157/#relation.

21. Federal Bureau of Investigation, Violent Gang Task Forces. https://www.fbi.gov/about-us/investigate/vc_majorthefts/gangs/violent-gangs-task-forces.

22. Federal Bureau of Investigation, National Gang Intelligence Center. https://www.fbi.gov/about-us/investigate/vc_majorthefts/gangs/ngic.

23. US General Accounting Office. 2000. "Seized Property and Forfeited Assets System Requirements." Washington, DC: US General Accounting Office; Moores, Eric. 2009. "Re-

forming the Civil Asset Forfeiture Reform Act," *Arizona Law Review* 51(3): 792–93. http://www.arizonalawreview.org/pdf/51-3/51arizlrev777.pdf; US Department of Justice. "Asset Forfeiture Program." http://www.justice.gov/jmd/afp/index.html.

24. US Department of Justice, Criminal Division. 2009. *Guide to Equitable Sharing for State and Local Law Enforcement Agencies.* "Asset Forfeiture and Money Laundering Section." Washington DC: US Justice Department. http://www.justice.gov/usao/ri/projects/es guidelines.pdf.

25. Williams, Marian R., Jefferson H. Holcomb, Tomislav V. Kovandzic, and Scott Bullock. 2010. *Policing for Profit: The Abuse of Civil Asset Forfeiture.* Arlington, VA: Institute for Justice. http://www.drugwarfacts.org/cms/forfeiture#sthash.sd5nfxnl.dp.

Chapter 10

Drugs in an International Perspective

Chapter Objective: Drug trafficking and smuggling are international problems that require an international response. The global drug market is described in this chapter, along with a description of policies that have been passed to address the growing problem.

Introduction

The international drug trade is an underground, covert black market through which illegal drugs are grown, processed, transported, and sold each day. According to the United Nations Office on Drugs and Crime, the industry is estimated to be worth more than $320 billion a year, or 0.9 percent of the world's gross domestic product. This figure constitutes about 14 percent of agricultural exports worldwide. Since the majority (if not all) of this is hidden, the true value remains unknown. The primary drugs that make up the drug trade include opiates (mostly heroin), cocaine, marijuana, and amphetamines. The market for marijuana and hashish is valued at $142 billion, followed by cocaine at $71 billion, and opiates at $65 billion. The international drug trade does not respect borders and is not based in one place, but it has become the primary source of income for millions of people in many countries. It is a large and lucrative market.

Illegal drugs are grown in many countries around the world, even in places where the drugs were not traditionally found. According to UNESCO's MOST program, the countries of the former Soviet Union now produce 25 times more hashish than the rest of the world and traffic it worldwide. Coca plantations, found in Bolivia, Peru, and Colombia, now exist in countries like Ecuador, Brazil, Venezuela, Panama, and Guyana, as well as other parts of the world. Opium poppy plantations, which were usually located in Laos, Myanmar, Thailand, Afghanistan, Iran, and Pakistan, are now appearing in Turkey, Egypt, Eastern Europe, Mexico, Central America, and Central Asia.

Once the drugs are grown in these countries, they are then transported to other countries around the globe where there is demand for the drugs. Some argue that the opening up of the former Soviet Union and China has led to the reopening of major drug routes that allow for easy transportation of drugs. There is an extensive network of roads and railways across Central Asia that can be used to traffic drugs. It is virtually impossible to watch over the borders that divide the states in Central Asia, so that drug traffickers are able to easily move their product without being detected.

Most countries, and international organizations, have tried to attack the problem. They have created eradication programs to destroy crops. Drug control and law enforcement efforts have been expanded. Education programs have been started to reduce demand. Despite these actions, more drugs are being produced and distributed now than ever before. It is almost impossible to estimate the exact quantities of illegal substances that are being produced, sold, and used, but officials in most nations agree that drugs continue to be brought into their countries at an alarming rate.

Much of the global drug trafficking can be traced to international organized criminal groups who are attracted to the market because of the enormous profits. Many of these crime groups formed and became truly organized during the Prohibition era in the US. They developed production facilities and distribution methods to supply an illegal product to the public. These groups now control the world's drug trafficking industry. The profits are used to fund other criminal activity or even terrorism. For example, it is widely accepted that Al-Qaeda has used the heroin trade to help fund terrorist acts.[1]

The illegal drug trade is very violent. Crime is common as groups vie for control of the black market. Murder occurs often, as do burglaries, robberies, and other crimes. Law enforcement from many countries must often work cooperatively in order to attack the groups who make up the drug trade. This is sometimes difficult, however, because laws vary widely from one country to another.

A large portion of the drugs grown and manufactured in other countries are smuggled into the US, one of the most lucrative drug markets. It has been estimated that the amount of drugs entering from Mexico into Arizona alone is in the thousands of tons.[2] In recent years, however, illicit drug consumption is increasing in Eastern Europe, Southeast Asia, and throughout Africa. In these countries, users are seeking to use drugs like ecstasy, cocaine, crack, and heroin. Cannabis and its derivatives are also popular drugs in most countries. The increased demand for these drugs means that they must be continually supplied, putting more demands on growers and producers.

People around the world are also showing more demand for synthetic drugs that are stronger and cost less than natural drugs. Synthetic drugs can easily be made in underground laboratories, and many crime groups have turned to making synthetic drugs to increase their profits.

There is still a lot unknown about drug smuggling throughout the world and the organizations that carry it out. It is very difficult to penetrate these groups and uncover information about them. This chapter provides an overview of the international drug trade and the impact it has on the availability of illegal drugs.

History of Drug Smuggling

Drug smuggling, or transporting illicit drugs into another country or across borders, is certainly not a new event. Even in the eighteenth century, there were controversies over drug imports. The **Opium Wars** provide one example of that. At that time, British citizens found they enjoyed Chinese tea and wanted to trade British goods for more tea. But the Chinese did not want any goods that the British offered. The British soon discovered that they could offer the Chinese opium in exchange for the tea. It was not long before opium that had been imported from Britain was readily available in China and the number of addicts rose dramatically. In 1839, China banned the British from importing opium but the British companies importing the drug were making large profits so they fought to end any restrictions imposed by the Chinese.

The British ordered its navy to force the Chinese ports to open. The Chinese emperor retaliated by confiscating a shipment of opium and then burned the ship. Britain then retaliated, destroying several coastal cities. At the end of the conflict, British merchants were able to convince the Chinese to allow trading rights in major ports. They also forced China to sign over the island of Hong Kong to Britain and to reimburse Britain for their losses resulting from the war.[3]

Only a few years later, in 1856, another opium war broke out between the two countries after China seized another British ship. After another scuffle between the nations, a treaty was signed in which China agreed to allow the importation of opium.[4]

French Connection

A more recent example of a drug smuggling operation was the **French Connection**. Prior to the 1970s, this was the largest drug trafficking operation in the world. It was estimated that the smuggling ring supplied over 90 percent of the illicit heroin being sold in the US. The French Connection was founded by French criminal Jean Jehan working alongside French-Italian organized crime groups in the 1930s.[5] The operation began in Turkey, where opium poppies were grown. From there, the drug was smuggled into southern France and made into heroin in clandestine labs. The drug was then smuggled into the US by French drug traffickers, where the drugs were sold to members of Italian organized crime families. The organized crime families sold the heroin to people on the local level in the US.

In 1972, US agents working alongside French law enforcement agencies broke up the French Connection smuggling ring. This demonstrated that law enforcement from different countries could cooperate and bring down international drug smuggling groups, sending a clear message to criminals that they could no longer hide their activities. Even though the drug route was destroyed, heroin was quickly smuggled into the US through other sources.[6]

Pizza Connection (1980–1982)

A significant drug smuggling ring was the **Pizza Connection** that was active throughout the 1980s. Here, members of the Italian organized crime groups, and in particular members of the Bonanno crime family, sold heroin imported from Southeast Asia's Golden Triangle (specifically from poppies grown in Afghanistan). The drugs were sold in pizza parlors in the US in an operation called the "Pizza Connection" by federal investigators.[7] The profits from the drug sales were held in bank accounts in Switzerland in violation of the Bank Secrecy Act. Organized crime groups from Italy, Switzerland, Spain, and Brazil were involved. This operation provided new evidence of the extent to which members of Italian organized crime cooperated with international crime groups to traffic in drugs and then launder the profits.[8]

US Response

In response to these drug trafficking operations, the US government sought to pass new laws to deter smuggling. President Nixon sought to learn more about drugs being smuggled into the US. He wanted to find a way to develop a coordinated approach to stop drug trafficking that included diplomatic, intelligence, and law enforcement personnel. To do this, he created the **Cabinet Committee on International Narcotics Control**. The goal of the committee was to fight international drug traffic and to eliminate drugs at their source.[9]

Nixon also announced **Operation Intercept**, which allowed border agents to perform searches of all individuals who were crossing the border into the US from Mexico. When the program ended it was replaced with **Operation Cooperation** that permitted US agents to be stationed in Mexico. This helped to increase the presence of American drug enforcement agents outside of the US.

Nixon was not the only president to seek international solutions to drug trafficking. In 1978, President Carter created the **Bureau of International Narcotics Matters** (BINM) to provide support for law enforcement agencies that were administering laws against international drug trafficking. Through the 1980s, the agency provided funds for many international anti-drug programs but directed more money into programs dealing with drug cultivation in Latin American countries. Even with the extra support, law enforcement agents were not able to stop the drug traffickers from Latin America. In the 1990s, the agency's focus turned to destroying the Mexican cartels.[10]

Throughout the 1970s, the US continued to give attention to international efforts to combat the production and trafficking of illicit drugs. In 1975, **Operation Condor** was a crop eradication program that allowed officials to destroy poppy fields. A similar operation in 1976, **Operation Trizo**, allowed Mexicans to fly planes provided by the US State Department over poppy fields to spray herbicides on them and destroy them. They also arrested many people who grew the poppies. Because so many people were arrested, the Mexican government requested that the operation be shut down in 1978.

Another international operation to attack drug smuggling from Colombia was **Operation Stopgap**, which started in 1975. In this program, DEA agents watched for suspicious boats off the coast of the country. They reported suspect vessels to the Coast Guard and the Navy, which then tracked the ships if they moved close to the US shore. During the course of this operation, over 1 million pounds of marijuana was seized. In another action, **Operation Banco**, the DEA and the FBI worked to break up a major drug smuggling group found in of Miami. In 1979, the DEA and Customs agents worked together in **Operation Boomer/Falcon** to fight drug smuggling in the Turks and Caicos Islands.

The DEA continued their battle against illicit drugs throughout the 1980s on both the domestic and international fronts. In the early 1980s, two projects, Operation Grouper and Operation Tiburon, worked to oppose cocaine smuggling from Colombia. The drug trade in Miami was the focus of Operation Swordfish in 1980.

Drug Smuggling Today

Today, criminal groups illegally smuggle heroin into the US that is made from poppies grown in Iran, Pakistan, and Afghanistan, in an area known as the Golden Crescent, and in Myanmar, China, Laos, and Thailand, an area called the Golden Triangle. The **Golden Crescent** is the origin of a large portion of the world's opiates. This area produces a highly pure form of the drug that is also very cheap. The profits from the sale of opium are used by groups to purchase guns and ammunition. The drug is transported from the Golden Crescent to Europe, the US, India, and Turkey, by way of commercial planes and cargo ships. The **Golden Triangle** is an area of about 150,000 square miles in Southeast Asia (from Myanmar to China's Yunnan province to Laos and Thailand), which produces opium and heroin. It is estimated that around 70 percent of global supplies of the drug come from this area. The area has an excellent climate and is full of fertile soil with cheap labor to produce mass quantities of the drug.[11]

In addition, drugs are also imported from Latin American countries and Mexico. Many drug cartels from this region have become successful in the drug smuggling operations, providing tons of illegal drugs to consumers in the US. The countries that produce large amounts of drugs are noted in Table 10.1.

Most drugs are smuggled into the US by land, primarily from Mexico but a smaller amount from Canada. In 2009, the Department of Justice estimated that 1,588,703 kilograms of illicit drugs were brought into the US by land routes. This also includes subterranean tunnels that cross the border. A much smaller amount of drugs is smuggled in through ports (bodies of water). The estimated number of kilograms of drugs brought into the US through the water was 24,737 kilograms. Finally, a smaller amount is also brought in through airports by use of low-flying or ultralight aircraft. This figure was 12,413 kilograms.[12]

Drug Cartels

It is a common misperception that a **drug cartel** is a large, single organization, but they are typically comprised of small, independent drug trafficking groups that are loosely organized and cooperate with each other to smuggle drugs. Some of the smaller groups will be responsible for producing

Table 10.1 Illicit Drugs by Country

Afghanistan	World's largest producer of opium
Bolivia	Third largest producer of coca and third largest producer of cocaine; produced 265 metric tons of pure cocaine in 2011
Brazil	Second largest consumer of cocaine in the world
Brunei	Drug trafficking of controlled substances carries a mandatory death penalty
Burma	World's third largest producer of illicit opium
Canada	Illicit producer of cannabis exported to US
China	Major transshipment point for heroin produced in the Golden Triangle
Colombia	World's largest coca cultivator; supplies cocaine to nearly all of the US market and the majority of other international markets
Germany	Source of precursor chemicals for South American cocaine processors
India	World's largest producer of licit (legal) opium for the pharmaceutical trade; but some is diverted to illicit drug markets
Kazakhstan	Cultivator for illicit cannabis and limited cultivation of opium poppy
Madagascar	Illicit producer of cannabis used for domestic consumption
Mexico	Major drug-producing country; world's second largest opium poppy cultivator; produces and distributes ecstasy; major supplier of heroin; largest supplier of marijuana and meth to US market
Morocco	One of the world's largest producers of illicit hashish
New Zealand	A significant consumer of amphetamines
Peru	World's second largest producer of coca leaf
Poland	Major illicit producer of synthetic drugs for the international market
Switzerland	Major international financial center often used for money laundering

Source: Central Intelligence Agency, The World Factbook, available at https://www.cia.gov/library/publications/the-world-factbook/.

the raw material (plants), whereas other will be responsible for transporting and delivering the drugs to the labs where they are processed. Yet other groups are responsible for storing the drugs and others take the drugs to be distributed (sold) on the streets. Some of the most important groups are responsible for bribing officials so that their operations are not broken up by law enforcement.

A smaller drug trafficking group may want to join in a cartel for many reasons. One is simply that the larger group has more resources, is more stable, and more successful at smuggling the drugs, which also means more profits. Working in the group will ensure the highest profit as opposed to working as smaller, individual groups. Together, the small groups can rely on the strengths of the other groups, so no one has to know and be able to operate in every task. The larger group may have more contacts, even international contacts that the smaller groups do not have, allowing for more sales.

Most cartels are organized into cells of about five to 50 members. The cells are not aware of the membership, activities, or location of the other cells. This way, if the members of one cell are arrested, they cannot provide information on other cells or the organization as a whole.

The cells operate with a chain of command that is similar to what exists in a legitimate business. The head of the cell will report to a regional director, who, in turn, reports to a designated individual in the home country. To communicate, cartels often use encryption devices that turn communications into indecipherable codes. This way, the cartels can operate secretly.

The cells are overseen by "managers" who know the cell's members and operations. The managers are chosen for this role because they are related to someone else in the organization. This helps to reduce the chances of theft or disobedience to the cartel. If someone does disobey the orders of the cartel, other family members would be physically harmed. The next level of worker is the middle managers who can be found in different cities throughout the US. These workers may be non-family members. In this case, they are friends of top-level leaders or were raised in the same region of the country so there is a high level of loyalty to the cartel. The lowest level of workers in the cartel are people who are responsible for specific tasks such as accountants, lawyers, enforcers, or pilots. The cartels will hire outsiders to perform these special tasks, and will cooperate with other criminal groups of other nationalities.

Colombian Cartels

By the mid-1970s, many organized crime groups in Colombia began to cooperate to create a new system of manufacturing drugs. They purchased coca leaves from poor farmers who grew them in the remote mountains of Peru and Bolivia. The leaves were then refined to make cocaine in labs in the remote jungles of Colombia. The cocaine was smuggled into the US, where millions of pounds were sold to customers.

In the 1990s, the Colombian cartels began to cooperate with Mexican drug traffickers. The Colombians carry the cocaine from Colombia into Mexico,

Sniffer dog by Steve Lovegrove via fotolia.com.

where Mexican drug organizations smuggle it into the US. To get the drugs past law enforcement, the cartels added chemical compounds to the cocaine to make it black and undetectable by drug-sniffing dogs.

Medellín Cartel

The first major Colombian cartel was the **Medellín Cartel**, based out of Medellín. This group came to light in the mid-1970s, eventually becoming the most powerful drug trafficking organization. One of the primary figures in the Colombian criminal groups was Carlos Rivas Lehder, a founding member of the cartel. While spending a short time in prison, Lehder met another drug trafficker from New England, George Jung. Together, they decided to use the same techniques they had used to traffic marijuana to traffic cocaine. They trafficked the drug by using small, private airplanes. To help with this endeavor, Lehder bought a strip of land in the Bahamas on which he built an airstrip. Planes carrying drugs could refuel here and then continue on to Miami. When the pair began their operations, cocaine cost $2,000 a kilo in Colombia, but sold for up to $55,000 a kilo in the US, which provided them with a huge profit margin.

Another Colombian drug trafficker, Pablo Escobar, saw how successful Lehder and Jung were, and began working closely with Lehder to expand the drug trade between the US and Colombia. To help their efforts, Lehder bribed government officials to "look the other way" so he could continue to smuggle drugs. When this became public, Lehder went into hiding, but was eventually captured. In 1987, the Colombian government extradited Lehder to the US, where he was convicted of trafficking in cocaine and sentenced to 135 years in federal prison.

When Lehder went to prison, Pablo Escobar became the head of the Medellín Cartel. He made it into the largest cocaine supplier to the US, smuggling millions of pounds of cocaine into the country. It continued to be a very violent organization. Hundreds of people were killed, including law enforcement, politicians, police, and innocent bystanders. The cartel relied on bombs and trained hit men known as *sicarios* who killed thousands of people who got in their way. They were accused of killing some prominent people in Colombia, including the justice minister, the head of Colombia's National Police Anti-Narcotics Unit, a newspaper editor, a presidential candidate, and a minister of justice. Escobar even announced bounties of $1,000–$3,000 on police officers. Most would agree that the Medellín Cartel was brought down because of their high profile and the extreme violence surrounding their organization.

Escobar evaded capture until December 1993, when he was shot and killed by Colombian police. But Escobar's death did not mark the end of the Colombian drug trafficking cartels. As the Medellín Cartel fell, the Cali Cartel took over.[13]

Cali Cartel

The **Cali Cartel** (based in Cali, Mexico) became the main smuggler of illicit drugs in the late 1980s after the demise of the Medellín Cartel. Like the Medellín Cartel, the Cali Cartel was not one single group but a collection of smaller groups who joined together. The members of this cartel were not as flamboyant as the Medellín Cartel and stayed largely out of the limelight. They trafficked drugs and laundered money quietly, avoiding publicity and violence, and to outsiders appeared to be a legitimate business. Like the Medellín Cartel, the Cali Cartel supplied most of the cocaine sold in the US and Europe. Cali moved most of its cocaine-productions to Bolivia and Peru, and changed its transportation routes to go through Venezuela and Central America.[14] The heroin sold by the Cali Cartel was a higher quality and cheaper than the heroin that came from Southeast Asia. In 1994 a gram of Colombian heroin was selling for $80 to $150 per gram, compared to $300 to $400 for the type from Southeast Asia.

The cartel established legitimate businesses as a way to form relationships with people in business, politics, law enforcement, and the media. Many of the members of the Cali organization were men who had been raised in poor neighborhoods but became successful businessmen. For this reason, they were admired throughout the country.[15] In 1995, the Colombian police, with the help of the CIA and DEA, captured six of the top seven leaders of the Cali Cartel. Many are in prison today for their crimes.[16]

Between these two Colombian cartels, drug distribution around the world was changed. The cartels made drug trafficking into an efficient and profitable business that was envied by many other groups.

Colombian Heroin Syndicates

During the 1980s, the Colombian cartels began to smuggle high-grade heroin to the US. Opium poppies grow well in parts of Colombia and the cartel provided poor farmers with seeds. The farmers would grow the poppies and sell them only to that cartel. The cartel gathered the poppies and transported the substance to secret labs, where the raw material was turned into a morphine base that was used to make heroin. The heroin was smuggled in small quantities into the US. Smugglers used hollowed-out shoes to transport the drug or sewed the drug into the lining of clothing. Some smugglers hid the drug in other shipments of commercial goods, whereas some found success by wrapping the drug in condoms and swallowing it.

Like the other drug cartels, the Colombian heroin trade is dominated by cartels that are made up of smaller groups that operate independently of each other. The Colombian heroin networks sell most of their product to customers in the US.

Contemporary Colombian Cartels

Law enforcement efforts against these early drug cartels have for the most part eradicated these groups from the drug trafficking business. While remnants of the organizations still exist, they are not as well organized and efficient as they once were. The Colombian drug trafficking groups have become more segmented and decentralized, making them more difficult for law enforcement to detect and control.[17] Despite this, the drug trade from Colombia has not stopped. The Columbians have begun to cooperate with Mexican groups to smuggle drugs.

Mexican Drug Trade

Many **Mexican drug cartels** have been trafficking drugs into the US for decades. One reason for this is that there is a substantial supply of marijuana plants in Mexico, as the plant grows easily there. In addition, the border between the US and Mexico is relatively open and it is easy for drug smugglers to carry drugs into the country. At the same time, a large portion of illegal drugs are brought into the US through the legal, official crossing sites. Because thousands of products are imported each day, it is easy to hide illegal drugs in with the legal goods.

In the 1980s, Mexican drug cartels helped the Colombian cartels smuggle marijuana into the US. This relationship helped the Colombians as it increased the efficiency of the operation. When the leaders of the Cali Cartel were arrested in the 1990s, the Mexican criminal groups became more involved in smuggling cocaine. By 1995, Mexican cartels dominated the cocaine market in the Midwestern and Western states in the US.[18]

Much of the cocaine sold in the US is smuggled into the country from Mexico. The drug is brought first from Colombia into Mexico either by air or sea. It is then taken by truck to Juárez or Guadalajara. From there, it is smuggled across the border to dealers in Los Angeles, Chicago, and Phoenix. Cartel members in those cities have arrangements with dealers to transport the drugs to smaller cities where it is sold to dealers and distributed to users.

According to the US State Department, over 90 percent of the cocaine that is confiscated in the US has come through Central America and/or Mexico. In 2011–2012, it was estimated that Mexican officials seized less than 2 percent of the cocaine that was thought to be brought into the country. In 2012, about three metric tons of cocaine was seized by officials. Meth is another drug smuggled from Mexico into the US. Officials have found massive meth labs in Mexico that are capable of producing hundreds of pounds of the drug at a time, and production of that drug seems to be climbing.[19]

Like other drug smuggling groups, the Mexican trafficking groups are extremely violent and corrupt. They often bribe government officials and law enforcement agents to "look the other way." The leadership relies on violence to enforce the organization's rules, as well as to deter other groups that may seek to sell drugs.

Much violence has erupted between the different trafficking groups that are each vying to keep their operations strong and to define and protect their territory. There is also tremendous violence between the trafficking groups and law enforcement.[20] This violence, called the Mexican Drug War, has resulted in about 60,000 deaths, as well as kidnappings, thefts, and a host of other crimes.[21] The violence resulting from drug trafficking in Mexico occurs frequently, has been brutal, and seems to be getting worse. The violence is concentrated along drug trafficking routes and in the northern border states in Mexico, but has also passed into US cities along the border. States like Arizona, Texas, and even Michigan (near the northern border with Canada) have reported increases in drug-related crimes. In fact, the Department of Justice reported that over 40 percent of all federal criminal cases filed in the nation last year were from judicial districts near the Mexican border, although many of these cases are a result of non-violent immigration violations.[22]

Many law enforcement groups, including the DEA, have been working to shut down the drug smuggling operations in Mexico since around the mid-1970s. To help them in this fight, the DEA has offices in Mexico City, Guadalajara, Hermosillo, Ciudad, Juárez, Matamoros, Mazatlán, Mérida, Monterrey, Nogales, Nuevo Laredo, and Tijuana. The American agents assist Mexican law enforcement officials to enforce international laws and also provide training and play an advisory role.[23] Congress has also held hearings and sought to take action against the violence. They have enacted resolutions and considered different legislative proposals. One action was in June 2015, when Congress wrote a bipartisan letter of concern asking the Secretary of State John Kerry to investigate the violence in Mexico as a threat to US personnel working in that country.[24]

There are five major Mexican drug cartels: Guadalajara, Juárez, Gulf, Sinaloa, and Tijuana cartels. Each of these is described below.

Guadalajara Cartel

The **Guadalajara Cartel** (or the Amezcua-Contreras organization) was founded in the 1970s and was one of the first to profit significantly from the cocaine trade. The cartel members worked with the Colombian cocaine cartels to transport heroin and cocaine into the US. At one time, it was estimated that the Guadalajara Cartel was responsible for about 70 percent of cocaine that was brought into the US.[25] It also traffics in massive quantities of methamphetamine as well as the precursor chemicals needed to produce methamphetamine.[26]

The Guadalajara Cartel was founded by Miguel Felix Gallardo, Ernesto Fonseca Carrillo, and Rafael Caro Quintero. The cartel began its downfall in 1985 when Enrique "Kiki" Camarena, a Drug Enforcement Agency (DEA) agent, was kidnapped and murdered. During the investigation into his death, officials uncovered rampant corruption among Mexican officials. Leaders from the cartel were arrested, and the remaining organization crumbled. The void was filled by other cartels, such as the Sinaloa Cartel, the Juárez Cartel, and the Tijuana Cartel.

Juárez Cartel

The **Juárez Cartel** operates in the Juárez-El Paso areas of Mexico and along the borders of western Texas and New Mexico and into Arizona. They smuggle cocaine, heroin, methamphetamine, and marijuana into the US through entry points in El Paso, Texas. The leader of the Juárez Cartel was Amado Carrillo

Fuentes. The cartel relies on members of the La Linea and the Barrio Azteca gangs to traffic drugs.

There is a lot of violence surrounding the cartel. Much of it began in January 2008 after one of the high-ranking members, Saulo Reyes Gamboa, was arrested and cooperated with US law enforcement. After he was arrested, there were a number of killings in Juárez that many thought were attempts by the Juárez Cartel to kill disloyal members. The Sinaloa Cartel, a rival organization of the Juárez Cartel, attempted to gain control of the Juárez drug-trafficking market by exploiting the power struggle within Juárez.[27]

Gulf Cartel

The **Gulf Cartel** is one of the oldest, and one of the largest, Mexican drug cartels. It was formed during Prohibition when it smuggled alcohol into the US. During the 1970s, the group turned to trafficking drugs, particularly cocaine. Today, its operations can be found on the Texas border. Its primary rival is the Sinaloa Cartel. It is known as being particularly violent.

In addition to smuggling cocaine, the Gulf Cartel is involved in other activities such as protection rackets (blackmailing businesses into paying for protection); kidnapping for ransom; human trafficking; bribery of law enforcement, elected officials, and journalists; theft; money laundering; trafficking in weapons; prostitution; and counterfeiting of products including clothing, TVs, video games, music, and movies. At one point, the Gulf Cartel was affiliated with the Los Zetas, but the relationship ended in 2010.

Sinaloa Cartel

The **Sinaloa Cartel** was created upon the breakup of the Guadalajara Cartel. It is one of the oldest Mexican drug cartels and specializes in trafficking marijuana but also traffics in cocaine and methamphetamine. The head of the Sinaloa Cartel was Joaquin Guzmán, also known as "El Chapo" Guzmán (for "shorty"). He was noted as being one of the most powerful men in the world, but also one of the richest men in Mexico, worth about a billion dollars. In 1993, he was sentenced to 20 years in prison for drug trafficking. He escaped from prison in 2001, and was able to evade law enforcement until February 2014. In July 2015, he escaped from prison again, this time through a tunnel that opened from his prison shower. In January 2016, he was again arrested and remains in custody.[28]

Tijuana Cartel (AFO)

The **Tijuana Cartel**, also known as the Arellano-Felix Organization (AFO), is one of Mexico's most powerful and violent drug-trafficking organizations.

It was established after the Guadalajara Cartel dissolved. This cartel operates primarily in Tijuana. The cartel smuggles cocaine, marijuana, heroin, and methamphetamine into the US.[29]

The Tijuana Cartel relies on trained paramilitary security forces and international mercenaries to train its members. They use members of violent street gangs from local towns in both Mexico and the US to kill anyone who tries to smuggle illicit drugs through their territory without paying a tax to the cartel. The cartel members watch over law enforcement's efforts by using radio scanners, cell phones, and other technology, and regularly bribe officials.

The cartel has weakened in recent years as many of its leaders have died or been imprisoned. In the late 2000, members of the Tijuana Cartel split off into two groups.[30] The leader of the cartel, Benjamin Arellano-Felix, was arrested in March 2002 and extradited to the US in 2011 to face charges there. The second in command, Eduardo Arellano-Felix, was arrested in October 2008.[31]

Mexican Drug Groups Today

These five drug trafficking organizations (DTOs) were the dominant Mexican cartels for many years. Recently, these groups have split into many smaller organizations. Some experts agree that these five major groups have split into anywhere from 9 to as many as 20 organizations. Today, it seems that the Sinaloa and the Los Zetas appear to be dominating the trade, but there are multiple trafficking groups. A new cartel, the Jalisco New Generation Cartel, is also receiving attention. See Table 10.2 for more information on these groups.

Table 10.2 New Mexican Cartels

Los Zetas: In the late 1990s the leader of the Gulf Cartel, Osiel Cardenas Guillen, hired some former military soldiers to protect him and work for the cartel. The 37 men became known as the Los Zetas. When Guillen was arrested, the Zetas set up their own drug trafficking operation. Many other people joined them, increasing their membership to around 300. In 2010, the Los Zetas began a war with the Gulf Cartel over some trade routes. Other groups eventually got involved, and thousands of people have died. The members are known to be brutal, savage, and extremely violent. The head of the organization, Muguel Angel Morales (El-40 or Z-40) is known to burn his enemies alive. They often use social media and display the bodies of victims (or body parts) to send messages to their enemies. The group was tied to a mass killing of 193 migrants in 2011 who were travelling through Northern Mexico. The Los Zetas have diversified their criminal activities and are involved in many crimes, including human trafficking, theft, extortion, and kidnapping.

Jalisco New Generation: This group, like the Los Zetas, are ruthless and violent. In 2011, they assassinated 35 members of a rival gang, including 12 women, and dumped their bodies alongside a busy road during rush hour. They also shot down an army helicopter using high-power weapons, killing all who were on board.

Beltran Leyva Organization (BLO): This organization was once part of the Sinaloa crime group, but have since split from them. The two groups are now rivals. In 2009, the group's leader was arrested, and his brother was arrested. The group has splintered. Two groups, specifically the Guerreros Unidos and the Los Rojos (among others) have roots in the BLO. The Guerreros traffic in cocaine as far north as Chicago. The Guerreros were linked to the kidnapping and murder of 43 Mexican teacher trainees whose bodies were burned.

Knights Templar: This trafficking group is a splinter group from La Familia Michoacana and has become a rival group. It began as a group claiming to protect citizens from other drug trafficking organizations and to be committed to social justice. The group is known for manufacturing and trafficking in methamphetamine. They are also known to extort local businesses and for illegal mining.

Source: June S. Beittel, July 22, 2015. Mexico: Organized Crime and Drug Trafficking Organizations. Congressional Research Service, Report 7-5700.

Drug Trafficking and Organized Crime

Recently, global transnational organized crime groups have emerged in countries such as the US, Russia, Poland, China, Mexico, Italy, and England, among others. These international, underground crime groups often cooperate with each other to commit serious, sometimes violent, crimes. Illegal drugs are found or grown on one continent, trafficked, and sold in other areas of the world. Organized crime is able to bribe government officials and infiltrate businesses to operate outside of the law to traffic in drugs. Criminal networks

Drug Trafficking by wellphoto via fotolio.com.

can change and adapt to meet the needs of the organization or adapt to new settings to allow for the easy flow of drugs from one place to another.

There are many reasons why drug use and organized crime have been on the rise. One is the increased globalization of drug consumption and higher rates of drug addiction. People in all parts of the world seek to use illegal drugs, creating an unlimited market. Another reason for the increase is the limited success of the War on Drugs in the US and similar policies in other countries. Despite new and tougher laws banning drugs, people continue to seek them out and use them. A third reason for the increase is the growth of drug cultivation and drug-smuggling routes. Drug traffickers are constantly seeking and finding new and more efficient ways to transport drugs from one place to another, often under the radar of law enforcement. Traffickers are constantly devising new ways to smuggle drugs. The fourth reason is the ineffective regional and international drug control policies that are passed regularly by international organizations. The laws often are not enforced in all countries and it is sometimes easy to identify those countries that have more lax enforcement. Fifth, there is increasing support for decriminalization and legalization policy alternatives.[32] More people are supporting legalized drugs or decriminalized drugs. Finally, at this point in our history there are more open borders and modern telecommunications than ever before. It is easy to travel from one place to another, and easier to communicate with people that are around the globe. For all of these reasons, organized drug crime is increasing.[33]

It is difficult for law enforcement to disrupt drug trafficking networks. Many times, law enforcement does not fully understand the individual networks and how they cooperate with each other. Each network is different so they are difficult to identify and track.[34] They change, adapt, and move frequently, so it is easy for law enforcement to miss when crimes are committed.

Terrorism and Illicit Drugs

It is clear that terrorist organizations need money to operate, and one place they can get that money is through the production and trafficking of illicit drugs. It is difficult to know the extent to which terrorist groups are involved in smuggling drugs, as terrorist groups operate largely in secret. But it is known that terrorist groups work with criminal groups to traffic opium, heroin, and cocaine, making a significant profit. The groups are then able to purchase weapons and support terrorist activity throughout the world.[35]

According to the United Nations Office on Drugs and Crime, it is almost impossible to know how much drug money is used to support terrorism. Moreover, the exact relationship between terrorist groups and drug trafficking groups is complex, constantly changing, and difficult to decipher. However, given the fact that the value of Afghanistan's 2006 opium harvest was somewhere around US$3.1 billion, even if the terrorist groups only received a small percentage it would be more than enough to fund terrorist activity.[36] The Department of State acknowledges that of the 59 terrorist organizations they have identified, about half have been linked to the global drug trade. They estimate the global drug trade generates around $400 billion each year.[37]

Groups

There are multiple international organizations that have the goal of reducing the international drug trade. Some of these are described here.

Global Commission on Drug Policy

The **Global Commission on Drug Policy** is an organization with an international membership of 22 representatives, including former world heads of state, governmental leaders, businesspeople, and writers. The members propose and support policies to reduce the harm caused by drugs in humane ways, and base those policies on informed, scientific knowledge. To do this, the commission members analyze basic assumptions and consequences of laws, evaluate the risks and benefits of different responses, and then develop evidence-based recommendations for reform. Some areas of concern to the commission are the current international approach to drug policies, policies regarding the production and supply chain (i.e., eradication, interdiction, money laundering, arms trafficking), criminal justice challenges (i.e., sentencing reform, legalization), organized crime, and demand reduction.

In June 2011, the members submitted a report on the War on Drugs in honor of the thirtieth anniversary of President Nixon's claim to launch a national War on Drugs. The report was critical of both US and international drug control policies, explaining that the punitive drug policies created by the government have failed and resulted in more harm. They recommended policy changes that included ending the criminalization of drug use and experimenting with legal regulation of drugs; providing a variety of treatment alternatives to those in need; investing in programs to prevent youth from taking drugs and also to prevent those who use drugs from developing more serious problems; initiating programs to undermine the power of violent criminal organizations; and implementing drug policies that are fiscally responsible and grounded in science.[38]

United Nations Commission on Narcotic Drugs

The **United Nations Commission on Narcotic Drugs** (CND) is the UN agency that makes policies on narcotics and psychotropic drugs. When the group was created in 1946, it was assigned the task of overseeing how international drug control treaties were being implemented. In 1991, the responsibilities of the agency changed and it became the governing body of the United Nations Office on Drugs and Crime (UNODC). The agency has 30 members that are selected by the UN's Economic and Social Council. The representatives represent different regions: Africa, Asia, Latin America/Caribbean, Eastern Europe, and Western Europe.

The commission meets each year in Vienna to consider recommendations made to the council regarding international policies for controlling illicit drugs. For example, in 2015 they were asked to consider a proposal from China to place ketamine as a Schedule I drug. In addition to this, the commission also tracks worldwide drug use patterns and makes recommendations for increasing the effectiveness of international drug control policies. At the same time, the agency oversees any international policies for reducing the demand for illicit drugs, including supply reduction policies. A key responsibility of the commission is to update the schedules of controlled drugs under the Single Convention on Narcotic Drugs and the Convention on Psychotropic Substances.[39]

United Nations Office on Drugs and Crime

The **United Nations Office on Drugs and Crime** (UNODC) is the office within the United Nations that is responsible for creating policies to combat the use of illicit drugs and its link to terrorism and other criminal activity. The office is located in Vienna, Austria, and has 21 field offices, along with a liaison office in New York City. The agency's responsibilities fall under three areas. The first is research and analysis of substance abuse policies; the second is promotion and support of international treaties among member nations that have been developed to attack drug activity; the third area is increasing cooperation among member states.

Many policies have been established by UNODC. One of those is the Global Program for Trafficking in Human Beings, which addressed the problems of kidnapping and smuggling of migrant workers for labor and the sex industry. Another program, the Global Program against Transnational Organized Crime, is a way for the UN to provide member states with current information, data, training, and policy strategies to address transnational organized crime. The Global Program against Corruption assists member nations to create new policies to reduce corruption in government. The Global Program against Terrorism helps members create new laws to prevent terrorist activity. Another program is the Legal Advisory Program that provides legal assistance to member nations that are developing legal frameworks to implement programs to fight drug use and other criminal activity. The UNODC's Global Assessment Program is concerned with the creation of initiatives to create policies that stop drug use through prevention and rehabilitation programs.[40]

World Federation Against Drugs

Based in Stockholm, Sweden, the **World Federation Against Drugs** (WFAD) is comprised of 89 nongovernmental organizations and individuals from around the world that aim to fight against illicit drugs. The group was formed in 2009, with the support of then US president George W. Bush. The goal of the WFAD is to create a drug-free world. The members of the WFAD agree that substance abuse is damaging societal values and threatening stable families, communities, and government institutions throughout the world. The members of WFAD agree that a drug-free world will promote peace and dignity, democracy, tolerance, equality, freedom, and justice. One of WFAD's tasks is to organize a biannual World Forum Against Drugs, a global conference that brings together people from all continents who seek to prevent drug abuse. WFAD opposes legalizing or decriminalization of cannabis or other recreational drugs. They also oppose injection rooms for heroin addicts.[41]

International Agreements

There have been many attempts to create some kind of an **international agreement** about drug trafficking. Even as far back as 1909, representatives from thirteen countries met in Shanghai to discuss creating a global narcotics control agreement. Most of the representatives at the meeting agreed that there was a need for drug control, but few tangible policies resulted from the meeting. Some of the policies they supported included a gradual suppression of opium smoking, a limit on the use of opium for medical purposes, and controls on its export and harmful derivatives.

In 1911, the US sought to have another international conference, which took place at The Hague in the Netherlands. The US sought to establish a global opium control policy. The US asked the other representatives to support an international policy for drug control that would place strict regulations on the production, manufacture, and distribution of opiates, standardize punishments for violations of drug laws, and provide for reciprocal rights to search ships that were thought to be used for smuggling drugs. Other nations expressed concerns about the costs that the policies would entail. They were untrusting of other nations and expressed concern that if they stopped producing and shipping drugs, other countries would increase their opiate operations and profit from the gaps in the drug market.

A third conference to discuss international drug policy was scheduled to meet at The Hague in June 1914, but before this could happen, World War I broke out, putting international drug control on hold for a few years.

United Nations Single Convention on Narcotic Drugs

One of the most significant international treaties is the **United Nations Single Convention on Narcotic Drugs** that was passed in 1961 (and that went into effect in December 1964). The treaty was written to reduce the production and trafficking of illicit narcotics and other drugs, and as a way to make international drug control policies more consistent between nations. This new treaty was the first international treaty to prohibit cannabis, a drug that had not been included in other international treaties.

The Single Convention categorized controlled substances into four schedules, unlike earlier treaties that had only two "groups" of drugs. The new schedules included increasingly strict regulations, but the convention also stressed the importance of these drugs for medical uses. A process was defined for adding new substances to the schedules, if needed. This would be decided by the Commission on Narcotic Drugs and the World Health Organization. These schedules are listed in Table 10.3.

Table 10.3 Four Drug Schedules in the 1961 Single Convention

- **Schedule I**—The substance is liable to similar abuse and productive of similar ill effects as the drugs already in Schedule I or Schedule II, or is convertible into a drug.
- **Schedule II**—The substance is liable to similar abuse and productive of similar ill effects as the drugs already in Schedule I or Schedule II, or is convertible into a drug.
- **Schedule III**—The preparation, because of the substances which it contains, is not liable to abuse and cannot produce ill effects; and the drug therein is not readily recoverable.
- **Schedule IV**—The drug, which is already in Schedule I, is particularly liable to abuse and to produce ill effects, and such liability is not offset by substantial therapeutic advantages.

The 1961 treaty remains in effect today. As of May 2013, about 184 countries have agreed to enforce the Single Convention. If a country agrees to abide by the treaty, they agree to pass laws in their countries that will permit law enforcement agencies to enforce the provisions of the treaty.[42]

United Nations Convention on Psychotropic Substances (1971)

The **United Nations Convention on Psychotropic Substances** is an agreement to control the availability of psychoactive drugs including amphetamines, barbiturates, benzodiazepines, and psychedelic drugs. The treaty, signed in Vienna, Austria, was the follow-up to the Single Convention on Narcotic Drugs, which did not include many of the newly developed drugs that were becoming popular at the time, particularly LSD and other hallucinogenic drugs. There are currently about 185 states participating in the treaty.[43]

United Nations International Conference on Drug Abuse and Illicit Trafficking (1987)

In 1987, the UN convened an International Conference on Drug Abuse and Illicit Trafficking in Vienna to establish international methods to combat the illicit drug problem on an international scale. The conference members considered a variety of possible options, including demand reduction, crop eradication, extradition, and the treatment and rehabilitation of addicts. There were three sessions, the first and third held in Vienna, and the second in Bolivia.

In the end, the committee members voted to accept a Declaration and the Comprehensive Multidisciplinary Outline of Future Activities in Drug Abuse Control. In this document, the committee members urged other governments to consider the framework provided by the UN when proposing drug control policies. As a way to increase resources for the UN Fund for Drug Abuse Control, the committee members asked member states to contribute funds.[44]

As a way to bring attention to the problem, the committee decided to observe June 26th of every year as the International Day Against Drug Abuse and Illicit Trafficking. Each year, the Day Against Drug Abuse has different theme, as noted in Table 10.4. One example was in 2013, when the theme was "Make Health Your 'New High' in Life, Not Drugs." The theme was geared toward educating the public, with a particular focus on youth, about the potential harmful effects of "bath salts," a newly emerging psychoactive substance. They wanted to make it clear that these new drugs were extremely dangerous and could cause death.[45]

Table 10.4 Themes for International Day against Drug Abuse

2012: "Global Action for Healthy Communities Without Drugs"

2011: "Say No!"

2010: "Think Health—Not Drugs"

> 2009: "Do Drugs Control Your Life? Your Life. Your Community. No Place for Drugs."
>
> 2008: "Do Drugs Control Your Life? Your Life. Your Community. No Place for Drugs."
>
> 2007: "Do Drugs Control Your Life? Your Life. Your Community. No Place for Drugs."
>
> 2006: "Value Yourself … Make Healthy Choices"
>
> 2005: "Drugs Is Not Child's Play"
>
> 2004: "Drugs: Treatment Works"
>
> 2003: "Let's Talk About Drugs"
>
> 2002: "Substance Abuse and HIV/AIDS"
>
> 2001: "Sports Against Drugs"
>
> 2000: "Facing Reality: Denial, Corruption and Violence"

United Nations Convention Against Illicit Traffic in Narcotic Drugs and Psychotropic Substances (1988)

The 1988 **United Nations Convention Against Illicit Traffic in Narcotic Drugs and Psychotropic Substances** provides the legal mechanisms for law enforcement to implement both the Single Convention on Narcotic Drugs and the Convention on Psychotropic Substances. The convention took effect on November 11, 1990, and has 188 member states participating.

The goal of the convention is to stop international drug traffickers from being able to traffic drugs and to deprive traffickers of any profits they may receive from the drug trade. States that agree to be part of the treaty must cooperate with law enforcement in any investigations and in the possible seizure of drug-related assets. Moreover, according to the treaty, participating countries must provide legal assistance to other countries if they seek to carry out searches and seizures, if requested.[46]

There are 34 articles in the treaty. They are listed in Table 10.5.

Table 10.5 Provisions of the 1988 Treaty

Article 1 Definitions

Article 2 Scope of the convention

Article 3 Offences and sanctions

Article 4 Jurisdiction

Article 5 Confiscation

Article 6 Extradition

Article 7 Mutual legal assistance

Article 8 Transfer of proceedings

Article 9 Other forms of co-operation and training

Article 10 International co-operation and assistance for transit States

Article 11 Controlled delivery

Article 12 Substances frequently used in the illicit manufacture of narcotic drugs or psychotropic substances

Article 13 Materials and equipment

Article 14 Measures to eradicate illicit cultivation of narcotic plants and to eliminate illicit demand for narcotic drugs and psychotropic substances

Article 15 Commercial carriers

Article 16 Commercial documents and labelling of exports

Article 17 Illicit traffic by sea

Article 18 Free trade zones and free ports

Article 19 The use of the mails

Article 20 Information to be furnished by Parties

Article 21 Functions of the Commission

Article 22 Functions of the Board

Article 23 Reports of the Board

Article 24 Application of stricter measures than those required by this Convention

Article 25 Non-derogation from earlier treaty rights and obligations

Article 26 Signature

Article 27 Ratification, acceptance, approval or act of formal confirmation

Article 28 Accession
Article 29 Entry into force
Article 30 Denunciation
Article 31 Amendments
Article 32 Settlement of disputes
Article 33 Authentic texts
Article 34 Depository

Conclusion

Drug trafficking is a global phenomenon. Drugs are grown in one country, processed in another, and sold in yet another. No country is immune from the global drug trade. The worldwide black market is violent, as groups fight each other to protect their territory and their drug sales, but also fight law enforcement as they attempt to enforce laws. The drug trade helps to fund terrorist activities and other organized crime groups. There have been many policies to combat the international black market, but none have been effective in reducing the amount of illicit drugs that are produced, smuggled, or sold to users. Despite this, there is no doubt that countries around the world will continue to battle the international market in the future.

Important Terms

Bureau of International Narcotics Matters
Cabinet Committee on International Narcotics Control
Cali Cartel
Drug Cartels
French Connection
Global Commission on Drug Policy
Golden Crescent
Golden Triangle
Guadalajara Cartel
Gulf Cartel
Juárez Cartel
Medellín Cartel
Mexican Drug Cartels
Operation Banco
Operation Boomer/Falcon
Operation Condor
Operation Cooperation
Operation Intercept

Operation Stopgap
Operation Trizo
Opium Wars
Pizza Connection
Sinaloa Cartel
Tijuana Cartel
United National Convention against
  Illicit Traffic in Narcotic Drugs
  and Psychotropic Substances
United Nations Commission on
  Narcotic Drugs
United Nations Convention on
  Psychotropic Substances
United Nations International
  Conference on Drug Abuse and
  Illicit Trafficking
United Nations Office on Drugs and
  Crime
United Nations Single Convention on
  Narcotic Drugs
World Federation Against Drugs

Review Questions

1. Describe some early smuggling operations that took place in the US.

2. What are the five major Mexican drug cartels? Give some examples of newer cartels.

3. Describe the Colombian drug cartels. How are they different from the Mexican groups?

4. Provide some examples of international treaties designed to stop international drug use. How could they be improved?

5. Describe how organized crime and terrorist groups benefit from the international drug trade.

6. What are some organizations that are active in the fight against international drug smuggling?

Endnotes

1. Shanty, F. "The Taliban, Al Qaeda, the Global Drug Trade, and Afghanistan as a Dominant Opium Source." University of South Australia, School of International Studies. http://www.picj.org/docs/issue3/The%20Taliban.pdf.

2. Potter, Mark. October 22, 2009. "Illegal Drugs Flow over and under US Border." NBC News. http://www.nbcnews.com/id/33433955/ns/us_news-crime_and_court/t/illegal-drugs-flow-over-under-us-border.

3. Fay, P. W. 1975. *The Opium War, 1840 1842*. Chapel Hill: University of North Carolina Press; Hernon, Ian. 2000. *The Savage Empire: Forgotten Wars of the 19th Century*. Thrupp, UK: Sutton Publishing.

4. Inglis, Brian. 1976. *The Opium War*. London: Hodder and Stoughton; Lovell, Julia. 2011. *The Opium War: Drugs, Dreams and the Making of China*. London: Picador.

5. Moore, Robin. 1972. *The French Connection*. Boston: Little, Brown; Maran, A. 2010. *Mafia: Inside the Dark Heart, the Rise and Fall of the Sicilian Mafia*. New York: St. Martin's Press.

6. Moore, Robin. 1972. *The French Connection*. Boston: Little Brown.

7. Alexander, Shana. 1998. *The Pizza Connection: Lawyers, Money, Drugs, Mafia*. New York: Weidenfeld and Nicolson; Havens, J. 1993. "'Pizza Connection' Legacy Examined." *Rock River Times*. http://rockrivertimes.com/1993/07/01/pizza-connection-legacy-examined/.

8. Marion, Nancy E. 2007. *Government versus Organized Crime*. New York: Prentice Hall; President's Commission on Organized Crime. 1984. *The Cash Connection: Organized Crime, Financial Institutions and Money Laundering*. https://www.ncjrs.gov/pdffiles1/Digitization/166517NCJRS.pdf; Reppetto, Thomas A. 2006. *Bringing Down the Mob: The War Against the American Mafia*. New York: H. Holt.

9. Goldberg, Peter. 1978. "The Federal Government's Response to Illicit Drugs, 1969–1978." Schaffer Library of Drug Policy, http://www.druglibrary.org/schaffer/library/studies/fada/fada1.htm; Nixon Presidential Library and Museum. "Cabinet Committee on International Narcotics Control." http://nixon.archives.gov/forresearchers/find/textual/central/subject/FG330.php; Nixon, Richard. September 7, 1971. "Memorandum Establishing the Cabinet Committee on International Narcotics Control." Online by Gerhard Peters and John T. Woolley. *The American Presidency Project*. http://www.presidency.ucsb.edu/ws/?pid=3139; Nixon, Richard. January 28, 1972. "Statement on Establishing the Office for Drug Abuse in Law Enforcement." Online by Gerhard Peters and John T. Woolley. *The American Presidency Project*. http://www.presidency.ucsb.edu/ws/?pid=3552.

10. "Bureau of International Narcotics and Law Enforcement Affairs." AllGov.com http://www.allgov.com/departments/department-of-state/bureau-of-international-narcotics; "Bureau of International Narcotics and Law Enforcement Affairs." US Department of State. http://www.state.gov/j/inl/.

11. UN Office on Drugs and Crime. 2010. "World Drug Report 2010." https://www.unodc.org/documents/wdr/WDR_2010/World_Drug_Report_2010_lo-res.pdf; UN Office on Drugs and Crime. 2011. "South-East Asia Opium Survey 2011, Lao PDR, Myanmar." http://www.unodc.org/documents/crop-monitoring/sea/SouthEastAsia_2011_web.pdf; Wiant, Jon. 1985. "Narcotics in the Golden Triangle." *Washington Quarterly* (Fall): 125–140.

12. US Department of Justice. February 2010. Drug Movement into and within the United States. https://www.justice.gov/archive/ndic/pubs38/38661/movement.htm.

13. Jonnes, Jill. 1996. *Hep-Cats, Narcs, and Pipe Dreams*. Baltimore: Johns Hopkins University Press; Langton, Jerry. 2012. *Gangland: The Rise of the Mexican Drug Cartels from El Paso to Vancouver*. Mississauga, ON: John Wiley and Sons; Nicaso, Antonio, 2005. *Angels, Mobsters and Narco-terrorists: The Rising Menace of Global Criminal Empires*. Mississauga, ON: John Wiley and Sons; Public Broadcasting System. "The Colombian Cartels." *Frontline*. http://www.pbs.org/wgbh/pages/frontline/shows/drugs/business/insice/colombian.html.

14. Shannon, Elaine. July 1, 1991. "The Cali Cartel: New Kings of Coke." *Time*. http://content.time.com/time/magazine/article/0,9171,973285,00.html.

15. Farah, Douglas. June 19, 1994. "Cali Cocaine Traffickers Fill Void Left by Medellin Cartel." *Sun Sentinel*; http://articles.sunsentinel.com.

16. Johnson, Tim. February 7, 2003. "Cali Cartel Still in 'Drug Kingpin' Business, U.S. Says." *Miami Herald*. http://www.latinamericanstudies.org/drugs/cali.htm; Rempel, William

C. 2011. *At the Devil's Table: The Untold Story of the Insider Who Brought down the Cali Cartel.* New York: Random House.

17. Kline, H. 1995. *Colombia: Democracy under Assault.* Boulder, CO: Westview.

18. Langton, Jerry. 2012. *Gangland: The Rise of the Mexican Drug Cartels from El Paso to Vancouver.* Mississauga, ON: J. Wiley and Sons, Canada.

19. *2013 International Narcotics Control Strategy Report (2013 INCSR).*

20. Beittel, June S. 2013. "Mexico's Drug Trafficking Organizations: Source and Scope of the Violence." *Congressional Research Service.* 1–50.

21. June S. Beittel, July 22, 2015. "Mexico: Organized Crime and Drug Trafficking Organizations." Congressional Research Service, report 7-5700. www.crs.gov.

22. Judicial Watch. August 5, 2014. "DOJ Report: Nearly Half of Fed Crimes Near Mexican Border." Available at http://www.judicialwatch.org/blog/2014/08/doj-report-nearly-half-fed-crimes-near-mexican-border.

23. Bewley-Taylor, David R. 2012. *International Drug Control: Consensus Fractured.* New York: Cambridge University Press; Leger, Donna Leinwand. June 12, 2013. "U.S. Cracks Down on Mexican Drug Trafficker's Family." *USA Today.* http://www.usatoday.com/story/news/world/2013/06/12/us-freeze-drug-kingpin-assets/2416191/.

24. June S. Beittel, July 22, 2015. "Mexico: Organized Crime and Drug Trafficking Organizations." Congressional Research Service, Report 7-5700.

25. Bunck, J. M., and M.R. Fowler. 2012. *Bribes, Bullets, and Intimidation: Drug Trafficking and the Law in Central America.* State College, PA: Penn State University Press; "The Five Most Famous Drug Cartels." 2012. *Coalition Against Drug Abuse.* http://drugabuse.com/the-five-most-famous-drug-cartels/.

26. Carpenter, Ted Galen. 2012. *The Fire Next Door: Mexico's Drug Violence and the Danger to America.* Washington, DC: Cato Institute; Elkridge, Chris. 1998. "The Mexican Cartels: A Challenge for the 21st Century." *Criminal Organizations* 12(1/2): 5–15.

27. Campbell, H. 2011. "No End in Sight: Violence in Ciudad Juárez." *NACLA Report on the Americas* 44(3): 19; Hill, S. 2010. "The War for Drugs: How Juárez Became the World's Most Dangerous City." *Boston Review* 35(4): 19–23; "Mexican Drug Cartels: An Update." 2010. *Stratford Analysis*, 4; "Mexico Security Memo: A New Juárez Cartel." 2012. *Stratford Analysis*, 32; Nergon, S. 2009. "Baghdad, Mexico." *Texas Monthly* 37(1): 60; "The Southwest Border Initiative 12 March 1997." Remarks of Thomas A. Constantine, Director, DEA.

28. Abernethy, Samantha. February 4, 2010. "Miguel Angel Caro Quintero, Former Sonoran Cartel Boss, Convicted in Denver." *Huff Post Denver.* http://www.huffingtonpost.com/2010/02/04/miguel-angel-caro-quinter_0_n_449654.html; Bewley-Taylor, David R. 2012. *International Drug Control.* Cambridge, MA: Cambridge University Press; Grayson, George W. 2010. *La Familia Drug Cartel: Implications for U.S.-Mexico Security.* Carlisle, PA: Strategic Studies Institute, US Army War College; US Senate Committee on Foreign Relations. March 12, 1997. *Mexico and the Southwest Border Initiative.* Statement of Thomas A. Constantine, Director, DEA. http://www.usdoj.gov/dea/pubs/congrtest.

29. "Mexican Drug Cartels." May 19, 2010. *NPR.* http://www.npr.org/templates/story/story.php?storyId=126890893; Vulliamy, Ed. November 1, 2008. "Tijuana Streets Flow with the Blood of Rival Drug Cartels." *The Guardian.* http://www.theguardian.com/world/2008/nov/02/mexico-drugs-trade-tijuana-cocaine.

30. Booth, William. May 24, 2012. "Mexico's Two Major Crime Cartels Now at War." *Washington Post.* http://www.washingtonpost.com/world/mexicos-two-major-crime-cartel-s-now-at-war/2010/08/25/gJQAUhKlmU_story.html; Diaz, Lizbeth. September 5, 2011.

"Tijuana Violence Slows as One Cartel Takes Control." *Reuters*. http://www.reuters.com/article/2011/09/05/us-mexico-drugs-tijuana-idUSTRE7844EX20110905.

31. Alexander, Harriet. October 20, 2013. "Francisco Rafael Arellano Felix: Head of Tijuana Cartel Shot Dead by Clown Gunmen." *The Telegraph*. http://www.telegraph.co.uk/news/worldnews/centralamericaandthecaribbean/mexico/10392239/Francisco-Rafael-Arellano-Felix-Head-of-Tijuana-Cartel-shot-dead-by-clown-gunmen.html; "Mexican Drug Lord Gets Life in Prison." November 5, 2007. *CBS News*. http://www.cbsnews.com/news/mexican-drug-lord-gets-life-in-prison/; "Mexico Seizes Top Drugs Suspect." October 27, 2008. *BBC News*. http://news.bbc.co.uk/go/pr/fr/-/2/hi/americas/7692319.stm; US Department of Justice, Office of Public Affairs. 2012. "Eduardo Arellano-Felix Extradited from Mexico to the United States to Face Charges." http://www.justice.gov/opa/pr/2012/August/12-crm-1072.html.

32. Bagley, B. August, 1–22, 2012. "Drug Trafficking and Organized Crime in the Americas: Major Trends in the 21st Century." *Woodrow Wilson International Center for Scholars Latin American Program*. http://www.wilsoncenter.org/sites/default/files/BB%20Final.pdf.

33. Drug Trafficking and Organized Crime in the Americas." 2012. Woodrow Wilson International Center for Scholars. http://www.wilsoncenter.org/sites/default/files/BB%20Final.pdf.

34. Ryan, Kennedy. 2013. "FBI: 24 Charged in Drug Trafficking Networks in Pasadena and Antelope Valley." *KTLA-5 News*, http://ktla.com/2013/12/12/fbi-24-charged-in-drug-trafficking-networks-in-pasadena-and-antelope-valley/#axzz2nPqSmxa9.

35. Bewley-Taylor, David R. 2012. *International Drug Control: Consensus Fractured*. Cambridge: Cambridge University Press; "Drug Trafficking and the Financing of Terrorism." 2007. United Nations Office on Drugs and Crime; Swarts, Phillip. September 20, 2013. "Terrorist Organizations Still Profit from Afghan Drug Trade." *Washington Times*. http://www.washingtontimes.com/news/2013/sep/20/terrorist-organizations-still-profit-afghan-drug-t/.

36. United Nations Office on Drugs and Crime. "Drug Trafficking and the Financing of Terrorism." https://www.undoc.org/undc/en/frontpage/drug-trafficking-and-the-financing-of-terrorism.html.

37. Remi L. Roy, October 26, 2014. "How Lucrative Illegal Drug Trafficking Finances International Terrorist Organizations" *The Fix*. http://www.alternet.org/drugs/how-lucrative-illegal-drug-trafficking-finances-international-terrorist-organizations.

38. "Global Commission on Drug Policies." January 25, 2011. *The War on Drugs*. http://newslanc.com/2011/01/25/global-commission-on-drug-policies/.

39. United Nations Department of Public Information. 1995. *Basic Facts about the U.N.* United Nations. "The Commission on Narcotic Drugs." http://www.unodc.org/unodc/en/commissions/CND/index.html; United Nations, Office on Drugs and Crime. "Twenty Years of Narcotics Control under the United Nations." http://www.unodc.org/unodc/en/data-and-analysis/bulletin/bulletin_1966–01–01_1_page002.html.

40. United Nations Office on Drugs and Crime. "United Nations Office on Drugs and Crime." http://www.unodc.org/pdf/unodc_brochure_2003.pdf.

41. World Federation Against Drugs. "Constitution of World Federation Against Drugs." http://www.wfad.se/about-wfad/wfad-declaration/35-wfad-declaration/51-constitution. World Federation Against Drugs. "Aims." http://www.wfad.se/about-wfad/aims. International Narcotics Control Board. "Single Convention on Narcotic Drugs, 1961." http://www.incb.org/incb/en/narcotic-drugs/1961_Convention.html; 2015. "INCB Encourages States to Consider the Abolition of the Death Penalty for Drug-Related Offenses." http://www.incb.org/documents/Publications/PressRelease/PR2014/press_release_050314.pdf.

42. United Nations. "Single Convention on Narcotic Drugs, 1961." https://www.unodc.org/pdf/convention_1961_en.pdf.

43. Osmanczyk, Edmund Jan. 1985. *Encyclopedia of the United Nations and International Agreements*. New York: Routledge; United Nations Office on Drugs and Crime. "Convention on Psychotropic Substances, 1971." http://www.unodc.org/unodc/en/treaties/psychotropics.html.

44. Reagan, Ronald. June 11, 1987. "Announcement of the United States Delegation to the International Conference on Drug Abuse and Illicit Trafficking"; Reagan, Ronald. 1987. "Remarks at a White House Briefing on the United Nationals International Conference on Drug Abuse and Illicit Trafficking"; United Nations General Assembly. December 7, 1987. A/Res/42/112. http://www.un.org/documents/ga/res/42/a42r112.htm; United Nations General Assembly, A/Res/42/126. http://www.un.org/en/ga/search/view_doc.asp?symbol=A/RES/42/126&Lang=E&Area=RESOLUTION.

45. United Nations. "International Day Against Drug Abuse and Illicit Trafficking: June 26." http://www.un.org/en/events/drugabuseday/index.shtml.

46. United Nations. "United Nations Convention Against Illicit Traffic in Narcotic Drugs and Psychotropic Substances, 1988." http://www.unodc.org/pdf/convention_1988_en.pdf.

Chapter 11

Drug Prevention and Treatment Programs

Chapter Objective: Most people addicted to drugs have a difficult time remaining drug-free and often relapse many times in their struggle against drugs. Treatment is complicated and arduous. This chapter reviews some of the concerns regarding drug treatment and different options that exist.

Introduction

As the number of people addicted to drugs increases, the search for ways to help users refrain from further drug use continues. Unfortunately, we know very little about addiction and ways to discourage future drug use. Our knowledge about why some people become addicted to substances and others do not is still developing, and we are still learning about the "best" way to help addicts become drug free. Even as early as the late 1800s, physicians debated the reasons for addiction and many began to consider substance addiction to be a physical disease that needed treatment as opposed to being the result of a person's weak moral character. Popular cures for drug addiction at this time emphasized detoxification programs whereby a patient's dosage of a drug would be reduced over time. In some cases, a user would consume large amounts of vitamins to help the detox process succeed. At the same time, many early "cures" for addiction would be what we would now call "quack cures." One popular treatment option in the early 1900s was the Towns Lambert Cure, named after Dr. Alexander Lambert. This involved giving patients large doses of hallucinogenic mushrooms over a two-day span.

As science advanced, so did our knowledge about why people become addicted to drugs and how to help those who suffer from drug dependence. Throughout the 1920s and 1930s, many more legitimate treatment options developed. For example, clinics provided morphine to heroin addicts, which would reduce their cravings for more drugs. Over time, experts continued to learn more about drug addiction. In 1970, the government put an emphasis on expanding our knowledge about drug use and addiction and federal funding was allocated to support research into the treatment of addiction. In 1972 the Drug Abuse Office and Treatment Act was passed that created the Special Action Office for Drug Abuse Prevention in the White House, which has the goal of preventing drug use.

Even today we continue to learn more about drug use and addiction and building new treatment options that help addicts learn to remain drug free. This chapter will focus on programs designed to help people refrain from drug use. This includes **prevention programs** that deter drug use before it begins (e.g., DARE), and **treatment programs** to help those who have developed an addiction to illicit drugs (e.g., drug courts). Medications are being developed to help an addict stay away from drugs, but some addicts are more successful with other treatment options such as support groups. The success of treatment centers, including the Betty Ford Center and the Hazelden Foundation, point to the critical services they provide. Other topics for this chapter include LifeRing Secular Recovery, Mandatory Treatment, the National Youth Anti-Drug Media Campaign, needle exchange programs, Phoenix House, Recovery Circles, and 12-step programs.

Drug Addiction Programs: Prevention and Treatment

Most drug addiction programs can be categorized as either a prevention program or a treatment program. Prevention programs are those that prevent a person from using drugs initially or ceasing to use drugs. Treatment programs are geared toward people who are already heavy users or addicts and help them learn to not use illegal drugs. These two types of programs are described below.

Prevention Programs

Prevention programs are those that have the goal of diverting people away from using illegal drugs and thus preventing any future drug-related problems that may arise. Sometimes these programs are called demand reduction programs as they reduce the demand for a drug. Many prevention programs are primary prevention programs, as they attempt to prevent people from using drugs at all. Other programs focus more on those people who have tried drugs, and maybe who use drugs occasionally, from continuing their use and possibly becoming addicted. These are called secondary prevention programs.

Many prevention programs focus on educating individuals about the dangers of drug use. Early prevention programs focused on the morality of drug use, teaching people that drug use was wrong for moral and ethical reasons. They sometimes also exaggerated the risks of using drugs, concentrating on the harmful effects of drugs. More recently, education-based prevention programs provide truthful information about the dangers of drug use. Most concentrate on providing this information to younger people who may be more open to prevention techniques before they ever try drugs. Once a young person begins to use drugs, prevention efforts are less likely to work. Typically, drug use peaks during a person's teenage years, but children as young as 12 or 13 have already used drugs. Because of this, most drug education programs begin in elementary-school. This way, the participants may understand the possible harm that could result from drug use and may be less likely to abuse drugs.

Other prevention programs include drug testing in schools or the workplace. Some recent prevention programs aim to reduce risk factors for drug use, such as poor school performance or parental or sibling drug use. Yet other programs attempt to increase protective factors, which are those factors that help a person avoid drug use, such as attendance in a religious setting or strong family ties. Prevention programs can also be speakers, such as doctors or recovered addicts, who speak to students or others about their experiences with illicit drugs. Some participants visit places such as hospitals, drug treatment centers, courtrooms, or jails. All of these programs have the same goal: to prevent illicit drug use and abuse. Some popular prevention techniques are listed in Table 11.1.

Table 11.1 Prevention Techniques

- Alternatives—This approach calls for the participation of target populations in constructive and healthy activities such as drug-free dances, youth/adult leadership activities, community drop-in centers, and community service activities that exclude drug use. Constructive and healthy activities are designed to offset the attraction to, or otherwise meet the needs usually addressed by alcohol and other drugs.

- Community-Based Process—This strategy enhances the ability of the community to more effectively provide prevention and treatment services for alcohol, tobacco, and drug-abuse disorders. Activities in this strategy include organizing, planning, enhancing efficiency and effectiveness of service implementation, interagency collaboration, coalition building, and networking. Some examples include community and volunteer training, multiagency coordination and collaboration, accessing programs and funding needed services, and community team building.
- Early Intervention—This approach uses activities that are designed to modify the behavior of an early substance abuser. It includes a wide spectrum of activities ranging from user education to formal intervention and referral to treatment provided by a substance-abuse professional.
- Education—This strategy builds critical life and social skills through structured learning processes. Critical life and social skills include decision making, peer resistance, coping with stress, problem solving, interpersonal communication, and systematic and judgmental abilities. Examples of this strategy include classroom and/or small group sessions, parenting and family-management classes, peer-leader/helper programs, educational programs for youth groups, and groups for children of substance abusers.
- Environmental—Programs of this nature challenge and change community standards, codes, and attitudes that tend to tolerate, accept, or support the use of drugs in the general population. This strategy is divided into two subcategories to permit distinction between activities that center on legal and regulatory initiatives and those that relate to the service and action-oriented initiatives. Some examples include promoting the review of drug-use policies in school; technical assistance to communities to maximize local enforcement procedures governing availability and distribution of alcohol, tobacco, and other drugs; modifying alcohol and tobacco advertising practices; and product-pricing strategies.
- Information—This approach provides knowledge and increases awareness of the nature and extent of drug use, abuse, and addiction, and their effects on individuals, families, and communities. Knowledge and awareness are promoted through available prevention

and treatment programs and services. Some examples include clear-inghouse/information resource centers, resource directories, media campaigns, brochures, radio/TV public-service announcements, speaking engagements, health fairs/health promotion, and telephone/computer information lines.

- Problem Identification and Referral—This strategy includes activities that identify those who have engaged in illegal or age-inappropriate use of tobacco or alcohol and persons who have begun to use illicit drugs. Effort is generated to assess whether the early alcohol and drug use of the individual can be reversed through education. It does not include any activity designed to determine if a person is in need of treatment. Some examples include employee-assistance programs, student-assistance programs, and educational programs related to driving while under the influence or driving while intoxicated. In-creased chances of substance use, stress, violence, trauma, and post-traumatic stress are among the reasons people are at greater risk of substance abuse, including relapse to alcohol and drug abuse, addic-tion, and cigarette smoking. Emotional strain caused by the September 11, 2001, terrorist attacks on the United States and threats of bioterrorism have led large numbers of Americans to seek treatment for substance-abuse problems. For example, "one year after the Okla-homa City bombing three times as many residents of that city reported increased drinking compared with residents of comparatively sized Indianapolis, Indiana. Understandably, rescue workers in Oklahoma City also experienced significant rates of substance abuse, depression, and suicide months and years after the bombing" (Columbia University Center of Addiction and Substance Abuse 2001).

Source: Richard E. Isralowitz. 2015. "Prevention" in Nancy E. Marion and Willard M. Oliver, eds. Drugs in American Society. Santa Barbara, CA: ABC-CLIO, pp. 755–759.

Keep a Clear Mind

There are a variety of drug education and prevention programs that exist today. One of those that has been successful in deterring drug use is **Keep a Clear Mind** (KACM). This program is geared toward older students between the ages of 8 and 12 and their parents. The program involves four weeks of ac-tivities that are to be completed by parents and their children together to show children the harmful effects of drug use and at the same time provide them with alternatives to drugs. Studies on the effectiveness of KACM indicate that 20 percent of parents noted that their children were more able to resist peer pressure to use alcohol, tobacco, and marijuana.

Project ALERT

Another anti-drug program geared toward older children is called **Project ALERT**, which is geared toward middle-school children around the ages of 11–14. This is a two-year program with 14 lessons that focus on the drugs that adolescents are most likely to use: alcohol, tobacco, marijuana, and inhalants. The program relies on a variety of techniques (videos, classroom discussions, role-playing, and small group activities), to teach resistance skills. Studies on Project ALERT indicate that it is effective in preventing youth from experimenting with drugs. After students completed the program they were less likely to use marijuana and cigarettes.[1]

Community Trials Intervention to Reduce High-Risk Drinking

A third successful education program is **Community Trials Intervention to Reduce High-Risk Drinking** (RHRD). This is a community-based program that focuses on reducing alcohol use by people of all ages and subsequent alcohol-related crimes (e.g., drinking and driving, underage drinking, or binge drinking). The program relies on increasing community awareness, responsible beverage service in restaurants and stores, preventing underage access to alcohol, increased enforcement, and community involvement. Analysis of this program found that there was a decline in self-reported events of drunk driving and binge drinking. There was also a decrease in emergency room visits for assault injuries related to alcohol.[2]

Drug Abuse Resistance Education

A popular drug education program is Drug Abuse Resistance Education, often referred to as the **DARE** program. It was originally developed in 1983 by the Los Angeles Police Department. The program seemed to have success and the federal government allocated funds to expand the program to all schools nationwide. With the extra money, many schools adopted the program. It was estimated that 75 to 80 percent of schools across the nation used the DARE program, eventually becoming the most popular school-based drug education program in schools.

The DARE program is a ten-week effort in which local police officers teach young students, generally in fifth and sixth grades, about the dangers of drug use, peer pressure, and ways to remain drug-free. For many reasons, the DARE program is not as popular as it once was and has been largely discontinued. Most studies of the program indicated that it did not reduce drug use in the long term. One study in 1994 by the Research Triangle Institute indicated that children who graduated from a DARE program were no more likely to stay drug-free than children who did not participate in the program. Instead, the study results seemed to indicate that a young person may have been even more curious to try drugs after learning about them in the program. Another study by the General Accountability Office (GAO) also found that the there was no difference between the drug use patterns found in fifth and sixth graders who graduated from a DARE program and those who did not. In total, these findings were interpreted to mean that DARE did not have a significant effect on preventing drug use by youth.

In addition to educating children about the dangers of drug use, the DARE program was a way to establish better relationships between the students and the police officers in their communities.

In response, changes were made to the program. In the new program, students are shown the effects that drugs have on the body. It also helps them develop their decision-making skills. Analysis of the revised DARE program shows that the new program is much more effective. Even though the federal government has stopped additional funding for DARE, the program continues to be popular in many schools today.[3] In fact, Presidents Bush and Obama have declared a National DARE day in April of each year to bring attention to the program.

National Youth Anti-Drug Advertising Campaign

Another attempt to educate people about the dangers of drug use was the **National Youth Anti-Drug Advertising Campaign** that was supported by the Partnership for a Drug-Free America and the Office of National Drug Control Policy between 1998 and 2004. Throughout these years, the media donated over $3 billion in free television and media coverage to run ads about the dangers of drug use. Congress also allocated around $1 billion on the anti-drug advertising campaign. Anti-drug messages appeared on television, in newspapers, magazines, on shopping bags, on videos, bumper stickers, and billboards. The goals were simple: to educate and enable youth to reject drug use, to prevent youth from ever using drugs, and to convince those who started to use drugs to stop.

The information presented in these ads was not always accurate. One study found that 94% of youth admitted to seeing the ads at least once a week, thus the campaign succeeded in sending a message. However, there did not seem to be any significant change in marijuana use patterns for the youth.[4]

Zero Tolerance Policies

Zero tolerance policies were adopted (and still exist) in many schools and workplaces. When these policies exist, a student or employee could be suspended or expelled (or fired) if they were caught in possession of drugs or consuming illicit drugs on school or work grounds or at events. Studies of these programs seem to show that zero tolerance policies, especially in schools, disproportionately affect youth of color. Evidence shows that black and Latino students are expelled more often than white students, and males more likely than females to be punished. Students with disabilities are almost three times more likely to receive a suspension than those without. Moreover, zero tolerance policies do not seem to make the schools any safer.[5] However, they do work to remove those who violate the rules and create a more conducive learning environment for other children and may have a deterrent effect on others.[6] Many schools continue to support zero tolerance but have become more flexible and evaluate events on a case-by-case basis.

Drug Testing Policies

Drug testing is a form of demand reduction, as it deters people from using drugs. Many schools and workplaces have instituted drug testing of its employees and students. These policies not only protect the school or employer, but also protect the worker and others in the work environment.

Many employees are required to pass a drug test before being hired. If they refuse, a company does not have to consider them for the position. Once hired, an employee can be subject to random drug testing, or tested based on observations by a supervisor. If an employee seems to be impaired or if they are found to be in possession of a drug, a manager may send an employee for testing. If the person is found to be under the influence, then further action could be taken. An employee may also be required to take a drug test in the case of an accident on the job. For example, if they were driving a vehicle that is in an accident, they will probably be required to take a drug test. If an employee tests positive, they could face additional discipline. Some employees are subject to random drug testing.

Drug testing is required by some jobs, especially those that involve operating heavy machinery or if the job involves public safety, such as those of bus drivers and those in the medical field. Some schools require testing of student athletes or if they suspect a student of drug use. Drug testing of federal government employees began in 1986 when President Reagan announced Executive Order 12564, in which he established a drug-free workplace. As part of this new program federal agencies were required to begin urine testing programs.

Those on probation or parole may be required to undergo drug testing. If they test positive, they may be sent (or returned) to prison. Athletes are drug tested to look for illegal substances, particularly performance-enhancing steroids. Since drugs are usually stable in frozen urine, the samples can be stored for long periods in case the results are appealed.

There are many methods used to test for drugs. The most common is urinalysis, but testing can also be done on an individual's hair, saliva, and sweat. The costs of these tests vary, as do their reliability, drugs detected, and detection period. In most cases, a drug test can identify if a person used marijuana, cocaine, barbiturates, LSD, methadone, opiates, amphetamines, and PCP. However, there are tests for other drugs as well. Alcohol does not remain in a person's blood a long enough time for most tests to detect it. Breathalyzers and oral fluid tests can detect current use only. Thus, while it is easy to detect if someone is under the influence of alcohol at the time, the use of alcohol is difficult to determine after that. Marijuana remains in the urine for weeks after use.[7]

These tests are accurate but take a few days to show results. Using a person's hair will show evidence of drug use over a longer time span, up to a few months. Tests on a person's saliva can show immediate results and are difficult to fake. Another way to test for drug use is sweat patches. These are applied to a person's skin to collect sweat samples. This can be over a few days or even a few weeks. If they are removed, the tester will know. Urine tests (urinalysis) are accurate but can easily be faked. Users may drink excess fluids to dilute their urine.

Random testing of students has been very controversial. Some argue that these policies assume that those being tested are guilty of drug use without reason. The Supreme Court has found that random testing of student athletes is acceptable in the case of *Vernonia School District v. Acton* (1995). In *Board of Ed v. Earls et al.* (2002), the Supreme Court decided that "drug testing policy was a reasonable means of supporting the school district's interest in preventing and deterring drug use among students and therefore did not constitute a violation of the Fourth Amendment."

Federal Demand Reduction Programs

The federal government has put an emphasis on reducing the demand for drugs. The DEA, for example, created a Demand Reduction Section within its agency that has as its goal to establish a public awareness education campaign for community leaders and to reach out to school-aged children with drug education and prevention programs. They also work with businesses and their employees to maintain a drug-free workplace. The section provides the public with current information about illicit drugs and collaborates with other agencies for prevention efforts.

More **federal drug demand reduction programs** are found in the Office of Justice Programs, part of the US Justice Department that also uses many different programs to lessen drug demand. Their programs are outlined in Table 11.2.

Table 11.2 Demand Reduction Programs in the Office of Justice Programs

1. Byrne Discretionary Grant Program: provides funding directly to public and private agencies and nonprofit organizations to support programs that prevent drug use.
2. Byrne Formula Grant Program: provides funding to states, which then make sub-grants to state and local governments to implement programs that improve anti-drug strategies.
3. Indian Alcohol and Substance Abuse Demonstration Program: provides funding for programs designed to reduce crimes associated with the use of alcohol and controlled substances in tribal communities.
4. Residential Substance Abuse Treatment Program: provides funding to improve the ability of states and local governments to provide residential substance abuse treatment for incarcerated inmates.
5. Weed and Seed Program: allocates money to communities that want to create ways to "weed out" drug use and then "seed" the neighborhood with programs for achieving economic revitalization.
6. Juvenile Justice Discretionary Grant Program: provides money to support research and training for programs to prevent juvenile drug use.
7. Delinquency Prevention Programs (formerly Title V Local Delinquency Prevention Incentive Grants): allocates funding and training for local delinquency prevention programs. This includes grant funding for programs to combat underage drinking.
8. Drug Prevention Demonstration Program: a program designed to develop and test programs that increase youth's perception that drug use is risky, harmful, and unattractive.

Treatment

Since drug addiction is considered by many to be a chronic disease, addicts must learn about their addiction and how to manage it over the course of their lifetime. They must learn about what triggers their drug use (what causes it) and any emotional issues that may contribute to their addiction. In order for treatment to be effective, it must help an abuser refrain from using drugs and then maintain a drug-free lifestyle so they can be a productive member of society.

There are many forms of treatment and there is no one perfect treatment program for all addicts. One drug abuse treatment program may be very successful for one person, but it may not be for another abuser. Every addict faces different personal issues, family situations, and environmental concerns. They have different health concerns and different levels of addiction. This means that every treatment program should be geared toward the individual. The most appropriated treatment matches the individual with the components of the program. Whether a treatment program succeeds depends on many factors, including things like the extent of the addiction, the drug involved, the addict's desire to be there, family support, or any additional medical or psychological disorders the addict may have. Most successful treatment involves some ongoing or continuing care. This is critical because this is the time during which addicts are most vulnerable to relapse.

Once the appropriate treatment plan is determined, figuring out how to pay for it can be another problem. Many healthcare plans limit the time addicts can stay in residential treatment, and many restrict the amount they will pay for medications. Many people cannot afford treatment. Some states have passed laws that require insurers to cover addiction treatment. Many employers have established programs that offer aftercare and insurance assistance to employees.

Some treatment is compulsory, or mandatory, drug treatment. This occurs when an addict is forced to enter into or complete a treatment program, most often after being charged with criminal behavior. In most situations, if an addict completes treatment for their drug abuse, the criminal charges against them may be dropped. If the offender commits another offense, they will then face punishment. Other individuals may be required to attend treatment as part of their sentence or as a condition for probation or parole. Some treatment take place within a prison, but some take place in the community.

Mandatory treatment is used because many addicts commit their crimes because of their drug use. The addict may deny their drug abuse caused the behavior, so they will be forced to enter.

Mandatory treatment programs are controversial, and their success is unclear. According to the National Institute on Drug Abuse, "most studies suggest that outcomes for those who are legally pressured to enter treatment are as good as or better than outcomes for those who entered treatment without legal pressure. Individuals under legal pressure also tend to have higher attendance rates and remain in treatment for longer periods, which can also have a positive impact on treatment outcomes." However, those who are forced to participate in treatment programs may not be open to changing their behaviors. It is well known that a person who is forced into treatment program who does not want to make changes will not do so. But in general, many addicts who participate in treatment programs will increase their chances of staying clean later on.[8]

Detoxification and Withdrawal

If the user has a severe addiction, they may be in need of **detoxification** to remove all of the drug from their body. A detox typically takes around 30 days. Some users may suffer from painful withdrawal symptoms, depending on the drug they were taking, past drug use, and other characteristics of the individual. Serious withdrawal symptoms may pose a risk to the individual, so a person may require medical care to prevent further harm. In some cases, increasingly smaller doses of the drug are given to the user to help ease any withdrawal symptoms they may experience. Sometimes medications like sedatives and anti-anxiety drugs may help to alleviate some of the symptoms.

Medication

Medication may also be used as part of a treatment program aimed at helping users stop taking drugs. These medications may block the withdrawal symptoms a user feels when they stop ingesting a drug, making it less likely they will use the drug again. Medications may also act to suppress the cravings that an addict feels when they stop using a drug. A user will not feel high from these medications, but they will not have the urge to use the drug so they are able to carry on their daily activities. The addict can gradually reduce the dosage over time with less discomfort than they would otherwise feel. These medications are often provided by medical personnel so they can be monitored and regulated.

Using medications to treat withdrawal symptoms is referred to as pharmacological drug treatment. What happens is that addicts will use one drug to prevent the use of another. It must be stressed that there are no drugs that will cure an addiction problem or prevent it, but some drugs can reduce or eliminate cravings for drugs, thereby reducing the chance that an addict will want to use again.

A common example of this is nicotine replacement therapy that is used by people who are trying to quit the use of tobacco (most often cigarettes). This is often referred to as "the patch" but there are also lozenges, gum (e.g., Nicorette), and tablets. Some argue that a user is simply trading one form of nicotine for another.

Another common medication that addicts use is methadone, which is a synthetic narcotic used to treat those addicted to heroin and other opiates. When an addict uses methadone, they get a "fix" that lasts longer than heroin so they can go longer before feeling the withdrawal symptoms. Methadone must be taken regularly.

Methadone maintenance programs are controversial. Some critics argue that a methadone user can develop psychological and physical dependency on methadone, meaning that they are simply replacing one addiction with another. Some abusers will use methadone in addition to the other drugs they are taking. It has been argued that a person could take methadone indefinitely.[9]

Another medication used to treat addicts is Naltrexone, sold under the trademarked name of Revia or Vivitrol. This drug was first synthesized in 1965 and is most often used to treat addictions to opiates. Taken orally, the drug can block the pleasurable effects of these drugs. Studies have shown that Naltrexone is extremely effective in combating opiate addiction. There have been reports of a five year, 95% success rate, allowing recovering addicts to lead stable lives.

In the early 1990s, it was discovered that the drug could also reduce an individual's craving for alcohol. The FDA approved the use of Naltrexone for this purpose.[10] Others studies have found that naltrexone is effective in treating those who suffer from compulsive shopping disorder, eating disorders, and tobacco addictions.[11]

Like all drugs, there are possible side effects from using Naltrexone. These include confusion, hallucination, blurred vision, severe vomiting, and diarrhea. It can also cause loss of appetite and anxiety for some. If taken in large doses, Naltrexone can cause liver damage. Naltrexone comes in the form of a tablet and can be taken at home or under supervision at a treatment center or clinic.[12]

Vaccines are being developed that prevent addicts from experiencing a pleasurable feeling from using a drug. One of these is Vivitrol, which seems to be helpful for those addicted to cocaine and tobacco.

A drug that is sometimes used to treat addictions to alcohol, cocaine, and methamphetamine is called Prometa. A person taking Prometa must take three prescription drugs while under a physician's care along with nutritional supplements. To date, the long-term effectiveness of Prometa has not been shown.[13]

Outpatient Drug Treatment Programs

Outpatient drug treatment occurs when patients receive treatment while they remain at home. Also called community-based treatment, this type of treatment is reasonable for people who have employment but are still in need of drug treatment.

Rehabilitation may occur in a residential (inpatient) setting for several days, weeks, or even months. The addict remains at the center and is not permitted to leave. It may also be as an outpatient, where the user visits a clinic regularly but does not reside there and can go home at night. Here the addict may receive counseling and group support to help addicts resume and maintain a drug-free lifestyle. If needed, medications can be used to block cravings or minimize the chance of relapse.

Residential Drug Treatment Programs

Many drug treatment programs are residential, where patients live in a facility for a period of time, anywhere from 1 month to 2 years. Here they receive treatment for their addictions, and their progress is monitored by medical personnel. Over time, the patient will assume more independence and will be able to "reenter" society. In most cases, a patient will be required to enroll in school or be employed in some capacity before they are permitted to leave the facility. In many cases there is an aftercare program located in the community that patients must attend.

Hospitals and other homes to treat alcoholism and opiate addiction have existed for a long time. They were sometimes called therapeutic communities (TC). One popular drug treatment program was Synanon. Here, patients were required to be completely removed from society for two years during which time they had to work and pursue an education. The founder, Charles Dederich, later said that an addict could never be cured, so many people were required to stay in the program their entire lives. Over time, the group became more like a cult. People joined who were not drug users and Dederich maintained control over them. Married couples were split up and forced to marry others. Children were sometimes separated from their parents, and former members were beaten. It eventually declared itself a religion in 1975. This and other residential treatment programs are described in Table 11.3.

Table 11.3 Residential Treatment Programs

Synanon

Synanon was founded in 1958 by Charles Dederich, a drinker who sought help from AA. When approached by a drug addict for help, he realized that AA did not help those addicted to drugs. Dederich adapted the 12-Step process found in AA to drug addicts. He added lectures and therapy to the original program. Clients would be served in a 2-year residential program. The approach seemed to be very effective. It had innovative principles based on behavior modification. However, because Dederich believed that addiction was a lifelong disorder, eventually there were no more graduates. The program became an alternative community, and it became very abusive.

By the 1970s, there were rumors about child abuse, illegal activities, and oppressive treatment of members. To make matters worse, Dederich was involved with some tax-related problems. An investigation of the community resulted with assault charges being brought against members. In 1980, Dederich agreed to a plea bargain on the conspiracy charges. He was forced to give up the leadership of the organization. By the 1990s, the organization had largely been dissolved. Dederich passed away in 1997.[14]

Phoenix House

Phoenix House was founded by Mitchell S. Rosenthall in 1967 as a treatment facility for drug addicts. It has become one of the country's largest private, nonprofit treatment providers. They provide both residential and outpatient treatment for 3,000 adults and teenagers in many locations in the US. The treatment programs in Phoenix House use self-help methods in a group setting. They see drug abuse as a disorder affecting the whole person. The goal of Phoenix House is to integrate their clients into society as drug-free and productive citizens.

Phoenix House provides services to all adults, but also special populations including veterans, adolescents, pregnant mothers, and children. They provide drug screening and prevention, mental health services, drug programs, detoxification services, and sober living and support services. The staff also helps to educate the community about drug use and addiction.[15]

In 1983, Phoenix House opened its first residential high school for addicted teenagers who have fallen behind. In 2005, the Phoenix House

Academy was designated as a "model program" by the US Department of Justice, and the federal government subsequently has listed the academy model in the Substance Abuse and Mental Health Services Administration's National Registry of Evidence-Based Programs and Practices.

Betty Ford Center

The Betty Ford Center is a hospital that is dedicated to treating those suffering from chemical dependency. The center was founded in 1982 and is located in Rancho Mirage, California, near the Eisenhower Medical Center. The center is named in honor of First Lady Betty Ford, wife of president Gerald Ford, after she fought addictions to prescription drugs and alcohol. Betty Ford admitted herself to a clinic in 1978, after her family persuaded her that she needed help. She was successfully treated and released from the hospital. Upon her release, Ford became active in the fight to raise awareness of alcohol and drug dependency issues and their treatment. Mrs. Ford sought to establish a treatment center that focused attention on special needs of women who have addictions. Ford and her friend, Ambassador Leonard Firestone, established the nonprofit Betty Ford Center. Since that time, the center has grown and has become an internationally recognized treatment facility.

The professionals at the Betty Ford Center believe that their patients who have become dependent on drugs are suffering from a chronic progressive disease that may lead to death if not treated. Their treatment programs involve family members in group therapy to treat not only the patient but also the family members who are also victims of the abuse.

The center treats male and female addicts. The specific treatment plans for each differ. They also offer a variety of programs to patients and their families. The goal is "treatment without shame."

In addition to the residential center, the Betty Ford Center also has an outpatient program that allows patients to continue to live in their home and work in the local community while receiving treatment for their addictions during the day. The program relies on a 12-step approach to recovery. The facility has also created a 90-day program for chronic relapsers, patients with a prolonged detoxification period, or those with multiple prior treatments. The center also has a children's program, which works with children ages seven through twelve who are not themselves addicted, but who have chemically dependent family members.[16]

Betty Ford and the center have helped to eliminate the stigma that is sometimes associated with drug abuse and alcohol dependency. Since the clinic has opened, it has treated over 90,000 patients, including celebrities such as Lindsay Lohan, Billy Joel, Elizabeth Taylor, and Kelsey Grammer.

Hazelden Foundation

The Hazelden Foundation is one of the most renowned addiction treatment facilities in the US. It is a nonprofit organization that relies on a multidimensional approach to treating patients who have become addicted to alcohol and other drugs. Hazelden also publishes literature related to addiction and recovery, and the Hazelden Foundation includes research facilities and a graduate school in addiction studies.

The first Hazelden facility was established in Center City, Minnesota, in 1948 to treat priests and other professionals who were addicted to alcohol. At the time, Hazelden took a simple approach to treating the patients. Residents were expected to make their beds, behave properly, talk with one another, and attend daily lectures on the 12 steps of Alcoholics Anonymous.

As the program grew, the Hazelden expanded its treatment options. It began to use the "Minnesota Model" for treating its patients. This treatment viewed alcoholism as a progressive disease that required lifelong abstinence. They also treated their patients with respect and created an environment of support for them. They also rely on the 12-step approach as part of the Minnesota Model, but other treatment options have also been added.

Over time, Hazelden has opened treatment centers in Chicago; New York City; Newberg, Oregon; and many locations in Minnesota. Since it first started, over 200,000 addicted individuals have been treated at Hazelden facilities.

Hazelden also has education and training programs. They have a certificate program for chemical dependency counselors and a Graduate School of Addiction Studies, which opened in 1999. In addition, Hazelden offers a Pastoral Training Program and Professional-in-Residence and Physician-in-Residence programs. The Butler Center for Research is also a part of the Hazelden Foundation. This group conducts clinical research, collaborating with other research centers, and disseminating scientific findings.

> In September 2013, the Hazelden Center merged with the Betty Ford Center. The new organization will be known as the Hazelden Betty Ford Foundation.[17]
>
> Source: Janzen, Rod A. 2001. *The Rise and Fall of Synanon: A California Utopia*. Baltimore: Johns Hopkins University Press; DeLeon, George. 1974. *Phoenix House: Studies in a Therapeutic Community 1968–1973*. New York: MSS Information Corp.; Betty Ford Center. "A Brief History of the Betty Ford Center." http://www.bettyfordcenter.org/welcome/ourhistory.php.; Hazelden. "Hazelden: Changing Lives. Every Day." http://www.hazelden.org/web/public/about_hazelden.page.

Behavioral Therapy

Behavioral therapy is effective for many addicts. This type of therapy provides a user with coping strategies through which they can identify situations that may trigger their drug use and learn how to cope with them without turning to drugs. An addict can learn how to manage their cravings for a drug and deal with any issues that may have caused the original addiction.

Self-Help Groups

For some addicts, taking part in **self-help groups** such as Alcoholics Anonymous (AA) or Narcotics Anonymous (NA) can help prevent relapse. These programs use a 12-step process that helps users understand their behavior. There are many types of support groups.

Alcohol Mutual Aid Societies

Mutual aid societies are abstinence-based groups that help people stop using alcohol. One of the first **alcohol mutual aid societies** was the Washingtonians, established in 1840 in Baltimore by six alcoholics. The members were mostly lower-, middle-, and working-class alcoholics who focused on helping individual users. They did not push for tighter legal restrictions on alcohol. They had rallies and speakers, but also had weekly meetings in which they provided support, encouragement, advice, and solidarity to other members. At these meetings, members told stories about how alcohol had harmed their lives along with the benefits of abstaining. If any members relapsed and drank, others provided emotional, financial, and medical support to help them. The Washingtonians dissolved in 1840s amid disagreements over membership, religious ties, and political ties.

Similar groups were formed in the early 1870s, called the Ribbon Reform Clubs. Examples included the Royal Ribbon Reform Club, the Blue Ribbon Reform Club, and the Red Ribbon Reform Club. They banned political discussions at all group events. It was expected that members would meet on a regular basis and provide mutual support to others. They also signed pledges of abstinence. To indicate their membership in a club, members wore ribbons on their lapels. This way, members would recognize others while traveling.

The Ribbon Reform Clubs appealed to lower- and middle-class drinkers. The Blue Ribbon Club meetings provided men with the male camaraderie often found in a saloon. Many found that the support meetings helped them remain abstinent.

Another alcohol mutual aid society was the Keeley Clubs, organized by recovering alcoholics affiliated with Leslie Keeley's institutes for inebriates. These started around 1890 and eventually were established nationally. Keeley believed that alcoholism was a disease and that it was necessary for an alcoholic to be treated with injections, behavior modification techniques, and a supportive therapeutic environment. Members of Keeley Clubs took part in morning meetings devoted to speeches, discussions, and mutual support. Keeley Clubs dissolved in the early twentieth century.[18]

Alcoholics Anonymous and 12-Step Programs

Alcoholics Anonymous (AA) is a program to help addicts who abuse alcohol. The program was originally founded in 1935 in Akron, Ohio, by Bill Wilson and Robert "Dr. Bob" Smith, two alcoholics who formed a mutual aid society, or support group, where members stood in front of others and made personal declarations or told their stories. In general, the organization supports abstinence, teaching its members to view themselves as being "allergic" to alcohol. They also avoid supporting any hard and fast answers to alcoholism and recovery. The group is comprised of local mutual support groups rather than a national organization for a more personal approach to treatment. Advice is given to members not by professionals, but by other alcoholic members who give stories of their own experiences. The group took the title "Alcoholics Anonymous" from the practice of members referring to themselves as "a nameless bunch of drunks." The only requirement for membership is the desire to stop drinking.

The organization provides addicts with an accessible and therapeutic environment to help them find support in their fight against their addiction. AA meetings generally consist of members sharing their experiences and wisdom as well as readings from *Alcoholics Anonymous* (also called *The Big Book*), the organization's basic text.

Alcoholics Anonymous Meeting by Photographee.eu via fotolia.com.

The program relies on a set of twelve principles for recovery that all patients must abide by. The steps are intended to help an addict recover from their addiction. The 12 steps for individuals who want to participate in the AA program are shown in Table 11.4, and the 12 traditions are found in Table 11.5. The traditions were developed as a way to prevent a hierarchical power structure from emerging among members.

Table 11.4 12 Steps of AA

Admitting that they are powerless over alcohol and that their lives have become unmanageable.

Coming to believe that a power greater than themselves could restore sanity to their lives.

Deciding to turn their wills and lives over to the care of God, however they understand him (their personal "higher power").

Making a moral inventory of themselves.

Admitting to their higher power, themselves, and to other people the exact nature of their wrongs.

Being ready to have their higher power remove these defects of character.

Asking the higher power to remove their shortcomings.

Making a list of all persons they have harmed, and becoming willing to make amends to them.

Making amends to such people wherever possible, unless doing so would cause harm to them or to others.

Continuing to take personal inventory and admitting when they are wrong.

Through prayer and meditation, working to improve conscious contact with their higher power.

Having had a spiritual awakening through these steps, trying to carry the message to other alcoholics, and to practice these principles in all aspects of their daily lives.

Source: Alcoholics Anonymous. http://www.aa.org/pages/en_US/twelve-steps-and-twelve-traditions.

Members are encouraged to attend weekly meetings. AA membership grew from 311,450 in 1970 to 907,575 in 1980. By 2006, there were somewhere around 2 million members. Today, groups vary and depend on the needs of the members. Some groups focus on God and spirituality, whereas other are more secularized. Some groups have limited their members by particular demographics, such as gender, age, language, or sexual orientation. AA has grown into the world's largest alcohol recovery group and most successful alcohol mutual aid society. AA is an international organization, but the central unit is the local meeting.[19]

Table 11.5 12 Traditions of AA

Our common welfare should come first; personal recovery depends upon AA unity.

For our group purpose there is but one ultimate authority—a loving God as He may express Himself in our group conscience. Our leaders are but trusted servants; they do not govern.

The only requirement for AA membership is a desire to stop drinking.

Each group should be autonomous except in matters affecting other groups or AA as a whole.

Each group has but one primary purpose—to carry its message to the alcoholic who still suffers.

An AA group ought never endorse, finance, or lend the AA name to any related facility or outside enterprise, lest problems of money, property, and prestige divert us from our primary purpose.

Every AA group ought to be fully self-supporting, declining outside contributions.

AA should remain forever nonprofessional, but our service centers may employ special workers.

AA, as such, ought never be organized; but we may create service boards or committees directly responsible to those they serve.

AA has no opinion on outside issues; hence the AA name ought never be drawn into public controversy.

Our public relations policy is based on attraction rather than promotion; we need always maintain personal anonymity at the level of press, radio, and films.

Anonymity is the spiritual foundation of all our traditions, ever reminding us to place principles before personalities.

Source: "Twelve Steps and Twelve Traditions." Alcoholics Anonymous. http://www.aa.org/pages/en_US/twelve-steps-and-twelve-traditions.

Other groups have emerged that are based on the 12-step process. Al-Anon and Alateen are groups that support spouses and children of alcoholics.

Al-Anon

Al-Anon is a support group for relatives and friends of alcoholics that helps them deal with the problems associated with other people's addiction to alcohol. The group was created in the 1940s after some family members were waiting for their loved ones to attend an AA meeting. The family members realized that alcoholism not only affected the individual who was drinking but also others close to them. The family members were looking for the same support as the members of AA received and formed their own organization. They began to share their experiences and provide support for each other. The group is now an international, nondenominational organization with tens of thousands of local chapters.

Al-Anon is independent of AA, but tied their mission to that of AA. At first, Al-Anon's publicly stated goals are to foster cooperation and understanding of the AA program, to help members live by the 12 steps and grow spiritually along with their alcoholic loved ones, and to welcome and give comfort to families of new AA members.

While Al-Anon is independent of AA, the Sixth Tradition of Al-Anon indicates that there should always be cooperation between the two organizations. Al-Anon holds weekly meetings for its members, which are much like those held by AA. Al-Anon members discuss their difficulties in dealing with an alcoholic, such as emotional stress and feelings of shame and personal failure. They abide by the 12 steps and 12 traditions of AA. They recognized that the effects of alcohol use can be a powerful impact on the entire family, not just the alcoholic.[20]

Alateen

Alateen is a support group for children and teenagers who have relatives or friends who abuse alcohol. Alateen was created in 1957 by a 17-year-old California teenager whose father was in AA and whose mother was in Al-Anon. He saw that Al-Anon helped many family members of alcoholics, but did not meet the needs of teenage relatives, particularly those between 12 and 20 years old.

The first Alateen group included the 17-year-old teen and five others who met in a room downstairs from the room where their parents were meeting. It grew quickly, and by 1963 there were over 200 Alateen groups. Alateen has expanded to have around 3,500 worldwide groups. Most Alateen groups are sponsored by a local Al-Anon group. Meetings are held at places such as community centers, churches, and schools, or other convenient and nonthreatening places for young people. The meetings provide support from others who may be facing similar situations or experiencing similar problems. These other members provide support and tips and share experiences to help them cope with the problems of living with an alcoholic.

Often, professionals will help the teenagers understand that they are not the cause of the problems and should not feel responsible in any way for other's choices to use alcohol, or for the behaviors that may result from the alcohol use. They tell the youth that they cannot control the behavior of others. They attempt to reinforce that they can have successful lives and positive experiences despite the problems caused by the alcohol abuse.[21]

SOS and LifeRing

James Christopher, an alcoholic, sought to form a non-religious organization to help alcoholics. He held the first meeting of a new group, called

Secular Organizations for Sobriety or Save Our Selves (SOS), in 1986 in California. This was a self-help organization for recovering alcoholics. SOS still exists in every state.[22] In 1997, some members of SOS split off and formed a new organization called **LifeRing**. This group (also called LifeRing Secular Recovery), is a nonprofit, mutual aid organization that is a nonspiritual 12-step abstinence program. The organization attempts to empower addicts to take the lead in their fights against addiction. They have meetings in the United States, Canada, and Europe. They have removed any spiritual component that is found in AA.

The basis of LifeRing's approach is their "Three-S" philosophy. The first "S" refers to sobriety, which is defined as the complete abstention from alcohol or other addictive drugs at all times. The second "S" refers to secularity, since LifeRing opposes spiritual elements and the submission to a higher power. This does not mean that members are opposed to religion. Rather, the group includes addicts from all religious backgrounds. The approach taken by LifeRing is that a person's recovery can be achieved through human, rather than divine, intervention. The third "S" in LifeRing's philosophy is self-help. LifeRing stresses the importance of individual motivation and effort to overcoming their addictions.[23]

Cocaine Anonymous

Cocaine Anonymous (CA) is a 12-step organization that is modeled on Alcoholics Anonymous but not affiliated with AA. Created in 1983, CA is a support group whose requirement for membership is simply a desire to quit using cocaine and other substances. People who are addicted to the drug share their experiences with others. It has an estimated 30,000 members.[24]

Narcotics Anonymous (NA)

Narcotics Anonymous (NA) is a **12-step program** for those suffering from an addiction to narcotics. The founders relied on the Alcoholics Anonymous (AA) model when it was founded in Southern California in 1953.

Similar to AA, NA encourages their members to attend regular meetings to help them stay clean. Addicts provide mutual support to each other. NA is not concerned with the particular substance being abused. Stressing that addiction is the problem, and not the particular substance, demonstrates that NA considers addiction to be a disease. The meetings are open to all addicts, regardless of their religious, social, racial, and ethnic backgrounds. The meetings typically take place in buildings run by public, religious, or civic organizations. Like AA, NA members must follow the 12 steps and 12 traditions that promote recovery from addiction.[25]

AA and NA often cooperate with each other, but they are not affiliated with each other. NA has no affiliations with treatment centers or correctional facilities. Similarly, NA does not employ professional counselors or therapists as they help addicts maintain their abstinence from all drugs, including alcohol.

Minnesota Model

The **Minnesota Model** is a treatment method for addicts that was developed during the late 1940s and 1950s by therapists in Minnesota. It is a multidisciplinary approach based on the premises of AA that includes professionals and family members into the treatment plan. They offer intensive counseling, group therapy, and guidance in lifestyle and behavioral issues. In the 1950s, the Hazelden Foundation adopted the model.

When it was first established, the Minnesota Model required a client to remain in a facility for 28 days. When this period was over, patients were required to complete follow-up treatment as a member in AA or another 12-step program. In recent years, the length of inpatient treatment has become more flexible and outpatient treatment is available. The core treatment philosophy has remained the same. This includes total abstinence, inclusion of the family in the treatment plan, and continued care after release as part of the treatment plan.[26]

The Minnesota Model includes several core principles. These were developed to treat alcoholics, but they are also used to treat those addicted to other drugs as well. These are listed in Table 11.6.

Table 11.6 Core Principles to the Minnesota Model

1. Alcoholism is an involuntary, primary disease that is diagnosable.
2. Because it is a progressive, chronic disease, untreated alcoholism will worsen without treatment.
3. Although it cannot be cured, alcoholism can be arrested.
4. Treatment outcomes cannot necessarily be predicted by the alcoholic's motivations for seeking treatment.
5. Successful alcoholism treatment must address physical, psychological, social, and spiritual dimensions.
6. Alcoholics should be treated with respect and dignity in a supportive environment if treatment is to succeed.

7. Alcoholics and other addicts are vulnerable to the abuse of other drugs; treatment for these addictions can be addressed as chemical dependence.
8. Alcoholism and chemical dependency are best treated with a multidisciplinary approach and individualized treatment plans.
9. A primary counselor, usually a recovering addict, is the best person to organize and implement an addict's treatment plan.
10. Recommended treatment combines 12-step work such as that found in AA, lectures, and individualized counseling.
11. The best follow-up group support structure for recovering addicts is AA.

Source: "The Minnesota Model." The Hazelden Betty Ford Foundation. http://www.hazeldenbettyford.org/articles/the-minnesota-model.

There are many other program designed to help addicts recover. These are outlined in Table 11.7.

Table 11.7 Recovery Programs

Moderation Management (MM): MM was created in 1994 by Audrey Kishline, and is centered around teaching alcoholics moderate their drinking as opposed to refraining from alcohol use. This approach has been criticized by many treatment professionals who believe that total abstinence is needed. Those in MM were encouraged to attend meetings, examine the reasons why they used drugs, establish goals and priorities, and periodically review their progress. Members were to abide by certain rules:

1. Never drink and drive.
2. Never drink when it would endanger oneself or others.

3. Avoid drinking every day.
4. Limit the amount of alcohol consumed per week.

In 2000, Kishline was involved in a drunk driving accident and killed two people.

Rational Recovery (RR): RR is a self-recovery movement that was founded in 1986. The organization places an emphasis on the "addictive voice recognition technique" (AVRT). Members are taught to recognize their addictive voice—any thinking that tempts a person to use alcohol or drugs. This way, an addict can identify the triggers that cause them to drink and then have power to deny those urges. There are no meetings or therapy, no abstinence requirements, and no use of medications to treat addiction. In recent years, some groups have broken off. One of those group that broke off formed a new entity called Self-Management and Recovery Training (SMART).

Secular Organizations for Sobriety (SOS): SOS, or Save Our Selves, was founded in 1986. It is a network of agencies that focus on personal responsibility for recovering from addiction while relying on the assistance of one's SOS group of choice. Membership meetings are available in many cities and in other countries. The organization's principles are embodied in its proposed steps to recovery:

1. Acknowledge one's alcoholism/addiction.
2. Reaffirm the presence of the disease and recommit to the knowledge that, no matter what, it is not possible to drink or use again.
3. Take whichever steps are necessary to maintain sobriety.
4. Recognize that life's uncertainties cannot be used as an excuse to use drugs or drink, and that life can be good without drugs.
5. As clean and sober individuals, be able to share thoughts and feelings with one another.
6. Maintaining sobriety should be the top priority.

Self-Management and Recovery Training (SMART): This group began operating in 1994 and seeks to help addicts gain the maturity and self-reliance to identify and then eliminate any self-destructive attitudes and behaviors that may result. They encouraging addicts to abstain from alcohol, develop emotional independence from others, and reduce their need for support groups.

Women for Sobriety (WFS): In 1975, WFS was created because of a need for a group that focused on the unique needs of female alcoholics. Although its principles are similar to those of AA, it defines its approach to recovery somewhat differently:

1. Accept responsibility for the disease and take charge of one's own life.
2. Remove negative thinking from one's life.
3. Develop a happy state of mind rather than waiting for it to just happen.
4. Understand problems so they do not become overwhelming.
5. Believe in oneself as a capable, compassionate, and caring woman.
6. Make one's life a great experience through conscious effort.
7. Embrace caring and love to change the world.
8. Focus on keeping one's priorities in order.
9. By viewing oneself as renewed, refuse to be submerged in the past.
10. Understand that love given is also returned.
11. Work to develop an enthusiasm for life.
12. Appreciate one's own competence.
13. Focus on being responsible for one's life and thoughts.

WFS groups originated in the United States, but there are also groups in Canada, Europe, Australia, and New Zealand.

Sources: Horvath, Tom. 2012. "If Not AA, Then What? SMART Recovery and the AA Alternatives." *Huffington Post.* http://www.huffingtonpost.com/tom-horvath-phd/addiction-treatment_b_1663494.html; Marlatt, G. Alan, ed. 1998. *Harm Reduction: Pragmatic Strategies for Managing High-Risk Behaviors.* New York: Guilford Press; Peele, Stanton. 2004. *7 Tools to Beat Addiction.* New York: Three Rivers Press; Rehab Centers. 2013. "Alternative Addiction Treatment for Drugs and Alcohol." http://therehabcenters.com/alternative-addiction-treatment/; Schaler, Jeffrey A. October 2002. "Addiction Is a Choice." *Psychiatric Times* 19(10): 54, 62. Stop Your Addiction. "Alternative Addiction Treatment." http://www.stopyouraddiction.com/addiction-treatment/alternative-addiction-treatment/; Trimpey, Jack. 1996. *Rational Recovery: The New Cure for Substance Addiction.* New York: Pocket Books.

Harm Reduction Programs

Harm reduction programs are policies that are intended to reduce the potential negative consequences of drug use, such as health, social, and economic consequences. They do not focus on reducing drug use or consumption but are geared toward reducing the possible harms associated with drug use for those people who are unable to abstain, or do not want to stop, using drugs. These programs help to lessen the possible dangers of using drugs.

The underlying concept behind harm reduction programs is that some people will not be able to stop using drugs, either because they are addicted or because they do not want to. Their continued use can lead to clear dangers to both the user and to family, friends, and the community. At this point, the attention can shift to increasing the safety of that drug use so that the least harm results from it. The success of a harm reduction program should not be based on how many people are no longer using drugs, but rather by changes in the number of deaths, crimes, and suffering caused by drug use.

An example of a popular harm reduction policy is a needle exchange program. Here, clean, sterile needles are provided to IV-drug users in exchange for their used ones. Many IV-drug users share needles with each other, spreading diseases such as HIV/AIDS. If users are given clean needles, it lessens the possibility that diseases will be passed from one person to another. It is thought that this program reduces the harm to the drug user and to society at large because it helps stop the spread of the disease.

Another example of a common harm reduction program is providing a safe area for people to use drugs. Some cities provide private rooms for users to inject drugs. This way, they will not be injecting in a public place where others, particularly children, may see it. Further, criminals will not be able to prey on the drug user who may not be able to defend themselves.

A third popular harm reduction program is called "Dance Safe." This program is popular in rave parties, where ecstasy pills are checked to determine their purity. This reduces chance that a user is taking a drug that is tainted with a harmful substance, thus protecting the user. It helps society by reducing the potential healthcare costs of the users and the chance that they may overdose.[27]

Harm reduction policies are often very controversial. Those who are opposed to them believe that these policies enable or encourage users to abuse drugs rather than helping them abstain from further use. They argue that harm reduction supports continued drug use. Another argument that is used against harm reduction policies is that these policies drain resources that could be used more effectively elsewhere. The third argument against harm reduction policies is that they result in more drug use in communities and thus threaten the public's safety. Drug users will move to places where these policies are popular, thus compromising the safety of these communities.

Needle Exchange Programs

The first **needle exchange program** was created in 1984 in Amsterdam by a group called the Junkie Union. In the United States, the first needle exchange program can be traced back to one man, Jon Parker, who distributed clean needles to addicts in New Haven, Connecticut, and to addicts in Boston. The first comprehensive program that provided clean syringes to addicts was established in Tacoma, Washington, in 1988. In 1998, New York was the first US city to use public money to fund a needle exchange program, but this was halted the next year after the federal government imposed a ban on its funding of needle exchange programs.

Drug Courts

Drug courts are used as sentencing alternatives for nonviolent drug offenders. They were first started in the late 1980s as a response to the growing number of drug-related cases. When a first-time offender is charged with a nonviolent drug offense, instead of being sent directly to a term in prison, the offender will instead be placed in a community-based treatment program that involves some kind of drug treatment. If the offender completes the treatment program without committing any further crimes, they will be released. If the offender does not complete the program, or commits another crime, a judge may send them to a correctional facility for the remainder of their original sentence.

Initial studies of drug courts indicate that they are very successful in keeping offenders off of drugs for the long term. Research indicates that the drug courts reduce crime as much as 35%. Moreover, the average recidivism rate is only 16% in the first year after completing the program and 27% in the second year. They have also been attributed with saving money. It has been estimated that drug courts can save anywhere between $4,000 and $12,000 per person.[28]

The treatment programs associated with the drug courts usually involve intensive treatment in the community. Many offenders may receive both drug treatment and mental health treatment. There will also be unannounced drug testing and probation supervision. The judges involved in drug courts receive extra training and develop expertise on drug abuse and treatment options.[29]

It appears that drug courts really do lower recidivism, or the chance that a person will be re-arrested and returned to prison. That means that there is less crime being committed by these people. They also save money because the of-fender is not going to prison and not committing more crime. They also seem to help addicts beat their addiction.[30]

By 2009, there were over 2,140 drug courts found across the US. Every state had already created a drug court or was planning to do so. Some jurisdictions have established drug courts for juvenile drug offenders. They are based on the same concept as those for adults but they are tailored to the special needs of young offenders. Not only do these juveniles receive drug treatment, they might also receive counseling, education, or other services.

Another type of alternative court is the family drug court. Here, parents who may be abusing drugs are provided treatment as a way to help the entire family deal with the drug abuse.

Drug Intervention Programs

A **drug intervention** occurs when family, friends, and other important people in a person's life come together to convince a drug abuser to seek help for their addiction. Often, the abuser is denying they have a problem, or may be facing painful withdrawal symptoms if they do not use the drug. The intervention is usually a face-to-face conversation that takes place in a neutral place, at a time when the user is sober. Sometimes a professional who has experience in addiction interventions will participate. This can be a counselor, social worker, or interventionist. The goal is to help the user agree to seek treatment.

There are three types of interventions. The first is primary prevention in-tervention, which is used for those with no or little experience with illicit drug use in the past. The goal is to prevent that person from using drugs at all, or to stop if they have started. Typically, these interventions are used for young people who have risk factors for drug use, such as family members (parents, siblings) who are using drugs. The second type of intervention is secondary prevention intervention. Here, the person has experienced some drug use. The goal in these interventions is to limit additional drug use, either the number of times it is used or the amount of the drug that is used. These interventions help to teach responsible drug use. This type these interventions is usually geared toward teenagers or young adults. The third type of intervention is a tertiary prevention, which is geared toward the serious user/abuser. The goal is to get the user to agree to treatment in the hopes that he/she will refrain from further drug use.

Another type of intervention is called a brief intervention. These are inter-ventions that are conducted by a healthcare specialist or a counselor in a clinical setting. The expert will perform a routine assessment of the user's drug use. If needed, the professional will discuss the possible consequences of drug abuse and addiction and will recommend treatment to the individual. The goal of this action is simply to increase the user's knowledge of drug use and motivate them to change.[31]

Conclusion

Drug prevention programs are designed to help people avert drug use before it becomes a problem. It has been argued that drug education programs are cost effective because it is cheaper to run an education program than deal with the consequences of long-term drug abuse. Thousands of people suffer from an addiction to a drug and most face serious hurdles in overcoming that addiction. There is no one perfect treatment option, and a treatment plan must fit the needs of the individual. There are many options for treatment, from residential to community-based, and each one provides a different approach to assist a user to become drug-free. In the end, not everyone wants to stop using drugs, but for those that do the road to sobriety can be long and difficult.

Important Terms

Al-Anon

Alateen

Alcohol Mutual Aid Societies

Alcoholics Anonymous

Behavioral Therapy

Cocaine Anonymous

Community Trials Intervention to Reduce High-Risk Drinking

DARE

Detoxification

Drug Courts

Drug Intervention

Drug Testing

Federal Demand Reduction Programs

Harm Reduction Programs

Keep a Clear Mind

LifeRing

Medications

Minnesota Model

Narcotics Anonymous

National Youth Anti-Drug Advertising Campaign

Needle Exchange Programs

Outpatient Drug Treatment

Prevention Programs

Project ALERT

Residential Drug Treatment

Self-Help Groups

Treatment Programs

Zero Tolerance Policies

Review Questions

1. What are the differences between drug demand reduction programs and drug treatment programs?

2. Give some examples of drug demand reduction programs

3. What are some drug treatment programs that are commonly used today?

4. If you could design a drug education program, what would it entail?

5. Why are treatment programs so diverse?

Endnotes

1. ProjectAlert.com. "Substance Abuse Prevention for Grades 7 & 8." http://www.project alert.com/.

2. Substance Abuse and Mental Health Services Administration, Prevention Research Center. "Community Trials Intervention to Reduce High-Risk Drinking." http://www.pire.org/CommunityTrials/index.htm.

3. Berman, Greg, and Aubrey Fox. 2009. "Lessons from the Battle over DARE: The Complicated Relationship between Research and Practice." New York: Center for Court Innovation; DARE. "About DARE." http://www.dare.com/home/about_dare.asp; "The DARE Program: A Review of Prevalence, User Satisfaction, and Effectiveness." 1994. Washington, DC: US Department of Justice, Office of Justice Programs, National Institute of Justice; "GAO Literature Review Reiterates Ineffectiveness of Original DARE." January 27, 2003. *Alcoholism & Drug Abuse Weekly* 15(4); Retsinas, Joan. March 12, 2001. "Decision to Cut Off US Aid to DARE Hailed." *Providence Business News.* 5B; Rosenbaum, Dennis. 1998. "Assessing the Effects of School-Based Drug Education: A Six-Year Multilevel Analysis of Project DARE." *Journal of Research in Crime and Delinquency* 35(4): 381–412.

4. Hornik, Robert, Lela Jacobsohn, Robert Orwin, Andrea Piesse, and Graham Kalton. 2008. "Effects of the National Youth Anti-Drug Media Campaign on Youths." *American Journal of Public Health* 98(12): 2229–2236.

5. Kang-Brown, Jacob, Jennifer Trone, Jennifer Fratello, and Tarika Daftary-Kapur. 2013. "A Generation Later: What We've Learned about Zero Tolerance in Schools." Vera Institute of Justice, Center on Youth Justice. http://www.vera.org/sites/default/files/resources/downloads/zero-tolerance-in-schools-policy-brief.pdf.

6. American Psychological Association Zero Tolerance Task Force. 2008. "Are Zero Tolerance Policies Effective in the Schools?" *American Psychologist* 63(9): 852–862.

7. National Institute on Drug Abuse. "Drug Testing." http:// http://www.drugabuse.gov/related-topics/drug-testing; Sawvel, Patty Jo, ed. 2006. *Student Drug Testing.* Farmington Hills, MI: Greenhaven; Verstraete, Alain. 2011. *Workplace Drug Testing.* London: Pharmaceutical Press.

8. National Institute on Drug Abuse. 2012. "Is Legally Mandated Treatment Effective?" http://www.drugabuse.gov/publications/principles-drug-abuse-treatment-criminal-justice-populations/legally-mandated-treatment-effective.

9. Cooper, Mary H. 1990. *The Business of Drugs*. Washington, DC: Congressional Quarterly; Yates, Rowdy, and Margaret S. Malloch. 2010. *Tackling Addiction: Pathways to Recovery*. Philadelphia, PA: Jessica Kingsley Publishers; Bart, Gavin. 2012. "Maintenance Medication for Opiate Addiction: The Foundation of Recovery." *Journal of Addictive Diseases* 31(3): 207–25.

10. O'Brien, Charles P., Laura A. Volpicelli, and Joseph R. Volpicelli. 1992. "Naltrexone in the Treatment of Alcoholism: A Clinical Review." *Alcohol* 13(1): 35–39; O'Malley, Stephanie. 2002. "Naltrexone and Alcoholism Treatment." Rockville, MD: US Department of Health and Human Services, Public Health Service, Substance Abuse and Mental Health Services Administration, Center for Substance Abuse Treatment; O'Malley, Stephanie S., Adam J. Jaffe, Grace Chang, Richard S. Schottenfeld, Roger E. Meyer, and Bruce Rounsaville. 1992. "Naltrexone and Coping Skills Therapy for Alcohol Dependence." *Archives of General Psychiatry* 49: 881–87.

11. Black, Donald W. 2007. "Compulsive Buying Disorder: A Review of the Evidence." *CNS Spectrum* 12(2): 124–32.

12. "Naltrexone." US National Library of Medicine/National Institutes of Health. http://www.nlm.nih.gov/medlineplus/druginfo/meds/a685041.html; US Department of Health and Human Services, Substance Abuse and Mental Health Services Administration, Center for Substance Abuse Treatment. 2009. "The Facts about Naltrexone for Treatment of Opioid Addiction." Washington, DC.

13. New York State Office of Alcoholism and Substance Abuse Services. 2007. "FYI Prometa." http://citesource.trincoll.edu/apa/apagovreportweb.pdf; Prometa. *Medical and Behavioral Health Policy Manual*. http://notes.bluecrossmn.com/web/medpolman.nsf/50c2d5c81dd37e6a862569bd0054c1b2/61c94b9ef44e3885862574860070464a/$FILE/Prometa.pdf.

14. Gerstel, David U. 1982. *Paradise, Incorporated—Synanon: A Personal Account*. Novato, CA: Presidio Press; Janzen, Rod A. 2001. *The Rise and Fall of Synanon: A California Utopia*. Baltimore: Johns Hopkins University Press; Mitchell, Dave, Cathy Mitchell, and Richard Ofshe. 1980. *The Light on Synanon: How a Country Weekly Exposed a Corporate Cult—and Won the Pulitzer Prize*. New York: Seaview Books.

15. DeLeon, George. 1974. *Phoenix House: Studies in a Therapeutic Community 1968–1973*. New York: MSS Information Corp; "Phoenix House Philosophy." October 22, 1989. *New York Times*. http://www.nytimes.com/1989/10/22/nyregion/phoenix-house-philosophy.html; "The Phoenix House Way." Phoenix House. http://www.phoenixhouse.org/.

16. Ashley, Jeffrey S. 2003. *Betty Ford: A Symbol of Strength*. New York: Nova History Publishers; Betty Ford Center. "A Brief History of the Betty Ford Center." http://www.bettyfordcenter.org/welcome/ourhistory.php; Betty Ford Center. "Alcohol and Drug Rehabilitation." http://www.bettyfordcenter.org/programs/index.php; Felci, Erica. September 24, 2013. "Betty Ford Center Merges with Hazelden Foundation." *USA Today*. http://www.usatoday.com/story/news/nation/2013/09/24/betty-ford-center-merges-with-hazelden-foundation/2865931/.

17. Felci, Erica. September 24, 2013. "Betty Ford Center Merges with Hazelden Foundation." *USA Today*. http://www.usatoday.com/story/news/nation/2013/09/24/betty-ford-center-merges-with-hazelden-foundation/2865931/; Hazelden. "Hazelden: Changing Lives. Every Day." http://www.hazelden.org/web/public/about_hazelden.page.

18. Betty Ford Center. 2011. "Significant Events in the History of Addiction Treatment and Recovery in America." http://www.bettyfordcenter.org/recovery/article.php?category= methods-techniques&post=significant-events-in-the-history-of-addiction-treatment-and-recovery-in-america; National Council on Alcoholism and Drug Dependence, Inc. "Mutual Aid/Self Help Support Groups." http://www.ncadd.org/index.php/get-help/ mutual-aid-support-groups; White, William. 2003. "Alcoholic Mutual Aid Societies." In J. Blocker and I. Tyrell, eds., *Alcohol and Temperance in Modern History*, 24–27. Santa Barbara, CA: ABC-CLIO.

19. Alcoholics Anonymous. 2001. *Alcoholics Anonymous: The Story of How Many Thousands of Men and Women Have Recovered from Alcoholism*. New York: Alcoholics Anonymous World Services; Alcoholics Anonymous. 2007. *Big Book*. S.I.: Works Publishing; B., Mel. 2007. *101 Meeting Starters: A Guide to Better Twelve Step Discussions*. Center City, MN: Hazelden; Blocker, Jack S. Jr., David M. Fahey, and Ian R. Tyrrell, eds. 2003. *Alcohol and Temperance in Modern History: An International Encyclopedia*. Santa Barbara, CA: ABC-CLIO.

20. Al-Anon. "Sixty Years of Hope." http://www.alanon.org.za/; Al-Anon. "Al-Anon's Twelve Suggested Steps." http://www.al-anon.alateen.org/the-twelve-steps; *How Al-Anon Works for Families and Friends of Alcoholics*. 1995. New York: Al-Anon Family Groups; *One Day at a Time in Al-Anon*. 2000. Virginia Beach, VA: Al-Anon Family Group Headquarters; Roth, Jeffrey D., and Emjay M. Tan. 2007. "Analysis of an Online Al-anon Meeting." *Journal of Groups in Addiction and Recovery* 2(1): 5–39; Timco, C., R. Cronkite, L. A. Kaskutas, A. Laudet, J. Roth, and R. H. Moos. 2013. "Al-Anon Family Groups: Newcomers and Members." *Journal of Studies on Alcohol and Drugs* 74(6): 965–76.

21. "About Alateen." http://www.al-anon.alateen.org/alaabout.html; Al-Anon/Alateen. "The 12 Steps of Alateen" http://www.al-anon.ab.ca/alateen/asteps.html; Al-Anon Family Groups. 2007. "Member Survey Results, Al-Anon Family Groups, Fall 2006." http://www. al-anon.alateen.org: "Twelve Traditions of Alateen." http://www.al-anon.alateen.org/ alatraditions.html.

22. Save Our Selves. "An Overview of SOS: A Self-Empowerment Approach to Recovery." http://www.sossobriety.org/overview.htm; Save Our Selves. "The SOS Story." http://www. sossobriety.org/james%20christopher.htm.

23. LifeRing. "About LifeRing." http://www.lifering.org; White, William L., and Martin Nicolaus. 2005. "Styles of Secular Recovery." *Counselor* (August): 58–60; Yates, Rowdy, and Margaret S. Malloch. 2010. *Tackling Addiction: Pathways to Recovery*. Philadelphia: Jessica Kingsley Publishers.

24. Cocaine Anonymous. "What Is Cocaine Anonymous?" http://www.ca.org; Cocaine Anonymous: New York. http://canewyork.org/; Cocaine Anonymous: Serving DC, Maryland, and Northern Virginia. http://www.tradition5.org/wmdvaca/.

25. Narcotics Anonymous. 1991. *White Booklet*. Center City, MN: Hazelden Publishing and Educational Services; Narcotics Anonymous. 1998. "Institutional Group Guide." http:// web.na.org/admin/include/spaw2/uploads/pdf/handbooks/IGG.pdf.

26. Spicer, Jerry. 1993. *The Minnesota Model: The Evolution of the Multidisciplinary Approach to Addiction Recovery*. Center City, MN: Hazelden Foundation; Yates, Rowdy, and Margaret S. Malloch. 2010. *Tackling Addiction: Pathways to Recovery*. Philadelphia, PA: Jessica Kingsley Publishers.

27. Ferner, Matt. November 27, 2013. "People Should Not Be Punished for Possessing Small Amounts of Any Drug." *Huffington Post*. http://www.huffingtonpost.com/news/drug-policy-alliance; Institute of Medicine of the National Academies. 2010. "Report Brief: Re-

ducing Harm." http://www.iom.edu/Reports/2010/Hepatitis-and-Liver-Cancer-A-National-Strategy-for-Prevention-and-Control-of-Hepatitis-B-and-C/Report-Brief-on-opportunities-for-harm-reduction.aspx; Marlatt, G. Alan, Mary E. Larimer, and Katie Witkiewitz. 2012. *Harm Reduction: Pragmatic Strategies for Managing High-Risk Behaviors*. New York: Guilford Press.

28. National Association of Drug Court Professionals, The Facts on Drug Courts. http://www.nadcp.org/sites/default/files/nadcp/Facts%20on%20Drug%20Courts%20.pdf.

29. Calahan, Joan B. 2013. *Adult Drug Courts: Brief Overview and Assessments*. New York: Nova Publishers; National Criminal Justice Reference Service, Office of Justice Programs. *Drug Courts*. https://www.ncjrs.gov/spotlight/drug_courts/summary.html; Office of National Drug Control Policy. "Drug Courts." http://www.whitehousedrugpolicy.gov/enforce/drugcourt.html; US Department of Justice, Office of Justice Programs. 2013. *Drug Courts*. https://ncjrs.gov/pdffiles1/nij/238527.pdf; West Huddleston III, C., Karen Freeman-Wilson, Douglas B. Marlowe, and Aaron Roussell. 2005. *Painting the Current Picture: A National Report Card on Drug Courts and Other Problem Solving Court Programs in the United States*. Bureau of Justice Assistance. http://www.ndci.org/publications/10697_PaintPict_fnl4.pdf.

30. National Association of Drug Court Professionals. "Drug Courts Work." http://www.nadcp.org/learn/facts-and-figures.

31. Mayo Clinic. August 13, 2013. "Intervention: Help a Loved One Overcome Addiction." http://www.mayoclinic.com/health/intervention/MH00127; Jay, Jeff, and Debra Jay. 2000. *Love First: A New Approach to Intervention for Alcoholism & Drug Addiction*. Center City, MN: Hazelden Foundation; Monti, Peter M., Suzanne Colby, and Tracy O'Leary, eds. *Adolescents, Alcohol, and Substance Abuse: Reaching Teens through Brief Interventions*. New York: Guilford Press, 2001.

Chapter 12

Looking to the Future

Chapter Objective: To introduce some ideas for reforming drug laws in the US and around the world.

Introduction

Illicit drugs have damaged the lives of users and non-users for hundreds, if not thousands, of years. Drug use and abuse is not a new problem but it is increasing and changing as traditional drugs become more potent and newer, more dangerous drugs are developed. The US and other countries around the world continue to battle drugs by making it illegal to manufacture, transport, possess, or use many substances, but the demand for illicit drugs does not diminish. People of all ages and from all parts of the world seek out drugs and continue to use them, even though they face criminal penalties for doing so.

The argument that the War on Drugs has failed is widespread. Governments have spent billions of dollars to fight drug production, trafficking, and demand, yet nothing has succeeded. Drug activities and use continue and are even rising. Thousands of people have spent portions of their lives in prison for drug offenses, ruining their families. The war has been called racist as minorities are sentenced to longer punishments than others. Thousands of people have been murdered, including not only those in the drug industry but also law enforcement and innocent citizens.

Critics of the War on Drugs argue that the majority of drug laws, both in the US and internationally, should either be repealed or modified and drugs either legalized or decriminalized. This is a very controversial proposal. While legalizing drugs would mean that the purity of substances would be regulated, sales could be taxed, the profits that support terrorist groups diminished, and abusers could seek out treatment easily, other problems would remain. Legalization would not eliminate all of the issues surrounding the drug trade. Even if drugs were legalized or decriminalized, there might still be an active black market, harmful drugs could be too readily available to people of all ages, and use might increase, resulting in a multitude of other social and economic problems.

There have been many calls to reform the current drug laws. An organization of law enforcement officials, called LEAP (Law Enforcement Against Prohibition) was formed in 2002 to support the idea that drug policies have failed and that we should eliminate laws that prohibit drugs for adults. Even former US president and Nobel Prize winner Jimmy Carter argued for revising the nation's drug laws. In 2011 Carter wrote an article for the *New York Times* in which he expanded on the failure of the War on Drugs. He wrote, "To make drug policies more humane and more effective, the American government should support and enact the reforms of the Global Commission on Drug Policy."[1]

When he wrote that, he was referring to a proposal made by the Global Commission on Drug Policy, an organization created in 2011 and comprised of political leaders who seek to re-think the world's drug policies. They accept that the global War on Drugs has failed, wasting enormous amounts of money and ruining lives. The commission members support global reforms of drug control policies and have suggested some ways for reducing international drug crimes. These are listed in Table 12.1.

Table 12.1 Recommendations from the Global Commission

1. End the criminalization, marginalization, and stigmatization of people who use drugs but who do no harm to others. Challenge rather than reinforce common misconceptions about drug markets, drug use, and drug dependence.
2. Encourage experimentation by governments with models of legal regulation of drugs to undermine the power of organized crime and safeguard the health and security of their citizens. This recommendation applies especially to cannabis, but we also encourage other experiments in decriminalization and legal regulation that can accomplish these objectives and provide models for others.
3. Offer health and treatment services to those in need. Ensure that a variety of treatment modalities are available, including not just methadone and buprenorphine treatment but also the heroin-assisted

treatment programs that have proven successful in many European countries and Canada. Implement syringe access and other harm reduction measures that have proven effective in reducing transmission of HIV and other blood-borne infections as well as fatal overdoses. Respect the human rights of people who use drugs. Abolish abusive practices carried out in the name of treatment—such as forced detention, forced labor, and physical or psychological abuse—that contravene human rights standards and norms or that remove the right to self-determination.

4. Apply much the same principles and policies stated above to people involved in the lower ends of illegal drug markets, such as farmers, couriers, and petty sellers. Many are themselves victims of violence and intimidation or are drug dependent. Arresting and incarcerating tens of millions of these people in recent decades has filled prisons and destroyed lives and families without reducing the availability of illicit drugs or the power of criminal organizations. There appears to be almost no limit to the number of people willing to engage in such activities to better their lives, provide for their families, or otherwise escape poverty. Drug control resources are better directed elsewhere.

5. Invest in activities that can both prevent young people from taking drugs in the first place and also prevent those who do use drugs from developing more serious problems. Eschew simplistic "just say no" messages and "zero tolerance" policies in favor of educational efforts grounded in credible information and prevention programs that focus on social skills and peer influences. The most successful prevention efforts may be those targeted at specific at-risk groups.

6. Focus repressive actions on violent criminal organizations, but do so in ways that undermine their power and reach while prioritizing the reduction of violence and intimidation. Law enforcement efforts should focus not on reducing drug markets per se but rather on reducing their harms to individuals, communities, and national security.

7. Begin the transformation of the global drug prohibition regime. Replace drug policies and strategies driven by ideology and political convenience with fiscally responsible policies and strategies grounded in science, health, security, and human rights—and adopt appropriate criteria for their evaluation. Review the scheduling of drugs that has resulted in obvious anomalies like the flawed catego-

rization of cannabis, coca leaf, and MDMA. Ensure that the international conventions are interpreted and/or revised to accommodate robust experimentation with harm reduction, decriminalization, and legal regulatory policies.[2]

Source: Global Commission on Drug Policy, 2011, "War on Drugs" http://www.globalcommissionondrugs.org/reports/war-on-drugs/.

Calls to reform drug laws have emanated from other places as well. The US Congress has considered legislation to either legalize medical marijuana, or to reschedule marijuana as a Schedule II drug. If that proposal were passed, there could be more research carried out to determine possible medical benefits. Other proposals in Congress have suggested removing all federal penalties for the possession, sale, and cultivation of marijuana, allowing officials in each state to decide how to regulate it. None of these proposals have had enough support in Congress to pass.

It is interesting note that on July 1, 2001, officials in Portugal decided to do just what the critics recommended. They implemented a new policy that decriminalized all drugs, including cocaine and heroin. The new laws still ban drug possession for personal use and drug use, but punishments for these offenses are considered to be only administrative violations and not criminal. Drug trafficking continues to be prosecuted as a criminal offense. Since the change was made, records indicate that the use of many types of drugs has actually decreased. The rate of individuals who reporting using what was once an illegal drug during their lifetime decreased for some age groups. For those between 13 and 15 years of age, the rate decreased from 14.1 percent in 2001 to 10.6 percent in 2006. For those who were 16–18 years old, the lifetime use rate also decreased, as did the use rates for psychoactive drugs. The total number of drug-related deaths in the country decreased after the law was implemented. Moreover, resources that had been spent in the past to prosecute and imprison drug offenders are instead being diverted and used to provide treatment programs to those who need it.

Benefits to Reforming Drug Laws

The idea that the drug laws in the US and around the world should be largely repealed and replaced with less stringent policies is difficult for some to support. But there are many arguments to support the change. What would really happen if drugs were either legalized or decriminalized is simply un-known, and chances are there would be some effects that were unintended or not anticipated. Nonetheless, there are many potential advantages to reforming drug laws. Some of these claims are described here.

1. Increased availability of treatment: If drugs are decriminalized or legalized, then addiction could be treated as a problem of public health and more treatment and counseling options would be more open and available than they currently are. The stigma associated with drug use would be elimi-nated and addicts would be able to seek medical care more easily.

2. Prison populations would decrease: The current drug policies result in mas-sive numbers of people around the world imprisoned for drug-related offenses. Many of those individuals have been sentenced to long prison terms for non-vi-olent crimes such as drug possession or use. This costs billions of dollars each year, and ruins the lives of the offender and their families. Instead of imprisoning users, states could rely more on alternatives to prison such as drug courts that provide for treatment or community-based treatment alternatives. This would allow states to spend valuable resources on other, more serious crimes.

3. Saving money: The US and other countries spend billions of dollars each year on drug control. Money must be spent on law enforcement, court costs, and punishing offenders. If laws were reformed, the federal government and states could save millions of dollars that are now being spent for drug prevention and criminal justice costs related to implementing anti-drug laws.

4. Crime would decrease: If drugs were available legally, the costs of the drug would decrease, so that users would be less likely to commit crimes of theft to feed their drug habits. Moreover, there would be less violent crime re-sulting from gangs and drug cartels who battle over turf and the market.

5. The purity of drugs would be more consistent and standardized: Many street drugs are cut (or mixed) with foreign substances which can cause more harm to a user than the drug itself. Moreover, the purity of street drugs is in-creasing, leading to overdoses. If drugs were regulated, the substance would be consistently the same purity, making the drugs safer for users and reducing the potential harm. The government could regulate doses, strengths, and purity of the drugs.

6. Increased hygiene: Under current policies, addicts who inject substances are sometimes forced to share needles with other drug users, spreading diseases such as hepatitis and HIV/AIDs. With legalized drugs, harm reduction programs such as providing sterile syringes to addicts could be implemented, reducing injuries to users.

7. Reduced organized crime and terrorist group activity: Legalizing drugs would destroy the underworld networks that fund terrorist groups. If the profits

from black market sales are significantly reduced or eliminated, organized crime groups would no longer be active in the drug trade. Moreover, without these profits, terrorist groups would not have the profits to fund their activities.

8. Education would continue: Even if drugs are legalized, education programs designed to discourage drug use would continue to be an important part of public policies. Schools would continue to reach out to young people, and communities may reach out to other populations to reinforce healthy living choices that do not contain drug use.

9. The choice to use drugs is a civil liberties issue: Adults should be permitted to choose if they want to use drugs or not. This should not be a government choice or regulated by anyone other than the individual. As long as an adult is not forced into using the drug, it should be their decision to ingest a substance that may alter their consciousness. Similar to tobacco and alcohol, which has the potential to result in serious health implications, a person of legal age should be permitted to make that decision.

10. Legal drugs could be taxed: If drugs were legalized, the sale or transfer of the substance could be taxed, bringing in thousands, if not millions of dollars to financially strapped federal, state, and local governments. This has been made obvious in Colorado recently. There, the tax money from the sale of legal and recreational marijuana has far exceeded what was predicted. The money can be used not only for treatment and education programs, but for infrastructure, healthcare, or any other budget item.

11. Some drugs may lead to more creativity: Many artists and religious thinkers have argued that drug use allows them to be more imaginative or more inspired and reach heights not achievable with other substances. While there may be no scientific proof for this claim, artists and other thinkers have relied on drugs to enhance their productivity for many years.

12. There may be medical benefits to drugs: For many years, people have argued that marijuana has medical benefits and is not addictive. Because of that, many states have legalized medical marijuana for patients who have been diagnosed with particular diseases. Other drugs may also have medical benefits that are not apparent yet.

Harms to Reforming Drug Laws

While many people support new policies that either legalize or decriminalize drugs, others maintain that the War on Drugs, or at least some current policies, are needed. Some of these arguments are explained here.

1. The impacts of legalizing drugs are unknown: A policy that legalizes all drugs, or even certain, less harmful drugs, could cause endless social and economic problems that society is not prepared to address. There may also be an increase in mental health problems with increased drug use. The effect that long-term or heavy drug use has on users has not been established, and the current healthcare system may not be set up to deal with that. There may also be social and economic implications of legalization that are unpredictable. Until we know more about the possible outcomes of legalization, it would be prudent to leave the laws as they are.

2. Drugs would be more available: If the US or the world legalized drugs, they would obviously be more readily accessible, leading to more use not only by legal adults but also by youth and children, a population that is more at risk when it comes to the potential dangers posed by drugs. This would lead to more problems in terms of crime, healthcare, and social concerns, but also to mental health issues.

3. The amount of drug-related violence would increase: Crime would not go down if drugs were legalized, as many people argue. Instead, crimes would change, or shift to other offenses when compared to what occurs now. People would drive and operate machinery while under the influence, resulting in thousands of fatalities. Legalizing drugs would not eliminate the theft caused by addicts who need money to buy drugs. They will still need money to buy drugs and would still commit theft or other crimes to get that money. There would still be addicts who exchange sex for drugs or money. There would still be assaults, kidnappings, and public intoxication. There would still be possession charges as some people would carry more than an allowable amount of drug on them, and there would still be people who manufacture drugs. Thus, crime will not decrease, but would change.

4. The black market for drugs would not disappear: If drugs were legalized, the underground sales of substances would continue to occur. Legalized drugs are highly taxed and therefore more expensive to purchase. Many people would rather buy the cheaper product and get more of it. Many people do not want a formal record of when they purchased a drug, how much they bought, and what drug they bought. They may also want more than an amount permitted by the law. Instead, they would prefer to purchase a quantity of a drug anonymously on the street. This also means that gang activity will continue.

Conclusion

This book has explained drug use in the US and globally and presented information on policies designed to address the problems associated with drug use. This chapter was designed to make readers think about the future of drug policies and if the trend toward legalization is a sound or useful one. It is safe to say that the War on Drugs will be in effect in the future, and that drug use will continue to remain illegal. However, as more people, agencies and organizations advocate for reforms, changes may occur in drug laws, the impacts of which are unknown.

Review Questions

1. Describe some of the recommendations made by the Global Commission on Drug Policy. Do you think they will work?

2. What are some possible benefits of legalizing or decriminalizing drugs?

3. Explain the possible harms of legalizing or decriminalizing drugs.

Endnotes

1. Carter, Jimmy. June 16, 2011. "Call Off the Global Drug War." *New York Times.* http://www.nytimes.com/2011/06/17/opinion/17carter.html?_r=0.

2. Global Commission on Drug Policy. 2011. "War on Drugs." http://online.wsj.com/public/resources/documents/GlobalCommissionReport0601.pdf.

Appendix

Effects of Drugs:
Physical and Behavioral Signs and Symptoms of Use

	Substance	Physical Symptoms	Behavior
Alcohol	Beer, Wine, Liquor	Slow or slightly elevated pulse, pupil size normal	Slurred speech, talkative, staggering, confusion, slow reaction time, often an odor of alcohol, nausea, vomiting, lowered inhibitions
Depressants	Barbiturates, Quaaludes, Valium, Xanax	Slow pulse	Slurred speech, slow reaction times, confusion, loss of coordination
Inhalants	Gasoline, solvents, aerosols, propane	Sometimes increased pulse rate	Confusion, slurred speech, bloodshot eyes, restrained behavior, flushed face, sometimes residue around the mouth and nose, heart palpitations
PCP	PCP, Kalamba	Increased pulse	Blank stare, sweating, rigid muscles, confusion, agitation, possibly violent, repetitive speech, some hallucinations

	Substance	Physical Symptoms	Behavior
Cannabis	Marijuana, hash	Increased pulse, pupils appear large	Bloodshot eyes, increased appetite, impaired perception of time and space, confusion, lowered inhibitions
Stimulants	Amphetamines, Methamphetamines	Increased pulse, pupils appear large	Excitable, loss of appetite, runny nose, dry mouth, euphoria, talkative, insomnia, irritability, dizziness, chest pain, high fever, convulsions, and cardiac arrest
Hallucinogens	Peyote, Mushrooms, LSD, MDMA	Fast pulse rate, pupils appear larger	Disorientation, paranoia, hallucinations, sweating, slurred speech, trouble concentrating
Narcotics	Opium, Morphine, Codeine, Heroin, Demerol	Slowed pulse, small pupil size	Slow speech, dry mouth, facial itching, track marks, sleepiness, nausea

Glossary

Addiction: Addiction occurs when a person becomes dependent on a drug and is unable to stop using. An addict will use a drug repeatedly, often for reasons other than to maintain their health. (1)

Addiction Liability: Some substances are more addictive than others. A drug's addiction liability refers to the likelihood that a drug will cause a chemical dependence in the user. (1)

Addictive Personality: Some users become addicted to drugs quickly. These people tend to have more risk factors for drug addiction than those who take longer to become addicted to drugs. (1)

Al-Anon: Al-Anon is a support group for relatives and friends of alcoholics that helps them handle the problems associated with another person's addiction to alcohol. The group was created in the 1940s after family members realized that alcoholism not only affected the addicted individual but also others close to them. Members share experiences and provide support for each other. The group is now an international, nondenominational organization with tens of thousands of local chapters. (11)

Alateen: Alateen is a support group for children and teenagers who have relatives or friends who abuse alcohol. Alateen was created in 1957 and now has around 3,500 worldwide groups. Most Alateen groups are sponsored by a local Al-Anon group. Meetings are held at places such as community centers, churches, and schools, or other convenient and nonthreatening places for young people. The meetings provide support from others who may be facing similar situations or experiencing similar problems. These other members provide support and tips and share experiences to help them cope with the problems of living with an alcoholic. Professionals often help members understand that they are not the cause of the loved one's problems and should not feel responsible in any way for another's choice to use alcohol, or for the behaviors that may result from the alcohol use. (11)

Alcohol: Alcohol is the most widely used depressant drug. It is easily available and legal in some circumstances. Alcohol affects brain functioning, lowers inhibitions, and impairs a person's judgment, coordination, reflexes, vision, and memory. Some users become violent, causing assaults and homicides. If used to excess, alcohol may also cause periods of memory loss. Alcohol poisoning will result in respiratory depression, coma, and possibly death. The long-term effects of alcohol use can include cirrhosis of the liver, heart disease, cancer, and brain damage. (4)

Alcohol, Drug Abuse, and Mental Health Reorganization Act: This bill restructured agencies dealing with alcohol, drug abuse, and mental health as a way to improve research about substance abuse and mental health and to provide more services to those affected by these diseases. (3)

Alcohol Mutual Aid Societies: Alcohol mutual aid societies are abstinence-based groups that help people stop using alcohol. One of the first alcohol mutual aid societies was the Washingtonians, established in 1840 in Baltimore. They had rallies and speakers, but also had weekly meetings in which they provided support, encouragement, advice, and solidarity to other members. Similar groups were formed in the early 1870s and called the Ribbon Reform Clubs. (11)

Alcoholics Anonymous: Alcoholics Anonymous (AA) is a program to help those addicted to alcohol manage their addiction. The program was originally founded in 1935. Today, the organization supports abstinence. It is comprised of local mutual-support groups rather than a national organization for a more personal approach to treatment. Advice is given to members not by professionals, but by other alcoholic members who give stories of their own experiences. The only requirement for membership is the desire to stop drinking. The program relies on a set of twelve principles for recovery that all members must abide by. The steps are intended to help an addict recover from their addiction. (11)

Amendment 20: In 2000, voters in Colorado accepted Amendment 20, which changed the state constitution to legalize medical marijuana. The new law allowed qualifying patients or their caregivers to legally possess up to six marijuana plants or two ounces of useable marijuana for medical reasons. (6)

Amendment 64: In 2012, Colorado voters chose to modify the state constitution for the second time and passed another ballot initiative, Amendment 64. Under the initiative, as of January 1, 2014, marijuana could be legally sold and used for recreational purposes. The users must be 21 years of age or older and cannot use the drug in a public place. Users can grow their own marijuana, up to six plants per adult, but the plants must be grown in an enclosed, locked space. No more than three plants can be in the flowering stage at one time. If a person grows marijuana plants, they are strictly prohibited from selling marijuana to another person. If a person wants to grow the drug for retail sale, they must be given a license from the state. All growers and sellers must keep track of all marijuana that is purchased and sold and report that information to the state each month. Anyone visiting Colorado may purchase and use the drug while in the state but cannot transport it to another state. (6)

American Society of Addiction Medicine: The American Society of Addiction Medicine (ASAM) is a nonprofit organization made up of physicians who treat patients with addiction problems. ASAM's mission is to increase the accessibility and quality of treatment for addiction. They also seek to educate physicians and other healthcare providers on issues pertaining to addiction and support research about addiction. They would like to establish addiction medicine as a specialty within the medical field. The organization exists on both the national and state levels. (8)

Amphetamine: A stimulant drug, amphetamines are synthesized from adrenaline and ephedrine and are difficult for a user's body to metabolize. Effects of this drug are an increased energy level and alertness, increased attention, well-being, euphoria, and sometimes a decreased appetite. Users may experience high blood pressure, irregular heartbeat, nausea, and vomiting. If used for a long time, users may experience irrational and paranoid behavior, psychotic episodes, or aggressiveness. Amphetamines can be used to treat depression, obesity, attention disorders, and narcolepsy. (4)

Analogue: Drug analogues are substances that are similar to a Schedule I or Schedule II drug in chemical structure and are intended to have a similar effect on a user's central nervous system as the Schedule I or II drug. To manufacture an analogue drug, a person only needs to slightly modify the chemical structure of an existing drug even in the smallest way to make a new form of the drug. If caught manufacturing an analogue drug, the offender could face harsh criminal penalties. (9)

Andean Trade Preference Act: Signed in 1991, this law provided financial assistance for four Andean countries (Bolivia, Colombia, Ecuador, and Peru) to assist them in their fight against drug production and trafficking. The law also allowed certain products to come into the US duty-free. It was thought that this would encourage farmers to refrain from growing coca and turn to a legitimate crop. (3)

Anomie Theory: A theory of drug use that focuses on societal goals and legitimate means to achieve these goals. When people are unable to achieve these goals, they have feelings of stress and strain and may use drugs as a way to cope. (1)

Antidepressants: Antidepressant are drugs that are prescribed to patients who have been diagnosed with moderate to severe depression, and include Prozac, Zoloft, or Paxil. For the most part, these drugs do not make users feel high but alter perception and mood. These drugs are also used to treat social anxiety, anxiety disorders, agitation, Obsessive-Compulsive Disorder, and posttraumatic stress disorder. Some antidepressants cause dizziness, anxiety, nausea, insomnia, restlessness, decreased sex drive, headaches, weight gain, tremors, sweating, sleepiness or fatigue, dry mouth, diarrhea, and constipation. They can also cause suicidal thoughts. (5)

Anti-Drug Abuse Act Amendments: These amendments were passed by Congress in 1988 to increase penalties for drug use. The law also included provisions to provide treatment for offenders. Another provision of the law created the Office of National Drug Control Policy (ONDCP) that would create and implement the nation's anti-drug use policies. The head of the ONDCP is referred to as the nation's drug czar. (3)

Asset Forfeiture: If a person is convicted of violating a federal or state drug law, the government can legally seize any property that was either used by the offender to commit the crime or that was purchased with the profits from the crime. This can include houses, cars, boats, weapons, art, or jewelry, among other items. When seized property is sold, any profit is placed into the Assets Forfeiture Fund that is held by the US Department of Justice.

Aviation Drug-Trafficking Control Act: This congressional law increased penalties for smuggling of illicit drugs. Any pilot whose aircraft contains, transports, or attempts to transport illegal substances could lose their license for five years. The Federal Aviation Administration could also strip an aircraft of its registration if it was used for transporting illegal substances. (3)

Bagging: A way for users to use inhalants that requires them to place a soaked cloth into a paper or plastic bag, allow the fumes to concentrate, then inhale them. This method has been blamed on suffocation deaths because of displacement of oxygen in the lungs. (4)

Bank Secrecy Act: A law passed in 1970 called the Bank Secrecy Act requires officials from the bank to report any large deposits of cash that they believe are linked to illegal activity to the federal government. Any bank that accepts these funds and does not make the report may be charged with money laundering. They risk criminal punishment and loss of their banking license. (6)

Barbiturates: Barbiturates are depressants that are called downers, sedatives, and tranquilizers. They slow down a person's central nervous system and brain activity, so they are often used to treat anxiety, agitation, insomnia, epilepsy, or muscle tension. The side effects of using barbiturates includes drowsiness, impaired judgment, diminished motor skills, amnesia, slurred speech, slowed reactions, and decreased reflex reactions. In higher doses, side effects may include vertigo, nightmares, aggression, coma, and cardiorespiratory arrest and an altered perception of time and space. Serious side effects include anemia, impaired liver function, headaches, blurred vision, and depression. (4)

Bath Salts: Bath salts are synthetic stimulants that are sold at convenience stores, head shops, or online that contain chemicals that have stimulant and hallucinogenic properties. Because they are made in a lab, street chemists are able to make new forms of these drugs as a way to keep them legal. As quickly as legislatures ban the product, chemists will make a slight change to the chemical compounds so it conforms with the law and can be considered legal. These are very dangerous substances, causing many users to hallucinate and carry out violent acts against themselves and others. (4)

Behavioral Therapy: Behavioral therapy is a type of therapy that provides addicts with coping strategies through which they can identify situations that may trigger their drug use and learn how to cope with them without turning to drugs. An addict can learn how to change their behavior to manage their cravings for a drug and deal with any issues that may have caused the original addiction. (11)

Benzodiazepines: Benzodiazepines are a type of sedative that are used to help people sleep. A widely used tranquilizer is Xanax, but other examples are Valium, Ativan, and Librium. On the street, these drugs are called candy, downers, sleeping pills, tranks, and benzos. (4)

Biological Theories: Biological theories of drug addiction are based on the notion that drug addiction is genetic, caused by a defect in the genetic makeup of users. A person's genes may affect how drugs affect a person, how much a person can tolerate, and how well the user's body metabolizes the drug. (1)

Black Tar Heroin: A type of heroin from Mexico that has impurities that cause it to be a dark color. The potency of this heroin is about the same as regular heroin but because of the impurities, there is a higher risk of side effects. Black tar heroin is often dissolved in water and injected, used as nose drops, used as a suppository, or drunk. It can also be ground into a powder that is snorted or heated on foil to create a smoke that is inhaled. (5)

Blood-Alcohol Content: The amount of alcohol in a person's body is measured by the blood-alcohol content, or BAC. This is specifically a measure of the percentage of alcohol that is present in a person's blood as measured in grams per 100 milliliters. If a person has a BAC of .08 or more, it means that they have .08 grams of alcohol in their blood (or 8/100 of 1 percent alcohol). At this stage, they are considered to be legally drunk. In all states in the US, a person with a BAC at or over .08 is not permitted to drive cars, aircrafts, or boats. They are also not permitted to operate heavy machinery. (4)

Boggs Act: Congress passed this law in 1951 to establish mandatory minimum sentences for those convicted of drug offenses. Under the law, any person who knowingly imported opiates, cocaine, or marijuana into the US could be fined up to $2,000 and be given a prison term of two to five years. This potential punishment also applied to anyone who knowingly received, concealed, bought, sold, transported, or conspired to traffic in drugs. Any person who committed these offenses more than once could face five years in prison, and those convicted of subsequent violations could face 10 to 20 years in prison. Anyone convicted more than once would not be eligible for suspended sentences or granted probation. (3)

Boylan Act: This law was passed in New York in 1914 and allowed courts to place drug users in state institutions to receive treatment for their addictions. The intent of the law was to reduce the availability and use of opiates for recreation, but in the end the law increased the availability of drugs on the black market. (3)

Bureau of Alcohol, Tobacco, and Firearms: When the Prohibition Unit disbanded, their responsibilities for enforcing anti-drug laws were given to the Bureau of Alcohol, Tobacco, and Firearms (BATF). The BATF (now BAFTE with the addition of explosives) is a federal law enforcement organization that is responsible for enforcing laws related to alcohol and tobacco products. When first created, the BATF had the authority to regulate the permitting, labeling, and marketing of tobacco and alcohol. However, their responsibilities changed when the Homeland Security Act of 2002 was passed. Now the BATFE focuses on illegal smuggling and trafficking of alcohol and tobacco. (8)

Bureau of Drug Abuse Control: The Bureau of Drug Abuse Control was established in 1965 by President Johnson and given the task of implementing the Drug Abuse Control Amendments Act. The first director of the agency was John Finlator, who publicly supported putting marijuana smokers in prison. To increase the public's support, Finlator invited Elvis Presley to the White House and arranged for him to receive a badge. The BDAC was responsible for enforcing the laws on depressants, stimulants, and hallucinogens. In 1968, the BDAC merged with the Federal Bureau of Narcotics to create the Bureau of Narcotics and Dangerous Drugs. (8)

Bureau of International Narcotics Matters: President Carter created the Bureau of International Narcotics Matters as a way to provide support to law enforcement agencies that were investigating international drug trafficking. During the 1980s, the agency provided money for many international anti-drug programs, with the bulk of the money going to programs to reduce drug cultivation in Latin American countries. Law enforcement agents were unable to stop the drug traffickers in these areas, and in the 1990s, the agency's focus turned to destroying the Mexican cartels. (10)

Bureau of Narcotics and Dangerous Drugs: In 1968, President Johnson consolidated the Federal Bureau of Narcotics and the Bureau of Drug Abuse Control to create the Bureau of Narcotics and Dangerous Drugs. The BNDD worked to control the availability of stimulants such as methamphetamines and hallucinogens. The BNDD focused on international trafficking and interstate violators. They provided training to local police departments on how to enforce illicit drug laws. They also oversaw over a half-million registrants licensed to distribute licit drugs. The agency was criticized for an increase in drug use, especially among youth. In 1973, the BNDD was abolished when President Nixon created a new federal agency—the Drug Enforcement Administration (DEA). (8)

Bush, George H. W.: President Bush continued Reagan's tough policies on illicit drugs, including tougher policies and an international approach to controlling drugs. He asked Congress for military and economic assistance to Andean countries as a way to reduce the traffic of cocaine into the US. In exchange, Andean leaders agreed to cooperate and increase anti-drug efforts in their countries. Bush also allowed military forces to go overseas and arrest drug dealers, even without the consent of the host country. (7)

Bush, George W.: President Bush had a comprehensive approach to illicit drugs. He worked with other nations to eradicate drugs at the source and stop the flow of drugs into the US. Bush cooperated with leaders of other countries to limit drug trafficking. But he also admitted that the most effective method for reducing drug use is to reduce the demand. He supported the Drug Abuse Resistance Education program (DARE) to education children about the dangers of drugs. Bush provided funds for drug testing of inmates, probationers, and parolees. For those users who were addicted to drugs, Bush proposed funding for treatment programs and provided additional funds to fund states' treatment programs for addicts and also for programs that incorporated faith-based elements into their programs. Bush increased funding for state drug courts. (7)

Cabinet Committee on International Narcotics Control: Set up by President Nixon, the goal of the committee was to fight international drug trafficking and to eliminate drugs at their source. (10)

Caffeinism: If a person ingests an excessive amount of caffeine, they could suffer from a caffeine overdose, called caffeinism. Symptoms include restlessness, dizziness, nausea, headaches, sleep disturbances, stomach irritation, irregular or rapid heartbeats, anxiety attacks, ringing ears, diarrhea, vomiting, light flashes, and difficulty breathing. Extreme use can cause convulsions, respiratory failure, and even death. (4)

Cali Cartel: The Cali Cartel, based in Cali, Mexico, became the primary drug smuggling group in the late 1980s after the demise of the Medellín Cartel. The Cali Cartel largely stayed out of the limelight and trafficked drugs and laundered money by avoiding publicity and violence. To outsiders, they appeared to be a legitimate business. The Cali Cartel supplied most of the cocaine sold in the US and Europe. Cali moved most of its cocaine production to Bolivia and Peru, and changed its transportation routes to go through Venezuela and Central America. The heroin sold by the Cali Cartel was a higher quality and cheaper than the heroin that came from Southeast Asia. In 1994, a gram of Colombian heroin was selling for $80 to $150 per gram, compared to $300 to $400 for the type from Southeast Asia. (10)

Cannabinoids: The chemical compounds in marijuana (and in particular delta-9-tetrahydrocannabinol or THC) that have psychoactive effects and can give users altered sensations and perceptions. (6)

Cannabis: "Cannabis" is a term that is often used interchangeably with marijuana, but it is actually another word for hemp. Cannabis is a flowering plant that is grown for its strong fibers (hemp). There are two primary types of cannabis plants. One is *Cannabis sativa,* a plant that has long stalks, sparse foliage, and slender leaves that is grown for industrial purposes, particularly for fiber. The second type of cannabis is the *Cannabis indica,* which originated in India. This plant usually grows to a height of four to five feet and has more and larger leaves. The leaves contain cannabinoids, the chemicals that have psychoactive properties. (6)

Carter, James E. "Jimmy": President Carter softened the government's position on marijuana and cocaine. Carter also cut back on international operations for reducing drug trafficking. Critics of Carter's policies pointed out that the global heroin supply could be traced largely to the failure of the DEA to interdict the drugs. (7)

Center for Substance Abuse Prevention: The Center for Substance Abuse Prevention (CSAP) is a federal agency housed within the Department of Health and Human Services and the Substance Abuse and Mental Health Services Administration. The mission of the agency is to reduce the use of illegal substances and the abuse of legal ones. To do this, it coordinates activities with other drug prevention agencies at the federal, state, and local levels. They also work with both public and private organizations. Together, these agencies seek to develop effective policies, programs, and services to prevent illegal drug use, prescription drug misuse and abuse, and alcohol and tobacco use by young people. (8)

Centers for Disease Control and Prevention: Founded in 1946, the Centers for Disease Control and Prevention (CDC) was created as the "nation's health protection agency." The agency works to prevent disease, injury, and disability. When it comes to drugs and drug use/abuse, the CDC works to reduce death and disease associated with tobacco use. The CDC also has a program that focuses on the dangers of alcohol use. Another program in the CDC spotlights illicit drug use, which educates the public about the dangers and consequences of illegal drugs. For addicts, the CDC helps with treatment options. (8)

Chemical Diversion and Trafficking Act: This law restricted access to precursor chemicals and tableting machines that are used to make other drugs. According to the law, companies are required to maintain detailed records about any transactions that include these materials. (3)

Clinton, William J. "Bill": Funding for drug interdiction declined during Clinton's first term of office—from about $1 billion to $569 million. This meant that there were fewer activities devoted to drug interdiction. Cocaine seizures dropped from 70,336 kilograms in 1992 to 37,181 in 1995. Clinton sought a military solution to the drug problem. He promised to give $75 million worth of military equipment to Colombia, Peru, Bolivia, Venezuela, and the Caribbean region. At the same time, Clinton supported the National Youth Anti-Drug Media Campaign. This was a program that targeted drug use among youth. It involved ads on television, radio, and other outlets that would send messages about the dangers of drug use. It also was aimed at parents and other adults as a way to encourage them to take actions to reduce drug abuse. (7)

Cocaine: Cocaine is a naturally occurring stimulant that is extracted from the coca plant, found primarily in South America. The plant is processed in secret labs and turned into a white powder, which is often diluted or "cut" with other ingredients. Cocaine is usually snorted or inhaled and causes a sense of euphoria, excitement, alertness, well-being, and increased confidence. Other effects include increased heart rate and blood pressure, muscle spasms, and convulsions. In high doses, a user may experience hallucinations, convulsions, seizures, and heart failure. Some users experience "cocaine nose," when the nasal membranes dissolve. (4)

Cocaine Anonymous: Cocaine Anonymous (CA) is a 12-step program that is modeled on Alcoholics Anonymous but not affiliated with AA. Created in 1983, CA is a support group whose requirement for membership is simply a desire to quit using cocaine and other substances. People who are addicted to the drug share their experiences with others. It has an estimated 30,000 members. (11)

Codeine: Codeine is the primary psychoactive element in opium and a mild version of morphine. It is often used to relieve mild to moderate levels of pain. The drug is also effective at treating diarrhea and is an effective cough suppressant. For these reasons, it is the most widely used narcotic in the world. Side effects of the drug include constipation, dizziness, itching, nausea, vomiting, and dry mouth. (5)

Codependency: Codependency refers to the behaviors that people develop if they are living with a person who is abusing drugs. These behaviors allow the abuser to continue his or her drug abusive patterns. The non-drug abuser is often forced to ignore their own needs and put the needs of the abuser at the forefront. Co-dependents help an abuser maintain their addiction. They will often make excuses to others for missed events, or attempt to maintain peace in the home, regardless of how it affects others. (1)

Combat Methamphetamine Epidemic Act: This law, passed in 2005, was meant to limit access to the drugs needed to make meth. The law required that pharmacies ensure that the drugs are sold only by the pharmacist to a person with a photo identification. Pharmacists must keep records of who purchases the drug and when. Sales of the drugs are limited to less than 7.5 grams within a 30-day period. (3)

Commission on Marihuana and Drug Abuse: President Nixon established the Commission on Marihuana and Drug Abuse (or the Shafer Commission) and asked it to recommend how to improve federal policy toward marijuana. The commission members carried out a comprehensive analysis of the drug by studying patterns of marijuana use and the possible addictive properties of the drug. They also examined the relationship between marijuana and violent behavior. They found that users are more likely to be passive, lethargic, and timid, and that there was no correlation between marijuana use and brain damage, violence, or crime. The committee recommended that marijuana use be discouraged but also that the government decriminalize simple possession of the drug. They recommended that penalties for nonprofit distribution of marijuana be removed. The Nixon administration did not agree with the recommendations of the committee and ignored their conclusions. (7)

Common Sense for Drug Policy: Common Sense for Drug Policy (CSDP) is a nonprofit organization that seeks to reform national drug policies, particularly in the areas of asset forfeiture, marijuana policy, mandatory sentencing for drug-related offenses, and needle exchange programs. CSDP provides local drug reform organizations with speakers and technical assistance to disseminate information about current laws, policies, and practices regarding marijuana. CSDP also supports policies that promote harm reduction. That includes syringe exchanges and expanding the availability of methadone and buprenorphine as a way to reduce harm to users and restrict the spread of HIV/AIDS and hepatitis C. (8)

Community Trials Intervention to Reduce High-Risk Drinking: This is a community-based drug prevention program that focuses on reducing alcohol use by people of all ages and subsequent alcohol-related crimes (e.g., drinking and driving, underage drinking, or binge drinking). The program relies on increasing community awareness, encouraging responsible beverage service in restaurants and stores, preventing underage access to alcohol, increasing enforcement, and promoting community involvement. Analysis of this program found that there was a decline in self-reported events of drunk driving and binge drinking. (11)

Compassionate Investigational New Drug Program: This program, run by the US government, allows certain physicians to prescribe medical marijuana to some of their patients. Those in the program receive low-potency marijuana cigarettes that are grown at the University of Mississippi. (6)

Comprehensive Drug Abuse Prevention and Control Act: Also known as the Controlled Substances Act (CSA), this law was one of the most significant pieces of federal legislation to regulate illicit drugs. The government placed drugs into one of five schedules based on their potential for abuse, their medical potential, and the potential of the drug to cause psychological and physical dependence. Those drugs placed into Schedule I were identified as having a high potential for abuse but no medical value, such as heroin, marijuana, and LSD. Schedule II drugs have a high potential for abuse and can lead to severe dependence on the part of the user and include methadone, oxycodone, and morphine. Schedule III drugs have less potential for abuse and have accepted medical uses. These drugs include Vicodin, Tylenol with codeine, ketamine, and anabolic steroids. Schedule IV drugs have a low potential for abuse and more medical functions. These include Xanax, Klonopin, and Valium. Schedule V substances have a low potential for abuse and consist primarily of preparations containing limited quantities of narcotics, such as cough syrups. (3)

Comprehensive Methamphetamine Control Act: When the use of methamphetamine increased throughout the early 1990s, Congress passed this law that focused on limiting the availability of the precursor chemicals that are needed to manufacture meth by increasing penalties for possession of these drugs. However, the law allowed some over-the-counter sales of precursor drugs. It also focused on limiting the trafficking of meth and importation of it from other countries, and on establishing a Methamphetamine Interagency Task Force to design, implement, and evaluate any education, prevention, and treatment practices regarding methamphetamines and other synthetic stimulants. (3)

Conflict Theory: A way to explain drug use by looking at societal divisions and power that exists in many cultures. Drug use may be understood by the lack of meaningful economic opportunities that exist in some communities, making residents feel powerless and alienated. (1)

Counterculture: During the late 1950s, youth who were opposed to values of mainstream society became part of a counterculture that opposed materialism, protested against the Vietnam War, lived in communes, and practiced free love. They also used many drugs, particularly psychoactive drugs like LSD. They were led by people like Timothy Leary and Jack Kerouac. (3)

Crack: Crack cocaine is a form of cocaine that is made when cocaine hydrochloride is dissolved in water and mixed with baking soda. The solution is boiled or heated in a microwave and then cooled, resulting in a yellowish-white product. Small chunks of the drug, called rocks, are heated in a small pipe or on a piece of foil. The smoke is inhaled by the user. As they are heated, the rocks make a "cracking" sound, giving the drug the name "crack." A user feels a sense of euphoria, excitement, and energy, and often do not eat or sleep for days. Users may also experience feeling of depression as the drug wears off. Some users will experience convulsions, heart attacks, and psychosis. (4)

Crime Control Act: This was a major anti-crime bill with many provisions, some of which focused on drugs. One section provided money for rural drug enforcement. Another section was the Drug-Free School Zone provision that required the US attorney general to develop policies for establishing and maintaining drug-free school zones. Another key provision was the Anabolic Steroids Control Act of 1990 that added steroids to Schedule III of the CSA. It also increased the potential fines and prison terms for knowingly distributing or possessing steroids. Another provision of the law was the Chemical Diversion and Trafficking Act that added to the list of precursor chemicals subject to federal laws. A similar provision focused on drug paraphernalia, making it illegal to sell, offer for sale, or to use the mail to transport, or import or export, drug paraphernalia. A section of the law was called Sentencing for Methamphetamine Offenses and required that the US Sentencing Commission amend the sentencing guidelines pertaining to offenses for smoking crystal methamphetamine. (3)

Cross-Addiction: If an addict uses a second drug to either replace the original drug to which they have formed an addiction, or they use two drugs at the same time, they may become cross-addicted. For example, a marijuana user may use alcohol if they are unable to purchase marijuana. Or that addict may use both drugs at the same time. (1)

Crossover Sensation: Crossover sensations are feelings experienced by LSD users in which they can "see" sounds and "hear" colors or lights. (5)

Cross-Tolerance: Cross-tolerance occurs when a user becomes tolerant to a particular drug and also develops a tolerance to another drug that is chemically similar. (1)

Cultivation: Cultivation means growing a controlled substance. Under state and federal laws (specifically the Controlled Substances Act), cultivating a controlled substance is illegal unless it is being done by a licensed pharmaceutical company (with the exception of marijuana in some states under state law). Some drugs, particularly marijuana, can easily be grown by a user and grow sites are found in warm climates, both indoors or outdoors. If a person is caught doing this, it is called cultivation of a drug, and is illegal. (9)

DARE: A popular drug education program is Drug Abuse Resistance Education, or DARE. Originally developed in 1983 by the Los Angeles Police Department, the program has become the most popular school-based drug education program in schools. It is a ten-week system in which local police officers teach young students in fifth and sixth grades about the dangers of drug use. Most studies of the program indicated that it did not reduce drug use in the long term and it is not as popular as it once was. (11)

Date Rape Drugs: Two drugs, Gamma-hydroxybutyrate (called GHB, liquid X, or easy lay) and Flunitrazepam (called Rohypnol or roofies), are called date rape drugs because they are easily put into a victim's drink and ingested by them, causing them to become weak, confused, dizzy, or unconscious. The victim can then be sexually abused without their knowledge or consent. These drugs are illegal but can be purchased easily on the black market. (4)

Dependence: Drug dependence occurs when a person is unable to control their use of a drug. They will crave the drug and may experience withdrawal symptoms. Drug dependence may be either physical dependence or psychological. (1)

Depressants: Depressants, also called downers, are drugs that slow the normal functions of a person's central nervous system. People who ingest depressants may be less aware of what is going on around them. Users may also have a lower energy level and lower pulse, blood pressure, and respiration, resulting in a sense of calm and reduced anxiety. Examples of depressants include alcohol, barbiturates, opiates (e.g., opium, morphine, heroin, codeine, methadone, Demerol, Percodan), sedatives, and tranquilizers. (4)

Detoxification: If the user has a severe addiction, they may be in need of detoxification to remove all of the drug from their body. A detox typically takes around 30 days. Some users may suffer from painful withdrawal symptoms, depending on the drug they were taking, past drug use, and other characteristics of the individual. Serious withdrawal symptoms may pose a risk to the individual, so a person may require medical care to prevent further harm. In some cases, increasingly smaller doses of the drug are given to the user to help ease any withdrawal symptoms they may experience. Sometimes medications like sedatives and anti-anxiety drugs may help to alleviate some of the symptoms. (11)

Differential Association: A sociological theory of drug use that explains that people who associate with others who place a value on deviant behavior will be more likely to exhibit those behaviors. In other words, if a person spends time with drug users, they are likely to also become a drug user. (1)

Differential Reinforcement: A sociological theory of drug use that suggests that drug use is justified through reinforcement and punishment. When drug users associate with other drug users, their behaviors are supported and continued drug use is justified. (1)

Disease Model of Addiction: The concept that an addict has a medical illness or condition that is the cause of their addiction. According to this idea, addicts are unable to control their drug use and are in need of medical treatment (and not punishment) in order to stop using. (1)

DMT: DMT is a hallucinogen that is naturally present in plants and animals including toads (in their venom), moth larvae, fish, and grubs in the Amazon. If the drug is injected or smoked, it creates powerful hallucinations. The drug can also be ingested in yage, a drink made from a vine in the Amazon Basin, and yopo, a snuff used by South American Indian tribes. However, the drug is often ingested by licking the toad or smoking it. Sometimes, the venom is harvested off the skin of the toads, dried, and then smoked. DMT is used by indigenous Amazonian Amerindian cultures in religious ceremonies and for healing purposes. (5)

Domestic Chemical Diversion Control Act: This bill, passed in 1993, eliminated a loophole that existed for purchasing of the drugs required to make methamphetamines bought over-the-counter. However, since the law applied to products that contained ephedrine but not pseudoephedrine, those who wanted to produce meth simply switched to using pseudoephedrine. (3)

Drug: A drug is a chemical substance that has an effect upon, or influences, a user's biological function. The substance is typically used to treat or prevent disease, but can also be used for pleasure. (1)

Drug Abuse: The use of a drug, either licit or illicit, in a way that is not prescribed by a physician. This can include the use of a drug if there is no diagnosed medical condition, or in a way that is not following the appropriate dosage. It can also be the use of a substance to achieve an altered state of mind, or to "get high." (1)

Drug Abuse and Treatment Act: This law, passed in 1972, reorganized federal drug agencies to make the federal government's response to drug abuse more effective. A new office, the Special Action Office of Drug Abuse Prevention, was created and given the responsibility to oversee all major federal drug-abuse prevention programs, education, treatment, rehabilitation, training, and research. Another agency, the National Drug Abuse Training Center, was created to develop, conduct, and support training programs related to drug abuse prevention. The third agency created in the bill was the National Institute on Drug Abuse (NIDA) that was given the responsibility to administer drug abuse programs assigned to the Secretary of Health, Education, and Welfare. (3)

Drug Abuse Control Amendments: As a response to an increase in drug use during the mid-1960s, Congress passed these laws to increase the number of substances that were regulated by the federal government. The new law regulated depressants (containing barbiturates), stimulants (containing amphetamines), and hallucinogens. Possession of these drugs without a license or prescription would be a federal offense. (3)

Drug Abuse Warning Network (DAWN): DAWN is collection of data from hospital emergency department visits and medical facilities to determine deaths and injuries related to drugs both nationally and for specific cities. It also includes events in which drugs were a contributing factor but not the primary cause of the event, like accidental consumption of drugs, adverse reactions, overdoses, suicides, or accidents. The original DAWN program was discontinued in 2011. (2)

Drug Cartels: Drug cartels are comprised of small, independent drug trafficking groups that join together and become loosely organized with other groups. They cooperate with each other to produce and smuggle drugs. In such an organization, some groups will be responsible for producing the raw material (plants), whereas other will be responsible for transporting and delivering the drugs to the labs where they are processed. Yet other groups are responsible for storing the drugs and others take the drugs to be distributed (sold) on the streets. Some of the most important groups are responsible for bribing officials so that their operations are not broken up by law enforcement.

Drug Courts: Drug courts are diversion programs that divert drug addicts from prison. When a first-time offender is charged with a nonviolent drug offense, instead of being sent directly to a custodial setting, the offender will instead be placed in a community-based treatment program that involves some kind of drug treatment. If the offender completes the treatment program without committing any further crimes, they will be released. If the offender does not complete the program, or commits another crime, a judge may send them to a correctional facility for the remainder of their original sentence. (11)

Drug Enforcement Administration: The DEA was created in 1973 when President Nixon reorganized existing agencies that enforced drug laws in some way. He sought to have a single federal agency to coordinate the government's drug control efforts. The DEA was tasked with coordinating all federal drug control efforts. Today, the DEA is the federal agency that enforces the nation's drug laws. Agents often cooperate with local law enforcement agencies and international agencies to exchange intelligence and expertise to investigate and prosecute those who have violated federal drug laws. The agency works to ensure that drugs produced for medical purposes are not diverted to the black market. DEA also has agents who serve as Demand Reduction Coordinators, who work with communities and organizations to help educate the public on the dangers of illicit drug use. (8)

Drug-Free America Act: This law was an attempt by Congress to eliminate drug use in the US. It allowed the president to increase taxes on any goods that were imported from countries that did not cooperate in efforts to halt drug production and trafficking. The law also gave law enforcement the ability to seize assets of drug dealers, and established anti-money laundering provisions. There were new federal mandatory minimum guidelines established for both drug possession and trafficking. (3)

Drug-Free America Foundation: The Drug-Free America Foundation, Inc., (DFAF) is a conservative, nonprofit organization that seeks to develop policies, both national and international, that reduce the use of, and addiction to, illegal drugs. The organization works to defeat any ballot initiatives to legalize drugs in any way, or those that propose a reduction in penalties associated with drugs. The group also encourages all citizens to remain drug-free. They advocate for abstinence-based drug education in schools and support law enforcement and drug interdiction efforts. (8)

Drug-Free Workplace Act: This 1988 law requires federal contractors and grantees both ensure a drug-free workplace as a condition of receiving the contract or grant from the federal government. A drug-free workplace is one in which employees are prohibited from manufacturing, distributing, dispensing, possessing, or using an illegal drug. If a federal contractor does not maintain a drug-free workplace, the contract may be terminated. (3)

Drug Intervention: A drug intervention occurs when family, friends, and other important people in a person's life come together to convince a drug abuser to seek help for their addiction. Often, the abuser is denying their problem, or may be facing painful withdrawal symptoms. The intervention usually starts with a conversation in a neutral place, at a time when the user is sober. Sometimes a professional who has experience in addiction interventions will participate. This can be a counselor, social worker, or interventionist. The goal is to help the user agree to seek treatment. (11)

Drug Kingpin Death Penalty Act: Under this law, the death penalty could be imposed against a person when an individual other than a participant in a criminal act dies. In 1994, the law was amended to allow for the death penalty against an individual who was considered to be a "drug kingpin," and who either played a significant role in the drug trade or who had control of the drug network. It was not necessary for that person to have actually carried out the crime that resulted in death. (3)

Drug Paraphernalia: This is any equipment, product, or material that is used to make, use, or hide illicit drugs, including bongs, grow kits, miniature spoons, roach clips, hookahs, or syringes. Paraphernalia can be products that are used to either ingest drugs or to conceal them (e.g., pipes or containers) or those items that are used by drug traffickers as they prepare substances for distribution (e.g., a scale or bags to package the drugs). (1)

Drug Policy Alliance Network: The Drug Policy Alliance Network is one of America's leading organizations that advocates for changes in US drug policy. The group maintains that current policies are rooted in outdated approaches, and these should be replaced by policies that are grounded in science, concerns over health, and a respect for human rights. The agency was formed in 2000 when two organizations that worked for drug policy reform—the Drug Policy Foundation, and the Lindesmith Center—merged. (8)

Drug Possession: Possession of a drug refers to knowingly or intentionally holding or having in one's possession a controlled substance (unless that substance was obtained directly, or pursuant to, a prescription from a doctor, who was serving as a professional when written). Whether a person is charged with drug possession depends partly on how much of the drug a person has, and how it is packaged. (9)

Drug Testing: Drug testing is a form of demand reduction because the intent is to deter people from using drugs. Many employees are required to pass a drug test before being hired. If they refuse, a company does not have to consider them. Once hired, an employee can be subject to random drug testing, or tested based on observations by a supervisor. An employee may also be required to take a drug test in the case of an accident on the job. Some schools require testing of student athletes or if they suspect a student of drug use. (11)

Drug Trafficking: A person found with a large amount of an illicit drug in their possession may be charged with drug trafficking (intent to sell). The amount depends on the drug. A person does not have to sell the drug—just possess the amount stated in the law. (9)

Drug Use Forecasting (DUF/ADAM): The ADAM study began in 1987 as the Drug Use Forecasting (DUF) Program, led by the National Institute of Justice. In 23 different sites, information is collected from juvenile and adult arrestees concerning their alcohol use, drug access, and drug markets. In 1997, the DUF Program was renamed the Arrestee Drug Abuse Monitoring (ADAM) Program and improved methods for collecting more accurate data. The program was terminated in 2003 but reinstated in 2006 as ADAM II, which used only ten sites. (2)

Drug Watch International: Drug Watch International (DWI) is a nonprofit group that was founded to support those who seek to live a drug-free lifestyle. DWI members believe that preventing drug abuse is the most practical, humane, and cost-effective way to address the consequences of drugs in our society. It is important that societal norms need to be developed that support drug-free attitudes, and acceptance of drugs and their destructive behavior need to be abolished. (8)

Drunk Driving: If a person who has used drugs chooses to operate an automobile, motorcycle, jet-skis, or boat (or any other type of machinery) while under the influence of an illegal substance, they can be charged with

Driving Under the Influence. Drivers often feel that they can control a vehicle, but their reflexes and coordination are affected by the drug and they are not able to do so. Some drugs, particularly sedatives, can result in dizziness and drowsiness. Marijuana slows a driver's perception of time, space, and distance. (9)

Durham-Humphrey Amendment: This act of Congress gave the Food and Drug Administration (FDA) the task of categorizing drugs as either a prescription drug or over-the-counter drug. The sale of prescription drugs was limited to those medically necessary and prescribed by a physician. (3)

E-cigarettes: Electronic cigarettes are battery-powered products that look like traditional cigarettes but do not contain tobacco. Instead, the user inhales a vapor instead of smoke. The device has a heating element in one end that heats a liquid solution that is inhaled. The liquid solution often contains nicotine along with other flavorings. When a person uses an e-cigarette, it is referred to as "vaping." (4)

Ecstasy: Ecstasy is categorized as a synthetic hallucinogen that is often used by young people at raves or nightclubs because it is perceived as a safe drug. Ecstasy causes the brain to flood with serotonin, the body's "happy chemical." Users report feeling euphoria and sensual arousal, often with an energizing effect. Some users will experience blurred vision, a fast heart rate, distorted perception and memory, and high blood pressure. (4)

Eisenhower, Dwight D.: President Eisenhower took a strong stance against drugs. In 1956, Eisenhower signed the Narcotic Control Act that increased the mandatory minimum sentences and established the death penalty for certain drug offenses. At the same time, Eisenhower supported treatment programs for those addicted to drugs. He signed legislation to make treatment an option for addicts. He also established a special committee to establish a new war on narcotic addiction at the local, national, and international level. (7)

Energy Drinks: These products claim to give a user energy, improve their concentration, and help them to lose weight. They have a high amount of caffeine and sugar, and sometimes vitamins or herbal supplements. These beverages usually contain three to five times the caffeine found in a can of soda. Some users claim to have had adverse reactions to the high doses of caffeine, including headaches, heart attacks, miscarriages, irregular heartbeats, diarrhea, vomiting, and even psychotic disorders and death. (4)

Fair Sentencing Act: This law was passed to reduce the disparity in sentencing between those convicted of different cocaine offenses. The sentences for possession of crack cocaine in the Anti-Drug Abuse Act of 1986 were more harsh than sentences for possession of powder cocaine. Many opponents pointed out that the discrepancy was racist, because crack-cocaine offenses were more often committed by black offenders whereas powder-cocaine offenses are most often committed by white offenders. Congress reduced the disparity in 2010 in the Fair Sentencing Act, which was signed by President Obama. (3)

Families Against Mandatory Minimums: Families Against Mandatory Minimums (FAMM) is a nonprofit, nonpartisan organization that questions the mandatory sentencing laws that exist on both the federal and state levels. Instead, FAMM supports a sentencing structure that can be individualized to the offender and the offense. The group's mission is to be a national voice for fair and proportionate sentencing laws. (8)

Federal Alcohol Control Administration: In 1933, President Roosevelt established the Federal Alcohol Control Administration (FACA) to oversee the legal alcohol industry and assist those who owned and operated wineries and distilleries. In 1935, the Supreme Court declared the FACA to be unconstitutional. (8)

Federal Bureau of Narcotics: Headed by Harry Anslinger, the Federal Bureau of Narcotics (FBN) was created in 1930 to enforce the nation's narcotics laws. FBN investigated those who were using drugs recreationally and those who were trafficking in illicit drugs. But it was given new responsibilities when the Marijuana Tax Act was passed in 1937. The FBN was criticized for intimidating physicians, and for its tough, anti-crime policies. The agency merged with the Bureau of Drug Abuse Control in 1968 and was renamed the Bureau of Narcotics and Dangerous Drugs. (8)

Federal Demand Reduction Programs: The federal government has put an emphasis on reducing the demand for drugs. The DEA created a Demand Reduction Section within its agency that makes the public more aware of the dangers of drugs. They work with community leaders and to reach out to school-aged children with drug education and prevention programs. They also work with businesses and their employees to maintain a drug-free workplace. The section provides the public with current information about illicit drugs and collaborates with other agencies for prevention efforts. (11)

Fetal Alcohol Syndrome: If a pregnant female drinks alcohol, the baby may exhibit birth defects such as low body weight, developmental delays, slowed growth, low intelligence, and problems with sight or hearing. Other infants may be missing fingers or toes, or have facial deformities or small brains. (2)

Flashbacks: Some LSD users experience brief episodes in which they feel the effects of the drug even though they have not recently ingested it. This can happen even many years after using the drug. They may experience hallucinations or halos of color or sparkling lights. (5)

Food, Drug, and Cosmetic Act: The Congress passed this law to protect the food supply and the quality of legal drugs. The law required that all consumable products have labels that listed the contents. Those selling medicines could no longer make false or exaggerated claims about the effects of a drug, and all drugs had to have labels with directions for safe use. The law also mandated that all drugs receive approval by the FDA before being sold to the public. (3)

Ford, Gerald R.: President Ford believed that drug abuse was one of the most serious problems in the US, and he continued the interdiction strategy that was the focus of the Nixon administration. Ford did not support a new executive-level office for drug abuse prevention. When Congress passed an amendment that created a new agency they called the Office of Drug Abuse Policy (ODAP), he did not hire any staff to run it. Ford signed the Alcohol and Drug Abuse Education Act Amendments and designated one week as "Drug Abuse Prevention Week." Ford sought to increase people's understanding of the dangers of using drugs. (7)

French Connection: This was the name given to the largest drug trafficking operation prior to the 1970s. It supplied an estimated 90 percent of the illicit heroin being sold in the US. The operation began in Turkey, where opium poppies were grown. They were smuggled into southern France to be made into heroin in clandestine labs. The drug was then transported into the US by French drug traffickers and sold to members of Italian organized crime families. The organized crime families sold the heroin to people on the local level in the US. In 1972, US agents working alongside French agencies broke up the French Connection. (10)

Gateway Drugs: These are "soft" drugs such as marijuana and alcohol that, some argue, will lead a user to abuse hard drugs such as cocaine and heroin. (1)

Gateway Hypothesis: The perspective that the use of soft drugs such as marijuana, alcohol, and tobacco makes it more likely that a person will use drugs that are more harmful. (1)

Global Commission on Drug Policy: The Global Commission on Drug Policy is an international organization with 22 representatives, including former world heads of state, governmental leaders, businesspeople, and writers. The members propose and support policies to reduce the harm caused by drugs in humane ways and base those policies on informed, scientific knowledge. To do this, the commission members analyze basic assumptions and consequences of laws, evaluate the risks and benefits of different responses, and then develop evidence-based recommendations for reform. (10)

Golden Crescent: The Golden Crescent is the area of the world from which a large portion of the world's opiates originates. This area produces a highly pure form of opium that is also very cheap. The drug is transported from the Golden Crescent to Europe, the US, India, and Turkey by way of commercial planes and cargo ships. (10)

Golden Triangle: The Golden Triangle is an area of about 150,000 square miles in Southeast Asia (stretching from Myanmar to China's Yunnan province to Laos and Thailand), which produces opium and heroin. It is estimated that around 70 percent of global supplies of the drug come from this area. The area has an excellent climate and fertile soil, with cheap labor to produce mass quantities of the drug. (10)

Green Rush: A state's Green Rush is the expansion of marijuana-related companies that appear as the drug is legalized in different states. (6)

Guadalajara Cartel: The Mexican Guadalajara Cartel was founded in the 1970s and was one of the first to profit significantly from the cocaine trade. The cartel members worked with Colombian cocaine cartels to transport heroin and cocaine into the US. It was estimated that the Guadalajara Cartel was responsible for about 70 percent of cocaine that was brought into the US, but also trafficked in massive quantities of methamphetamine and precursor chemicals needed to produce methamphetamine. The cartel began to fall apart after Enrique "Kiki" Camarena, a Drug Enforcement Agency (DEA) agent, was kidnapped and murdered. Many cartel leaders were arrested and the organization crumbled. (10)

Gulf Cartel: The Gulf Cartel is one of the oldest and one of the largest Mexican drug smuggling groups. It was formed during Prohibition when it smuggled alcohol into the US. During the 1970s, the group turned to trafficking drugs, particularly cocaine. Today, its operations can be found on the Texas border. In addition to smuggling cocaine, the Gulf Cartel is involved in other activities such as protection rackets (blackmailing businesses into paying for protection); kidnapping for ransom; human trafficking; bribery of law enforcement, elected officials, and journalists; theft; money laundering; trafficking in weapons; prostitution; and counterfeiting of products including clothing, TVs, video games, music, and movies. They are known to be particularly violent. (10)

Gutka: Another tobacco product is gutka, a sweet, chewable, smokeless tobacco product that is often mixed with spicy and fruity ingredients. Gutka may also contain parts of the areca nut and have other flavors mixed in such as cardamom, turmeric, cloves, saffron, and mustard seed. A user will place a small quantity of the product between their teeth and gums or lip. The user then sucks or chews on the mixture, spitting out small pieces of tobacco or other ingredients. (4)

Hallucinogens: Hallucinogens, or psychedelics, are drugs that distort a user's senses and their perception of people and events, and in some cases may even cause a user to see or hear things that are not real. Examples of these drugs are LSD, psilocybin, phencyclidine (PCP), mescaline, peyote, ketamine, and psilocin. Some hallucinogens occur naturally, while others are manufactured in a lab. (5)

Hard Drug: Drugs that are thought to be highly addictive and potentially harmful to a user. They are often responsible for causing a user's death. Examples of hard drugs include heroin and morphine, cocaine, crack, and amphetamines (methamphetamine, crystal meth). (1)

Harm Reduction Programs: Harm reduction programs are policies that are intended to reduce the potential negative consequences of drug use, including health, social, and economic consequences. They do not focus on reducing drug use or consumption. These programs help to lessen the possible dangers of using drugs. This is based on the premise that some people will not be able to stop using drugs, either because they are addicted or because they do not want to, but their continued use can lead to dangers to both the user and to family, friends, and the community. The attention should shift to reducing the harm from that behavior and not trying to prevent the act. The success of a harm reduction program should not be based on how many people are no longer using drugs, but rather by changes in the number of deaths, crime, and suffering. (11)

Harrison Narcotics Act: The Harrison Narcotics Act was passed by Congress in 1914 as the first major anti-drug law passed by the federal government. The law required that every person who purchased narcotics keep records for up to two years. Local revenue offices were required to keep copies of all narcotics orders, and pharmacists could only sell medications that contained opium, cocaine, or their derivatives to those with a doctor's prescription. A retail dealer or physician who dispensed the drugs had to have a tax stamp, and every person that sold narcotics had to register with the federal government. (3)

Hashish/Hash: Hashish is a powerful drug that comes from the cannabis plant and contains a high concentration of THC. Hashish oil also comes from the cannabis plant and is extracted from the plant by use of a solvent. Hash can be crumbled and smoked in a pipe, hookah, or bong, or it can be baked into foods such as brownies or cookies to make an edible product.

When ingested in any of these methods, the hash can have various effects on users, including euphoria, relaxed inhibitions, increased appetite, disoriented behavior, altered coordination of reflexes, and altered perception of time and distance. The effects of hash last between 2 and 4 hours. (6)

Hemp: Hemp is the fibrous product found in the *Cannabis sativa* plant. The strong fibers from the plant are often used to make rope because of its great strength. The leaves of this plant have very little THC, and cannot be used as a psychoactive drug. The seeds of the plant have high nutritional value with high levels of fatty acids (linoleic acid-omega-6 and alpha-linolenic acid-omega-3), vitamin B, and dietary fiber. Hemp is used as an ingredient in many foods such as energy bars, salad dressing, milk, and protein shakes. Hemp is also found in cereal, frozen waffles, and ice cream. The oil from the hemp seen contains gamma-linolenic acid (GLA), which is used to treat ailments such as neurodermatitis, arthritis, and premenstrual syndrome. (6)

Heroin: Heroin is a powerful, fast-acting drug that is highly addictive but used as a recreational drug that is often deadly because it is so potent. It is a drug that is considered by the US government to have no medical purpose with a high chance for addiction and is therefore found in Schedule I of the Controlled Substances Act. The short-term effects of heroin include a feeling of euphoria and relaxation. Users will often "nod off" or doze. Some users will feel drowsy and have poor motor coordination, slurred speech, facial itching and scratching, dry mouth, deepening of voice, constricted pupils, impairment of night vision, and dizziness. Heroin users may also have mood changes, an inability to concentrate, apathy, mental confusion, giddiness, fearfulness, and anxiety. If a user ingests too much heroin, it can lead to respiratory depression, clammy skin, seizures, and possibly coma and death. (5)

High-Intensity Drug-Trafficking Areas: Certain places within the US have been identified as high-intensity drug-trafficking areas, or "HIDTAs." Once a city is given this designation, officials will be provided with federal assistance to fund programs geared toward alleviating drug-related problems. They also support more cooperation between federal, state, and local law enforcement agencies to fight drug trafficking. (1)

Hillory J. Farias and Samantha Reid Date-Rape Drug Prohibition Act: In 2000, GHB (or gamma hydroxybutyric acid) became an illegal Schedule I drug when President Clinton signed this bill. The drug can still be used for legitimate purposes.

Huffing: One way to ingest inhalants is by soaking a cloth with the substance and then holding it close to the nose so it can be inhaled. (4)

Ibogaine: Ibogaine is a drug that comes from the root of the African shrub *Tabernanthe iboga*, which grows in the Congo Basin. The bark is dried and pounded into a powder. The plant is used by indigenous groups as a stimulant in healing and initiation ceremonies. In high doses it is a powerful psychedelic that causes an increased sense of colors, with some users reporting seeing spectrums or rainbow-like auras to appear around objects. Other users are able to stay awake and alert for days after consuming the drug. With a higher dose, the user will experience slight nausea, dizziness, and a lack of muscular control. If one gram is consumed, the user may experience hallucinations that can last for days. (5)

Inhalants: Drugs categorized as inhalants are intentionally inhaled by a user to produce a feeling of being high. Over 1,000 substances are considered to be inhalants, many of which are available in most homes and are cheap to buy. Since they are household products, they are legal to purchase. Inhalants suppress the central nervous system and decrease a user's respiration rate and blood pressure. They also lead to a distorted perception of time and space. There are four types of inhalants that includes volatile solvents, aerosols (sprays that contain propellants), gasses (found in many common items such as lighters, propane tanks, whipped cream dispensers, and refrigerants), and nitrates.

International Narcotics Control Act: This law allocated federal funds to combat the international drug trade, with a focus on halting the production of cocaine in South America. Congress authorized $115 million in 1990 for narcotics control assistance with another $125 million for military and law enforcement assistance to the South American countries of Colombia, Peru, and Bolivia. A major portion of the bill was crop substitution programs that would provide alternate employment for people who grow coca. (3)

Johnson, Lyndon B.: Johnson sought to take action to address the increasing use of drugs in the US. He asked Congress to pass the Drug Abuse Control Amendments that would set tighter controls over the production and distribution of amphetamines, barbiturates, and other psychoactive drugs. Congress agreed. The new law also included provisions to deter the diversion of depressant and stimulant drugs from legal channels and into the illicit market. At the same time, Johnson sought to increase rehabilitation for drug offenders and in 1966 worked for the Narcotics Addict Rehabilitation Act that provided rehabilitation for addicts. Early in 1968, Johnson proposed a plan to reorganize the federal agencies that played a role in drug enforcement and in doing so, created the Bureau of Narcotics and Dangerous Drugs. Johnson also thought it was important to give more attention to educating people about the dangers of drug abuse. (7)

Juárez Cartel: This Mexican drug cartel operates in the Juárez area of Mexico and along the borders of western Texas and New Mexico and into Arizona. They smuggle cocaine, heroin, methamphetamine, and marijuana into the US, using violence to carry out their operations. (10)

Keep a Clear Mind: Keep a Clear Mind is a drug education and prevention program that is geared toward older students between the ages of 8 and 12 years old and their parents. The program involves four weeks of activities that are to be completed by parents and their children together to show children the harmful effects of drug use and at the same time provide them with alternatives to drugs. Studies on the effectiveness of KACM indicate that 20 percent of parents noted that their children were more able to resist peer pressure to use alcohol, tobacco, and marijuana. (11)

Kennedy, John F.: In his 1962 State of the Union Address, President Kennedy discussed the problem of illicit drug use across the nation and called for government action. In September of 1962, Kennedy convened a White House Conference on Narcotic and Drug Abuse. It became apparent that the attendees, experts in their fields, knew little about illicit narcotics and the drug trade, the effects of drug use on the body, or even why people use drugs. Kennedy also appointed a President's Advisory Commission on Narcotics and Drug Abuse in 1963. The commission studied illicit narcotics use, including any existing research, possible effects, likelihood of addiction, and treatment options. (7)

Ketamine: Ketamine was originally developed as an anesthetic, but today is used as an animal tranquilizer by veterinarians. It has become a popular drug for those attending dance clubs and raves. Once ingested, ketamine acts quickly on the body. Users will have a short burst of energy, but they may also become euphoric, delirious, and dizzy. It also causes feelings of detachment from pain or their environment, and can also cause high blood pressure, and depression. In high doses, it can cause an experience temporary paralysis, anxiety, hyperventilation, black-outs, and psychosis. Long-term, heavy use may cause damage to memory and cause irreversible damage to the lining of the bladder and urinary tract. Ketamine can cause amnesia that can make users vulnerable to becoming the victim of an unwanted sexual event. Because of this, is it sometimes used as a date rape drug. (5)

Khat: Khat is a stimulant drug that is found in the East African shrub *Catha edulis*. The drug reportedly increases energy and suppress the appetite of those who use it, and can also produce a sense of euphoria and elation. In larger doses, the user may experience hallucinations, delusions, increased heart rate, exhaustion, hyperactivity, insomnia, and gastric disorders. If used for an extended time, a user may experience tooth decay and gum disease, constipation, ulcers and inflammation of the stomach. Users may also experience an increase in blood pressure, irregular heartbeat, heart attacks, and strokes. (4)

Labeling Theory: A sociological theory of drug use which suggests that individuals are labeled as drug addicts based not only on their drug use but also on their race, socioeconomic status, or other characteristics. Once a person is labeled as a drug user, they take on that identity and continue to use drugs. (1)

LifeRing: LifeRing is a nonprofit mutual aid organization that is a nonspiritual, 12-step abstinence program. The organization attempts to empower addicts to take responsibility in their fight against their addiction. They have meetings in the United States, Canada, and Europe. They have removed any spiritual component that is found in AA. The basis of LifeRing's approach is their "Three-S" philosophy: sobriety, secularity, and self-help. (11)

LSD: Lysergic acid diethylamide, or LSD, is a powerful synthesized psychoactive drug that is usually found as small squares of paper or pressed into sugar cubes. The exact effects of this drug are unpredictable and depend in part on the mood of the user or the environment in which the drug is ingested. Typically, a user will experience perceptual distortions, elevated body temperature, and an increased heart rate and blood pressure. Some users report that they can "see" sounds and "hear" colors or lights, and others report that their perception of time is distorted, so that a few seconds may feel like an hour. Other users have intense hallucinations, leading to feelings of panic, despair, and fear of insanity. (5)

Manufacturing: Manufacturing is the making of an illegal drug. Under state and federal laws (specifically the Controlled Substances Act), manufacturing a controlled substance is illegal unless it is being done by a licensed pharmaceutical company (with the exception of marijuana in some states under state law). Some drugs, such as methamphetamine, are manufactured or made in a home lab. Manufacturing a drug can be very easy but also very dangerous since the chemicals involved can cause an explosion. (9)

Marihuana Tax Act: Passed by Congress in 1937, this law effectively prohibited the recreational use of marijuana in the US. Anyone who sold marijuana had to purchase a stamp from the Treasury Department and pay a tax for every sale or transfer of marijuana. In addition, anyone who grew, transported, prescribed, or sold marijuana had to register with the federal government. (3, 6)

Marijuana: Marijuana is the most widely used illegal drug in the world. The psychoactive agent, delta 9-tetrahydrocannabinol (THC), is found in the leaves of the cannabis plant. The leaves are commonly smoked but can also be eaten in cookies, brownies, or other food products. Users report changes in perception, feelings of relaxation, and a distorted sense of time. Some become paranoid and experience impaired memory with difficulty concentrating and slowed reaction to time. There will be a moderate increase in a user's heart rate, and they may experience red eyes, a dry mouth, and increased appetite. (5)

Marijuana Rebate: Some of the money collected by the state of Colorado through taxes on the sale of legalized marijuana was distributed to local governments in areas where there were retail marijuana sales in this program called the marijuana rebate. (6)

Medellín Cartel: The first major Colombian cartel was the Medellín Cartel, based out of Medellín. This group appeared in the mid-1970s and became the most powerful drug trafficking organization. One of the founding members was Carlos Rivas Lehder, who smuggled cocaine into the US by small, private airplanes, landing in Bahamas to refuel. The most well-known leader was Pablo Escobar. He expanded the drug trade between the US and Colombia by bribing officials and using violence. He made the organization into the largest cocaine supplier to the US, smuggling in millions of pounds of cocaine. In 1993, Escobar was shot and killed by Colombian police. (10)

Medication: Medication may be used as part of a treatment program to help helping users stop taking drugs. These medications may block the withdrawal symptoms a user feels when they stop ingesting a drug, making it less likely they will use the drug again. Medications may also act to suppress the cravings that an addict feels when they stop using a drug. A user will not feel high from these medications but they will not have the urge to use the drug so they are able to carry on their daily activities. The addict can gradually reduce the dosage over time with less discomfort than they would otherwise feel. These medications are often provided by medical personnel so they can be monitored and regulated. Using medications to treat withdrawal symptoms is referred to as pharmacological drug treatment. (11)

Mescaline: Mescaline is a hallucinogenic agent found in the peyote cactus. It is usually ingested orally in the form of powder, a tablet, a capsule, or liquid. The effects of mescaline differ, depending on the user, the situation, the dose, the potency, and the user's experience with the drug. The effects can include an altered visual perception and an increased body temperature, heart rate, and blood pressure. There may also be nausea, loss of appetite, sleeplessness, numbness, weakness, and body tremors. Some users have experienced terrifying thoughts and anxiety, fear of insanity, fear of death, or fear of losing control. The drug has been used by the American Indians in the Native American Church as part of their religious ceremonies and they have been granted permission to use it as part of their ceremonial rites. (5)

Meth Labs: Meth is easily manufactured in a home, apartment, garage, or car, using common household products and drugs that are found in over-the-counter decongestants. These sites where meth is made are referred to as meth labs. (4)

Methamphetamine: A type of amphetamine, methamphetamine, or "meth," is a powerfully addicting drug that is made in laboratories. It is an odorless, tasteless drug that comes in many forms, including a powder, which can be smoked, snorted, or injected. It can also be dissolved in water or alcohol and injected. "Crystal meth" or "ice" is a concentrated, smokeable form of meth that resembles small pieces of translucent glass. Meth can cause a user to feel more alert, have heightened energy levels, and have an overall sense of well-being. If used for an extended time, a user may experience hallucinations, paranoia, or obsessive picking of the skin. Acute users may also experience irregular heart rhythm, heart attacks, or stroke and irreversible damage to their brain. A common symptom in addicts is "meth mouth," caused by drying of a user's gums and salivary glands, causing the enamel on the teeth to rot and the teeth to decay. (4)

Methaqualone: This is a synthetic depressant sometimes referred to as "Quaalude." At one time, Quaaludes were thought to be non-addictive and safe to use, but this is not the case. These drugs were contributing factors in the deaths of Freddie Prinze and Elvis Presley. (4)

Mexican Drug Cartels: In the 1980s, Mexican drug cartels helped the Colombian cartels smuggle marijuana into the US. When the leaders of the Cali Cartel were arrested in the 1990s, the Mexican criminal groups became more involved in smuggling cocaine and quickly dominated the cocaine market in the Midwestern and Western states in the US. Today, much of the cocaine sold in the US is smuggled from Mexico. They also produce thousands of pounds of meth that is also sold in the US. The Mexican trafficking groups are extremely violent and corrupt. Much violence has erupted between the different trafficking groups and between the drug cartels and law enforcement. (10)

Minnesota Model: The Minnesota Model is a treatment method for addicts that was developed during the late 1940s and 1950s in Minnesota. It is a multidisciplinary approach that includes professionals and family members into the treatment plan. They offer intensive counseling, group therapy, and guidance in lifestyle and behavioral issues. Today, the length of inpatient treatment is flexible and outpatient treatment is available. The core treatment philosophy includes total abstinence, inclusion of the family in the treatment plan, and continued care after release. (11)

Monitoring the Future Study: This is a survey conducted each year by the National Institute on Drug Abuse (part of the National Institutes of Health). This is a survey of about 50,000 students in public and private schools about their drug use, with follow-up surveys sent to respondents through age of 55. The study provides a longitudinal analysis of drug use patterns. (2)

Morphine: A derivative of opium, morphine is one of the most powerful natural pain relievers that exists. It is a Schedule II drug under the Controlled Substances Act and is highly addictive. Morphine addiction is very serious and the withdrawal process must be gradual or it may result in a stroke, heart attack, or death of the user. Withdrawal symptoms include runny nose, sweating, headaches, irritability, loss of appetite, body aches, severe abdominal pain, nausea, vomiting, and severe drug cravings. Morphine addiction is often treated with naloxone and naltrexone that block its effect, or methadone. (5)

Mothers Against Drunk Driving: Mothers Against Drunk Driving (MADD) is a nonprofit organization whose mission is to stop drunk driving, support victims affected by it, and prevent underage drinking. MADD has grown into one of the nation's most prominent anti-drunk driving organizations. The group seeks to change the laws for underage drinkers so that a young driver with any measurable amount of alcohol in their system would be illegal. For drivers who are 21 or over, MADD has programs to encourage more responsible alcohol consumption. One of those is the "designated driver" program, whereby one individual is chosen from a group of drinkers as the person who will remain sober and drive others home. MADD also continues to promote awareness of the dangers of driving while under the influence through public service announcements. (8)

Narcotic Addict Rehabilitation Act: This act provided for rehabilitation and treatment of drug addicts instead of punishment. Drug addicts could be committed civilly before their trial or sentencing. This was the first law to provide for alternative methods of punishments and treatment programs for drug offenders. (3)

Narcotic Control Act: This 1956 law increased penalties for offenders convicted of drug trafficking and dealing. The act authorized narcotic agents to use surveillance techniques to identify suspects, to carry guns, and to arrest suspected violators of drug laws without a warrant. It also mandated that anyone identified as an addict, user, or a person with a drug-related offense had to register with the Treasury Department before leaving the country. (3)

Narcotic Drugs Import and Export Act: When passed by Congress, this law governed international commerce in controlled substances. It established tougher restrictions on the importation of narcotics, which were banned unless they were intended to be used as medicine. The act also created the Federal Narcotics Control Board that would determine if drug exports were legal and if drug imports were necessary. (3)

Narcotics Anonymous: Narcotics Anonymous (NA) is a 12-step program for those suffering from an addiction to narcotics. The founders relied on the Alcoholics Anonymous (AA) model when it was founded in Southern California in 1953. NA encourages their members to attend regular meetings where addicts provide support to each other and help them stay clean. Stressing that addiction is the problem, and not the particular substance, demonstrates that NA considers addiction to be a disease. The meetings are open to all addicts, regardless of their religious, social, racial, and ethnic backgrounds. The meetings typically take place in buildings run by public, religious, or civic organizations. Members of NA must follow the 12 steps that promote recovery from addiction. (11)

National Clearinghouse for Alcohol and Drug Information: This is an agency that collects information on patterns of drug use and then disseminates it to researchers and the public. The organization is overseen by the Center for Substance Abuse Prevention, part of the Substance Abuse and Mental Health Services Administration of the US Department of Health and Human Services. (2)

National Council on Alcoholism and Drug Dependence: The National Council on Alcoholism and Drug Dependence (NCADD) is the largest public health advocacy group in the US for problems related to alcoholism and drug use. NCADD was founded in 1944 and originally called the National Committee for Education on Alcoholism (NCEA). (8)

National Drug Policy Board: The National Drug Policy Board was created on March 26, 1987, by President Reagan. The board members were asked to create a National Drug Control Policy that would reduce the availability and use of illegal drugs in the US. Their plan was to include international approaches and new strategies for law enforcement, alongside new policies for drug prevention, education, treatment, and rehabilitation. Another task for the board was to find a way to collect information concerning patterns of drug use across the country and to support additional research. The board was asked to provide advice to the president and to Congress on policies that should be implemented to reduce illicit drug use and abuse. (7)

National Institute on Alcohol Abuse and Alcoholism: The National Institute on Alcohol Abuse and Alcoholism (NIAAA) was formed in 1970 by Nixon. The agency was the first one to focus on alcohol use since the Prohibition Bureau. The agency was responsible for research on alcohol use. President Reagan reorganized the agency after it was criticized, moving it to the National Institutes of Health. The reorganization made the NIAAA into a research organization. (8)

National Institute on Drug Abuse: The National Institute on Drug Abuse (NIDA) is the federal agency that carries out government research on drug abuse and addiction. NIDA's mission is to advance knowledge on addiction and drug abuse, so their research focuses on how drugs work in the brain and body. They develop and test new treatment and prevention approaches, and detect and respond to emerging drug abuse trends. In 1975, NIDA began the Monitoring the Future Survey. (8)

National Minimum Drinking Age Act: This 1984 law required states to raise their legal drinking age for alcohol to 21 years. If a state did not comply, they would not receive federal funds for highway construction. The goal of the new law was to decrease deaths caused by drunk drivers. (3)

National Narcotics Border Interdiction System: Established in 1983 by President Reagan, the National Narcotics Border Interdiction System (NNBIS) monitored suspected drug smuggling activity at the border and then arrested those involved, seizing any contraband. The NNBIS worked closely with the Drug Enforcement Administration (DEA) and the Department of Justice. In 1984, the NNBIS was criticized after the head of the DEA, Frances Mullen Jr., claimed that the NNBIS hindered the DEA from doing its job. In 1985, the General Accountability Office announced that the NNBIS was largely ineffective in halting drug traffickers. (8)

National Organization for the Reform of Marijuana Laws: Founded in 1970, the National Organization for the Reform of Marijuana Laws (NORML) is a nonprofit advocacy group that lobbies to change the legal status of marijuana in the US on both the state and federal level. It is the oldest and largest organization advocating for the reform of the nation's marijuana laws. NORMAL does not believe marijuana should be completely unregulated. Instead, they support laws that remove criminal penalties for private possession of the drug and for casual nonprofit transfers of small amounts of the drug. It supports a controlled market for marijuana, where consumers could purchase it from safe, legal, and regulated sources. (8)

National Research Council Report on Drug Enforcement Activities: In 2001, the National Research Council filed a report criticizing the government's War on Drugs. They accused the federal government of spending billions to fund drug-enforcement programs, but there was little evidence to show that the programs worked. The chairman of the committee noted that it was unacceptable that the government should spend such a high amount to fund the programs without evidence that they worked. Further, the council argued that the nation's drug enforcement measures are not based on scientific principles. (7)

National Survey on Drug Use and Health: A survey completed each year by the US Department of Health and Human Services (the Substance Abuse and Mental Health Services Administration) of 70,000 young people to track their drug use behaviors. They collect information on the use and abuse of alcohol, tobacco, and illegal substances. (2)

National Youth Anti-Drug Advertising Campaign: An attempt to educate people about the dangers of drug use was the National Youth Anti-Drug Advertising Campaign. Media outlets donated over $3 billion in free television and media time to run ads about the dangers of drug use. Anti-drug messages appeared on television, in newspapers, magazines, on shopping bags, on videos, bumper stickers, and billboards. The goals were simple: to educate and enable youth to reject drug use, to prevent youth from ever using drugs, and convincing those who started to use drugs to stop. There did not seem to be any significant change in marijuana use patterns for the youth after the ads ran. (11)

Natural Theories: Theories of drug use and addiction that center on the idea that drug addictions are a consequence of an innate need in human nature to alter one's consciousness. (1)

Needle Exchange Programs: A needle exchange program is a harm reduction program that provides clean syringes to addicts. Since some addicts either cannot or will not stop using drugs, the goal becomes making the harm done by the use as small as possible. Providing clean needles helps to prevent the spread of diseases from one user to the next. (11)

Neonatal Abstinence Syndrome: This syndrome occurs when an unborn baby becomes addicted to an illegal drug after the mother uses it while pregnant. The newborn may also suffer from withdrawal symptoms after birth. (2)

Nicotine: Nicotine is a naturally occurring drug found in the tobacco plant. It is present in cigarettes (as shredded tobacco leaves), cigars (as whole tobacco leaves), pipe tobacco, or smokeless tobacco products (i.e., snuff and chewing tobacco), and gums. Nicotine is one of the most addictive and one of the most widely abused drugs. Use of nicotine will cause an increased heart rate, respiration, and blood pressure. Long-term effects include a decreased sense of smell and taste, frequent colds, bleeding gums and mouth sores, wheezing, coughing, bad breath, yellow-stained teeth and fingers, gastric ulcers, chronic bronchitis, emphysema, heart disease, chronic obstructive pulmonary disease (COPD), stroke, and cancer. (4)

Nixon, Richard M.: President Nixon was the self-proclaimed "law-and-order president" who believed that drug abuse was a sickness instead of a crime. He was the first president to focus on reducing demand and improving treatment over punishing offenders. After the 1968 campaign, Nixon changed his policies on drug abuse and moved toward tougher policies on drug users. He proposed a new agency that would centralize all federal efforts for drug policies. The new agency was the Special Action Office for Drug Abuse Prevention (SAODAP). Despite evidence that marijuana did not cause a person to become violent, nor was it addictive, Nixon maintained that marijuana was a dangerous drug. He took an international focus to the drug problem and met with leaders of other countries to seek their help in stopping drug trafficking into the US. Nixon also sought to increase punishments for drug traffickers. Before he left office, Nixon reorganized offices for a second time, this time creating the Drug Enforcement Administration (DEA). (7)

Non-opiate Analgesics: These drugs have no psychoactive effects but are effective pain-killers, albeit much weaker than opiates. Common non-opiate analgesics include acetylsalicylic acid (marketed as Aspirin), acetaminophen, and ibuprofen, each of which is available in over-the-counter products. While these drugs are relatively safe, they can still be misused. If abused, a person can experience liver problems, damage to the stomach lining, or even death. (5)

Obama, Barack H.: President Obama called the War on Drugs "an utter failure." He supported changing the mandatory minimum sentences for drug offenders to lower the mandatory prison sentences for low-level, nonviolent drug offenders. Instead, these offenders would receive drug treatment. Obama also ordered federal prosecutors to back away from prosecuting recreational users of certain drugs. Obama took action to help federal inmates who had been convicted of charges relating to crack cocaine. He commuted the sentences of over a thousand federal inmates who had been convicted of charges related to crack cocaine. Obama sought to ensure that drug addicts could receive treatment. He also sought to learn more about addiction. Obama's strategy also included drug prevention and treatment on a global level. He proposed alternative crops for farmers in some areas that are known for producing drugs. (7)

Office for Drug Abuse Law Enforcement: President Nixon established the Office for Drug Abuse Law Enforcement (ODALE) on January 28, 1972, to remove drug traffickers from the streets. Agents were asked to collect and review information about drug traffickers, and then assist local agencies to detect, arrest, and prosecute heroin traffickers. The organization was not effective and was consolidated with other federal anti-drug agencies (the Bureau of Narcotics and Dangerous Drugs, the Office of National Narcotics Intelligence, and the Customs Service Investigation Unit) to become the Drug Enforcement Administration. (8)

Office of National Drug Control Policy: Created by the Anti-Drug Abuse Act of 1988, the Office of National Drug Control Policy (ONDCP) is an agency housed within the Executive Office of the President that oversees the government's anti-drug plan. The office is headed by the director, more commonly known as the "Drug Czar." Two new offices were also created: the Office for Demand Reduction that helps to coordinate prevention, treatment, and recovery policies for federal agencies and the Office of Supply Reduction that coordinates the international policies. The ONDCP publishes the National Drug Control Strategy that outlines the administration's priorities and goals for drug reduction. This provides a plan to reduce illicit drug use and availability in the US, along with plans to reduce the manufacture and distribution of illicit drugs and the crime and violence associated with it. Another goal is to reduce the health consequences that result from the use of illicit drugs. (8)

Operation Banco: During Operation Banco, the DEA and the FBI worked jointly to break up a major drug smuggling group found in of Miami during the 1970s. (10)

Operation Boomer/Falcon: In 1979, the DEA and Customs agents worked together to fight drug smuggling in the Turks and Caicos Islands. (10)

Operation Condor: This anti-drug action was a crop eradication program that allowed DEA officials to destroy poppy fields in Mexico. (10)

Operation Cooperation: During the Nixon administration, Operation Cooperation permitted US agents to be stationed in Mexico. This helped to increase the presence of American drug enforcement agents outside of the US. (10)

Operation Intercept: Created by President Nixon, Operation Intercept was a program that allowed US border agents to perform searches of all individuals who were crossing the border into the US from Mexico. (10)

Operation Stopgap: An international operation to attack drugs being smuggled from Colombia was Operation Stopgap, which began in 1975. DEA agents watched for suspicious boats off the coast of the US. They reported suspect vessels to the Coast Guard and the Navy, which then tracked the ships if they moved close to thc US shore. During the course of this operation, over 1 million pounds of marijuana was seized. (10)

Operation Trizo: In 1976, Operation Trizo allowed Mexicans to fly planes provided by the US State Department over poppy fields to spray herbicides on them and destroy them. They also arrested poppy growers. Because so many people were arrested, the Mexican government requested that the operation be shut down in 1978. (10)

Opiates: The term "opiates" refers to all products and derivatives from the opium poppy, including morphine and codeine, the natural opiates; heroin, a semisynthetic drug; oxycodone (painkillers OxyContin and Percocet); and thebaine, an opiate that is not frequently abused. Other drugs that are made from the opium plant include hydromorphone, ketobemidone, tildine, and hydrocodone. (5)

Opium Poppy Control Act: Passed in 1942, this federal law placed strict controls on the production of domestic opium by requiring that all opium poppy growers in the US obtain a license from the government. There were also new limits on the amount of opium the growers could produce. (3)

Opium Wars: In the eighteenth century, the British sought to offer the Chinese opium in exchange for tea. When British opium became was readily available in China, the number of addicts rose dramatically. In 1839, China banned the British from importing opium but the British opium companies fought to end any restrictions imposed by the Chinese. At the end of the conflict, British merchants convinced the Chinese to allow trading rights in major ports. A few years later, another opium war broke out between the two countries. In the end, a treaty was signed that allowed the British to import opium into China. (10)

Organized Crime Drug Enforcement Task Force Program: The Organized Crime Drug Enforcement Task Forces (OCDETF) Program was established in 1982 to disrupt the structures of organized drug dealers. The OCDETF brought together many different agencies that each had the goal of reducing drug-related crime. These agencies collected and shared intelligence on trafficking organizations, using that information to go after organized traffickers. This approach created a national, coordinated attack against drug traffickers. (8)

Outpatient Drug Treatment: Outpatient drug treatment programs are those where patients receive treatment while they remain at home. Also called community-based treatment, this type of treatment is reasonable for people who have employment but are still in need of drug treatment. (11)

Over-the-Counter Drug: Drugs that can be sold legally to adults, possessed by them, and used by them for medicinal reasons. There are sometimes limits on who can purchase an OTC drug and how much they can buy. (1)

Oxycodone: Oxycodone is a semisynthetic opiate that is a powerful painkiller often used for cancer patients. It is made from thebaine, a naturally occurring ingredient in opium. Oxycodone has accepted medical uses but is also highly addictive so it has been classified as a Schedule II drug under the Controlled Substances Act. Addicts will crush pills into a powder and snort it, or mix it with water and inject it. They will experience a rapid and intense rush with feelings of well-being, relaxation, drowsiness, and sleepiness. Some users will also experience dizziness, nausea, constipation, and sweating. If a large quantity of the drug is ingested, it could lead to coma and death. (5)

PCP: Phencyclidine, or PCP, is a synthetic drug that was once used by doctors as an anesthetic and as an anesthetic by veterinarians. PCP is available as a tablet, powder, or liquid. Some users dissolve the powder in water or alcohol and spray it onto another product such as marijuana or tobacco, which is then smoked. The drug can also be injected. PCP has been called "the world's most dangerous drug" because of the intense effects. Users will often be unable to feel pain and have poor or impaired muscle coordination. A user's speech is often slurred, they may be dizzy, stagger when they walk, and have bloodshot eyes. They may also have shallow breathing, sweating, and feelings of being unattached or in a trance. Others who use the drug report nausea, vomiting, blurred vision, and drooling. Many times, users will report periods of blackout and not remember their actions while under the effects of the drug. PCP use is also linked to hostile or violent behavior or even suicidal thoughts. With higher doses, a user may become comatose or have convulsions, resulting in their death. (5)

Peyote: Peyote is a small, spineless cactus that grows in the southwestern US and the northern part of Mexico. The top of the cactus has small, disc-shaped "buttons" that contain the hallucinogenic substance mescaline. These buttons are sliced from the cactus and dried. The buttons can be chewed or soaked in water to produce an intoxicating liquid that can be mixed with other beverages or injected. (5)

Pharmacology: The study of how drugs affect a user's biological systems. Experts in this field study the chemical properties of drugs, the biological effects of drug use, and any therapeutic uses of drugs. (1)

Pizza Connection: The Pizza Connection was a drug smuggling operation during the 1980s. Members of the Italian organized crime groups, and in particular members of the Bonanno crime family, sold heroin imported from Southeast Asia's Golden Triangle (specifically from poppies grown in Afghanistan). The drugs were sold in pizza parlors in the US. The profits from the drug sales were held in bank accounts in Switzerland in violation of the Bank Secrecy Act. Organized crime groups from Italy, Switzerland, Spain, and Brazil were involved. This operation provided new evidence of the extent to which members of Italian organized crime cooperated with international crime groups to traffic in drugs and then launder the profits. (10)

Poppers: Poppers are a type of inhalants that are often used by older adolescents or adults. A user will experience an immediate feeling of being high, but will later experience drowsiness, lightheadedness and agitation as the drug wears off. A user may experience slurred speech, nausea, headaches, or impaired motor coordination. Some may lose consciousness. Users may also have watery eyes or a rash around the mouth. Chronic inhalant users may exhibit anxiety, excitability, irritability, or restlessness. Some users will suffer irreversible physical and mental damage from using poppers. (4)

Porter Narcotic Farm Act: This law, passed in 1929, created two "narcotic farms," or prison hospitals in Kentucky and Texas, where drug addicts were treated instead of punished. The hospitals were operated by the US Public Health Service and the Federal Bureau of Prisons. The institutions did not have high success rates and they were turned into traditional prisons in 1975. (3)

Possession: A person is in possession of a drug if they own, control, or use it. Those convicted of a drug possession charge may be fined or incarcerated, or both. (1)

President's Advisory Commission on Narcotic and Drug Abuse: President Kennedy established the President's Advisory Commission on Narcotic and Drug Abuse in 1963. The committee members were asked to recommend legislation that would prevent the abuse of both narcotic and nonnarcotic drugs (mostly barbiturates and amphetamines) by Americans. They were also to recommend new ways to provide rehabilitation and treatment for habitual drug users, and how to improve law enforcement programs related to narcotic drugs. The committee members recommended a federal civil commitment statute to allow for treatment of users. At the same time, the group recommended that illegal drug trafficking should receive more attention from the federal government, that the federal government should have the power and the responsibility to prevent the importation, manufacture, and transfer of illegal narcotic drugs in a more coordinated approach. (7)

President's Drug Advisory Council: In 1989, President Bush created the Drug Advisory Council that was given the task of making drug use "socially unacceptable" through a process called "denormalization." The members of the committee were to come up with ways to explain the National Drug Control Strategy to citizens. They could do this by working with the media, but also by sponsoring forums and seminars. In 1991 Bush extended the council until 1993. (7)

Prevention Programs: Prevention programs attempt to deter drug use before it begins. Sometimes these programs are called Demand Reduction programs as they reduce the demand for a drug. Many prevention programs are primary prevention programs, because they attempt to prevent people from using drugs at all. Secondary prevention programs focus more on those people who have tried drugs, and maybe who use drugs occasionally, from continuing their use and possibly becoming addicted. (11)

Prohibition: Created by the Eighteenth Amendment of the US Constitution, Prohibition was a time in the US when the manufacture, sale, or transportation of intoxicating liquor was illegal, as was the importation and exportation of alcohol into and out of the United States and all of its territories. (3)

Prohibition Unit: The Prohibition Unit was formed in 1919 and was the federal agency that enforced Prohibition and the Volstead Act from 1919 until 1933. The Narcotics Division of the Prohibition Unit successfully enforced provisions of the Harrison Narcotics Act and other drug laws. Prohibition agents could seize and sell any vehicles that were used to transport illegal liquor and could close any establishment that was used to manufacture or sell illegal alcohol. They could also arrest anyone who was manufacturing, transporting, or using alcohol. The Prohibition Unit was underfunded, understaffed, in some cases unethical. Prohibition was repealed in 1933 and the Prohibition Bureau was shut down. (8)

Project ALERT: A drug prevention program geared toward older children is called Project ALERT. This is a two-year program with 14 lessons that focus on the drugs that adolescents are most likely to use: alcohol, tobacco, marijuana, and inhalants. The program uses a variety of techniques (videos, classroom discussions, role-playing, and small group activities) to teach resistance skills. Studies on Project ALERT indicate that it is effective in preventing youth from experimenting with drugs. After students completed the program they were less likely to use marijuana and cigarettes. (11)

Proposition 215: In 1996, California became the first state to pass a bill to legalize medical marijuana when the voters passed **Proposition 215**, the Compassionate Use Act. Under the law, residents can possess and cultivate marijuana for medical purposes if they have a doctor's recommendation. Since then, more states and the District of Columbia have passed laws allowing for medical marijuana. (6)

Psilocybin and Psilocin: Psilocybin and psilocin are the hallucinogenic substances found in some mushrooms found in South America and the southwestern US. The effects of these drugs depend on the type of mushroom consumed, the processes used to extract the drug, and the dosage, but the effects may include nausea and drowsiness, hallucinations, and distorted perceptions. Some users report feeling anxiety and agitation, even panic, and may display psychotic behavior. (5)

Public Intoxication: Most people think of being under the influence of alcohol when they hear the term "public intoxication," but the term refers to being under the influence of any drug, including cocaine, methamphetamine, or any other substance. It is illegal to be visibly under the influence of drugs in public. If someone is, they can be arrested by law enforcement and be charged with public intoxication, sometimes called "drunk and disorderly." Each state has set a threshold level for intoxication based on a person's blood-alcohol content (BAC). In most cases public intoxication is a misdemeanor crime. (9)

Pure Food and Drug Act: A law passed by Congress in 1906 that required vendors label all food, medicine, or other products that were sold to, and consumed by, the general public. It made it illegal for a person to transport mislabeled foods or drugs across state lines. (3)

Purity: A drug's purity is the concentration of the active ingredient found in it. Many drugs are cut, or mixed, with foreign substances or adulterants such as starch, sucrose, or even rat poison. (1)

Quasi-legal Drug: Drugs such as marijuana that are both legal and illegal at the same time. Marijuana is currently illegal in the federal system, but many states have declared its use to be legal under some circumstances. (1)

Reagan, Ronald W.: President Reagan believed that illicit drugs was one of the most serious problems facing the nation, and promised to crack down on the production, trafficking, and use of these substances. Domestically, Reagan hired new federal drug law enforcement agents, provided for training, intelligence, and equipment to law enforcement agencies, and worked with Congress to increase punishments for drug offenses. At the same time, Reagan also focused just as much attention on treatment options for addicts. The president also cracked down on drug production and smuggling and cut off supplies of illicit drugs coming into the country. He authorized intelligence agencies to break up international drug rings. (7)

Residential Drug Treatment: Rehabilitation may occur in a residential or inpatient setting where the addict remains at the center and is not permitted to leave. Here an addict may receive counseling or group support to help them resume and maintain a drug-free lifestyle. The residential program may take weeks, or even months. If needed, medications can be used to block cravings or minimize the chance of relapse. (11)

Reverse Tolerance: When a small quantity of a drug produces the same effects on a user as a larger dose did in the past. This often happens when a user has not ingested a drug for an extended period. This can cause a drug overdose in the user. (1)

Rockefeller Drug Laws: This refers to a series of laws passed during the 1970s by the New York State Legislature during Governor Nelson Rockefeller's tenure. The laws were very harsh and set high punishments for those convicted of using illicit drugs. Offenders faced mandatory sentences of 15 years to life in prison with no option for probation/parole, and no plea bargaining. (3)

Salvia: Salvia, or salvinorin A or divinorin A, is a naturally occurring hallucinogen that is grown in Mexico and South America. The leaves are dried and then smoked. Users experience hallucinogens, visions, and altered visual perception that is similar to those experienced with LSD. The effects are felt by the user within a minute or two after ingestion. The effects are intense and are usually over within an hour. (5)

Self-Help Groups: For some addicts, taking part in help self-help groups such as Alcoholics Anonymous (AA) or Narcotics Anonymous (NA) can help prevent relapse. These programs use a 12-step process that help users understand their behavior. There are many types of support groups that not only help addicts but also their families. (11)

Shisha: Shisha is a flavored tobacco mixture that is burned in a hookah or water pipe. Often sweetened with honey, molasses, or fruit, the mixture is heated in a pipe. The smoke passes through water to cool before it is inhaled by the user. The smoke from shisha can have the same amount of tar and nicotine as found in 20 cigarettes and may also contain high levels of carbon monoxide. In some cases, the tobacco mixture may include drugs such as narcotics. (4)

Sinaloa Cartel: The Sinaloa Cartel was founded when the Guadalajara Cartel broke apart. It specializes in trafficking marijuana but also traffics in cocaine and methamphetamine. The head of the Sinaloa Cartel was Joaquin Guzman, also known as "El Chapo" Guzman (for "shorty"). He was noted as being one of the richest men in Mexico, worth about a billion dollars. In 1993, he was sentenced to 20 years in prison for drug trafficking. He escaped from prison in 2001, and was able to evade law enforcement until February 2014. In July 2015, he escaped from prison again, this time through a tunnel that opened from his prison shower. In January 2016, he was again arrested and remains in custody. (10)

Smoking Opium Exclusion Act: Passed by Congress in 1909, this law banned the importation of opium for smoking into the US. If convicted, an offender faced a fine of up to $5,000 or a sentence of two years in prison. This was the first law that restricted trafficking of drugs into the US. (3)

Sociological Theories: Theories of drug use based on the idea that use of illegal substances is a learned behavior. Examples include Anomie Theory, Differential Reinforcement, Labeling Theory, Differential Association, and Conflict Theory. (1)

Soft Drug: These are drugs that are thought to be either non-addictive or only mildly addictive. They are usually more socially acceptable and have lower criminal penalties associated with them. Examples include caffeine, alcohol, nicotine, and marijuana. (1)

Special Narcotic Committee: The Special Narcotic Committee was formed in 1918 to study the emerging problems of narcotics control and to make recommendations for new laws. The SNC concluded that there were over 1 million drug addicts in the country and that the country's per capita consumption of opium was higher than in any other industrialized nation. The committee found a need for more government action to provide treatment for addicts who might become violent without medical care. They proposed a new law that tightened the government's restrictions over narcotics. The new law created an extra tax of one cent per ounce of narcotics a person possessed. In the end, the SNC spread fear about narcotics addiction and about drug users and traffickers. (7)

Steroids: Steroids are synthetic derivatives of testosterone. Use of these drugs can promote muscle growth, so they can enhance a person's athletic performance and improve a person's body shape. They do not make people feel high, but can make users feel euphoric, friendly, and more energetic. At the same time, they can also feel more aggressive and experience increased sexual desire. They can also cause hair growth and a deepening of the user's voice. Steroids can be injected into the body or through a nasal spray, skin patches, or creams. Some are taken orally in a pill form. Low doses of steroids are used to treat some medical conditions. Women who use steroids are more likely to experience increased muscle development and a decrease in body fat. They may also see changes in their voice, more facial hair, irregular or absent menstrual cycles and shrinking of the breasts. Male users may experience premature balding, impotence, or gynecomastia (an abnormal enlargement of breasts). Common side effects also include a high blood pressure, reduced sperm count, and testicular atrophy. In both men and women, steroid use is associated with acne, liver problems, and cardiovascular disease, and a reduced level of good cholesterol. (5)

Stimulants: Stimulants are drugs that speed up a user's central nervous system. After ingesting a stimulant, a person's mood will be elevated; they may feel more alert and energetic. Users feel less tired and are able to stay awake for longer periods of time than is typical. These drugs may also suppress a user's appetite, and increase blood pressure, heart rate, and respiration. Examples are caffeine, nicotine, cocaine, and amphetamines. (4)

Students Against Destructive Decisions: Students Against Destructive Decisions (SADD). The organization asks young people and their parents sign a contract in which the youth pledges to make safe decisions about drinking and driving, and any parent who signs pledge agrees to either pick up their child, no questions asked, from any place and at any hour, or pay for a taxi to bring their child home. Parents must also promise to seek safe transportation home if they have had too much to drink. There are approximately 10,000 chapters in middle schools, high schools, and colleges around the country. (8)

Substance Abuse and Mental Health Services Administration (SAMHSA): The Substance Abuse and Mental Health Services Administration (SAMHSA) is a federal agency housed in the US Department of Health and Human Services that funds research into helping individuals with substance abuse problems. There are four primary programs found in the agency: the Center for Mental Health Services, the Center for Substance Abuse Prevention, the Center for Substance Abuse Treatment, and the Office of Applied Studies. Other major programs include National Survey on Drug Use and Health, the Drug Abuse Warning Network, and the Drug and Alcohol Services Information System. Today, SAMHSA carries out a survey of to determine trends in substance abuse and provide information about the use of illicit drugs, alcohol, and tobacco. (8)

Surgeon General's Reports on Tobacco: In 1964, the US Surgeon General published the first report on tobacco use, entitled *Smoking and Health.* The document was based on many years of research and included over 7,000 articles about smoking, health, and disease. The final report concluded that there were multiple health effects that were caused by smoking tobacco, including lung and laryngeal cancer, chronic bronchitis, emphysema, and coronary artery disease. In response, the committee concluded that smoking tobacco was a health hazard and that some kind of action should be taken. The report was a serious blow to the tobacco industry. Similar reports were issued almost every year after this. (7)

Synthetic Cannabis: Synthetic cannabis is comprised of dried plant leaves or herbal mixtures that have been sprayed with synthetic cannabinoids (the ingredient in marijuana that causes a user to feel "high"). The drug is sold as fake (and therefore legal) marijuana. The synthetic spray is comprised of many different compounds, but is enough chemically different from marijuana that the laws regulating marijuana (and cannabinoids) do not apply. The sprayed material is sold in small bags using names such as K2 or spice. These drugs are not regulated by the DEA and can be sold to anyone of any age. The packs are often labeled as potpourri and carry the warning "Not for Human Consumption." Users often display paranoia or panic attacks, or will carry out violent acts when under the influence. Some users have committed suicide after using the drug. (4)

Synthetic Drug Abuse Prevention Act: In response to drug manufacturers who are producing synthetic marijuana, an extremely dangerous drug, Congress passed a law to increase regulations of these drugs. When this was signed into law, 26 types of synthetic cannabinoids were placed into Schedule I of the Controlled Substances Act. (3)

Syrup: "Syrup" is a recreational drug that is popular in the hip-hop community. The main ingredient in this mixture is prescription-strength cough syrup that contains codeine and promethazine (an antihistamine). The cough syrup is mixed with soda such as Sprite, 7Up, or Mountain Dew. It can also be mixed with a sport drink or Kool-Aid. The mixture is also referred to as sizzurp, lean, drank, purple drank, and other names. The references to purple have to do with the color of the cough syrup, which has a purple color.

THC: Delta-9-tetrahydrocannabinol, or THC, is the chemical found in marijuana that makes a user feel "high." The concentration of THC in marijuana is the percentage of THC per dry weight of material. The effect of the THC on a user will depend on how the user ingests the drug, the amount ingested, and characteristics of the individual. Low doses of THC can produce feelings of relaxation, euphoria, hunger, enjoyment, relief of pain, heightened sensations, and altered perceptions. In high doses, or with prolonged use, THC can produce hallucinations, paranoia, psychosis, image distortion, learning and memory impairment, and mood swings. (6)

Tijuana Cartel: The Tijuana Cartel, also known as the Arellano Felix Organization (AFO), is one of Mexico's most powerful and violent drug-trafficking organizations. The cartel smuggles cocaine, marijuana, heroin, and methamphetamine to the US, relying on paramilitary security forces and international mercenaries to train its members. They use members of violent street gangs from local towns in both Mexico and the US to kill anyone who tries to smuggle illicit drugs through their territory without paying a tax to the cartel. The cartel members watch over law enforcement's efforts by using radio scanners, cell phones, and other technology, and regularly bribe officials. (10)

Tobacco Institute: The Tobacco Institute was formed when some tobacco companies met at the Plaza Hotel of New York City in December 1953. They decided that the Tobacco Institute would act as a public relations organization. They issued pamphlets, letters to newspaper editors, magazine articles, newsletters, advertisements, and white papers that attempted to counteract the negative research on the effects of using tobacco. It also paid scientists for favorable medical journal articles and letters to the press. The institute gathered intelligence regarding public attitudes towards smoking. It then used that information to formulate legislative strategies for its own lobbyists to use against efforts inimical to tobacco company interests. The Tobacco Institute was discontinued as part of the Tobacco Master Settlement Agreement in 1998. (8)

Tolerance: Over time, a drug user may need to use more of a drug to experience the same high. Many drug users become desensitized to the effects of a drug as their body adapts to it. (1)

Tranquilizers: Tranquilizers are used as antianxiety medications because they have a calming effect on a user. Minor tranquilizers are used for sedation and anxiety. Major tranquilizers (neuroleptics) were developed to treat of psychiatric disorders such as schizophrenia. These drugs combat hallucinations and delusions, and make a user feel less stress and fear. (4)

Treatment Programs: Treatment programs for addicts help them learn how to manage their addiction so they can live a drug-free lifestyle. They must learn about what triggers their drug use (what causes it) and any emotional issues that may contribute to it. Treatment must help an abuser refrain from using drugs. There are many forms of treatment and every treatment program should be geared toward the individual. The most effective treatment program will match the individual with the program that is right for them. (11)

Trip: This refers to the effects experienced by a person who has used LSD or other hallucinogenic drugs. These may include perceptual distortions, elevated body temperature, increased heart rate and blood pressure, and insomnia. (5)

Tweaking: Some drug users, particularly those who use meth, will sometimes refuse to eat or sleep for days at a time. During these periods, some addicts experience hallucinations, anxiety, paranoia, and a tendency to repeat behaviors, a pattern referred to as "**tweaking**." (4)

United Nations Commission on Narcotic Drugs: The UN Commission on Narcotic Drugs (CND) is the UN agency that makes policies on narcotics and psychotropic drugs. The agency was created in 1946, and given the task of overseeing how international drug control treaties were being implemented. In 1991, the responsibilities of the agency changed and it became the governing body of the United Nations Office on Drugs and Crime

(UNODC). The agency has 30 members that are selected by the UN's Economic and Social Council. The representatives represent different regions: Africa, Asia, Latin America/Caribbean, Eastern Europe, and Western Europe. The commission meets each year in Vienna to consider recommendations on international drug control policies. (10)

United Nations Convention against Illicit Traffic in Narcotic Drugs and Psychotropic Substances: The 1988 United Nations Convention Against Illicit Traffic in Narcotic Drugs and Psychotropic Substances provides the legal mechanisms for law enforcement to implement both the Single Convention on Narcotic Drugs and the Convention on Psychotropic Substances. The convention took effect on November 11, 1990, and has 188 member states participating. The goal is to stop international drug traffickers from being able to traffic drugs and to deprive traffickers of profits from the drug trade. (10)

United Nations Convention on Psychotropic Substances: The UN Convention on Psychotropic Substances is an agreement to limit the availability of psychoactive drugs including amphetamines, barbiturates, benzodiazepines, and psychedelic drugs. The treaty was the follow-up to the Single Convention on Narcotic Drugs, which did not include many of the newly developed drugs that were becoming popular at the time, particularly LSD and other hallucinogenic drugs. There are currently about 185 states participating in the treaty. (10)

United Nations International Conference on Drug Abuse and Illicit Trafficking: In 1987, the UN convened an International Conference on Drug Abuse and Illicit Trafficking to establish international cooperation in combating the illicit drug problem on an international scale. The committee members agreed to a document in which they urged other governments to consider the framework provided by the UN when proposing drug control policies. As a way to increase resources for the UN Fund for Drug Abuse Control, the committee members asked member states to contribute funds. The committee decided to observe June 26 of every year as the International Day Against Drug Abuse and Illicit Trafficking. (10)

United Nations Office on Drugs and Crime: The UN Office on Drugs and Crime (UNODC) is the office within the UN that is responsible for creating policies to combat the use of illicit drugs. It is also concerned with the link between drugs and terrorism and other criminal activity. The main office is located in Vienna, Austria, along with 21 field offices, and a liaison office in New York City. The agency's responsibilities fall under three areas. The first is research and analysis of substance abuse policies; the second is promotion and support of international treaties among member nations that have been developed to attack drug activity; the third area is increasing cooperation among member states. (10)

United Nations Single Convention on Narcotic Drugs: One of the most significant international treaties is the United Nations Single Convention on Narcotic Drugs that was passed in 1961 (and went into effect in December 1964). The treaty was meant to reduce the production and trafficking of illicit narcotics and other drugs, and as a way to make international drug control policies more consistent between nations. This new treaty was the first international treaty to prohibit cannabis, a drug that had not been included in other international treaties. It also categorized controlled substances into four schedules. The new schedules increased regulations. (10)

US Coast Guard: The Coast Guard is a federal law enforcement agency that oversees rivers, ports, and the high seas. In 2012, the Coast Guard seized 107 metric tons of cocaine that was headed for the US. (8)

US Customs and Border Protection: The US Customs and Border Protection (CBP) helps to protect the country's borders from intrusion by terrorists and weapons smuggling. They are the lead agency for preventing drug trafficking through ports, including airports, seaports, and land borders. The strategy behind the CBP's activities is supply reduction, or reducing the amount of drugs that flow into the country from other nations. This is accomplished through interdiction and deterrence of drug smuggling. (8)

US Immigration and Customs Enforcement: US Immigration and Customs Enforcement (ICE) is a federal agency whose mission is to protect national security, public safety, and the integrity of US borders through the criminal and civil enforcement of federal law. They are responsible for, among other things, stopping illegal activities stemming from smuggling. This includes investigation of crimes involving narcotics smuggling. ICE is one of the lead agencies in regards to narcotics investigations and enforcement. ICE works closely with other agencies and the Office of National Drug Control Policy. Additionally, ICE participates in organized crime drug enforcement task forces. (8)

Violent Crime Control and Law Enforcement Act: This law, passed in 1994, was a large bill that made many changes in the criminal justice system, some of which had to do with drugs. One provision of the law was related to drug courts. This created a grant program so that states could create drug courts. Drug treatment for inmates was also part of the bill, as was drug testing of federal offenders placed on post-conviction release. Drug trafficking in rural areas was the topic of one portion of the bill. Congress provided federal funds for rural drug enforcement assistance. The Rural Drug Enforcement Task Force was also established in some areas. (3)

Webb-Kenyon Act: Passed by Congress in 1913, the Webb-Kenyon Act criminalized transporting alcohol from a wet state (where alcohol is legal) into a dry state (where alcohol was banned). The law was originally vetoed by President Taft, but Congress overrode his veto and it became law. (3)

White House Conference for a Drug-Free America: In 1987, President Reagan sponsored the Conference for a Drug-Free America as a way for experts to discuss drug abuse education, prevention, and treatment, and the production, trafficking, and distribution of illicit drugs. The role that parents and other family members play in drug abuse patterns was also a topic of discussion. Other areas of concern to those attending the conference were the circumstances that contributed to youth drug use. The goal was to make recommendations for new laws and actions to combat some of the issues raised during the conference. (7)

White House Conference on Narcotics and Drug Abuse: In 1962, the White House held a conference to learn more about narcotics and drug abuse in the country. The conference lasted two days and was attended by about 500 people with different backgrounds including police, psychiatrists, and government officials. In the end, the meeting showed how little officials knew about narcotics and drug abuse. (7)

Whitney Act: A law passed by the New York State Legislature in 1917 that permitted doctors to treat addicts as they saw fit. This meant that doctors could prescribe maintenance prescriptions to addicts if it was intended to wean that person off of the drugs. Moreover, any addicts who violated drug laws could be paroled to the care of a physician for outpatient treatment instead of being sent to a correctional facility. (3)

Withdrawal: If a person who is addicted to a drug or has used a drug for an extended time stops using it, they may experience withdrawal symptoms. These symptoms may include tremors, nausea, diarrhea, anxiety, headaches, restlessness, fatigue, depression, convulsions, delirium, and even death. (1)

World Federation Against Drugs: Based in Stockholm, Sweden, the World Federation Against Drugs (WFAD) is comprised of 89 nongovernmental organizations and individuals from around the world that seek to fight against illicit drugs. The group was formed in 2009, with the support of then US President Bush. The members of the WFAD agree that substance abuse is damaging societal values and threatening stable families, communities, and government institutions throughout the world. The members of WFAD agree that a drug-free world will promote peace and dignity, democracy, tolerance, equality, freedom, and justice. (10)

Youth Risk Behavior Survey: The Youth Risk Behavior Surveillance System began in 1990 to track high-risk behavior and use of illegal substances by students in grades 9–12. It monitors behaviors that could lead to death, disability, and social problems, such violent acts, sexual behavior, tobacco and alcohol use, unhealthy dietary patterns, and inadequate physical activity. The survey is carried out every other year by the Center for Disease Control. The survey has collected information on over 3.8 million students since it began. (2)

Zero Tolerance Policies: Zero tolerance policies mandate that students or employees can be suspended or expelled (or fired) if caught in possession of drugs, or consuming illicit drugs on school or work grounds or at events. Studies of these programs show that zero tolerance policies, especially in schools, disproportionately affect youth of color and do not seem to make schools any safer. (11)

Index